COUSIN BEEDIE
And COUSIN HOT

COUSIN BEEDIE
And COUSIN HOT

My Life with the Carter Family of Plains, Georgia by **Hugh Carter** *as told to Frances Spatz Leighton*

PRENTICE-HALL, INC./Englewood Cliffs, New Jersey

COUSIN BEEDIE AND COUSIN HOT:
My Life with the Carter Family
of Plains, Georgia,
by Hugh Carter as told to
Frances Spatz Leighton

Copyright © 1978 by Hugh Carter and
Frances Spatz Leighton

Printed in the United States of America

Prentice-Hall International, Inc., London
Prentice-Hall of Australia, Pty. Ltd., Sydney
Prentice-Hall of Canada, Ltd., Toronto
Prentice-Hall of India Private Ltd., New Delhi
Prentice-Hall of Japan, Inc., Tokyo
Prentice-Hall of Southeast Asia Pte. Ltd., Singapore
Whitehall Books Limited, Wellington, New Zealand

10   9   8   7   6   5   4   3   2   1

Library of Congress Cataloging in Publication Data

Carter, Hugh Alton
  Cousin Beedie and Cousin Hot.

  Includes index.
  1. Carter family. 2. Carter, Hugh Alton, 1920-
3. Legislators—Georgia—Biography. 4. Carter,
Jimmy, 1924-   5. Plains, Ga.—Biography. I. Leighton, Frances Spatz. II. Title.
E874.C34 973.926'092'2   78-4975
ISBN 0-13-185470-4

*To Alton Carter, who was the heart of Plains
and whose heart belonged to Plains ... my father.
He passed away January 18, 1978.*

An Acknowledgment

I want to pay special tribute to the four people in the world closest to my heart—my wonderful wife, Ruth, my two loving daughters, Laurie and Connie, and my distinguished son, Hugh, Jr. My sincere thanks to Ruth, Connie, and Laurie for their help in collecting information for my book. So that they would not influence me in what I said, I want the reader to know that not a word of this book was shown them during its writing, nor will they get to read it until it appears in print.

And in the case of Hugh, Jr., because he works at the White House, I did not even tell him I was writing a book until it was nearly finished.

CONTENTS

Part Five CAMELOT SOUTHERN STYLE

COUSIN BEEDIE
And COUSIN HOT

Part One

COUSIN BEEDIE, COUSIN HOT

1·COUSIN BEEDIE, COUSIN HOT

The first time that Jimmy came back to Plains after moving into the White House, he visited around town and his first stop was at my store—Hugh Carter's Antiques—to say hello to me and my daddy, his Uncle Alton.

Behind him came his entourage of Secret Service men, reporters, and cameramen. I looked at this character whom I used to boss around when he was Cousin Hot, a kid four years younger than me, and suddenly I blurted out, "I don't know what to say. You're making me nervous."

The President of the United States looked at me and laughed, "That's all right, Beedie, you used to make *me* nervous."

Alice in Wonderland had nothing on Cousin Beedie and Cousin Hot. Little barefoot Hot has gone through the looking glass to find himself President of the United States. I have gone through the looking glass and emerged as Worm King of America and a state senator.

I'm glad I became those things before Cousin Hot became President or they would be saying I was cashing in on his fame. No, each of us made it on our own from that never-never land we lived in so long ago—can it be a half century?

Jimmy and I kid each other quite a bit when we are together. For one thing, I was *president* before he was—president of the sophomore class at Georgia Southwestern College.

He also is a Jimmy-come-lately in sports, being famous now, I tell him, as the manager and pitcher of the White House Staffers. That's the softball team that plays the Press Stars whenever the President comes to Plains.

The star of the Press team is Billy Carter, and this is one of the funniest and never-ending Minor League World Series going. The teams take their game very seriously—it's cutthroat on both sides. In fact, last summer both teams brought in ringers, and it turned into a showdown between Bigfoot, for the White House gang, and Dave the Ringer, for the Press Stars. Bigfoot scored two home runs and Dave the Ringer topped him with three, to win for the Press Stars team, 11-9. Cousin Hot vowed to stay till he won.

Fortunately, the next day the President managed to play a winning game, 19–17, enabling him to return to Washington in honor and not go back on his vow that he would not leave Plains until he had won a game.

When a tourist spectator, hearing all the lunatic hostility between the teams, asked if they were playing a grudge game, the President laughed and said, "Every game is a grudge game."

It's fun to play a guessing game after a man has made it to the presidency and speculate on whether he would still have made it had he done this or that.

There was that crucial time that Jimmy was running for U. S. Congress against Bo Calloway. He quit the race to run for governor. Had he not quit, would he have made it to the House of Representatives on Capitol Hill and be there still today?

I think he would. I think he would have been a congressman for several terms and then tried for the Senate. Jimmy did have aspirations to become a United States senator. I seriously doubt that he would be in the White House now had he followed that route.

But knowing how ambitious Jimmy is, he would be planning to run for President someday.

I'm glad he did it before some other southerner beat him to the punch.

Jimmy Carter is the first southern President the nation has had since Zachary Taylor—over 120 years ago.

You had probably never heard of me before Jimmy became President but Jimmy and I have always worked side by side in politics. As a matter of fact, I now sit in the very seat that Jimmy occupied when he was a Georgia state senator. When you're a *state* senator your name is not a household word.

The reason you don't know me better today is that I am just a *state* senator and not a *U.S.* senator. And the reason I'm not a *U.S.* senator is an interesting story involving Jimmy—Cousin Hot. You'll read about it in the book, eventually, and it is the one thing over which I could, if I let myself, feel a little bitterness.

When I see all the abuse Jimmy is taking from the Congress I remember how I used to run interference for him on the state level as his floor leader in the Senate while he was governor. Had he appointed me senator to the U. S. Senate when Senator Richard Russell died, there is a good chance that I might have been there today, in Washington, helping to run interference for him as I did before.

A chief executive of a state or of a nation has to have a loyal supporter fighting for his program. I am proud that I helped get Cousin Jimmy's whole program through the Georgia state legislature during his term of office there.

I sometimes wonder what would have happened if he had appointed me U.S. senator and I was now in the Senate as his right arm, as I was in Georgia.

Some who are reading this book will say, well why didn't Cousin Hugh run for office on his own if he wanted to be a U.S. senator? The answer is that in 1971 I almost did run. But what I found out is that running for the Senate is a game for millionaires and I didn't feel that I was in that league.

But right away, let me assure you that the book for the most part is not too political and not at all bitter but lively and full of life as I have lived it.

It's time that someone told the truth—the complete truth about Jimmy and our whole Carter clan and all the relationships involving Jimmy. Which members get along and which don't. How the members treat each other, goad each other, help each other, enjoy each other, and just what kind of atmosphere exists in Plains.

Miz Lillian, when she reads the book and finds out how I told that she's not the easiest person to get along with, may not be talking to me. But then, as the book explains, for months at a time she wouldn't be talking to me.

I tell the truth about Billy Carter, too, who started out as a pampered child, ran away to the Marines, and took a child bride of fifteen.

Because this is a family history, I will tell about the position of Billy in his family and the influence that Jimmy and Billy had on each other.

And there will be the life stories of Jimmy's other siblings—sister Gloria and sister Ruth. Most of all, I want to take the reader back to when we were barefoot boys known to our families as Cousin Beedie and Cousin Hot.

I think southerners make more of a big thing over names. We really can almost taste a name as it rolls over our tongues. We pull out the name, and say it lovingly.

We're very big on words of endearment, too, and I call my wife "Sugar" and "Honey" a lot, as Jimmy does too with Rosalynn. My father was "Uncle Buddy" to Cousin Jimmy. My daddy became sort of a father substitute to the President when his own father died in 1953. Daddy Alton was Jimmy's father's older brother.

In fact, as you will see, Alton became head of the whole Carter family when Jimmy's and my grandfather was shot in a senseless murder. But for now, I just want to give you a little of the flavor of our family. How it sounds when we get together at family reunions. An outsider would hardly realize who we're talking to or what to make of it.

To hear me say "Cousin Hot," you might think that I was referring to that flashily dressed man in the corner rather than the casually dressed President of the United States. Of course, if I were in public I would call Cousin Hot "Mr. President."

Amy, Jimmy's young daughter, has her own names for her grandmothers. Her name for Rosalynn's mother is "Mama Allie." She calls her daddy's mother "Grandmamma."

Only one person reverses the informality in the family, and that is Rosalynn, who can never bring herself to call her mother-in-law "Mother." Instead, she calls her "Miss Lillian," very formally. You will understand that relationship more as we get into the book.

Everyone has nicknames in the Carter clan. Jimmy calls Rosalynn "Rosie." Rosalynn is not too fond of this and only Jimmy can get away with it. Most people don't know where her name comes from.

It comes from her grandmother on her mother's side. Her name was Rosa. That's why Rosalynn's name is pronounced Rose-a-lynn instead of Roz-a-lynn. Her mother, Miss Allie, just added a "Lynn" to her own mother's name.

My own wife, who will probably clobber me for telling it, had to share her nickname with a candy bar—"Baby Ruth."

Once we liked the sound of a word and it fitted the person, he or she was stuck with it. When Gloria was born, Jimmy couldn't pronounce her name so he called her "Go-Go." This has remained her nickname all her life. I call her Go-Go now and so do many other people in Plains.

Jimmy's nickname, "Hot," is actually short for "Hotshot." His daddy was right in calling him that because he certainly did become a hotshot.

Jimmy's sister, Ruth, had a nickname, too—"Boopy-doop." It's rare that we call her that. It just doesn't seem right to call an evangelist preacher "Boopy-doop."

My own nickname of "Beedie," which the President and others

call me, was given me by a nursemaid who would croon about my going "beddy-bye, beedie-bye." The Beedie stuck.

My son, Hugh, Jr., grew up with the nickname of Sonny.

It seems that nicknames have always existed in our family—Swift, Turk, Beedie, Snaggum, Hot.

Jimmy's dad's nickname was Turk. He received this appellation because he was "low-slung like a turtle," according to Mr. Joe Bacon, Sr., an elderly gentleman who used to be his friend. How "Turtle" became "Turk" is one of those southern mysteries.

Swift was Turk's brother and my daddy. The amusing thing is that the whole town called Daddy "Swift" before he got married and then he slowed down so much, in his walking and work pattern, that they switched to "Buddy." But as a young kid trying to get ahead and being the sole support of his mother, brothers, and sisters, Daddy seemed to be racing with the wind.

Snaggum was my brother Donnel's nickname. He earned it for being able to catch anything in midair. But in his adult life he settled for just snagging a good news story. Today he's vice-president of the Knight-Ridder chain of newspapers.

Buckshot—that's Billy Carter's nickname. It was given to him by his daddy, my Uncle Earl, because he was just a little feller, so much smaller than anyone else in the family. But more recently Billy has gone by a nickname that he gave himself, Castiron, for his ability to drink vast amounts of beer and bourbon. Billy also uses *Castiron* as his identification when he talks on his CB radio.

When it comes to nicknames, the Secret Service beats the Carter family at picking descriptive names. Their name for Jimmy, during the campaign, I learned, was "Dasher." I don't think they were referring to Santa's reindeer so much as they were commenting on how fast Jimmy moves and how rarely he sits still.

Each member of Jimmy's family is completely different from every other one. If you know Jimmy, you still are not prepared for Brother Billy's outspokenness. And if you know the evangelistic Ruth, you are still not ready to recognize the woman coming at you on a motorcycle, in black leather jacket, as her sister, Gloria.

Jimmy is certainly not the motorcycle type either. There is only one time that I saw him riding a motorbike. That was when he was running for governor and it had a big "Carter for Governor" bumper sticker on it.

I guess Gloria and her husband, Walter, had taught him how to ride the motorbike but I don't believe he ever went back for seconds.

Jimmy's father, my Uncle Earl, was thirty years old when Jimmy was born. He was forty-three when Billy was born. Uncle Earl was not a tall man—5′ 8″—and weighed about 175 pounds.

Uncle Earl was a good sportsman—good at baseball and good at tennis. He was also a good community teamworker. He was a member of the County School Board and he taught Sunday School.

His reward was that the district elected him to serve in the Georgia House of Representatives in 1952—a two-year term. He only lived for one year of it and died in 1953. When he died, the town honored him for having helped bring electricity to the farms of Georgia.

He had served as one of the original REA—Rural Electrification Association—directors. How well I remember the days of our childhood before electricity. We used kerosene lamps for light. There was no electric heat, no automatic milkers or time-savers.

But when electricity came, everything changed for the better. No more did Jimmy and I have to pump water by hand for our kitchen needs. Suddenly we had refrigerators and the luxury of hot water. It was great!

Jimmy says that he can remember six lickings that his father gave him, all with switches from a peach tree. If you've been switched with a sharp peach tree switch, you know you've gotten a licking and you're still smarting for hours. Jimmy's brother, Billy, can remember no such spankings even though presumably he deserved them every bit as much as Jimmy. But Billy was never spanked.

The difference was in Uncle Earl's attitude toward the two boys. In our family it was a little joke that according to Uncle Earl, Jimmy could do no right and Billy could do no wrong—meaning that Jimmy got spanked and Billy didn't. Uncle Earl expected perfection of Jimmy, his firstborn, but when Billy came along as the child of his later life, he put away that old peach-switch thinking.

Perhaps this was the greatest spur to Jimmy to reach for perfection in order to stay out of trouble, and it may have helped goad him to the heights.

We didn't know that Uncle Earl was near the end of his life but maybe he felt it and something in him wanted to make the most of being close to a child of his own flesh. He had missed the boat with Jimmy. He wasn't going to do it again with Billy. They were inseparable.

From the time little Billy was toddling around, he was following his daddy, and when Uncle Earl went to the State House as a representative, he took Billy with him, saying it would be a good experience for Billy to learn about political life.

I think that the most surprised person in the world to see Jimmy sworn in as President, had he lived, would have been Uncle Earl.

Though Billy had every opportunity and was practically pushed into public life, he seemed to be immune to politics, whereas Jimmy, who seemed to be headed into a military career or a business career, or anything other than politics, became, eventually, the master politician.

I know just how much of a master politician he is, because I was his floor leader getting his bills passed when he was governor. It wasn't easy. There was bad blood between Governor Jimmy Carter and Lieutenant Governor Lester Maddox. I had to somehow get along with Maddox and not make him a worse enemy to Jimmy than he already was.

I'm not belaboring politics—I'll just give a few highlights of days when Jimmy was governor, state senator, candidate for President, and finally, President.

I visited him recently at the White House. It's a different kind of view that the reader will get because I was there, not as a visiting head of state, but just plain folks, member of the family, with my wife, Ruth.

My son, Hugh, Jr., was already there of course. He works at the White House. I think you heard about him when his White House colleagues gave him a new nickname—Cousin Cheap. That's because he's the efficiency expert and the one who took out all those TV sets that everyone was enjoying. But what people don't know, however, is that Hugh, Jr., is also the man who keeps the liaison with former presidents. He spent some time with former President Ford recently and they're close friends.

The book tells the truth about how the various members of the Carter family feel about religion and explains the whole fuss that resulted in many of the Baptist members of Jimmy's old church packing up and marching off to start a brand-new church. I know about that all right because I was the marcher at the head of the line.

This is a book about a loser who becomes a winner. It's a great success story but it's more than that. Most of all, it's a human interest story of the people behind the scenes in politics; it's a family saga that goes back into the roots of this particular family.

We don't have horse thieves but we do have murders and high drama.

I think people are more curious these days about what their political leaders are really like, and I want to share my memoirs of growing up with a President of the United States. There are so many questions people ask me about Jimmy Carter.

Is he really open-minded or a secret bigot? Is he really that hot about religion? Did he ever have a girl friend other than Rosalynn?

And what kind of wife is Rosalynn? And what are Rosalynn's relationships with other female members of the family? And does Jimmy have any enemies in Plains?

And did he ever play with black children, as a child?

But most of all, I am asked this question by the tourists who come into my antique store:

How religious is Jimmy?

To talk about the Carters is to talk about religious differences. That, as all other frequently asked questions, will be answered in good time.

Ours is a typical American family with skeletons in the family closet, passions of jealousy and competitiveness, loyalties, and even an occasional divorce.

But it is a strong family, with much good in it. We are a family who want to succeed, but not at the price of flaunting any law of God or man. Though we are an earthy family with earthy humor, most of us have a strong communion with God.

In this book, I hope the reader will see all facets in the making of a President. I think that what this book illustrates is that while no presidential family is perfect, out of its striving can come great leadership from one of its members.

I'm proud that in this case the leader is my first cousin.

2·PLAINS–
HOMETOWN, U.S.A.

Spring and early summer is the time to see Plains. That's when the honeysuckle blooms in abundance and strangers stand transfixed for an hour at a time, just breathing in the air. There is no bloom that is sweeter and it wafts its perfume so that it seems to follow wherever you go.

There are actually two kinds of honeysuckle blooms around Plains. The most fragrant is the one that grows on a vine that covers fences and clings to the branches of trees. The bloom is predominantly yellow and white.

The other honeysuckle grows wild in the woods and is about eighteen inches tall. It produces single stick blooms which are red.

My daddy used to take Jimmy and me for a ride on Sunday afternoon. We would visit the plum orchards in Webster County and pick ripe plums. Other times, we would stop the car and eat blackberries right off the bushes. If Jimmy and I found enough, we would take the surplus home for our mothers to make jelly.

Daddy taught us to pick a handkerchief full of blossoms of a plant called a sweet shrub and crush them for the fragrant odor. They grow along streams and many people dig them up and grow them successfully around their patios or pools.

I was born August 13, 1920, in Plains, Georgia, within a stone's throw of where Jimmy's house is now. Of course, his home was not there at that time—it was built before he ran for governor.

My daddy, Alton Carter, lived in the same spot, though not in the same house in which I was born.

Daddy had come to Plains in 1904 as head of his family at the age of fifteen. Our home was about a half mile from Daddy's general merchandise store and I can remember him walking back and forth to work every day.

We got a Model-T Ford. Later, we had a Model-A Ford with a rumble seat. Cousin Hot rode with us often.

Jimmy thought I was pretty lucky because my daddy used to take me on buying trips to Atlanta to obtain dry goods for the store. H. Mendel and Co. was one of the main stores he bought from. As a small boy, I would ride up and down on the elevator while my daddy selected the goods.

We usually packed the things purchased in the back of the car and brought them home with us. I also went to Albany, Georgia, with my father to buy dry goods. In Albany he bought goods from Hofmayer Dry Goods Company.

At Christmastime we sold toys. About three weeks before Christmas the toys would have been shipped in large wooden boxes and on a certain night all the family and the clerks would meet at the store to open the wooden boxes and mark the prices.

This was a big night in Plains. Many people, especially children, would watch through the windows and doors as we marked and hung up the toys. Cousin Hot would try to be around at this time. Every day after school, the store would be full of children, Jimmy among them, looking at the toys and selecting things which they truly hoped would be under their tree on Christmas morn.

This was life in Plains about a half century ago.

When I was boy about ten years old, I used to ride my bicycle to the drugstore and buy frozen candy bars for a nickel. I also sometimes bought a cup of ice cream with yellow sherbet in the bottom of the cup.

Dr. L. E. Godwin was the druggist and operated the drugstore. Sometimes his pesky little daughter would be hanging around. She was a girl and therefore not worthy of notice.

How could I know that in 1941 I would marry that same little girl and would be taking notice of her every day from then on?

I remember the iceboxes in Jimmy's house and mine that were used for preserving food. The icebox would hold fifty or a hundred pounds of ice. This was usually delivered twice a week by an ice truck. Most of the iceboxes were made of oak wood.

Now, in my antique shop, after all of these years, this is the one item that is perhaps most in demand as an antique. People refinish them to bring out the grain in the oak wood and make liquor cabinets of them.

Jimmy was always fascinated by his family history and he gathered many stories about how things used to be done in Plains from his grandparents and from my daddy. I saved what Jimmy told the people of Des Moines, Iowa, during the recent campaign:

11

There is no way for me to describe how I feel coming to Iowa. As our host was talking about change and opposition to change, and agriculture and farm land and historical developments, I thought about two or three weeks ago. I went down to our farm near Plains with one of the television network correspondents, and we were in the cemetery there where our ancestors are buried who were born in 1787—we haven't moved very far.

And I thought about my own children's great-grandfather who helped to clear that land and he went down into the swamp and he told me when I first came home from the Navy that it was so hot down there that he never wore trousers, he had long shirts and they came down to about his knees.

And he used to plant corn–before it was possible even to get a mule and a plow through the new fields–by poking a hole in the ground and dropping in a corn grain and then hoeing around the stalk as it came up. "Mr. Captain," as we used to call my wife's grandfather, never did like change either.

I asked Mr. Captain what was the thing that bothered him most and he said, well, he thought the thing that bothered him most was women's styles. He said when he was a young man that women wore their dresses very carefully and that you couldn't even see their instep. Nowadays, the dresses don't even cover up their step-ins.

What is life like in Plains today for the average citizen and what was it like a hundred years ago? Let me tell a little about this town of Jimmy's and mine.

Long ago this part of what is now Georgia was inhabited by the Creek Indians. In 1827, however, the federal government moved these Indians out of this area under the Treaty of Washington. The Creeks and Cherokees had to walk to Oklahoma.

As early as 1840, there were three white settlements in this area, Plains of Dura, Magnolia Springs, and a smaller settlement around Lebanon Cemetery.

Plains of Dura had its name shortened to Plains when the railroad was built through the area in 1885 to draw all the settlements together. H. L. Hudson was the first settler in Plains and he donated the land for the depot, which was the first building in the town.

Hudson was also the first postmaster and the first railroad agent. He also built the first house in Plains, which is currently owned by Mrs. B. J. Wise.

The ancestor of the famed Dr. Thomas Wise, Dr. B. T. Wise, was the first mayor and Plains had its first charter on December 17, 1896.

The first telephone system began its operation in 1909, and 1919 saw Plains as a thriving agricultural community and great shipper of hogs and cattle.

The *great* number of six hundred population was reached in 1920 and Plains became a boomtown. A new schoolhouse was built for three hundred students after the passage of a $50,000 bond issue. Then a hospital was built at a cost of $75,000. And then there was a two-story hotel in the center of town to board the newcoming visitors to the bustling town of Plains.

The Depression hit Plains in 1929 and took away the boomtown quality. Plains then became a quiet, sleepy community and has remained so ever since. As for Cousin Hot and me, we never did notice that Plains was not a "boomtown." We thought it was a fine town and an exciting place to live.

When Jimmy and his family returned to Plains, after his father died in 1953, he first lived in what was known as the Housing Project for several years till he could get on his feet. The rent was something like forty dollars a month.

But then, sometime in 1956, Jimmy took a step up in the world, moved out of the Housing Project and into a house about a mile from Plains en route to the Lebanon Cemetery and on the road that leads to the farmhouse where Jimmy had lived as a child.

The house was built around 1880, according to my daddy—Alton Carter—and it was here when the Carter family moved to Plains.

It is built of big wide, heart-pine boards. The rooms are very large and the ceilings are very high. There is a big wide hall down the middle of the house, and all the side rooms open into the hall. The kitchen and porch are on the back of the house but there is also a front porch. All houses used to have a lot of porches.

I personally went up to the attic room one day and felt relieved to come down. The old chimneys gave it an atmosphere and I told myself that the noises had probably been birds or bats that had been trapped in the chimneys and were trying to get out. Rosalynn told my wife, Ruth, that she saw a strange white dog outside one day.

The house was originally built by the Rylander family. Ed Stewart married one of the Rylander girls and it is believed that she acquired

13

the house and lived there with her husband, Ed, and had one daughter. Ed Stewart, who died in 1939, had built a ram in his pasture for pumping water.

Very few people nowadays know what a ram is. It requires no electricity of gasoline or power of any kind other than the force of water. It builds up its own pressure and pumps water. I can remember as a small boy going to Stewart's pasture with a gang of boys and having picnics and playing around the ram.

After Ed Stewart died, Mr. and Mrs. Howard Pantall moved into the Stewart house, and after they moved Dr. Thad Wise, one of the famous Wise doctors, lived there until he died. Dr. Thad had a pond down in the general vicinity of where the ram used to be.

In my time a tragedy was added to the history of the house. One day some boys were playing in a boat at the pond and a young boy named John Sewell fell from the boat and drowned. Some of us were called from town to administer artificial respiration but he had been in the water too long and we were unable to revive him.

After Dr. Thad died, the house was vacant for some time and Jimmy and his family moved in.

Jimmy and Rosalynn did not live in the house too long because Cousin Jimmy built his new house in town in the sixties and moved.

Now all the tour buses slow down when they go past the old house to tell tourists that President Jimmy Carter once lived there for several years.

Looking back, I realize there were a lot of fires at Plains—too many to be justified by the law of averages. For example, the school gymnasium burned down in 1940 when Jimmy was a junior. After that the only place big enough to hold the junior and senior proms of Jimmy's class was his family's Pond House, which was something his daddy had built to provide family entertainment,. and possibly business entertainment.

It had the family pool table and Ping-Pong table in a game room and it had a big ballroom for dancing. The ballroom had a jukebox and no coins had to be put in to change or play the records.

Then mysteriously the Pond House also burned down. It is a great mystery that remains unsolved.

Another strange fire took place at Rosalynn Smith's house some years before she married Jimmy. It seemed to have been started in a coat closet. Fortunately, the fire was put out before the whole house went up in flames.

Our house—the first house I knew as a baby—burned when I was only one year old. Dad had to build another.

Daddy's mule barn also burned mysteriously in the night back in 1946. I lived very close to it at that time. I had just gotten out of the Army the night it lighted the sky.

More recently, my antique warehouse burned in the autumn of 1976. In fact, I stopped having auctions because of that great loss. I have no explanation of all the fires that have been sustained in Plains. It is very strange and mysterious.

Two important landmarks concerned with the birth and infancy of the President also burned down. First is the Cook House on Church Street where Jimmy was brought from the hospital as a newborn infant and where he lived for a few months. It was across the street from the Methodist Church, which Rosalynn used to go to before marrying Jimmy, and which she was married in.

Also gone because of a fire is the next house the infant Cousin Hot lived in, the Lunsford House on Bond Street.

I hope that the strange fires of Plains are a thing of the past. Jimmy's home is well guarded by Secret Service men, and nowadays the Secret Service kind of keeps an eye on the town.

When Jimmy built his new one-level rambler house, in 1962, he chose a style quite like the house that I had built. Mine was on Bottsford Road. His on Woodland Drive.

My house is located on a thirty-acre lot of woods about two miles from Jimmy's home. Some distance behind my home is the World's Largest Worm Farm—about three acres of worm beds—plus parking and feed storage sheds. I also have a bluegill and bass fish pond on the property.

Here is a description of Jimmy Carter's home. His living room is medium sized with formal wallpaper. He has turquoise and white French provincial furniture and a gold rug. On a table sits a Grecian bust, and on the walls are a pair of landscapes and a massive portrait of Amy which is hung over the couch.

The dining room has a medium-sized table with straight-backed chairs. Crystal and silver adorn the sideboard and at the far end of the room a Chinese screen is hung on the wall.

When he's home in Plains, Jimmy spends most of his time in the high-ceilinged family room which is behind the living room. This spacious room is paneled and contains hundreds of books and family photos. There are more paintings of Amy and the other children. It contains comfortable furniture for relaxing.

The family room or den opens onto a large patio. The small back lawn is where Amy's trampoline is located. Jimmy does not have a swimming pool as yet. I have a figure-eight pool and a greenhouse.

Jimmy's home has four bedrooms and just recently they converted the carport into a large office for Jimmy. They built another garage that has a large room over it for guests. There is also a beautiful terrace.

My house and Cousin Jimmy's house were built by the same builders, Ralph and Charlie Wiggins. Both are brick and ranch style and are probably of about the same value. Although mine was built a few years before Jimmy's, I would say that each is worth around $100,000.

When Jimmy became governor in 1971, and then when he was elected President in 1976, Plains began to really prosper. The town began to enlarge and as southern hospitality prevails here, visitors come from all over the world.

Plains presently takes up four pages in the district telephone book. At a good brisk walk, it should take you no more than one-half hour to cover the town—to see where Jimmy lived when he first returned from the Navy, to see where First Brother Billy lived until recently, to see where the President's home is located, to see where Jimmy's uncle and my daddy, Alton Carter, lived.

It has been estimated that some 25 percent of the tourists who come to Plains spend no money on souvenirs and the like, but the rest spend from five to fifteen dollars each. Occasionally a big spender will go hog-wild spending fifty or a hundred dollars, or even more, and very often a dealer will come in wishing to purchase items wholesale to sell in his own store back home.

At one time the Plains area was largely dependent on the mobile-home industry. Unfortunately, the business failed and at the height of the recession, there had been about 30 percent unemployment. Unemployment decreased drastically, to 10 percent in 1977.

Jimmy has done a lot for the businessmen of Plains, even though some tend to forget it. Before he ran for the presidency there was an empty store building that no one even wanted to rent, but as a result of the boom, at this writing it is bringing $650 per month rent.

Four of our storefronts had been empty for more than thirty years and used as either warehouses or storage rooms. Now all are filled. Nothing is available for renting.

City zoning laws are now becoming very strict about new businesses. The big problem is finding land that is suitable to build on near the business district. Plains looks like a movie set with extras wandering around the street. Everyone says the town especially resembles TV's version of Dodge City in the Matt Dillon series.

The main town is one row of stores, several of them two stories high. We want to retain this appearance.

Plains is not as bigoted as you might think. We have had black councilmen for some years. The first black elected to the town council was Henry Jackson. He was later defeated. The next black elected was Bowman Wiley, who is still in office.

People who had never heard of Plains are suddenly dropping in. One day a dark and swarthy man and his beautiful wife and five-year-old son came wandering in and browsed around. Something about them looked familiar to my daddy but he didn't want to be nosy. After about an hour, they bought an $85 cut glass bowl and a $12 car horn and a few other souvenirs.

Suddenly, when they spoke, it was obvious who they were— Johnny Cash and his wife, June, and their son.

The news media and Secret Service stay in Americus or Albany, especially when the President is in the area. Some even stay in the Plains area when President Carter is not in Plains, just to keep an eye on things.

Tourists, their cars and Winnebagos swarm like ants in Plains. The tour buses run wild. I understand at least five firms or individuals have been licensed and each is allowed to operate three vehicles locally. Only one of the firms is allowed by the Public Service Commission of the state to operate *in and out* of the town limits.

One thousand to two thousand tourists sign the visitors' book each day in the depot, and in my Hugh Carter's Antique Store, I notice that some 2,000 to 5,000 sign my visitors' book on Saturday and Sunday.

Along the tour one can see the Plains High School that was built in 1921 where Cousin Jimmy and I graduated, and both of our families attended. The tour also includes seeing "Hugh Carter's Antique Shop—the Best Known Antique Shop in the World," and Billy Carter's gas station, which is now doing fantastically well, also.

There are often long lines of cars waiting to buy gas from Billy Carter, just to say they bought gasoline from him. Often they will go inside hoping to get a glimpse of him or to purchase Billy Beer or some other item coming from his store.

Along the tour one can stop in one of the two grocery stores which now sell Jimmy Carter souvenirs, and when you get hungry along your "long" tour you can stop in one or the other of the two restaurants for some delicious ice cream or some Southern-style, pit-cured barbecue, whatever suits your fancy.

Going a little farther out of town, the Carter Worm Farm may be of interest to you. It's the largest fish bait industry in the world and as there is good fishing in southern Georgia, you'll probably want to try your luck with the best bait.

Then there is the Jimmy Carter Presidential Campaign Headquarters, the old train depot which has been converted. After most primaries Jimmy came back to Plains and made many historic speeches from that depot platform. Throngs of people were always waiting for him to return to give him their best wishes and to congratulate him, and to touch him.

Everyone would gather in the old depot on primary election nights and watch the results come in on two television sets. As Jimmy won the primaries one by one, the crowds grew larger.

On final election night, the huge crowd stayed up all night waiting for Jimmy Carter to return from his headquarters in Atlanta. It was a glorious occasion.

Visitors will also want to see the President's peanut and fertilizer businesses. And the Plains Cotton Warehouse, a business similar in many respects to Jimmy's. Nearly everyone coming to Plains wants to see and shake hands with at least one of the Carter family and most want an autograph.

My father, Alton Carter, who was eighty-nine years old when he died on January 18, 1978, enjoyed meeting and talking to people in my antique shop with me. Now I do it alone. Sometimes, however, I need to find a bit of seclusion for my personal life and my family, so I disappear for a day.

Approximately 1.8 million people are projected to visit Plains in the next twelve months. This should be about 900,000 cars and I'm sure most of them will fill up on gas from Billy Carter's filling station. However, these 1.8 million might want to be aware of a few quaint laws that are still on the books so as not to do anything illegal in the town of Plains.

For example, it is illegal to shoot a slingshot, bow and arrow, or any firearm in the city limits or in the cemetery. Also, you can't start a house for immoral purposes. And another thing you can't do now that in olden days you could is rent a horse and buggy to go to Americus, ten miles away, for twenty-five cents.

Jimmy relishes all the stories about our town, and the folklore of Plains is full of true stories about the various adventures of the Carter family. For example, in 1915 Oscar Williams and my daddy, Alton Carter, drove to a dance twenty miles away in a Maxwell car that Williams owned. They had car trouble and actually pushed the car all the way back to Plains—almost the whole twenty miles.

Oscar Williams died not long ago and to the end, he always told the story of the car and how lucky it was that Daddy finally married in 1916, so they wouldn't have to go looking for girls as far away as Macon, Georgia.

One of the stories in Plains involves Daddy Alton's wine-making activity. For years Daddy Alton made wine in the shed in back of his house. Many nights he and his wife, my stepmother, Betty, stayed up into the wee hours peeling peaches or apples for the wine. He also made scuppernong wine.

He could make wine out of just about anything and pear wine was one of his specialties. He put the wine into those beautiful old antique bottles that used to be embalming bottles when our store was an undertaking parlor.

Daddy had, of course, scalded and sterilized the bottles before the wine got in, but when you finish your wine, you have a beautiful antique bottle—I forget how old they are.

One day Daddy wanted a corroborating opinion on how the wine was coming, so he asked a friend, hurrying by on his way to work, to test it. The friend kept standing there, just sipping and sipping, and never did make it to work.

The town of Plains has not yet gotten over what happened in 1913. The Uriah McTyier family was prominent in nearby Bottsford. They were big farmers and well respected.

The Laster family were white tenant farmers, all of whom worked for the McTyiers, except for one of the Laster sons, Roscoe, who had struck out to make his fortune.

One day, someone called Mrs. McTyier long-distance from Florida and told her there was an important message for her. Roscoe would be arriving in Plains on the local passenger train and would Mrs. McTyier notify the Laster family to meet the train at 3:30 p.m.

Mrs. McTyier got excited and told the Lasters that Roscoe Laster had died and that his *body* was coming in on the train and to have someone there to meet the body. Why else would someone have done the phoning for him?

So the Lasters had Ross Dean, the local undertaker, there at the station as the hour drew nearer with funeral hearse, drawn by two gray horses, all ready to take the body off the train and deliver it to the undertaker's parlor.

It was a big event in those days when a coffin came to town on the train and it always drew a large and curious crowd of spectators.

This particular death had drawn even more interest because the man was young, he had gone off to seek his fortune in Florida, something others only dreamed of doing, and because his family was connected with the prominent McTyier family.

People from far and wide—about 150 strong—were gathered there at the depot in Plains to see Roscoe's body arrive in a box. Daddy was there, too. Also, Uncle Earl—Jimmy's daddy. Everyone was looking very long-faced and solemn.

Well, the train pulled in, smoke puffing out of the smokestack, coal cinders flying everywhere, steam blowing off under the engine. The ladies were holding their handkerchiefs to their eyes and the gentlemen had removed their hats.

The door of the baggage car opened slowly, but instead of Roscoe in a box, out stepped Roscoe from the coach, with a suitcase in hand. He was the picture of success in new suit, tie, and celluloid collar. It was an hour before the young "adventurer" knew what all the cheering and whooping was about and why people were hugging and kissing him or just trying to touch him.

It was one of Plains's shining hours.

It's a different kind of history that has been made in this corner of Georgia today. The state has stretched itself and produced a President, and not an exalted President, but a man of the land, a man who leads a simple life and returns to his familiar haunts.

The tourists see him walking in the distance and wonder what he is doing. I'll tell you.

Anytime you see Jimmy Carter walking in a field, his head is always bent. This doesn't mean he is deep in prayer. What it does mean is that he is looking for arrowheads as he relaxes. Collecting arrowheads and other Indian artifacts is his favorite hobby and he loves to talk about the life-style of the Creeks and Cherokees who once lived here and trod the very land he walks.

He also likes old maps and stories of the old settlers.

Land values are an interesting subject in a President's hometown. After Jimmy Carter became President, land speculators tried to make a fortune selling land for $5.00 to $11.00 per square inch.

In 1880 to 1910, land in this part of Georgia sold for about $1.25 to $5.00 per acre.

Real estate is booming today. A lot worth $1,500 a couple of years ago sold for $22,500 a few days before this writing. Also, a house in town recently valued at about $10,000 before Jimmy became President sold for $58,000.

Although my father farmed all of my boyhood years, I did not work in the fields very much, only picking cotton, shaking peanuts occasionally, and other odd chores, such as stacking oats or cutting sprouts of corn.

I worked for the most part at the general store. My Dad ran the general store and farmed as well. He also bought and sold mules.

About 1938 Daddy went into the mule business. There were no tractors then to amount to anything and most of the farming was with mules.

Dad's top year in the mule business was when he sold about eight hundred mules. Usually he would sell between five hundred and eight hundred per year. He liked to try to average fifty dollars profit per mule. Once he sold a mule, if he ever saw that mule again, he had the ability to remember him, what he paid for him, and what he had sold him for.

This was amazing considering the thousands of mules he sold. He really knew his mules!

One Sunday, he bought a high-priced mule in Atlanta. He paid $275 for him and hauled him to Plains. Two days later he went to the barn and this mule was stretched out dead. Daddy claimed that it was because he bought him on a Sunday, a day when he shouldn't have been buying mules.

Rev. Isaac Johnson, a retired black preacher who lives in Plains, says he and his family used to work occasionally on the farms operated by Daddy and Uncle Earl—Jimmy's father.

He can remember when farm labor was only paid fifteen to fifty cents per day for stacking peanuts to dry before thrashing. Uncle Earl paid one cent per stack and Daddy paid two cents per stack. I asked Daddy about it, but he said he didn't remember this.

Rev. Johnson said that his family—a large one—could put up about three hundred stacks of peanuts per day. He said that at noon, when he was working on the Carter farms, Mrs. Nina Carter— Jimmy's and my grandmother—used to hand them food occasionally out the back door—pones of corn bread and buttermilk. Johnson said they always looked forward to this.

He said he and his family always liked to work for Alton and Earl Carter because they were fair to their employees and always treated them well. He did mention, however, that of the two brothers, Alton—my father—was his favorite.

Those hardworking days are gone from Plains and fewer workers are needed. Now men don't stack peanuts anymore. They combine them with big machinery in the fields as they are dug from the ground. The peanuts are then taken to town in trailers for drying by huge gas dryers.

Jimmy and I both had a healthy interest in the peach and pecan trees which are very plentiful in this area. Even during the presidential campaign, Jimmy did a little peeling of peaches so that the big supply would be frozen and not wasted. Jimmy and I would gather pecans back in the thirties. Fifteen cents per pound was a good price for nuts then, now pecans sell for seventy-five cents to a dollar per pound.

Another phase of country life that Jimmy and I were acquainted with was hog-butchering time. Since we had no refrigeration when we were boys, we had to wait until cold weather set in before killing the hogs. We would usually shoot them with a .22 rifle.

Today, the only way to get to Plains is by automobile. There are no trains (except freight trains), no buses, no cabs, no airplane service. There is, however, a charter air service about four miles north of Plains, called Petecraft Aviation Services, Inc., which is operated by a pleasant fellow named Tom Peterson.

You can land a private plane on Tom's airfield or you can charter Tom Peterson's services to take you most anywhere.

Jimmy used Tom's charter service extensively during the presidential campaign. He and Tom are great friends and Jimmy has great confidence in Tom's ability to fly.

In 1977, on one of Jimmy's stops at my antique shop to see me, Tom had just brought in a poster for me to display advertising a plane ride over Plains and the President's home for five dollars.

Jimmy looked at the poster with pride and said, "Oh, you have a *new* service here in Plains—and I frankly think five dollars is a reasonable price to charge for a plane ride."

Later in that same conversation, Jimmy told me he had almost decided to drop plans to build a helicopter pad near his home and that he would probably always land his copter at Peterson's field, because the Secret Service can drive him the four miles to his home in just a few minutes.

It's hard to keep Plains just a sleepy little town when high-pressure entrepreneurs like Larry Flynt, the publisher of the formerly sex-oriented magazine *Hustler*, comes down and buys its newspaper.

The town of Plains was really rocked to wake up and find that its weekly family-type newspaper, *The Plains Georgia Monitor*, had been bought by Flynt for a good price. I think that Editor Sam Simpson is staying, and that he will continue to do a good job.

What the Town Council has agreed on is that we don't want Plains to become a town of chrome and plastic like Johnson City, near LBJ's ranch, became.

Someday, Jimmy will be back and we've promised the town will be the same. He will walk hand in hand with Rosalynn as he did before. I will look out my store and I will call out as he goes by, "Hi, Cousin Hot."

Everything will be back to normal.

3 · TWO TOM SAWYERS

I am not going to say Jimmy and I were little angels. He was forever pulling his sisters' hair and I was forever having fist fights with by brother Donnel.

When Hot was nine and I was thirteen, he was spending the night with me once when we decided to have a little fun. We stuffed a long silk stocking of Mother's with cotton so that in the dark it resembled a snake.

We tied a long string to it and we hid on our front porch. We put the "snake" in the ditch out in front of the house. When we would hear someone coming down the sidewalk, we would pull slowly on the string and the "snake" would come slowly out of the ditch and across the sidewalk in front of the startled pedestrian.

Most of them would holler and start looking for a stick to kill the snake. Of course, we would keep pulling until the snake disappeared.

After the person was out of sight, we would sneak off the porch and plant the "snake" back in the ditch until the next victim appeared.

Sometimes, the poor frightened soul would start running and could still be heard hollering off in the distance—which pleased us very much. Snakes were an important part of childhood.

Jimmy and I killed any number of them.

There are still many snakes around Plains, Georgia, of which the rattlesnake and the moccasin are the most deadly. Other snakes, not so dangerous, are coach whips, black snakes, green snakes, rat snakes. I remember the day, not too many years ago, when my wife and son, Hugh, Jr., and Buck Sproull and I were fishing in a nearby swamp.

I almost stepped right on a big rattlesnake. By some miracle Buck saw it in time and whacked it in the head, killing it before it could strike me. That was a tense moment.

Buck, incidentally, who was a buddy of both Hot and me, is now a rural mail delivery man at Colbert, Georgia.

Dad would take Jimmy and me fishing occasionally when I was a boy. One afternoon an eel grabbed my line down at Hall's Bridge on the Kinchafoonee Creek. I was only about ten years old and the eel looked so much like a snake that I refused to take it off the hook.

When I got home, mother fried the eel and I discovered that eel is a delicious fish.

When we were kids, hunting was the exciting thing to do. Our fathers taught us to hunt. We were anxious to grow old enough to go out hunting with them. I remember one day when Jimmy was eight and I was twelve and we were going to make a big day of it.

Jimmy got to my house about 9:00 in the morning and we struck out for Rabbit Branch, about a mile and a half from my home. We had to go through the very woods where the presidential home is now located, in order to get to Rabbit Branch.

It was springtime and the road was long and winding through woods full of blooming dogwood trees. On that particular day we weren't after rabbits, birds, or any other animal. We were going to hunt for certain flowering shrubs to give to my mother because she had said she would like to plant some in the front yard.

We boys did not consider it odd to pick off a lot of sweet-smelling shrubs to tie in our handkerchiefs and bruise for the sweet aroma. We even took sweet shrubs to school and swapped them for marbles or bananas or gave them to our girl friends or the teacher.

So we were thinking about what we'd do with all the newfound wealth when suddenly there was a timber rattler right in front of us. They are a very poisonous kind of rattlesnake whose venom can kill. This one had thirteen rattles but at that moment we were not counting rattles, we were falling back as fast as we could go.

Then Jimmy found a good heavy stick and I, being the older, had to tackle and kill the beast. It never dawned on us to wait until the snake went its way and let us go ours. Killing a snake was considered an act of bravery and soon we were cutting off those thirteen rattles— one for every year.

We came home in triumph with something for everyone—plants for mother, sweet shrubs for the teacher, and rattles to scare girls with, and of course enough stories to last a week. Mother had a good noonday dinner ready for us—and my mouth waters as I remember exactly what Hot and I ate as we bragged about our great adventure.

Everything had been raised on the fields right around us, made according to Mother's own recipes. One of her favorite dishes that the whole family, including Jimmy, liked was Irish potatoes sliced and fried with onions on top of the wood stove. Mother had fixed it for us that day along with fried chicken, rice and gravy, hot biscuits, iced tea, corn bread, and pecan pie for dessert.

Hot always ate the drumsticks. My favorite parts were the chicken wings—and I was amused to read some time ago that this was also the favorite food of Elizabeth Taylor and that she would even have fried chicken wings flown to her wherever she was.

After dinner, we went out to the patch of woods behind our house—we had about two acres of trees—and worked at one of our favorite pastimes, town building. We were great town builders. We would rake leaves into streets and stores and houses. The street would be about three feet wide.

The main building for us was the barbershop. We would bring soap and water along to play barber. We would lather our faces and rake the lather off with a stick. Of course, neither of us was old enough to have a single hair on our chin but we had high hopes.

We also had play money to pay for shaves and haircuts and other things. We built the grocery store and shopped there for licorice sticks. We had a drugstore with a soda fountain, a hardware store, an ice house, a courthouse and a theater which we called a "moving picture house." We spent the entire afternoon in our town.

That little patch of woods is still there behind my father's house. I oftentimes look at it and ponder the days Jimmy and I used to play.

Jimmy was born in the Wise Hospital but at the time his mother and daddy had rooms in the E. E. Cook house across the street from the Methodist Church. This was in 1924, October 1. Two years later his family moved to the Lunsford house which later burned down. It was located just below the house presently occupied by Mrs. Y. T. Sheffield.

About 1927 they moved to the Ballew or McGarrah house, where our postmaster, J. R. McGarrah, now lives. In 1928 they moved to the farm which is about two and a half miles west of Plains near Archery. Jimmy was four years old when they moved to the farm, and he spent most of his early life there in a wooden clapboard house.

On the way from my house in Plains to this early childhood farm home, I would pass the Lebanon Cemetery, used by all the churches in Plains to bury their dead. Jimmy's father, Earl, is buried there. So is my mother, Annie Laurie, and our grandmother, Nina Pratt Carter, and now my father, Alton Carter.

The clapboard house was on a dirt road which continued on from Archery to Preston. That road is paved now but the house still stands and is occupied by Mr. and Mrs. T. R. Downer.

I remember how good it was to be in that house in the summer. The ceilings were high and so it was cool. But in the winter it was very cold. The house was heated with fireplaces and they gave off a cheery glow as if to apologize for not being able to heat the rooms.

There was always a problem of having enough wood. Wood cut with a saw or ax was used for fuel; oak, pine, and fat pine for starting the fire. Some hickory was used because it was slow-burning and kept the fire from going out. Hickory was also used for making ax handles and hoe handles for farm tools.

I remember the wood stove in Aunt Lillian's kitchen. I often visited and ate delicious meals cooked by Aunt Lillian, as I called Jimmy's mother. She was an excellent cook but she was also an avid reader. I used to wonder how she could enjoy her food because she nearly always read a book or magazine while she was eating. Jimmy also acquired this habit early in life.

There was no indoor toilet, but rather an outdoor privy. Newspapers or a Sears catalog was the accessory. I didn't know that rolls of toilet paper existed in those days.

If I wanted a drink of water or to wash my hands, I pumped it from a hand pump. Great progress was made later when a windmill was installed and there was running water in the house.

However, with running water came problems. If not drained when there was a freeze, the pipes were filled with solid ice and burst. There were no hot water heaters and water had to be heated on the wood stove in pans for bathing.

The front yard was not a lawn but rather earth swept clean with a brush broom. Chickens roamed the yard scratching up any grass that tried to grow. Hens' nests could be found almost anywhere. Jimmy found the eggs and any not needed by the family were taken to town on Saturday and sold in the store or commissary.

I remember eating chicken pie and baked sweet potatoes at Jimmy's house. Afterward we would go out in the yard and play under the trees. Jimmy had pecan trees, fig trees, chinaberry, and magnolias.

In the back of the pasture on Jimmy's farm there was a homemade swimming pool about five feet wide and fifteen feet long boarded on the sides. The water in it was about five feet deep. Jimmy, Willard

Slappey, also a first cousin, and I would go skinny-dipping in it.

Then we would go horseback riding. Jimmy was a very good horseman but one day Willard was thrown from the horse and he broke his arm in two places. Willard and I didn't do much horseback riding after that.

Jimmy had a way with animals and he was never without a pet that I can remember. Even now, at the White House, in partnership with daughter Amy, he has a dog named Grits and a Siamese cat named Misty Malarky Ying-Yang—the latter means bad and good.

When Cousin Hot was no more than two or three years old he was seriously ill at the hospital with some stomach ailment. I believe it was colitis. Anyway, he was on the danger list, but sick as he was he kept saying he wanted a billy goat.

One of the nurses at Wise Sanitarium went scouting for goats and found a young billy goat and brought it to him. It was kept right in Jimmy's hospital room and it is credited with having given Jimmy the will to live.

I have many memories of Jimmy's pony that was named Lady. Jimmy was very jealous of anyone else getting too chummy with Lady and he trained her to resist doing anything for anyone else. Jimmy could make Lady trot and run and pull a cart, but with anyone else the pony would balk and go straight into the barn no matter how they pulled and tugged.

Jimmy even once kept a baby alligator under his bed. It was good insurance against his sisters snooping around his room. I can't remember what happened to the alligator but I rather think his father took it away when it outgrew the box it lived in.

Eventually Jimmy had a second pony and he named it Lady Lee.

Until I was six or seven years old, my name was Hugh Inman Carter. Young as I was I decided that I had to have my name changed so it would be similar to my father's. I got Dad to go to the State Capitol in Atlanta, where the official state records were kept at that time, and order my name changed legally and officially to Hugh Alton Carter.

But before Dad went to the Capitol, I had to make my peace with my grandmother Nina who had given me that weird middle name, Inman. She was understanding of a small boy who wanted to be like his daddy.

The population of Plains at the time Jimmy was born was 550 people. It only advanced by 100 between that important date and January

1977, when that little babe, having weathered fifty-two years, was sworn in as President of the United States.

When Jimmy was born, peanuts were already the major crop of the town, followed by peaches, watermelons, cotton, and cantaloupes. Eggs were also shipped out in large quantity.

I well remember the world into which Jimmy was born in 1924. The world of his farm. The world of one hundred blacks whose lives revolved around his family because they worked the farm and they bought their groceries at the commissary run by his father.

Jimmy was the oldest, the firstborn, who was two years old before his first sister came along. His earliest memories were of farm bells ringing. Workers were awakened every morning at 4:00 by that farm bell that told them it was time to get to the fields.

The going rate for labor in those days was one dollar per day. Women got 75 cents and children 25 cents.

The hardest work on Uncle Earl's plantation was "shaking" the peanut plants free of dirt and stacking them. The peanut plants were plowed up with mule power. Workers followed along behind the plows picking up the vines, shaking them and making stacks about ten yards apart. They were left to dry before harvesting. Georgia produces 40 percent of all peanuts grown in the United States—more than any other two states combined.

Tourists going through Plains ask to see how peanuts grow and are harvested. They grow underground like potatoes.

Peanuts are better for the ground than potatoes, however, because they are a legume, which means they have little nodules on the roots which enrich the soil. Each vine produces about fifty or sixty nuts. When the nuts come out of the ground they contain about 35 percent moisture. A delicious dish is to boil them in salty water for about an hour when they still contain this moisture. The result is called *boiled peanuts.*

Jimmy and I both boiled peanuts on Saturdays when we were very young. You could make about $5.00 profit on a Saturday selling sacks of peanuts for 5 cents each as we did—$2.50 apiece looked good to us.

Uncle Earl also raised sugarcane and cotton. A lot of sugarcane was grown back in those days. Cane grinding was a big thing to attend late in the afternoon or night and I would go over to watch with Jimmy. A mule would walk around in a circle in harness as manpower for the grinder. The cane was ground and the juice was boiled to make syrup.

The juice was a delicacy to drink. Several families would go to a cane grinding on the same night and this became quite a social occasion that we looked forward to.

One of the meanest jobs Jimmy had to work at on the farm was mopping cotton to kill the boll weevils. Molasses, water, and arsenic were mixed together and applied with the help of a rag mop. It had to be rubbed on each stalk of cotton by hand. The molasses would get all over him and cause a sticky mess, and a poisonous one.

Another crop Uncle Earl raised in large supply was sweet potatoes. They were dug out of the ground in fall and placed in a pile, covered with pine straw and boards to protect them during the winter.

When Jimmy was five, the depression of 1929 had begun and from then until 1933, when Franklin Roosevelt became President, living was hard and there was little hope that things would get easier. Peanuts were being sold by farmers for only about a penny per pound. People were hungry. Labor was very cheap and would be paid mostly with food.

I remember my mother paid our maid and cook 50 cents per week and her meals. Jimmy's nursemaid, Annie Mae, who took care of all the Carter kids, got 50 cents a week, too. However, his mother's cook was handsomely paid—one dollar a week and all she could eat.

In comparison, an acre of peanuts would yield about seven hundred pounds so if you got one cent per pound that was only seven dollars per acre for a lot of work and a lot of worry about the weather.

Both my mother and Aunt Lillian had plenty of help with their housework from among the black female domestic workers of the town. My nanny, who also took care of brother Don, was named Mary Bishop.

As we grew up—Jimmy and I—we followed the same tradition of colored help in the kitchen. Emma Harvey, who used to cook in my house, later cooked for Rosalynn and Jimmy.

Lillian Pickett, who cooked for Jimmy and Rosalynn, now cooks in a restaurant in Plains.

Rachel Clark, the black woman who used to nurse Jimmy, still lives in Plains and I talked with her just the other day about those early years when she and her husband, Jack Clark, used to live in one of the tenant houses on Uncle Earl's farm.

As kids, we all loved Jack and Rachel. Rachel would stop to tell all of us stories and we felt close to her. Rachel prides herself on the fact that she spent so much time with Jimmy in his early years. She said, "I have to pinch myself to make me believe he is now President of the United States."

Rachel recalled that when she was cooking for Jimmy's family she was always spanking Billy for the mischief he got into but not Jimmy.

It was probably Aunt Lillian's attitude toward black people that influenced Jimmy to play with black kids when that was almost a taboo thing in Plains. When we were growing up, blacks did not enter the front door of a house but had to go around to the back door.

Aunt Lillian was fiercely kind to the black children who played with Jimmy. She bought clothes for Edmund Hollis, whose nickname was Pap. In spite of the segregation rules, she insisted that Jimmy's black friends go along with them to occasional movies and to the circus. Usually the black kids would refuse to go because they didn't want to get into trouble with movie and circus managements.

One friend, Alvin "A.D." Davis, would go to the circus but refused to sit with them so that he wouldn't get into trouble. He would automatically disappear and they would spot him later in the segregated section for blacks. When it was time to go home, A.D., whose nickname was Knock, would suddenly reappear at their side.

Aunt Lillian deserved a lot of credit for being the first person in Plains to try to lower the color barrier and succeed. In her house black boys could sit and eat at the same table with Jimmy, play in his room with him, and even lie on his bed.

Jimmy's father and my father did not share Aunt Lillian's feelings, and the black children I played with were those who were along when I played with Jimmy. From what I could see, though Uncle Earl had the traditional southern segregationist attitude, he just ignored the black children that Aunt Lillian permitted in the house and did not try to change her.

Or if he ever had tried, he probably had given up because Aunt Lillian was very strong-willed.

But Uncle Earl was a very kindly man toward the blacks and they would come to him when they were in trouble and needed money. They would also come to Daddy Alton.

When any little boy had big problems, Aunt Lillian took a special interest. That was the case with Rembert Forrest, whose mother died when he was five. On top of that, Rembert himself developed pneumonia. Aunt Lillian became a second mother to Rembert and nursed him and made Jimmy play with him.

He became a good friend of Jimmy's and in later years they kept in touch.

Though there was a depression, one reason Cousin Hot and I did not suffer too much was that we had all the good eating we could wish for just by having fun—that's what hunting and fishing was for us. We would go fishing at night sometimes and put out set hooks. Catfish and suckers and jacks were the main fish we caught.

It was fun to muddy the creek so that the fish would have to come to the top for air and then we would catch them by spearing them. We also gigged suckers with spears using flashlights at night in the spring of the year.

Often we would come upon a hidden moonshine still while hunting in the fall and winter. We kept the secret and it was part of the sport to watch how moonshine was made. But always from a distance.

Even before we could hold a gun, our fathers took us on dove shoots in the morning at sunrise and our job would be to run and pick up the fallen birds. The way it was done in those days is that fields would be baited with wheat and corn and then on the morning of the hunt about twenty-five to thirty hunters would surround the field. When the doves came in to feed in the early light of day, they would be shot on the wing.

This was a great sport back in those days. It was legal to hunt doves at any time of the day and baiting of fields had not been outlawed yet.

I was never very good at quail hunting as I didn't have any good dogs and would not have been able to handle them well even if I did.

When Jimmy and I, and Cody Timmerman, a buddy, eventually were old enough to handle the guns, we shot doves at a particular water hole near Plains where the birds would fly in for water late in the afternoon.

Jimmy still kids me about one of my hunting experiences, which involved Miz Minnie and Miz Florence Wise, two sisters who owned the woods out Highway 280, just out of the Plains city limits on the east side of town toward Americus.

Miz Minnie and Miz Florence were very strict and they did not allow anyone to hunt squirrels in their woods. But as boys, some of us would slip in there late in the afternoon with our .22-caliber rifles and shoot a squirrel or two.

I must have been in high school when this incident happened. I was trespassing in the Wises' woods late one afternoon with Cody

Timmerman when Florence Wise came through the woods. Cody saw her before I did and he quietly disappeared behind a tree. Miz Florence confronted me and the dead squirrel dangling from my hand. I thought I was being fairly gallant when I quickly offered to give her the squirrel but she tossed her head with disdain and proceeded to give me the scolding of my life.

The gist of her lecture was that it was the same thing as if she had gone downtown and taken some cloth out of my daddy's store without permission and without paying for it.

I listened to all this silently and felt like two cents.

But suddenly something in me snapped and I started lecturing her—because she had refused my fair and square offer to let her have the squirrel to take home and cook. Since she had spurned my generous offer and was still telling me haughtily what I had done that was wrong, I took it upon myself to tell her what she had done that was wrong.

I reminded her that her cows had just a few days before broken out of her pasture and into our fields, damaging my father's corn crop by eating a great number of the young stalks.

I described the damage, warming to my subject, and asked heatedly if she thought one small squirrel was more valuable than all the corn her cows had eaten and all the ears of corn that would never be in that field because her cows had destroyed them before they had even had a chance to live and grow.

As Miz Florence went stalking off, I went stalking back and found Cody doubled up with laughter behind a tree. We replayed the scene for Jimmy and every now and then he would have me repeat the incident and laugh all over again.

Once a year a Sunday School teacher, Mr. O. V. Hogsed, took youngsters to spend the night at an old millhouse about three miles north of Plains. We fished during the day in the pond and cooked the fish at night for supper. We slept on the floor in the millhouse and always threw corncobs at each other after the lights went out.

Other than Mr. Hogsed's much anticipated shindig, we did our own programming.

Of course, we had our responsibilities. For example, Jimmy, Willard, Donnel, and I used to have certain nights to stay with our grandmother (Nina Carter) who lived alone in her home behind the Methodist Church in Plains. It kept her from being lonely or afraid and it was good training for us.

Jimmy's night was Friday night. My night was Tuesday night. On those nights when we stayed with "Mama"—she wouldn't let us call her Grandmother—we would play out under the streetlights with other kids in the neighborhood.

Jimmy had his daytime responsibilities. He carried buckets of water to black workers on the farm and he hoed Bermuda grass out of the cotton and peanuts. He and I collected old newspapers in Plains and sold them to the markets to wrap fish in.

We also gathered up scrap iron and sold it to a junk dealer for 20 cents per hundred pounds. All to make our spending money.

I had a responsibility, too. Nearly everyone had a cow in those days and so did we. I always had to do the milking at my house. My brother Donnel, being older and smarter than I was, made like he couldn't learn to milk. But anyway, he had to cut the fat splinters to start the fires and bring in the coal and wood.

And sometimes he would fix the cow feed for me while I milked. So it evened out.

I remember one time Jimmy spent the night with me. I had a little trick that I played on everyone I could. I asked him to kneel down close to the cow's bag and I would show him where the milk came out.

When he did, I gave his face a good dousing with fresh cow's milk directly from the bag. He didn't see the humor of it.

Every morning after milking I would have to walk the cow from my home to the pasture so that she could eat grass all day. Then in the afternoon I would have to go get her. Whenever I could, I persuaded my brother to do these chores for me.

Daddy had the general store in town and I worked in the store from the time I was big enough to make change and stand on a wooden box to sell cold drinks—at five cents each. Later, I sold vinegar, pumped from a barrel, and bulk coffee at fifteen cents per pound. Also, ground coffee beans when needed.

Tobacco was fifteen cents per plug, but if a person wanted a nickel's worth, you could cut one third plug for him. We sold sugar at five cents per pound in bulk, or you could buy five or ten pounds in a white cloth bag. One day Dad's bookkeeper caught a man trying to take a ten pound bag of sugar out of the store under his coat.

When I was twelve or thirteen years old I began to help take inventory. Everything in the store had to be counted at the end of every year. This was always a big job. Jimmy helped us in the store at this job from time to time. Our fathers always gave us jobs to make our spending money. They would always pay us. It helped to teach us the value of a dollar early in life.

On Saturdays when they were in high school, my brother, Donnel, and cousin, Willard Slappey, ran the hot dog, hamburger, and ice cream stand in the old bank building which my Dad had bought. Then when Donnel went off to college, Willard and I operated the stand. After Willard went off to school, Jimmy and I operated it.

Sometimes one or the other of us could not do our ice cream vending on a particular Saturday and the other would get a friend to help. One day Jimmy got Rembert Forrest as his helper. Instead of splitting the money as Jimmy and I did, Jimmy was going to pay Rembert a straight salary of thirty-five cents.

Unfortunately, it hadn't been a completely successful day and Jimmy failed to sell all his ice cream. Being a sharp businessman, even at an early age, Jimmy tried to get Rem to take his pay in leftover ice cream. However, although Rem loved ice cream, he didn't think much of having to eat seven ice cream cones all at one time.

I believe he said no. However, so persuasive was little Jimmy that I wouldn't be surprised to learn, even at this late date, that Rem ended up eating a lot of melted ice cream.

Even though I was trying to make money by selling ice cream in the town on Saturdays with Cousin Jimmy, I was not excused from my morning chore of milking the cow. Mother would awaken me about 6:00 A.M.—I slept in the large upstairs room with Brother Don—and I would hurry out and find the cow in the wooded area about a hundred yards behind the house and milk the creature.

By the time I got the bucket of milk back to the house, I had started to wake up a little and Mother had breakfast ready for all of us.

But before I would eat, I would call Cousin Hot. I would crank the phone to signal the operator and she would connect me with Jimmy's house.

I would check to see whether Jimmy and his mother were making their share of the boiled custard—boiling sweet milk with the proper ingredients—for the ice cream. Jimmy and his mother would make one three-gallon freezer full of ice cream and one-gallon freezer, and my mother and I would make the same amount. Hot and I would go to town with eight gallons to sell on the street.

So that Jimmy and I could be together for the making of the ice cream, we would take turns bringing our share of the boiled custard to each other's home early in the morning. Then we would laugh and talk as we froze and packed the ice cream for sale.

Since we had four different freezers, we made four different kinds of ice cream—strawberry, in season, peach, in season, cherry, in season, and vanilla, always.

Guided by our mothers, we added a bit of red coloring to the strawberry and cherry to make it more tempting.

Before Jimmy would get to my house with his boiled custard, the iceman would have left two big blocks of ice—a total of two hundred pounds. It took a lot of ice to freeze and then pack the ice cream for hardening, so that it would stay hard while we sold it. It had to be firm so that it could be placed on a cone.

We used the old-style crank ice cream freezers with dashers turning on the inside as Jimmy and I cranked the handle on the outside.

At first it would be fun, but it would get tougher and tougher to sit there and keep turning until the custard began to harden. We were relieved when it was thick enough for the fruit to be added, but that made it harder to turn than ever.

The ice was a problem, too. The large cakes had to be crushed in a burlap bag and the chips put around the ice cream container between it and the walls of the wooden freezer bucket.

We had to mix salt with the ice as we put it in the freezer to speed the freezing. Salt also was added to the ice when we packed the ice cream for transporting it to town.

It took about thirty minutes to make a freezer of ice cream which meant that we were ready in a little more than an hour since each of us made two freezers full. Our reward was the ice cream we scraped off the dasher. The final thing we would do before we left his place or mine, after that heavy work, was to take a quick bath and put on our good clothes. We wanted to look our best at our stand in Plains.

We had to remember to bring along the double-decker ice cream cones that we had bought a few days before.

Our final responsibility as soon as we got to town was to rush over and borrow five dollars' worth of change from daddy's store. We learned early that entrepreneurs always used someone else's money to go into business.

Already there would be a crowd of kids waiting at our stand in the old bank building. They would plunk down their nickel and we would put one dip on each side of the cone and top if off with one dip in the middle on top—customer's choice of flavors. Many came back for seconds.

Our best customer was Harold Sproull, who would buy at least three cones in the course of the afternoon.

If business got slack, I would pull rank on Hot and order him to run out and drum up trade. Since I was older and taller, my will prevailed. Old Hot hated it but would run up and down the street hollering, "I SCREAM, YOU SCREAM, WE ALL SCREAM FOR ICE CREAM! Rush on down to Carter's ice cream stand and get three dips for a nickel."

Now and then I would take pity on Jimmy and do it myself, but most of the time I made him do the vocal advertising.

Another rhyme we used to advertise was this: "Ice cream, made in the shade, sold in the sun, old Chic Tyson, ain't got none." Chic Tyson was an older fellow who operated a fish stand down the street and didn't sell ice cream.

I can only remember one or two times that we failed to sell out our supply of ice cream. In fact, we usually were done with it by four or five o'clock in the afternoon.

The hotter the weather, the faster the sales. After paying all expenses and returning the five dollars change to our personal banker, my much amused dad, we would divide the profits. On a really good day we would make up to five dollars each. But that was after we added the five-cent hot dogs and the five-cent hamburgers to our menu. We had an efficient little operation. One would scoop ice cream while the other flipped hamburgers. We would cook the hamburgers on a small oil stove, using a big iron frying pan. We would buy the ground beef from Mr. Kennedy down on the corner, who ran a small market.

As we had seen our mothers do, to "extend" the meat, we would mix the ground beef with bread and chopped onions. The odor was very tempting as Hot and I fried the meat over a hot fire. We didn't worry too much if we couldn't get hamburger buns. We just got a loaf of bread and put the hamburger between two slices.

We might sell as many as fifty to a hundred hamburgers and hot dogs during a Saturday's business. It seemed that anything we sold was a nickel—including a big bag of boiled peanuts.

The reward after the hard day's work was to hitchhike to Americus and see a Western movie at the old Rylander Theater. Tom Mix, Buck Jones, and Ken Maynard were our favorite western stars. Another thing that drew us like a magnet, week after week, was the serial which was continued from time to time and left the hero hanging on the edge of a cliff by his fingernails at the end of each episode.

The cost of the movie was only two nickels—a thin dime.

Cousin Hot and I never worried about the dangers of hitchhiking home because we knew everyone and everyone knew us. The worst that could happen would be that we would have to walk a little before a car came that was going to Plains.

There was a big junction at Abbets Place and the road to Plains that was the best spot to stand with our thumbs stuck out. If it was getting late and nobody came and it looked like we were stuck, we would have to resort to calling his mother or mine to come after us. But this only happened occasionally.

Uncle Earl was a very kind man and he liked to make children happy at Christmastime. Especially the poor. He would throw a big party a few days before Christmas each year at the Elks Club and there would be lots of hot dogs and ice cream to eat, and I believe peanuts and some kind of punch.

No child left empty-handed. Uncle Earl gave a gift to each child and made sure the poorer children got the best gifts, toys and dolls and teddy bears.

There was one Christmas Jimmy couldn't have come to the party if he'd wanted to—that was when he had the measles and had to stay in a darkened room. Before the Christmas holiday was over so did his sisters, Gloria and Ruth. Jimmy was only about five at the time and it was mighty gloomy for him to have to go through Christmas without chasing around the tree and sneaking a look at presents.

A family tradition for all Carters was to leave a snack for Santa Claus. This taught us, our parents said, to look out for anyone who was nice to us and give him something in return. At my house and Jimmy's, Santa found cookies and a big glass of milk. And once at least, Santa found the ultimate child's tribute—a licorice stick.

4 · BAREFOOT
AND HAPPY

Nostalgia fills me as I remember the many things we did that so few kids do today. I feel sorry for all the children growing up in cities today who cannot begin to know the simple joys and inventiveness of the games their President played as a farm child. No parent instructed Jimmy and me in what to do to amuse ourselves. They didn't have to.

We flew kites that we made ourselves. We caught June bugs and tied thread to their legs so they could be our pets. We caught lightning bugs out under the streetlights and put them in jars to watch them light up.

We rolled barrel hoops with a stiff wire. We played king of the mountain on sawdust piles. We hunted in piles of trash in the stream for penny winkle worms—a fish bait—which we sold to the local fishermen for fifty cents per hundred.

Both Jimmy and I had battery-operated radios in our homes, with a round speaker, separate from the receiver, sitting on top. We would invite in the neighbors when there were prizefights or programs of special interest. I can remember we thought Lowell Thomas was the best newscaster of the day.

One of Jimmy's favorite orchestras as a boy was Glenn Miller.

Then there were overnight excursions to a nearby small creek. We always took bacon, eggs, and other items that we could cook easily and we would spend the night. Of course, we took along our blankets and a canvas tent, if available.

Sometimes when there was a pile of sand near a creek, we'd take some of it and dam up the creek to make a swimming hole, and go skinny-dipping.

We felt that we weren't hurting the creek because the sand would soon be worn away by the flow of water.

Jimmy and I would take turns going to each other's houses. I liked going over to Jimmy's at Archery for horseback riding and, of course, for walking the rails.

At the time, I did not think that railroad tracks in front of the house might lower its real-estate value. I thought he was mighty lucky to have the Seaboard Railroad tracks so conveniently close. We would have a contest to see who could walk the most rails without falling off.

A single rail was about twenty-five feet long. We had a superstitious idea that if you could walk nine rails without falling off, you could make a wish and the wish would come true. It was supposed to be more effective than wishing on the first star.

Hot could beat me walking rails because he was younger and lighter than I was—but more important, his feet were always larger. We always walked the rails barefooted, and Jimmy was very good at gripping them with his toes. Looking back, I wonder if Jimmy ever used his wish to ask for the presidency.

I know my favorite wishes ran to toys, trips, and other boyish adventures.

There were a lot of freight trains during the course of the day, but only one passenger train a day, which was called "The Butt Head" because the engine was rounded in front. But I remember the earlier trains before "The Butt Head" were the old type with smokestacks, fed by coal.

Cousin Hot and I used to put pennies on the track and let the train run over them to flatten them. These made very impressive gifts for girls. If we had no pennies, we collected any pieces of metal we could find to see what the train could do to them. Sometimes they would come out like the shape of a state or an animal.

We could spend a whole afternoon doing things along the railroad tracks. The telegraph wires followed the railroad tracks and birds would sit on the wires and we would shoot at them with our slingshots or flips. We made our own slingshots and flips out of rubber tire inner tubes and the leather tongues of old shoes.

Naturally, there were a lot of nice smooth stones along the railroad track so we were never out of ammunition. If only the birds had stayed still, we would have had good hunting.

Jimmy's favorite hunting activity did not always involve birds however, but arrowheads. He was fascinated by arrowheads and the thought that an Indian had held this thing in his hand, had made it, and used it to bring home food. If I wanted to please Hot, I would suggest we go arrowhead hunting.

We would wander through the fields and pastures heads down scanning every bit of stone that poked its head up from the earth. I don't think Jimmy ever gave any of his away, and he probably still has them. I know he still goes arrowhead hunting with Rosalynn and the boys.

I did not have Jimmy's feelings about arrowheads. He would be very excited when he found one. I would be thinking of what I could do with mine.

I would give them to my current girl friend. Or I would trade them for something good to eat—like scuppernong grapes or plums.

If I got really lucky, I would swap an arrowhead for marbles, which were something I collected and needed because I played marbles a lot.

For some reason, Jimmy never offered to trade anything for my arrowheads so I hung on to mine until a good offer came along. Jimmy held on to every arrowhead tenaciously and did not trade them away.

He also collected old bottles and had a most impressive collection of them which tourists and visitors could look at when he was governor. I'm sure that people did not know that one of the greatest sites for finding antique bottles in Georgia, and other places, is in the ground where outhouses once stood. Men who secretly drank would toss their empty pints in the outdoor privy away from prying eyes.

Whenever Jimmy and I would be walking along a creek, Jimmy would keep an eye out for old disreputable-looking bottles. He would rinse them off and some would look very nice, especially the blues and whites.

At our houses, we boys used to build hens' nests out of orange or lemon crates that had two compartments. We would nail the nests up off the ground to protect the chickens and the eggs from dogs. We would put a board against the tree leading up to the nest to help the hen get up there.

On Saturdays we took the extra eggs to town and traded them for groceries at the grocery store.

A favorite trick of children would be to slip an egg or two from a hen's nest and bring the one or two eggs to town to swap for a penny or two of candy. Since eggs cost fifteen cents per dozen it was an even deal.

The favorite candy for Jimmy and me was licorice or hard stick candy—lemon and peppermint sticks about four and a half inches long and a little bigger around than a pencil.

My mother, Annie Laurie, and her sister-in-law, Miz Lillian, who was married to Jimmy's father, were certainly different. Miz Lillian was never content to be just a homemaker. She was always out and around taking care of the sick, investigating the needs of the poor. When she wasn't busy outside the home, she was deep in some book.

My mother, on the other hand, seemed to live only for her family and their welfare. Mother would darn our socks with tender loving care so that they wouldn't hurt where the darn was. I don't believe many mothers know that art anymore.

Mother would encourage us—Donnel and me—to sit down and tell her about our day at school and everything we felt and thought. Miz Lillian did not have time to delve into her children's lives in the same way. She would be reading a book at the table and she would tell them to read a book. Everyone at the Jimmy Carter table read a book while eating except Uncle Earl.

The only way Cousin Jimmy could get out of work around the house was to say he was reading. Aunt Lillian was so anxious for her children to be well read that she would go do a household chore herself rather than interfere with Jimmy's learning process.

Unfortunately, the same dodge wouldn't work for me and if I said I was reading, I'm sure my Dad would have said, "Well, stop reading and take care of this."

Aunt Lillian seemed to me to be a little ashamed that her husband was not keeping up the family tradition of book reading and she would explain to us that Uncle Earl's eyes were bothering him and that was why he wasn't reading. But the truth of the matter was that he didn't care to read at the table.

Nor did we at our house. We would have interesting conversations at the table about events of the day. It would be really amusing to have lunch or dinner at Jimmy's house. I did not read at the table and had no book with me, so I would study my plate and just look around while everyone else read.

After Jimmy ate, he would throw himself down on the couch and read a little more until his food digested. Then he would jump up and we would go out and continue our games.

Jimmy still is reading at the table at the White House, whenever he doesn't have company, and now little Amy has the habit. Other guests were shocked when Amy brought a little book right along with her to read at a formal function for the Mexican head of state. But I wasn't at all surprised. I would have been surprised if she *hadn't* brought a book.

I think that one reason Jimmy was a little shy in childhood, in the same way that Amy is today, is that he was not trained to talk at the dinner table. Talking was forbidden at the table, other than the saying of the blessing. He did not learn to hold general conversations at mealtimes.

Life with father was sometimes pretty rough for Jimmy. Uncle Earl was very stern and forceful as a father and was the complete boss. So Jimmy did not protest when his daddy used the mule shears to cut Jimmy's hair. Unfortunately electricity had just been brought in and these were new electric clippers.

Uncle Earl wasn't used to them and he made a clean path right across the top of poor Hot's head. Jimmy didn't know what to expect next. He had a sinking sensation that whatever it was, it wasn't going to improve his appearance for an upcoming trip to his grandparents in Columbus.

Uncle Earl proceeded to clip off all the rest of Jimmy's hair—to Jimmy's consternation.

Jimmy was no longer sure he wanted to go to Columbus but his dad got him a cap and off he went. It's a family story that Grandmom reported that Jimmy had been a perfect little guest for a whole week with one exception—his little cap had seemed to be glued to him. For some peculiar reason, he had refused to ever take it off—not to eat at the table and not even when he climbed into bed.

To know the kind of awesome feeling that Jimmy and his family had about their daddy, you have only to know what happened when Uncle Earl took the grand step of being measured for a tailor-made suit. When it was delivered Uncle Earl put it on and became more ridiculous-looking with every moment.

The suit was huge and obviously made for some other man or just a botched-up job. Yet nobody dared laugh, and off they went to church as solemn as can be.

The President's father was rather a strange man. In his independence, he was a lot like Billy is today—both in attitude toward life and wanting a good time.

I never saw him drink and Jimmy's sisters have said they never saw him drink, but he himself decided not to be a deacon of the church.

My daddy, his older brother, never took a drink of hard liquor.

Come to think of it, there was a little similarity in the situation between Daddy Alton and his younger brother, Earl, and Cousin

Jimmy and his younger brother, Billy. The younger brothers made up for the older brothers, in cutting up, turning away from the strait-laced approach to life.

Jimmy's daddy brought home or built everything he could think of for having fun. A tennis court, a Ping-Pong table, horses, a pond for swimming, and then the Pond House for dancing and housing over-night guests.

On the subject of religion and church, Jimmy's daddy stood some-where between his sons, Jimmy and Billy. Jimmy attended everything the church had to offer and Billy stayed away completely. Uncle Earl would not go to sermons, which he thought boring, but would go to the Sunday School classes, which he thought were stimulating.

So what he'd do is leave church before the sermon began and ride around in his car or sit around the filling station, just like Billy used to do until the tourists drove him out.

Both Jimmy and I had pool tables in our homes. Jimmy's daddy used to startle guests by letting little Gloria, Jimmy's sister, play awhile with the guests. She would usually beat them, to their shock and amazement.

Daddy told my brother, Don, and me that he was giving us a pool table so that we would stay out of pool halls. We certainly did, es-pecially since it proved to me that it was not too interesting a game.

Much more interesting to me on long winter evenings was a game we would play as a family, "I Spy." You give the first letter of the thing you spied as a clue and the next person would take if from there.

We also had a form of shuffleboard with steel balls, three balls for each turn. It had holes with different scores and the one who scored 10,000 points first won.

One night, as I recall, Dad and Mother had gone off somewhere and left Brother Donnel to baby-sit me—he was three years older. Dad had warned us to be good and not to fight.

We used to fight at the drop of a hat, settling any argument with our fists.

That night, for a change, we weren't really fighting. We were just sort of wrestling, Don trying to get me to get up from the sofa and go to bed. Unfortunately, as Dad and Mother got home and approached the house, Dad looked in the window and thought he saw us fighting.

He ordered Don to go cut a switch off the peach tree in the backyard and then he gave us each a good switching.

It was much more fun to play with Jimmy, who was younger, than with Donnel, who was older and tougher.

Marbles was one of my favorite outdoor sports. We would dig five holes shaped like the number 7. You had to start at the towline, go around and land in every hole, and back to the towline. When you "rang" a hole, you got another shot.

The first one back to the towline won. The loser, as penalty, had to put his fist down on the ground and let the winner shoot it with a marble. This was called knucks. Dad, incidentally, said he used to play this type of marbles when he was a boy.

Some kids play dominoes, but I was not fond of that game. Better than dominoes was a card game called Rook or Go Fishing.

Jimmy and I would have wars with tops. The more top-owners who played, the better the war. We would try to hit someone else's top with our own spinning top, and that was called nulling.

Then we had "rubber gun fights" with rubber guns made of scrap lumber and clothespins. We would cut strips of rubber inner tube to shoot in the gun.

This was a big sport. We would choose up sides and have big fights. If someone hit you with a rubber you were considered "dead" and out of the fight.

Jimmy played with me in both these games, as did all the other boys in the neighborhood.

We also liked to play football on the lawn in front of the Logan house after school.

Then other times we would play a game called scrub, which was similar to baseball. We used a homemade ball made of a rubber center with a ball of string wound tightly around it. Our bat was homemade and made of hickory wood.

We would all take positions like in a baseball game. If you caught a fly or put a man out by yourself, you took his place in home and got a chance to bat. Three men would be in home-place waiting to bat at all times.

If a man got out by an assist in which two or more put him out, then you would move up in position until you got to the catcher position and then you would move in to bat.

Summers are long in Georgia and sometimes Jimmy and I would go to the huge sawdust pile near town to spend the night under the stars, cooking out. I don't know why a sawdust mountain was such an attraction, but it was. The names of the streams that we liked to explore were Kinchafoonee Creek, Rabbit Branch, Choctawhatchee Creek (I wouldn't like to bet money on my spelling on that one), Thrasher's Branch, and Shirley's swimming pool—I think all of us learned to swim there.

No, we didn't have snow but we did have sawdust piles. We didn't need sleds to take advantage of them. We would take a piece of cardboard or a wide board, sit on it, and slide down. This would keep us occupied, finding new ways of going down—backward, forward, belly-slamming. Eyes closed.

At night I would hardly want to go inside because I was so fascinated by the positions of the stars in the sky. Grandmother Nina was sure I would become an astronomer.

I recall that in the old days, dove hunting was Jimmy's favorite sport. He was a very good shot. We would go out together into a cornfield and he would bring them down with a .12-gauge automatic. It would be beautiful hiking along finding a likely field.

Jimmy and I would find a persimmon tree during the season they were ripe and hang around it, making faces and eating all we could hold. Persimmons are delicious fruit but those that were not quite ripe would make our mouths feel as if they had turned inside out and we would make horrible faces.

Raccoons and possums also liked persimmons and when we went possum and coon hunting, with Dad and some of his friends who had the proper coon dogs, the dogs would invariably tree a coon up a persimmon tree.

Jimmy loved hunting and fishing so much that he would go coon hunting with the husband of his nanny, Rachel Clark. And with Rachel, he would go fishing, carrying both his fishing pole and hers. They would sit for hours on the side of the creek and wait for the fish to bite while she told him folktales.

He and Rachel had a warm friendship, and even today, as President, he still sees her and calls her Rachel as he did when she called him Little Jimmy.

Having a nanny didn't mean that Jimmy was being raised in luxury. Since Aunt Lillian was away from home so much, someone had to look after the children. Besides, Rachel more than earned her keep in picking cotton on Uncle Earl's farm and Jimmy would pick cotton right along with her.

Jimmy and I always considered ourselves pretty big but there were times when the older kids made us feel very small. That was every Friday afternoon over possibly a month's span in the summer when the "Plains Theater" season was on. I doubt that the adults knew that there was a theater season but there was.

Hot and I were discriminated against because we were not permitted to act in these shows but were forced to pay two cents apiece to see the wretched performance.

I don't know what the actors did with all the money they received from us and from other small-fry that included Buck Sproull, and his brother Charles and a few others of us second-class citizens. The actors, whom I must say were filled with self-importance as they bustled around preparing for the big event, included Willard Slappey (our cousin), Donnel Carter (my brother), Oliver Spann (a friend), and Elva Mills—the only girl who was considered worthy enough to get a chance at show biz.

The actors had spent so much time on costumes and curtains and settings that the performances were pretty well unrehearsed. Lines were supplied and suggested back and forth which added to the general merriment. Each playlet was sillier than the rest but the one that I remember best because it seemed to be a favorite, brought back by popular demand each year, was the wedding scene.

One of the fellows was dressed up as the bride and the girl was dressed up as the groom and the others were members of the wedding party. The theater curtain made out of burlap sacks would squeak open on a wire. And there would be my brother, Donnel—he'll probably disown me for this—talking in falsetto as the nervous, shy bride. Anything that could go wrong at a wedding did—and purposely—tripping over the train, a drunken groom arriving late, somebody objecting and trying to stop the wedding.

Though Jimmy laughed a lot to watch those clowns on stage, I don't believe he's going to invite that particular entourage to repeat their triumph as state dinner entertainment in the East Room of the White House. But on the other hand, one never knows.

5 · WE GO TO SCHOOL

The school building still stands where Jimmy and I went to school all our elementary and high school days—eleven years' worth. We had only eleven grades then—not twelve as now.

My point of pride at school was that I was trusted to ring the bell to change classes and dismiss school. That was because I was reliable and had a very fine pocket watch that my daddy had given me.

I can remember how Jimmy and I dressed. Short pants and barefoot.

For a little while Jimmy was also wearing squirrels on his head— live squirrels. A mother squirrel had been killed, leaving two babies behind, and Jimmy raised them. They would climb all over him and ride on his head. I believe it was Jimmy's daddy who brought the baby squirrels home to him.

At first he had to hand-feed them. He had saved their lives because they could never have survived without their mother if Jimmy hadn't lavished tender loving care on them.

In my early days at school I sported knicker pants that buckled and bloused down over the knee. I wore a tie to school and a wool cap with a visor. We weren't allowed to go to school barefooted, but as soon as school was out in the afternoon, off came Jimmy's and my shoes and there I was with my splendid dignified tie and my bare toes hanging out.

Dressing up for us meant that we wore either a long tie or a bow tie and a long-sleeve shirt. Dressing up also meant we wore a belt to hold up our pants. And we wore socks and high-topped shoes. I have a picture of Jimmy in this hated getup.

When Jimmy was about twelve or thirteen, he went through an Indian phase in which he wrapped a band around his head, rode his ponies shirtless, and of course, went barefoot. Which was to say, he wore blue jeans and little else.

It was about this time that Billy was born. Now Jimmy was no longer the only boy in the family.

At this point I was not of much help to him because I was suddenly interested in dressing up and strutting around in front of girls.

When Jimmy was nineteen and Billy was six they started to have a close relationship, though it was still somewhat like father and son. Jimmy would take little Billy boating. By now Jimmy was wearing white T-shirts and blue jeans or shirt top and pants of some kind.

I remember when we would get our hair cut about once every six weeks, we would have to sit on a board across the arms of the barber's chair. It was Mr. Wellons who used to cut Jimmy's hair and mine.

We used to see a lot of fights at recess, two boys and occasionally two girls would be involved in a fight over some member of the opposite sex.

The teacher would usually come out and stop the fight and then paddle the participants—if they were boys. The girls would have to sit in a corner the rest of the day.

But though Jimmy didn't have fistfights, it didn't mean he wore a halo. As a matter of fact, Mrs. Alma Coller, who used to teach Jimmy when she was Miss Alma Hall, remembers that she did have to spank Jimmy in the fourth grade.

She remembers him as full of mischief and, in fact, his grades in "deportment" in the first five grades show that he was something less than perfect. But by the sixth grade he was all straightened out and getting A's.

In fact, he was almost a straight-A student from the fifth grade on. The only subject which he couldn't seem to get the hang of was music, in which he got C's.

In high school Cousin Hot was a straight-A student except for physical education, in which he got B's. He even got A's in such subjects as shorthand, typing, and woodworking.

Jimmy rarely missed a day of school and was hardly ever late. He still follows this practice of being everywhere on time. I have never known him to be late for anything that he planned to do. Someone checked the record when he was running for President and found he had been late for school only twelve times during his entire seven years in elementary school.

Music was not my strong suit, either. Brother Donnel could play the trumpet. I remember when I was in the eighth grade and he was a senior in high school, I was dazzled by how well he could play "Song of India" on the trumpet.

For a while, I thought that maybe I could do something with piano lessons. But after six months the piano and I both gave up and I promptly forgot every note I'd learned and every finger position.

I was seven years old when I faced my great ordeal of the piano lessons. Looking back I feel sympathy for Mrs. Ida Lee Timmerman, who had to put up with me and the assault on her ears.

One afternoon I played hooky from my music lessons to take a ride in an airplane with my brother for the bargain price of a dollar each.

When Mother found out about it, she said, "If you don't think any more of music than that, you can stop taking music." *That* was music to my ears. However, years later I wished over and over again that I could play the piano. It really was a mistake to give up.

I don't remember Jimmy having learned to play any instrument either. Maybe the fact that he didn't have to practice piano every day influenced me not to want to practice either. However, he too showed an interest in music later in life. He collected unusual records. He was pleased that his wife took violin lessons and he encouraged Amy to study violin at the White House so that he could listen to them play duets.

In my own family, I have encouraged my children to play piano.

Looking back, I can see that Jimmy was starting to be a politician and picking up political techniques at an early age. Copying his grandpa, Jim-Jack, Jimmy would stick out his hand and say, "Hello, I'm Jimmy Carter," even when he was in the first grade.

He may have been shy about reciting in class, but he had no shyness about going up to every stranger who came to town. With his puckish little grin, he won the hearts of adults, who would stand around and talk with him.

I would stand off and watch this with admiration. I had no shyness about reciting in class or dealing with strangers in my daddy's store, but I didn't approach strangers on my own.

Going to the county fair every year was a big event in the life of every Plains child. I would save a little money all during the year for two big reasons—the county fair in October in Americus and the trip to Americus at Christmastime to do Christmas shopping.

Five dollars was considered an ample amount for the fair, and five dollars was considered an adequate amount for Christmas shopping— for the whole family.

A dollar stretched an amazing length in those days—the thirties. We only exchanged gifts in the immediate family. Christmas cards were exchanged with Jimmy's family.

At the fair we would ride all the rides—the Ferris Wheel, the Flying Jenny, the Swings, the Tilt-&-Whirl. There were always a lot of dirty sideshows and gambling booths. If Daddy was with us, we would not get anywhere near the side shows but we did play bingo occasionally.

Jimmy loved all his lady schoolteachers as a boy. I remember when he had Mrs. Eleanor Forrest in the first grade and he wanted to show her how he felt, he offered her his mother's diamond ring.

When she showed surprise, he said that was all right, his daddy could get his mother another one. And undoubtedly, Uncle Earl could have because he was a very successful man. There was a saying around town that everything Earl Carter touched turned to money.

I remember one time when I was in the third grade, I jokingly put on a girl's hat. The girl's name was Sara Wise. My teacher, Miss Tot Hudson, made me wear that hat the rest of the day.

That was awful punishment and worse than being paddled. Not only that, but I had to stand in a corner of the schoolroom all day while wearing that blasted hat.

When we were just elementary school kids, Jimmy and I and other boys used to play underneath the schoolhouse, crawling around in the dirt, to the consternation of our teachers. We would always slip under the schoolhouse to eat our home-packed lunch at noon.

Swapping items at lunch was a big deal—frowned upon but practiced every day. A sandwich for a piece of fruit. Candy for a pickle.

I lived in a day, as did Jimmy, when paddling at school was the main form of punishment. The teacher would take a student out in the hall and you could hear the licks all over the school building. Jimmy was such a cautious fellow he rarely got spanked at school.

But his father, who was even harder to please than any schoolteacher, made up for it with switchings with a peach switch. Jimmy's Aunt Sissy Dolvin, the sister of Miz Lillian, remembers one of the times Jimmy got the peach switch. He had been given his usual penny to put into the collection plate. But instead of putting it in the plate, he had come home with two pennies.

His daddy made him take both pennies back to the minister on foot—about three miles.

Sissy is not a Baptist like the rest of the family. She is an elder in the Presbyterian Church at Roswell.

In all my years at school as a boy I never did get a paddling by my schoolteacher. I remember one time my teacher in the fifth grade gave me B's all the way down on my report card because I played hooky one day and shot doves all day long. I usually got all A's.

I often remember those days of dove hunting with Cousin Hot. I remember one winter nonschool morning in particular. We were going hunting with Uncle Earl and my daddy. We were up before daylight and went uptown to meet other hunters at Ross Dean's undertaking parlor.

It may seem strange to be eating in an undertaking establishment, but that's where we had coffee and doughnuts without a thought of the dearly departed.

It was a terribly cold morning and Jimmy and I both wore two or three pairs of wool socks, two pairs of pants, and a scarf wrapped around our ears and under our chins. Over the scarf we wore our stocking caps, which also came down over our ears.

Under all this, we had on "long-handles", as we called our long underwear which covered our bodies tightly from neck to ankles. We both had on leather gloves.

I had a small .410-gauge shotgun. Jimmy had a .20-gauge double barrel gun; Daddy and Earl had automatic .16-gauge guns.

The dove field that morning was located at Archery—not too far from Jimmy's home, about a half a mile. It was behind E. H. Watson's house. At that time Watson was a section foreman for the Seaboard Railroad, which went right in front of Jimmy's house.

We got into cars and it was a relief to get out of that intense cold. It was still dark when we got to the dove field. The field, as usual, was baited to attract the birds. Of course, now it would be unthinkable to bait a dove field with grain, but back then it was not.

We all built a little fire to warm our hands. Each of us had brought along some fat splinters to start the fire going and Hot and I ran around and found some dry cornstalks to add to the tinder pile for a faster burn.

I believe it was the coldest morning I have ever seen. It must have been about twelve or fifteen degrees and that is about as cold as it ever gets in this part of Georgia.

When dawn began to break, birds started to fly in and Hot and I began to bring one down occasionally. We felt mighty big because Daddy and Uncle Earl were unable to shoot a single bird, as it was so cold that the oil on their automatic guns froze and would not work.

Here we are, Cousin Beedie and Cousin Hot,
when I was five, and the future President was
an open-mouthed one year of age.

Plains, Ga. — Home of President Jimmy Carter in 1905

Plains in 1905, the year after the Carters settled here. It hasn't changed too much. It still looks like a mock-up for a Western movie set.

The drugstore was much a part of the early life of Cousin Hot and me. I did not, of course, dream I would grow up to marry the druggist's daughter.
Dr. L. E. Godwin, Sr., is standing at the left. The man closest to the camera at right is J. Robert McGarrah, who became the Postmaster of Plains and who we thought might marry Miss Allie, Rosalynn Carter's mother.

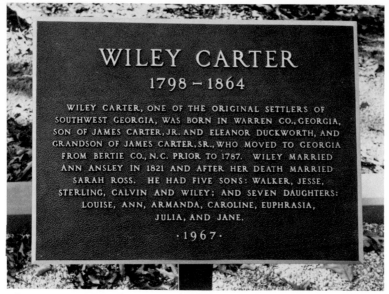

WILEY CARTER
1798 – 1864

WILEY CARTER, ONE OF THE ORIGINAL SETTLERS OF
SOUTHWEST GEORGIA, WAS BORN IN WARREN CO., GEORGIA,
SON OF JAMES CARTER, JR. AND ELEANOR DUCKWORTH, AND
GRANDSON OF JAMES CARTER, SR., WHO MOVED TO GEORGIA
FROM BERTIE CO., N.C. PRIOR TO 1787. WILEY MARRIED
ANN ANSLEY IN 1821 AND AFTER HER DEATH MARRIED
SARAH ROSS. HE HAD FIVE SONS: WALKER, JESSE,
STERLING, CALVIN AND WILEY; AND SEVEN DAUGHTERS:
LOUISE, ANN, ARMANDA, CAROLINE, EUPHRASIA,
JULIA, AND JANE.

·1967·

This is the marker in the Carter Family Cemetery in Schley County,
eleven miles north of Plains on State Highway 153. Wiley Carter was the
President's and my great-great-grandfather.

Jimmy taped several hours of my father's reminiscences of our family genealogy. Here Jimmy Carter and Daddy Alton look over the historic Rock House in
MacDuffie County, Georgia. The roots of the Carter family go back to this
house built by Thomas Ansley in 1785.

I own the original of the only formal portrait of Jimmy Carter's father, Earl. It is the most borrowed picture I own.

I'm so happy to have this picture of Daddy Alton on his last birthday, August 17, 1977, his eighty-ninth. He had come to work as usual in my antique shop. His mind was as sharp as a twenty-year-old's.

This is probably the most complete photo of our combined families in existence. It was taken Christmas 1943. I am not in the picture because I was in the Army at the time. The house is the first the Carters lived in when they came to Plains in 1904. Left to right, standing: Wade Lowery, now dead (uncle); Alton Carter, now dead (my dad); W. D. Fleming, now dead (uncle); Don Carter (my brother); Jimmy Carter, wearing Annapolis uniform (Cousin Hot); Willard Slappey (cousin); Earl Carter, now dead (Jimmy's dad, my uncle); Jack Slappey, now dead (uncle). Left to right, sitting: Lillian Carter (Jimmy's mother, my aunt); Lula Fleming (my aunt, my dad's sister); Jeanette Lowery (my aunt, my dad's sister); Ethel Slappey, now dead (my aunt, my dad's sister); Ruth Carter Stapleton (Jimmy's younger sister, my cousin); Nina Lowery Middleton (my cousin), holding her baby, Mary Louise; Gloria Carter Spann (Jimmy's older sister, my cousin); Mrs. Hugh Carter, holding Hugh Carter, Jr. (my wife, Ruth, and our son). The little boy in the front is Billy Carter (Jimmy's brother, my cousin).

A second Christmas 1943 picture. Left to right, standing: Don Carter
Jimmy Carter, Willard Slappey. Left to right, sitting: Ruth Carter
Stapleton, Gloria Carter Spann, Billy Carter
(little boy standing), Nina Lowery Middleton,
holding her baby, and my wife, Ruth Carter,
holding our son, Hugh Carter, Jr.

This is Jimmy's and my beloved teacher Julia
Coleman, made famous by Jimmy Carter. I'm
sorry she did not live to hear him pay tribute to
her influence in his inaugural address.

This is a snapshot I took of my family in our house. Left to right: my wife, Ruth; Laurie Gay Carter Tharpe; Connie Carter Collins; Mrs. Hugh Carter, Jr. (my son's ex-wife); Hugh Carter, Jr.

When I snapped this picture of my son Hugh Carter, Jr., in 1965, I little dreamed he would one day be working at the White House and that another member of the Carter family would be President.

I occupy the same seat in the Georgia legislature that Jimmy Carter did when he was a state senator from 1963 to 1967.

They finally tried holding the guns over the fire long enough to get them thawed a bit. But the guns would still fire only one time instead of the usual five times.

Jimmy was the star that morning. He bagged twelve birds. I only brought down six. At least we had good eating at our houses that night.

When we grew older and were allowed to shoot a rifle or shotgun, Hot and I would go squirrel hunting. We would get up early in the morning and be in the woods when light appeared—the time of day when squirrels move around the most.

Because of his size—5'3" in high school, though he grew three inches his first year in college—Jimmy was not great in sports. In this field I had him beat, though my time in high school was ahead of his. I played first base on the baseball team and ran the 100- and 220-yard dash in track. I also broad-jumped. I won the district championship in singles tennis in 1937 and Cody Timmerman and I won the district doubles championship in the same year. There were about ninety high schools in our district.

Northern children do not realize how good it feels to be a "barefoot boy with cheeks of tan", as that old poem goes. As kids, Jimmy and I were usually barefoot and I would almost bet Cousin Hot wanders around the family quarters of the White House today barefoot, when he is relaxing, just as he did when he was governor.

To show that being barefoot does not hamper one's ability to run, when I was in high school I always ran barefoot in competitions and I won the district track meet broad-jump competing against ninety schools in 1937. I jumped 17 feet 11 inches in my bare feet.

The next year, I did even better at college, jumping 20 feet 4 inches for Georgia Southwestern. But by then, as a college man, I was wearing track shoes.

Although Jimmy was not the greatest sportsman in the world, he was spunky. He would show off his bike riding technique in front of a girl and fall off and scrape his arm. He was forever getting banged up. He would fall out of a tree and hurt himself and he would be forever getting bruised on a basketball court.

Basketball was Jimmy's best sport on the Plains team, even though he was a shortie compared to the big guys. Maybe, to make up for his size, he played even more intensely, in forward position. He was a fast runner.

He wasn't only good by Plains's standards, and when he went to Southwestern College he made the college team.

We certainly were well chaperoned at high school dances. My class was chaperoned and so was Jimmy's. When Jimmy's junior and senior proms were held at the Carter Pond House, there would be not one but three chaperones, and to keep fellows and their girls from necking, a bell would be rung every five or six minutes to signal time to change partners or have refreshments or pause for intermission.

Of the three people Jimmy Carter has said influenced him most, in preparing for the presidency, Miss Julia Coleman was the only person outside his family—the other two being his father and mother.

Miss Coleman is also the person next to my father, mother, and brother who most influenced me toward success in my own way. I think if every schoolchild was made to memorize Rudyard Kipling's poem "If", as she made us memorize it, it might excite many more youngsters to fight for success and take defeat in stride until success eventually comes.

Julia Coleman in her own life was a great story. She had been stricken with polio and walked with a little difficulty because it had left her slightly deformed. That is probably the reason she never married but she gave her life to children, anyway, and she lived through the excitement of their adventures. I know that our triumphs were her triumphs and a great thrill was to impress Miss Coleman with a job well done that we didn't think we could handle. She always thought we *could* handle it.

She taught us to memorize. To look for deeper meanings, to open our minds to poetry. And she made us stand up and recite poems from memory. Jimmy was shy and hated to get up to recite. Maybe his size had something to do with it.

If Miss Coleman had not forced him and encouraged him to do it, who knows whether Cousin Hot would ever have gotten the courage to stand up in public and speak. But Miss Coleman gave him the courage and made a debater of him as well. In those early shaky experiences, Jimmy spent a great deal of time in preparation and had all his facts but could not find his tongue to present them with conviction. Slowly, under Miss Julia's tender encouragement, he started to loosen up a little.

Miss Julia coached the debating team and from her Jimmy and I both learned how to reach for the right expression, how to argue politely but effectively, and to get our point over to the judges.

I know that I owe a lot of my success in achieving the state senatorship to the early training and encouragement I received from Miss Julia.

I loved to argue and was active in the Debate Club under Miss Julia's direction. I also acted in a one-act play and won a medal as best boy actor in the Third District in the role of the warden in the play *The Valiant*.

It was Miss Julia who had coached me.

Miss Julia was such an unusual person that I cannot help talk about her. She had become a member of Plains School faculty back in 1912 and was, in her way, a women's libber—she had fought to get public approval for girls to wear basketball suits.

We had five high school teachers—Miss Julia Coleman, Mr. Y. T. Sheffield, Mrs. Carolyn Webb, Mr. Chester, and Mr. Simpson.

I took French in high school from Mrs. Webb and Mr. Chester. Later I took two quarters of French in college. It was a big help to me when I was in France during World War II.

I took vocational education under Mr. Simpson and made a knife as my year's project. I remember he gave me a B grade and I was heartsick because I thought I should have gotten an A.

One day one of our teachers made the newspaper in a most amusing way—amusing to all but her. It was Mrs. Carolyn Webb who got her finger caught in a hole that someone had cut in a wooden desk. She stayed a "prisoner" for a couple of hours before someone decided to cut her desk and get her finger out.

Among teachers, next to Julia Coleman, I guess Y. T. Sheffield had the greatest influence on both Cousin Hot and me. He taught us math—algebra and geometry—and coached basketball and track and baseball.

It was Miss Julia who brought Sheffield, who was so important in Jimmy's and my life, to our town.

There is a tragic note to his story. Sheffield retired in 1965 and took his own life two years later.

It was a sad ending for the man who was at one time considered the number one high school basketball coach in all of Georgia.

Miss Julia was like a crusader about books, encouraging us to read as many as we could and actually requiring that we read a certain number of books per month.

It was very amusing that Miss Julia wanted Jimmy to read *War and Peace* when he was only twelve years old. He had thought it would be a book about American Indians.

I think Jimmy learned a lot from the book about biting off just the amount that he could handle. He built his political career carefully step by step. He didn't say, "I'm going to run for President" out of the blue. First he said, "I'm going to run for state senator." Then after he had thoroughly mastered that job, he had decided to try for the governorship—not without early failure. And not until he had learned how to run a state did he decide it was time to run a country and that he was capable of doing so.

Often Jimmy would talk about the great effect *War and Peace* had on him, how it made him see that the course of world history was changed by Napoleon's retreat from Russia, and even as a grown political man, he was still talking about it and how it showed that wars did not affect just the generals but, more importantly, the average person.

Nor could generals win wars. As he once stated it, "The point of the book is that the course of human events are not determined by the leaders of a nation or a state, like presidents or governors or senators.

"They are controlled by common ordinary people."

It wasn't just reading that Miss Coleman forced on Jimmy. She told him and others of us who came under her influence that there were two other doors to the world of beauty that must be opened, and she opened them—the world of art and the world of classical music.

Miss Coleman opened those doors and Jimmy walked through. He memorized many paintings as well as works of great composers.

When Miss Julia died several years ago, Brother Donnel found a letter she had written him which showed her bold spirit, even though she was growing old and blind and realized that she might "soon have to reside in some home for aging people."

What I liked about the letter is that she said, "I am not joining in the current line, 'Stop the World, I Want to Get Off.' Yes I miss the old days. But never mind—I like this NOW of ours.

"I am well aware of a host of evils, negations, confusions and conflict. But I still see much good shining through the mists. I deplore all the evil, but I firmly believe in the ultimate triumph of the Greater Good."

At least Miss Julia was honored while she was alive.

I'll never forget the elaborate plans we made to celebrate "Julia Coleman Day" when our beloved Miss Julia decided to retire as superintendent.

The date was May 19, 1949, and participating in the big event was my wife, Ruth, Mrs. Allie Smith, Rosalynn Carter's mother, Mrs. Eleanor Forrest, Jimmy's first-grade teacher, and many others.

My brother, Donnel, who is now vice-president of the Knight-Ridder newspaper chain, went overboard in his handling of the publicity for Julia Coleman Day and sent the story of her thirty-five years of teaching to the Atlanta *Journal*, the Macon *Telegraph*, the Columbus *Ledger*, the Albany *Herald*, the Associated Press, the United Press, and the International News Service, as well as the Atlanta *Constitution*. I don't think there was anyone in the state who didn't know that there were big doings at Plains.

I still cherish the story that Don wrote and am going to quote part of it.

Perhaps reading it, the reader will understand why she was one of the three persons Jimmy Carter gave most credit to, when he became President:

> ... *Plains High School, under this lady's leadership, has achieved a position of eminence in the education world. It was designated by the Georgia State Dept. of Education as one of the three model or laboratory schools in Ga. For years, it did experimental work which was later adopted into the state's program of education.*
>
> *One of Miss Coleman's unique accomplishments has been the developing and landscaping of the school campus. Shrubbery and flowers have been planted in "The Friendship Garden" by the boys and girls of the school.*
>
> *A special section of the campus has been set aside as "Baby Row." Here a new plant of some variety is established in honor of each new baby in the community. The School thinks of it as being planted by the "Little Citizens" of the town.*
>
> *On at least two occasions, national honors have been bestowed on Miss Julia's school. The Junior Garden Clubs of America recognized it with an award for its campus program, and the magazine* Current Events *gave it special honors for citizenship.*
>
> *Miss Coleman, known and loved by all the community, chose the life of the small town in preference to more lucrative offers from larger cities. Each boy and girl who has been in her school has learned to appreciate her help and guidance and has known her influence in finding a better and fuller life.*

I'm sure that even as a small boy, Jimmy Carter realized, because of the example of Julia Coleman, that a person could come from a very small town and still be of great importance. I know that I thought of her every time someone would say, "How can a man from a little peanut town of Plains think that he can become President?" A man who had been under the influence of Miss Coleman *would* think so. Would know that he could and would have the *confidence.*

I want to tell you, too, what my wife, as president of the PTA on that great day of honor to Miss Julia, said in her speech:

> *... I shudder to think of the many positions "Miss Julia" could have taken far away from us and received double and triple the salary she has received here; but being the person she is and having the love for the welfare of boys and girls that she has, I'm sure "Miss Julia" must have considered the job involved and not the salary.*
>
> *This reminds me of the story of a young man who had the job of being a missionary in a foreign country, and received a salary of only six hundred dollars a year. He was a brilliant young man, well educated, receiving top honors in all his classes.*
>
> *His qualifications were exactly what a big oil company was looking for, to do a job they had in a foreign country.*
>
> *They offered him up to fifteen thousand dollars to take this job but he refused. They couldn't understand and asked him what was wrong. He said, "It's not a question of salary. That is magnificent. The job is too little. I'd rather have a big job with a little salary than a small job with a big salary."*

I have but one regret when I think of Miss Julia and it brings tears to my eyes—the fact that she did not live to see her prize student become President of the United States. She died in July 1973. But had she known, she wouldn't have been surprised.

Part Two

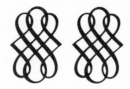

TWO PATHS
DIVERGE

6 · LOVE AND MARRIAGE

All of his boyhood, Jimmy had a dream and that dream was to be an admiral. Unfortunately, he didn't make it and had to settle for being Commander in Chief instead. But, back in those days, when he was getting out of Plains High School, his one burning ambition was to attend Annapolis Naval Academy, as step one of the big goal.

He was distressed that Plains High School had not provided all that he would need to get into the Academy. But he was not going to let that stop him. He first took a year at Georgia Southwestern College in Americus to get certain courses he needed in preparation for attending the Naval Academy.

Then he took a year at Georgia Tech at Atlanta for other courses he would need, and he was in Naval ROTC while there. He told me one time that the year at Georgia Tech was the hardest year of his life scholastically. When he finally got into the Naval Academy, Jimmy was a very happy fellow.

The Naval Academy was no snap either. Jimmy told me that he worked so hard at the Academy, he didn't have time even to think about girls, so his life as a midshipman was woefully free of romantic attachments. That's why his holidays at Plains with his old friends meant so much to him. He was trying to make up for lost time. Until he succumbed to the charms of his sister's best friend, Rosalynn Smith!

The way most biographies of Jimmy Carter read, you would think that the President had only one romance in his life—Rosalynn Smith—and that he never looked at another girl until he spotted her.

The truth of the matter is that another girl was his first love and it is a touching story which showed him early in life that you don't always get what you want or win in the game of hearts.

Eloise Ratliff was called Teenie by all her friends. It was good she was tiny because Jimmy was no giant—only 5′3″ in high school. Jimmy fell for the pretty dark-haired Teenie. The thing she had going for her was something that still impresses him in any woman—she read a lot of books.

Together they would read and share their thinking on what we kids called "heavy books," which meant that they were not easy to read like the Tom Swift series or the Tarzan stories.

This didn't mean that Jimmy didn't read the adventure stories, too. In fact, I think he read all of Edgar Rice Burroughs.

For a while it seemed like Jimmy and Teenie were inseparable, but then came the competition from one with a more affluent lifestyle and a more flamboyant personality than Jimmy's. His name was Lonnie Taylor and he was taller and handsomer than Jimmy, dark-haired, and most of all, he had an Austin car of his own. Lonnie was the only person in Jimmy's class of '41 to have a car, although Jimmy had the use of his Dad's car a few hours on Sundays.

Heavy books and a perky grin could not compete with a tall handsome owner of the only car in the gang. Not only did Jimmy lose his girl to that Austin car, but also his own chance to be valedictorian of the class.

Jimmy should have been valedictorian because he had the grades for it, but in just one mad moment he made a wrong decision. Lonnie got almost all the fellows in the senior class to play hooky on April Fools' Day in 1941 and go to a movie at Americus in his car.

Such a thing could not be kept secret and when Miss Julia Coleman, the superintendent, heard of it, she decided that the fitting punishment for Jimmy was that Jimmy could not take his place as valedictorian. The one who was valedictorian was Teenie Ratliff.

There is something that is not clear in my mind—and that is, what happened to Jimmy's scholarship? When Jimmy was slated to graduate as valedictorian, he was to receive a scholarship to Georgia Southwestern College. But when the superintendent demoted him for his prank, the scholarship was in question, and Teenie Ratliff was awarded it instead.

I have a feeling—and this is confirmed by someone who knew Jimmy well in those days—Jimmy himself wanted his old girl friend to get the scholarship.

Teenie's parents were not as affluent and this may have been the only way to make sure she would have a chance to get two years of college. Jimmy knew his daddy would send him to college anyway.

Jimmy was very ethical and fair-minded even in high school. A winner was a winner. He was warmhearted, always wanting to look out for friends and for the less fortunate. Jimmy was never bitter about Miss Julia Coleman's stern punishment for his one breach of conduct. Instead he said that he had been wrong and he had paid the price. He never turned against her or her memory and in his inaugural speech in January 1977, I felt transported back to our childhood, as I heard Jimmy say, quoting Miss Julia Coleman, "We must adjust to changing times and still hold to unchanging principles."

He read from the Bible used in the inauguaration of the first President in 1789 and his choice of verse from prophet Micah explains perfectly how Jimmy tries to live: "He hath shown thee, O Man, what is good, and what doth the Lord require of thee, but to do justly and to love mercy and to walk humbly with thy God."

Miss Julia had lived to see Jimmy become the governor of his state but only her spirit attended the presidential inauguration.

Teenie ended up marrying Lonnie Taylor and everything went well for them. Teenie presented him with two children born exactly one year apart to the day—Tommy and Patricia.

Lonnie was still the front-runner of the graduating class—the first in the gang to have his own plane.

Then in July of 1948, almost exactly two years after Jimmy, too, had gotten married, Lonnie took his whole family for an airplane ride, including a few in-laws—Teenie's sister, Lorraine, and her brother, Bobby.

Some said there were too many in the light plane. I remember the wreck well. It occurred in a small wooded pine thicket a few miles from Butler, Georgia, which is about forty miles north of Plains.

Ruth and I went to the wreck site. The engine plowed at a steep angle into the ground and the plane was almost completely demolished on ground contact. No one knows exactly what caused the wreck, but all in the small plane were killed.

I will never forget the day of the funeral when four caskets lay in a row in front of the church. It was one of the saddest days the town had ever experienced. I don't think there was a dry eye in town. I can never erase that picture from my mind, though I wish I could.

There were six people dead in those four coffins. The boy, Tommy, was buried in the coffin with his father, and the little girl, Patricia, was buried with her mother. Everyone said at least the parents and the children would not be alone.

Today, their graves are only thirty yards from where Jimmy's daddy is buried in Lebanon Cemetery, about two miles west of Plains.

I have tried to figure out how Jimmy's interest in the Navy got started. I'm pretty sure it started with his Uncle Tom who was the brother of Jimmy's mother and Aunt Sissy. It's too bad that Tom Gordy didn't live to see Jimmy become President.

Tom was Jimmy's idol because he was traveling and adventuring all over the world. When we were just kids, Jimmy would be receiving postcards from far-off places wherever Tom's ship was taking him.

I think this is why Jimmy determined that he, too, would join the Navy and see the world. Only he was going to be an admiral with men to command. As it turned out, any traveling around the world that Jimmy did in the Navy was as a married man.

If Aunt Lillian had had her way Jimmy would have married Marguerite Wise, the daughter of Dr. Bowman Wise, one of the medical brothers whom Aunt Lillian almost worshiped.

Marguerite was a lovely girl, and in fact, resembled Rosalynn, whom he did marry. Marguerite today is married to Dr. Robert Cato, of Macon, Georgia, who is very successful and has a fine medical practice.

After the *National Enquirer* had unearthed the fact that Marguerite was an old girl friend of Jimmy's, I was invited to a party given by Mrs. Sara Turpin of Americus in honor of Dr. Sam Wise of Maryland, her brother, and a former boyhood friend of mine who used to live in Plains.

Sam is a first cousin of Marguerite and his father was Dr. Thad Wise.

I was happy to see that Marguerite Cato was also at the party for it was like old times. But Marguerite was very upset that the *Enquirer* had quoted her as saying, "If ever there was a reason for not marrying Jimmy Carter, that reason was Miss Lillian.

"I can understand anyone not getting along with her. I fully understand why Rosalynn didn't want to return to Plains. It would be like going back to Hell!"

Of course, the *Enquirer* article was an important topic of conversation at the party. Marguerite insisted that she had been misquoted and that the whole thing had been very embarrassing for her.

The same article also quoted me as saying, "Certainly there is a feud between Miss Lillian and Rosalynn. We Carters are a hardheaded bunch. We're also born leaders.

"When you put those characteristics together, there are bound to be fireworks—and that's just what happens between Miss Lillian and Rosalynn."

Marguerite told me later that she had written to the President and apologized for any embarrassment she might have caused him and to tell him that she had been misquoted.

I told her not to worry about it. I offered her a small gold peanut to wear on her lapel but Marguerite was so nervous and upset that she would not accept even this symbol of Jimmy for fear that it would be misunderstood.

It's interesting that two of the people dearest to Jimmy's heart both lost their fathers when they were about thirteen years old. That's how old his brother, Billy, was when Uncle Earl died and how old Rosalynn was when her father died.

Jimmy has great compassion for those who suffer a great loss and it's further interesting that Jimmy's close friend in the White House—perhaps his closest friend, press secretary Jody Powell—also lost his father in an untimely death, when he was fairly young.

Maybe it was because she didn't have a father around when she was a teen-ager to hug her and show her affection that Rosalynn was so shy that she avoided dating because she didn't want anyone to kiss her. According to one of her brothers, pretty as she was, she would hide when fellows came to the house to see her and pretend she wasn't home. Sometimes she would hide outside, behind the house.

If it hadn't been for Jimmy's sister, Ruth, Rosalynn's best friend, guiding Rosalynn and smoothing the way for her to be thrown in contact with Jimmy, I wonder if she would be First Lady today. I credit Ruth for making the romance possible.

But the one place Rosalynn was not shy around Plains was answering questions in class. I'm told, however, that at Georgia Southwestern, from which she graduated two years later, her shyness at talking in front of a large group of people troubled her deeply when she had to recite in class.

Rosalynn, as I said, was thirteen when her father died. Her brother Jerry was eleven, Murray eight, and baby Alethea was three. The cause of death had been leukemia.

Her mother, Allie, had fallen in love with Edgar Smith when she was only about fourteen or fifteen. Edgar had been the school-bus driver. He was, I believe, nine years older than she. Edgar did not go to college but Allie did. She studied home economics at Georgia State College for Women and then came home to marry the man she loved, who had become the town's mechanic.

Edgar also did a little farming on some land he owned. When he died Allie rented it out.

Every family has its favorite Christmas stories and the Carter clan is no different. One of the cutest stories is that of Rosalynn Carter when she was a little girl growing up, and had to cope with the fact that Allie Smith, her mother, had a birthday the day before Christmas.

One year, Rosalynn wanted to give her mother one more expensive gift instead of two less expensive ones. So it happened on December 24, Miss Allie opened a beautifully wrapped box to find one fur-lined bedroom slipper and the next day unwrapped a differently wrapped Christmas package to find the second single fur-lined bedroom slipper.

Rosalynn was a good little girl, when she was growing up, but she was a rascal as a little tyke of three or four. Her brother Jerry was only one or two when this happened.

Her mother heard a commotion in the chicken coop and rushed in to find that Rosalynn was busily tar-and-feathering herself and her baby brother. There had been an open can of tar around and somehow she knew just the use to make of it.

Rosalynn went to Georgia Southwestern, which is a two-year junior college in Americus. I believe the family story goes that she was planning to go on to a university afterward to complete her education but she chose Jimmy and marriage instead.

The way I remember Allie Smith, her mother, telling the story, Rosalynn had made out her application to the university but had never mailed it, because Jimmy had proposed and she had said yes.

Miss Allie was one of the most respected women in town, though in modest circumstances. She worked to support Rosalynn and the younger children and Rosalynn added to the family earnings by working at the local beauty parlor, after school and Saturdays.

But since she hadn't taken a beautician's course, Rosalynn was not permitted to set hair. Instead she could only give hair washings and tidy up the parlor.

The first date of Jimmy and Rosalynn took place in 1945. Jimmy was a midshipman on leave from Annapolis. According to the family gossip, Aunt Lillian hit the ceiling when Jimmy came home with his glowing account of Rosalynn and his avowed goal of marrying her.

She commented with characteristic bluntness that Rosalynn was not good enough for her son and not good enough to enter the Carter family.

Jimmy always makes his own decisions and he made it in the case of Rosalynn, proposing to her twice before she said yes. Though Aunt

Lillian said openly that Jimmy was marrying a girl "from the wrong side of the tracks," Jimmy's father went around proudly telling what a lovely girl his son was lucky enough to be getting.

It was Rosalynn's own savings, incidentally, that made it possible for her to go to college. That is an interesting story. Actually, Rosalynn's father, Edgar, left a little money when he died and Miss Allie put that money aside for college educations for her children.

Allie was determined not to touch that money until Rosalynn was ready for college. And she didn't. Instead, she sewed—especially bridal gowns and difficult things like men's overcoats and jackets, and then she worked at the post office. Rosalynn saved most of her money for college, and if she had not married Jimmy, she would probably have finished putting herself through school.

The Smith family has something to be proud of—all the children went to college and Rosalynn, as a matter of fact, is the only one who did not graduate from a university.

Murray became a math teacher and athletic coach. Jerry received an engineering degree and practices his craft in Indiana, and Alethea, the baby of the family, since graduation has worked for various banks in Atlanta and Americus.

There are several versions including Miz Lillian's of how Jimmy and Rosalynn finally got together. According to Aunt Lillian, Rosalynn had had a schoolgirl's crush on Jimmy for two years before he noticed her, and the way she tells it, he first noticed her at a dance Jimmy and his friends held at the Pond House, where they danced to the music of the jukebox.

In Rosalynn's version, Jimmy saw Ruth and Rosalynn together and to be kind, said, "You girls can get yourselves somebody for dates and come to our party, if you like." The girls had found the invitation less than enthusiastic but they were thrilled to be invited at all to a party of the older crowd. So they did rustle up dates and show up at the dance.

In Aunt Lillian's version, Jimmy eventually danced with Rosalynn and bragged, "Don't you think my date tonight is pretty?"

Rosalynn is supposed to have snapped back at Jimmy, "I don't think she's half as pretty as I am," and Jimmy, taken by surprise, took a real good look at Rosalynn for the first time and liked what he saw.

According to Miz Lillian, Jimmy never dated any other person after that.

The way Rosalynn tells the story, she fell in love with Jimmy when he came home on leave from the Naval Academy in the summer of 1945 in his sparkling dress white uniform as a midshipman. But though she had eyes only for Jimmy, Jimmy didn't know she was alive.

The whole summer faded away and even though Jimmy almost fell over her around his house, since she and his sister, Ruth, were best friends, he did not seem to notice.

When there were only a few days left before Jimmy had to return to Annapolis to start his senior year, Rosalynn and Ruth tried a desperate measure to get Jimmy to notice Rosalynn. The girls offered to help Jimmy clean up the Pond House.

Even though Rosalynn worked like a galley slave all day, Jimmy still wasn't noticing and, weary and crestfallen, she had to hurry to clean up and get to a Methodist church activity that night.

I'm not clear but I believe Ruth and Rosalynn were standing in the churchyard when Jimmy and his friend came by in the friend's car and stopped. The friend was someone Ruth dated.

Jimmy walked over and asked if Rosalynn would like to go to a movie. Rosalynn was so excited and stunned she could hardly answer yes.

This is the way Cousin Jimmy described it one time when in 1971 he was getting ready to celebrate his twenty-fifth wedding anniversary: "Twenty-six years ago, I was driving by the Plains Methodist Church and a young girl, who was quite a bit younger than I was, was in the front of the church and I was looking for a blind date to go to a movie.

"I was home as a senior at Annapolis and Rosalynn Smith was out there and, in desperation as I couldn't find any older girl to go with me, I asked her for a date. When I got home that night I went in to see my mother who was getting ready to go to bed, and she said, 'Well, how did you like Rosalynn?', and I said, 'She's the one I want to marry.'"

He cut off the story at that point, never telling what Lillian's many comments had been. He simply added, "A year later we were married and next month we will celebrate our twenty-fifth anniversary. And I think today I love her more than I did the first time I saw her."

No matter which version is correct, what happened next is that Jimmy got back to the Naval Academy and started writing to Rosalynn every other day and so did she. But Rosalynn was determined not to get carried away.

She was studying to be an interior decorator and she was determined to finish college. When Jimmy came home that Christmas of 1945, he proposed and she said no. She softened it by saying she still had to make up her mind about whether to have a career.

When Jimmy came home on his next leave, Washington's Birthday, Jimmy asked her again and this time she said yes. It hadn't taken her very long to decide that Jimmy was more important than college.

They were married as soon as Jimmy graduated from the Naval Academy and there is a family picture showing that both Rosalynn and Miz Lillian were at the graduation and jointly pinned his insignia on him. Usually only one loving female has this honor.

Jimmy had given Rosalynn a Naval Academy ring instead of an engagement ring and he slipped a simple wedding band on her finger on July 7, 1946.

As I see it, Jimmy Carter is thrust between two strong-willed, dynamic women. He has been trying to please both of them, ever since that day when he was commissioned into the Navy and both his wife and mother stood up to pin his insignia on him.

It is touching that Jimmy and Rosalynn each yielded something to the other to make the union a success. Jimmy married Rosalynn in her Methodist Church but then Rosalynn became a Baptist to please Jimmy and his family.

7 · THE BIGGER WORLD

When Jimmy and Rosalynn got married, I was already married. In fact, Jimmy was the usher at my wedding. Like Jimmy, I had not paid any attention all through eleven years of school to the girl who was destined to be my wife.

She had been under my nose all that time but I had had a blind spot where Ruth Godwin was concerned. She was just the daughter of the town druggist. She was a grade behind me in school, and I ran with girls in my own school class.

I had to go away to college—Georgia Southwestern—in Americus and come back in my freshman year to discover this lovely girl I had left behind. She was a senior in high school and I could hardly believe she was the same girl I had vaguely noticed in the halls.

It took a dance at Magnolia Springs to give me a good look at her. That is the same place where Jimmy and Rosalynn would later court. I love to dance and I asked Ruth to dance with me. Though she had come with another boy, she did dance and we jitterbugged, trucking around the floor.

As happened with Jimmy later, after one date I gave up all other feminine interests and put my Plains senior class ring on Ruth's finger as my symbol of engagement. The auspicious occasion for changing the class ring for an authentic engagement ring was the Georgia-Auburn game of 1941. I can't remember who won. I was too stunned by my own game plan.

I had stopped the car as we approached the stadium and had said, "I have something to show you." It was my mother's engagement ring, which I had inherited from her. I had taken it to a jeweler and he had reset the two-carat stone in a different setting.

Ruth and I could hardly keep our minds on the game. This was a much more beautiful game—and yet it was scary because it was for keeps. We were married Christmas Day, 1941.

The times we were living in had gotten a lot scarier. Pearl Harbor had cast its shadow. We were at war and we didn't know for how long.

When I graduated from the University of Georgia I was lucky to get a job immediately as an accountant with the Southern Bell Telephone Company. The company had a policy of making accountants learn the business from the ground up and so I was shifted to Columbus, Georgia, where I went to work in June 1941, climbing poles and doing construction work.

In October I was transferred to Jackson, Mississippi, and came back to Plains to marry Ruth and take my bride back after the 1941 Christmas holidays. I was happy that I was a full accountant by then and not still climbing poles.

In the spring of 1942 Daddy flew to Mississippi to see me, so I knew he had something important in mind. He said, "Hugh, if you can come home, I wish you would. I need you now in the store. So if you ever plan to take over from me, now would be a good time."

I was happy to have the invitation to come back to Plains. I knew that I wanted to spend my life there someday, but it had been good to get away for a while and see life in other places.

I knew that because of his health, Daddy could use me near and I had another reason for welcoming the chance to go back. Ruth was pregnant with our first child and I wanted it to be born in Plains as I had been. I worked for my father until the following spring when I was drafted into the Army, not to return from France until October 1, 1945—which, by coincidence, was Jimmy's birthday.

Hugh, Jr., was eight months old when I was drafted and it was sad to have to part with my wife and small son. I was in the Army for three years. Ruth and Sonny visited me when I was in Advanced Communication School at Fort Bliss, Texas, after I had been in the Army a little over a year.

The Army trained me as a radio operator and I attended Advanced Code School at Ft. Bliss and also was given some tactical training there. We rented a small apartment in El Paso for a few weeks and that was the only bliss at Fort Bliss.

Most of the time that I was in training at El Paso, it was grim. My searchlight outfit would go out on the desert in southern New Mexico for field training under hardship conditions. We would stay out for two weeks at a time and be given only one quart of water a day for bathing, shaving, drinking, and everything.

They were toughening us up for overseas duty and they were succeeding. Big sandstorms would come up which would never produce rain, and sand covered everything including the food we ate. I was glad when that phase was over.

Sonny, my son, by this time was about a year and a half old and amazing everyone by walking and talking like a three-year-old. In the fall of 1944 I was accepted in Officer Candidate School at Fort Benning, which was only forty-five miles from my home in Plains. There followed the toughest training I had ever had in my life.

I received my commission as a second lieutenant in the Infantry in February of 1945 and I was immediately sent overseas. I received one battle star in connection with my service in Europe.

I was in Rennes, France, in 1945. Our division was reorganizing, after being plastered in the Battle of the Bulge. At the time, we were also considered as the reserve backup for one of our Army units holding the Germans in at Lorient, France—a pocket of Germans with their backs to the sea.

As a lieutenant I was officer of the day that day and in charge of the regimental guard detail for the night. We had men walking guard posts throughout the regimental area.

Everyone was a little nervous and jumpy as occasionally a German patrol would break out of the pocket at Lorient and infiltrate the American lines in the reserve area to do as much damage to our headquarter units as possible.

We were very strict about using the correct password, especially at night. The password was changed daily. When a person was stopped by a guard he shouted out the first part of the password for the day (the guard shouted first, then the person being challenged was supposed to give the correct reply).

That day the password was "grapefruit." The guard challenged a man coming into one of the headquarter areas. The guard called out "*Grape.*" The man being challenged was supposed to answer with "Fruit" if he knew the password.

He didn't know it so the guard assumed he was the enemy and shot him. Fortunately, he shot the man in the shoulder and he did not die. He turned out to be one of our own men.

After the war ended in Europe, we stayed there near Lorient for some time. I was still regimental communications officer, in charge of all communications throughout the regiment.

Of course one thing we had to worry about, even though the war was over, was booby traps, as the Germans had left many in houses, and everywhere. Also many of the roads and streets were mined and we had to be very careful as to where we walked and rode.

The Germans liked to leave a picture crooked on the wall with a booby trap attached. If you straightened the picture, which you have a natural instinct to do when you see one crooked, the booby trap would explode and kill you and anyone else in the room.

We had several accidents of this nature. As a communications man, I was always interested in German communication equipment, how it worked, etc. I often found German telephones but I would always inspect them carefully before I touched them to see if any wires were attached which might be a booby trap.

Nothing toughens a man more than seeing comrades die, and one died in my arms. It happened in an area we were in that was covered with ammunition left by combat troops. We warned the men not to touch any of the ammo. One of the men in our company took a 20-mm German shell and opened it and struck a match to the powder. It exploded, wounding him critically.

We were eating chow at the time and one of the men ran to me and said, "Lieutenant, come quickly, one of the men is hurt."

I had heard the explosion. I reached the wounded man in about two minutes and instructed someone to call an ambulance immediately so that he could be transported to the aid station. I gave the man first aid but he was bleeding badly. He was still conscious.

He looked up at me and said, "Lieutenant, I'm sorry I disobeyed your order." I cradled him in my arms and told him it was all right. He opened his mouth once more and whispered, "I wish I could see my mother."

Those were his last words. He was dead. The ambulance arrived—too late.

I was a different man when I returned to the States from France in October of 1945, after the hostilities were over—older, sadder, tougher, and momentarily jaded. My little son hardly recognized me and did not want to come near me. I was determined to lose that toughness as quickly as possible.

Laurie Gay was born October 23, 1946, the month after Sonny turned four. She was named for my mother, who had died when I was nineteen years old. Connie came along six years later.

I was not mustered out of the Army until the following year, May 11, 1946.

I was glad to be back in time to see Jimmy's happiness at having fallen in love at last and to be there for his wedding in '46.

I was especially delighted with Jimmy's wedding. It forged

another link in the friendship of Cousin Hot and Cousin Beedie—our wives were also related.

Rosalynn's mother's daddy, Captain John William Murray—also called Uncle Captain around Plains—was Ruth's daddy's uncle. Miss Allie and Ruth's daddy were first cousins. I believe this makes Rosalynn and Ruth what we call second cousins. And they have always had a wonderful friendship of their own, which did not depend on Jimmy and me.

Maybe some of their friendship came from the fact that the shared background between Rosalynn Carter and my wife, Ruth, is every bit as colorful as Jimmy's and mine. Their first ancestor to reach American shores was John Kleckley, the fifth-generation grandfather, who came to America in 1750 from Germany.

He came for religious reasons, as a Protestant escaping the Roman Catholic domination of southern Germany. It was one of the worst voyages in colonial history. About a hundred shipmates perished from starvation—John's wife among them—leaving the man with three small children when they set foot on Cape Fear in North Carolina.

Somehow John Kleckley and his little family survived a march of several hundred miles until they settled in Saxe-Gotha, South Carolina, on a two-hundred acre farm. Kleckley and his son, John, Jr., fought in the Revolutionary War in the Battle of Cowpens and other battlefields. He died in 1790.

Katherine Kleckley, wife of John, Jr., was kidnapped by Indians on the warpath in the Saxe-Gotha territory in 1773 and almost put to death. But so courageous was she that the Indians spared her life.

Eventually, she was able to escape and returned home with her startling story.

The third-generation maternal grandfather of Rosalynn Carter was John, Jr., and Katherine's son, Jacob Kleckley, who came to Oglethorpe, Georgia, with a dual career—preaching and medicine.

He became very wealthy from selling patent medicines, and when he died in 1862 he owned a thousand acres and several dozen slaves. Rev. Jacob Kleckley is credited with founding the first Lutheran Church in central Georgia.

Rosalynn also had ministers on her father's side. Her great-great-grandfather was Rev. George Lynch Smith. He was a circuit-riding preacher belonging to the Disciples of Christ denomination.

However, so independent was he that when the church tried to

73

lay down rules for his ministry, he broke away and founded a denomination known today as the Nondenominational Fellowship of Christian Churches (Independent).

Rosalynn's great-grandfather on her father's side, Wilburn Juriston Smith, son of the minister born in 1853, became an important man around Plains in spite of great adversity. He had wanted to become a full-fledged doctor but he was severely injured by a mule and was unable to go to medical school. For years, he could not even walk but had to crawl on hands and knees. So he taught himself medicine by reading medical textbooks and "unofficially" treated patients who came to his home.

It was a happy day for him when he was finally able to be fitted for a specially designed back brace, enabling him to walk. Doc Smith died in 1918.

Almost everyone knows and has read about Ensign Jimmy's grilling by Admiral Hyman Rickover, which influenced his life, but most people don't know the whole flow of Cousin Hot's early career, after Annapolis and until his return to Plains.

Jimmy's first assignment after Annapolis was at Pensacola, Florida, where Jimmy was assigned to fly blimps. He hated it. He had not entered the Navy to become an admiral of a floating balloon.

The next assignment was a little better. It was at Norfolk, Virginia, where Jimmy spent two years on experimental gunnery ships—the *Wyoming* and the *Mississippi*—as electronics officer. Still Jimmy wasn't all that thrilled. He though of quitting the Navy. He thought of getting a Rhodes Scholarship, which would at least get him one step out of the country toward his ambition of seeing the world. But he failed to get the scholarship.

Submarines next became his driving ambition. In 1948 Jimmy was accepted into submarine school and he studied at New Haven, Connecticut, graduating third in a class of fifty-two.

Immediately afterward, he was bound for Hawaii aboard ship. Jimmy was perfectly fine when confined to a submarine under the water but he had terrible seasickness above water for the five days his ship struck stormy seas.

Several recent Presidents have had some harrowing experience in the military which might have resulted in death. Jimmy, too, had an incident in which he almost lost his life.

One stormy night Jimmy was on duty on the bridge of the *U.S.S. Pomfret* holding the rail to keep his balance as the deck under him rocked crazily. An enormous thirty-foot wave washed over him, suddenly and unexpectedly, and swept him overboard. He kept swimming not knowing if he was in the ocean or above the deck of the ship. Or even if anyone realized his plight.

When the water subsided, miraculously, he was able to grab a five-inch gun and hang on, some twenty-five or thirty feet from the bridge where he had been standing when the wave hit. Sometime afterward, the *Pomfret* heard a radio message for all ships in the Pacific to be on the lookout for pieces of the *Pomfret* "believed to have sunk seven hundred miles south of Midway Island."

The irony was they could not even message that the *Pomfret* was "alive and well" and still above water, because the radio was damaged.

After his tour of duty on the *Pomfret*, Jimmy was assigned to a prototype strike submarine, the K-1. And from that, he went into Admiral Rickover's nuclear submarine program, having to first be approved by Admiral Rickover in person.

It was then, when Jimmy could have thought life was just a bowl of cherries and he would be quickly climbing the ladder of success within the Navy, that he received word his father had cancer and could not be expected to live.

The year was 1953 and Jimmy was now the father of three children: Jeff, who had just been born the year before; Chip, who was three; and Jack, who was six.

Jimmy has always been grateful that he was able to see his father before he died and have a heart-to-heart talk with him. Without it, he would have been tormented all his life in not knowing what his father's last wishes had been. As it was, he knew that his father was counting on him to look after Billy and his mother and the family business.

I don't believe people realize how profound an effect his father's death had on Jimmy. They had grown apart for some years and Rosalynn had not wanted to live in Plains again—ever. But when Uncle Earl died, Jimmy suddenly changed and returned, as if to make it up to him, and take over the responsibility for his mother and young Billy, who was still only a kid.

After Uncle Earl's death, when Jimmy told Rosalynn that he was going to give up his Navy career and become the same kind of man in the community that his father had been, I am told that Rosalynn burst

75

into tears. She had thought they were on a straight course to wonderful military life, and her dream was shattered. And even worse, she knew that in Plains she might still be regarded as a little girl by Jimmy's mother and her own mother, and not the coequal head of the family.

Rosalynn knew how to dry her tears and hide her disappointment. Only years later did she tell how really shattered she had been. Jimmy, however, had said frankly it was the biggest fight he and Rosalynn ever had—the argument over whether to return to Plains.

8 · IT'S DADDY BEEDIE, DADDY HOT

Jimmy used to say that his first child, Jack, was the ugliest baby he had ever seen. And then he'd laugh, because son Jack turned into a very cute little boy as soon as he had gotten himself straightened out.

What had happened is that he was a breech baby and the doctors had tried to turn him around in the womb. It hadn't worked and baby Jack came out foot first and his face looked as if he'd been in a prizefight.

Fortunately, Chip and Jeffrey and Amy have been perfectly ordinary births—no trouble at all. But the shadow of that first agony hung over Rosalynn just a little bit on the later births.

Jimmy proved he was a compassionate husband by being especially gentle and helpful to Rosalynn after every baby. He would treat her like a queen and insist on getting up and taking care of those nighttime feedings, until she was completely rested.

Jimmy loves to reminisce about where he was when each of his sons was born. All of them were born while Cousin Hot was in the Navy. Jack, the oldest, who is twenty-nine, was born in Virginia. Chip, the second, twenty-six years old, was born in Hawaii. The youngest of the boys, Jeff, twenty-four, was born in Connecticut. Jimmy points out that Amy, the only daughter, is the only child to follow the family tradition of having been born in Georgia.

Jimmy turned into a much tougher father than I was. Maybe because he had three sons and no girls until the boys were almost grown, and I had two little girls and one son, mine was a no-spank household. My little girls were gentle creatures and my one son, Hugh, Jr., was too busy with his many projects to get into trouble.

Jimmy was a lot like his own father, as it turned out, spanking his boys when he felt they needed it. Just as Jimmy used to have to go out and bring in the switch that his daddy would use, so he had his three boys cut their own switches. If they picked switches that weren't big enough, he did not laugh. He threw the little-bitty switch away and went out and picked his own and it would be a little rougher than if they had brought in a medium-sized switch to begin with. But Jimmy didn't only use a peach switch. He used a paddle. What he was trying to do was to discipline his sons to become bookworms like himself and get good grades.

But Chip was not like his Dad. He would disappoint his father by getting low grades and Jimmy would decree that he couldn't watch his favorite television shows for a week or so.

I'm not sure that Jimmy's technique worked too well. He didn't want his sons to smoke, and when he caught twelve-year-old Chip smoking, he paddled him. Chip grew up to be a chain smoker.

I had not been switched with a peach switch more than once or twice, plus an occasional spank with my father's hand, so I did not switch my little boy, Hugh, Jr. I would just sit and talk with him if I did not like what he was doing and keep talking until Sonny indicated he understood, and would keep it in mind for his future behavior.

I think I was lucky, too, in having a son who was so interested in the worm business that he could find excitement in being on his own and bossing his own little crew.

Though I did not give Hugh, Jr., an allowance, Jimmy did give allowances based on age. A ten-year old got 50¢, a nine-year old, 45¢, and so forth.

When the boys graduated to little warehouse jobs, they received a salary of $2.50 a week. They felt it was not enough.

My son, on the other hand, felt that his earning capacity was unlimited. He was a real businessman in the worm business making money on the amount of worms he prepared and shipped and a bonus for the work he supervised that was done by other little boys. I think it is the greatest thing that parents can do for their children to make them feel they are in charge of something.

Hugh, Jr., has never had to be in rebellion against anyone. For that reason, I believe, he never became involved in drugs or juvenile pranks that land many of today's kids in trouble with the law.

Rosalynn, to my knowledge, never used physical force with her sons, except for a little swat, perhaps, if they weren't minding her. She was a stickler for neatness and insisted that they keep their rooms neat. If they didn't, they were confined to their rooms where they could tidy up after they got over being mad and read until they were out of the doghouse with their mother.

Television privileges might be taken away as a punishment, but reading never was.

Jimmy was very strict about having dinner on time. Whatever they were doing the children had to drop and be seated at 6:00 sharp. Unlike Jimmy's own family meals, however, as a child, there was no restriction on talking, and Chip, Jeff, and Jack could read or talk, as they chose, or any combination thereof.

So they're not always reading in the Carter family anymore. In fact, through the years Jimmy and his sons developed a kind of game that they play at the table, even with company, in which they argue the opposite side from which they believe.

But not necessarily. The point is to confuse each other so that nobody knows what side they are really on. Cousin Jimmy is good at this kind of arguing and Rosalynn gets very frustrated because it is not her idea of humor. She wants to know what people really believe but Jimmy loves to tease his little "Rosie."

Jimmy was a great one for helping his sons with their homework. He practically memorized their textbooks and would discuss the subjects with them in detail. He would also try to expand their minds by reading poetry aloud to them—especially Dylan Thomas.

I was not much on helping my kids with homework except for math, but—just like my dad had taken me, I would take my son squirrel hunting. We would go in different directions and then meet back at the designated place at a certain time. Now and then I would hear a shot in the distance but there was no way of telling who had bagged the most squirrels until we met—usually it was Hugh, Jr.

I feel especially sympathetic toward Jeff because he had so much medical trouble. It all started with a broken jaw that did not set properly, sustained in an accident. It had to be rebroken, and by some fluke, that injured the eardrum.

He has had to have an artificial eardrum and bone grafts in his chin. Jeff has risen above all he has suffered and he is a very hard-working student. When this book comes out, he may already have graduated from George Washington University.

In our household, we, too, lived through serious medical problems with our son.

We had noticed when Hugh, Jr., was six years old that one leg was a bit shorter than the other and his heel on the short leg was not as developed as the other.

The solution specialists chose was to put staples in the bone in the long leg and slow up the growth until the short leg caught up, then remove the staples, and they would grow on evenly after that.

Today he stands 6′2″ tall and walks without a bit of limp.

I thought of Jimmy so many times in the adventures I have shared with my son.

As soon as Sonny was old enough—four or five—I started doing with him all the things Jimmy and I used to do. We walked along the creeks and gathered sweet shrub blossoms and we fished and hunted. We also watched the trains go by and he was awed by them.

One day when Sonny was five he disappeared and we frantically hunted for him, fearing that he had run away from home. Eventually after searching woods and streams I found him in the heart of town, on the platform of the old train depot talking to everyone and watching the train switch tracks, just as Jimmy had done.

I learned the fierceness of father-love. I was raising a few chickens and we had a mean rooster that did not like children. One day Laurie went in the chicken pen to gather the eggs and this rooster jumped on her, drawing blood. I heard Laurie cry out and I ran into the pen with a stick and swung at the rooster and knocked his head completely off.

I remember another time when the specter of death really hung over Sonny. Sonny felt about sandpiles the way Jimmy used to feel about sawdust piles—he loved to slide down them.

One Wednesday afternoon—the day on which the general store was closed—I had taken him with me to get a load of sand at Jackson's Sand Pit, a few miles from Plains.

As I shoveled sand into the truck, Hugh, Jr., was having fun sliding down huge inclines. Suddenly I realized he was missing. I looked and saw a whole bank of sand had caved in on him.

I searched and searched but could not see even a shoe sticking out. I was horrified as I realized he might be smothering to death. Yet I dare not use the shovel.

Covered with a cold sweat of fear, I dug frantically with my hands until I had located him and uncovered his nose. As I pulled him out, I sank to the ground hugging him and thanking God for having spared his life.

When Hugh, Jr., was about six or seven I began raising crickets as bait for fishermen. I would pay him to go out in his granddaddy's oat field with several other white and black children and catch crickets, which we had a ready market for.

I would let him report to me the number that each person caught and I would pay them accordingly. At that early age he was learning the value of a dollar by the amount of time it took to earn a dollar. Also, just as our fathers had done with Jimmy and me, I was letting Sonny earn his own spending money.

I remember an incident that taught little Hugh an important lesson. One small boy who was bringing his crickets to Hugh, Jr., for counting seemed to outshine all the rest of his little crew.

Hugh, Jr., was paying the little boy almost double what anyone else was getting. Then we found that after we left the cricket house, he was slipping in the back window and stealing the same crickets out of the box and would bring them back to us and sell them to us the second time. We didn't know how long this had gone on before we got wise, but it did give us all a laugh, in spite of the expense. It also impressed little Hugh with the fact that you can't get away with wrongdoing for long and that finally the truth will catch up with you.

When he was about eleven years old, Hugh, Jr., began to help Daddy Alton and me take inventory at the general store at the end of the year and he was invaluable to me in helping me raise and sell fishing worms, which I added to my cricket business.

Sonny was already quite levelheaded at that early age. We had several women and one man working daily at the worm farm in the rear of our home and I taught Sonny at that early age to also supervise the counting of the worms.

Sonny was certainly busy in the summer because he also continued to grade, count, and pack all the crickets to be shipped.

He was earning quite a bit of money for a little boy and he could have frittered it away but he learned to save. His credo became: "Never waste a dollar. Never buy anything that you don't need or really want. No matter how cheap an item is, it is not cheap at any price if you don't need it."

By 1956 and '57, our worm business had flourished and now it was a family affair. Hugh, Jr., was in charge of all packing and shipping and he was sending crickets and worms all over the country.

His mother, Ruth, did all the office work, answering the hundreds of letters that we received in response to our national advertising in sporting and farm magazines. She also processed the orders and made the labels to turn over to Hugh, Jr., for handling in the packing house.

In 1957 Sonny was especially busy because, besides the worm

business, as a fifteen-year-old, he was very involved in high school activities. Y. T. Sheffield, who had been my coach and Jimmy's, was now coaching Hugh, Jr., in basketball and track.

And on top of that, we were building a new house and a much larger worm and cricket farm about a mile and a quarter south of Plains. We were already being singled out by writers as one of the originators of the cricket-worm combination business and we were fast moving toward the title of the world's largest worm suppliers.

All during the time Hugh, Jr., was growing up, his cousin, Jimmy Carter, was his hero. Jimmy was the scoutmaster and Hugh, Jr., strove to impress him. At school he tried to emulate him and when there was a contest on who could read the most books, Sonny won.

He adopted the Jimmy Carter habit of reading a book while eating lunch!

He also once impressed scoutmaster Jimmy with a birdhouse he made. I remember how hard he worked at it, even painting it with great care.

No wonder Hugh, Jr., gets so much done at the White House. He was always a great one for budgeting his time, even in grade school. His sixth-grade teacher, Mrs. Nancy Sheppard, once told me that she had never seen anybody use his time so precisely as Sonny.

He had so many things he wanted to do after he got out of school every day that he used even two or three available minutes to do homework. She said that often there would be a five-minute lapse before a bell would ring after a class and while everyone else was stacking their books and sitting around, Sonny would be feverishly getting his homework done.

He was the same way in his work with the worm farm. Sonny would work so hard and long that he would stretch out and fall asleep on top of the cricket boxes. I would carry him in the house sound asleep.

Hugh, Jr., had to take a lot of ribbing at school about the fact that he was in the worm business, but it did not stop his popularity, because he took it with good grace and learned to make jokes about it himself.

For a time I thought that maybe Hugh, Jr., was going to become the musician I never could be.

Sonny and Johnny Hendricks, his best friend in Plains, would sometimes sit up all night working toward developing their own band. Sonny played the drums and Johnny—whose nickname was Brown—played the electric guitar.

Ruth and I thought we would go out of our minds trying to sleep with that Plains version of Elvis Presley. Eventually, they found a fellow who could play the piano and the quality of their music certainly improved.

A few years later, after he had matured a bit, he turned into the most generous person in the world, bringing back gifts of necklaces of uncut emeralds for his mother and sisters and even buying his sister Connie a set of yellow Tupperware that she thought was the most beautiful thing in the world.

Because of his love of antiques, acquired in our antique business, he ended up with the most unusual but charming apartment—an old icebox refurbished, a three-legged chair, copper kettles, an old mahogany fern stand, and many antique planters in which he raised a beautiful assortment of plants.

In his senior year at Plains High School, he was editor of his school annual and was selected star student of his senior class. He graduated as valedictorian and chose Georgia Tech as the college he would attend. He finished in the top third of his class.

Like other boys his age, Hugh, Jr., was drafted into the Army for two years of military service. During that military sojourn, he married a lovely girl, Joan Samuelson, whom he met at Auburn University while visiting his boyhood friend, Johnny Hendricks.

Ruth and I were very saddened when, some years later, he and Joan were divorced. They had no children. It was the second divorce in the Carter family; Jimmy's sister Gloria got the first one.

After Hugh, Jr.'s, discharge from the Army as first lieutenant, he went back to school, attended Wharton School of Business in Philadelphia, receiving his master's degree in two years.

You can't tell me that overwork kills people—for Carters, it keeps them young. Take my daddy, Jimmy's uncle, who became eighty-nine August 17, 1977, and died in January 1978. He hardly took off time for his birthday and continued to be at work every day of his life, except Sundays, from 8:00 A.M. to 6:00 P.M. until shortly before his passing.

Jimmy has said he hopes he has some of that "Uncle Buddy long lifeblood" in his veins.

Two things besides hard work kept Daddy Alton alive and kicking. One was baseball. Nobody loved baseball more than Daddy, and he could tell you almost any baseball fact you could ask him—even way back to the first baseball games in the sport's history.

When Connie was in high school, Daddy had made such a sports fan of her that all of us—she, Ruth and I, Betty and Granddaddy

Alton—would pile into the car just about every Wednesday afternoon during the summer and go to Atlanta to the Braves baseball game 135 miles away.

The second grand passion for Daddy was the study of our family tree and history. He worked on it all the time that he was not waiting on customers or listening to a ball game. And he traced the Carters way back to the *Mayflower!*

Reporters found Alton Carter an amazing man to talk to since he knew just about everybody in the state of Georgia or at least some of their kinfolks.

Maybe it was also being married to a woman twenty-two years younger than himself that kept Daddy Alton so spry and happy. He lived alone for five years after Mother died and then he took a bride from a neighboring town, Parrott, Georgia.

Betty Jennings was a schoolteacher and had never been married. Daddy was fifty-seven and she was thirty-five when they married in June 1945. I was still overseas at the time in the military, so I could not be present. But I was happy that my father had found happiness again. The Carters have always placed learning and teachers on a very high plane and again Daddy had chosen a wife from the teaching profession.

Their life was extremely happy, although they had no children, and they shared every interest. To the end of Daddy's life, they went out to dinner together at restaurants, like newlyweds, and fought over baseball games—a passion they both shared.

Connie was Granddaddy's girl and Granddaddy Alton used to take her along on his mule-buying trips. He would drive an old beat-up red car.

Connie would be scared to death to ride with him but she would go anyway.

Unfortunately, Connie was present when Daddy added some of the quaint markings to his car. She took it stoically. Braving life and limb on the back roads of Plains was one thing but Connie refused to go along with another suggestion of her Granddaddy's—that she learn to ride a horse.

My Daddy Alton was helping me teach Connie about money earned through hard work—he had a deal with her that he would give her a dollar every time she made all A's on her report card.

By the time she was in the third grade, she had almost twenty dollars. But her Granddaddy had taught her so well about saving money for things she would want in the future that she hoarded her dollar bills and refused to use them.

Some years went by and one day she unearthed her money and found that it had just about rotted. I asked her what the experience had taught her and whether the experience had shown that money should be used to buy things.

"No," she said. "It means you should always put your money in the bank."

A new generation of Carter cousins were friends when my kids were growing up and going to school with Jimmy's kids. Jimmy's youngest son, Jeff, and Connie, my youngest, were special friends. One Christmas, Connie and Jeff were both acting in the Christmas nativity scene and Jeff had to dress up like a shepherd.

Connie was going to go caroling with him after they were through and so she wore a pair of warm slacks. When she saw she was the only one in church wearing them, she ran out of the church because she was embarrassed, but Jeff followed her out to the car. He insisted that she have the courage to be different, saying, "By golly, if I can wear this ladies' cloak and look like a shepherd, you can certainly wear a pair of pants into church and look like a girl."

A high-water mark for Connie was to go to the Governor's Mansion for a party that Jimmy's three sons were giving. Connie felt very adult about that.

None of Jimmy's sons were the dedicated scholars their father was but they were all bright enough. In the tenth grade, Connie and Jeff would be working together on geometry problems, and he had a quick grasp for figures. Though I was really the cousin of Jimmy's children, they always called me Uncle Hugh and my wife, Aunt Ruth.

Connie had Jimmy as her Sunday school teacher for four or five years, when she was in the Junior Department at Plains Baptist Church. In those day, Connie would play the piano and Jimmy would lead the singing.

Sometimes, Jimmy would pick a number that Connie found very hard to play and she would rebel but she usually would plod through any song or hymn that "Uncle Jimmy" wanted. She would practice the piano hours at a time to show Jimmy how good she could be in playing the "quiet music," the music played while everyone was assembling before the church service.

Connie was thrilled when Jimmy came to her wedding reception even though he was running for the presidency. He had to fly down after a fund-raising dinner in Atlanta to make it. But before the wedding the Secret Service was all over the place walking around with wires in their ears and walkie-talkies and never smiling.

Quite a few Carters came—Rosalynn, whom Connie calls Aunt Rosalynn, Billy and his wife, Sybil, and Aunt Lillian.

But it was Laurie's eldest child, Carter, the five-year-old ring bearer, who stole the show. Everyone was making a fuss over him and he was telling everything he knew when a guest asked him what country he lived in.

Carter replied without a moment's hesitation, "Jimmy Carter's."

When he saw what an uproar he had caused, Carter did a little thinking and decided to check up to make sure he wasn't making any mistakes. He went over to Jimmy, pulled on his pants leg, and said, "Cousin Jimmy, are you going to be the next President?"

Jimmy knelt down and hugged Carter. "I sure hope so," he said.

"Well, you better," said Carter, "because I promised."

It was a beautiful ceremony but my mind flashed back to those golden years when Connie was that little girl glued to the telephone. She and Jeff Carter used to talk together on the phone for at least an hour every night and there would be a lot of giggling on Connie's part.

I could not help but register that Jeff and another little boy in class, James Harper, were always getting in trouble at school for drawing monsters in their notebooks instead of studying. Jeff was a great reader of science fiction. He'd come down to my general store and see what was new in supernatural comic books.

When the new ones came in, he would just sit and read without buying until we closed the store at 6:00 and I would have to shoo him out.

Going back still further, Jeff used to sit behind Connie in the first grade, when she wore braids, and he would delight in wedging a braid in the crack between their desks so that she would be jerked back down when she started to get up.

Laurie loved Uncle Jimmy and Aunt Rosalynn as much as Connie did, but she had a special feeling about Rosalynn. That was because they both had a special interest in art. Laurie's paintings hang in places of honor in our home. Also, she just admired Rosalynn, her special look and her way of creating beauty around her in her home.

Both my daughters made their decision to be baptized into the Plains Baptist Church at the same age—nine. Both sailed through school with almost straight A's and graduated as valedictorians.

Each went on to be an outstanding university student—dean's list. Connie graduated from the University of Georgia *summa cum laude.*

When they were little tykes, seeing their big brother making all that money in the worm business, I took them along and they would sit happily for hours in a big box of shredded paper, watching how Daddy packed worms.

It was a big thrill when I finally let Laurie dig worms for Daddy at a dollar an hour, for an hour or two. She had no squeamishness about handling wiggly worms. Connie would never touch a worm.

Everything was fun around the girls. They used to call the bubbles in the iced tea "money," and would compete for the privilege of stirring the sugar in the iced tea in the pitcher at the table to make "money." Once one of them got up on the dining room table and stirred so hard the pitcher broke and tea flew in all directions. We all had a big laugh.

Busy as he was earning money, Sonny managed to be a complete clown around the house and dream up all sorts of tricks to play on his sisters. He once had little Connie crying because she believed him when he said he had planted a frog under her plate. He had run a tube under the tablecloth which was connected to a device under her plate at one end and a rubber hollow bulb at his end. Every time he squeezed the hollow bulb it made her plate jump.

He had a set of plastic ice cubes with real insects molded into them. He would drop them into someone's iced tea and when they got it half drunk, would shout, "Look out! You have a bug in your tea."

Jimmy has told me how thrilling it is to watch a little girl grow and develop. I know what he means. I was doubly blessed, having two girls, to see how each unfolded in her own way.

Laurie was more like Amy, quiet and reserved. Yet very sweet and concerned with the welfare of everyone—and every stray dog.

Connie was outgoing and fun loving—a regular little clown. One of the pictures of her that I most cherish is Connie with her stuffed monkey doll sticking her finger in it and pretending that it is biting her. She was a cheerleader at school and had enough of a writing flair to be on the staff of the *Annual*.

She was so much fun to be around that she was not only elected president of her sorority—*Kappa Alpha Theta*—but also was presented with the "Beautiful Intangible Award," the highest award of her sorority.

I remember one course in college when she was working on her master's degree in education. Her professor had given her the task of instructing a child who had no interest or incentive in his schoolwork.

One day, out of the blue she called me saying it was an emergency and telling me to ship her immediately some big fat worms and mail her under separate cover all my brochures on raising worms.

As she told me later, when she had dumped out all the worms on the table for the little boy to see, it was as if he had suddenly come to life. He grew excited and wanted to learn all about worms. And he had not gone back into his shell after that.

The curiosity about worms had led to other curiosities, and the learning process had begun for him.

When Connie fell in love and married Leon Collins, Leon got up at the rehearsal dinner and made the sweetest tribute to Connie that I have ever heard a prospective husband make to his future bride.

The Carter family believes in developing its children in whatever direction their talents would indicate. Jimmy is developing Amy's talents right now in dance and languages and music. My daughter Laurie started tap and ballet lessons when she was four years old.

Eventually she switched her interests to art and studied painting. Most of the paintings in our home were done by Laurie when she was thirteen and fourteen years old. But you would never guess it.

One year when there was an art show in Americus featuring the paintings of Lamar Dodd, local artists were invited to bring paintings to see if they would qualify for exhibition. One of Laurie's was selected to be exhibited in the same room with Dodd's paintings. It was described by the officials as "superb."

For a time, Laurie was almost decided to become a medical doctor, but then she met Thomas Edwin Tharpe. She was married in Plains with all the Carters present and she lived first in Atlanta and then Americus, where she and Ed have recently bought a beautiful old six-bedroom house. Ed is vice-president of the Citizens Bank of Americus.

Now Laurie has her hands full with three children but for a time she did teach biology on the high school level in Atlanta.

Laurie is becoming more like her idol, Aunt Rosalynn, every day. Her latest project is interior decorating. She and Ed have renovated their huge almost-hundred-year-old house and she is in complete charge of the decor. Like Rosalynn, too, she is keeping up with music and plays classical music on her piano, especially Bach and Chopin.

These are the things I remember. And I sometimes think, as I see crowds of children trooping by, who knows which of them belongs to a future presidential family?

9 • STARTING FROM PEANUTS

It was almost as if Uncle Earl was guiding his son from on high, the way Jimmy did everything he could to follow in his father's footsteps. He joined the Lions Club and became very active in it, not only in town but throughout the state. That membership led him to organize his first civic project, the construction of a public swimming pool, which is still in use in Plains.

In a way, the swimming pool, small as it was, taught Jimmy how to raise funds—a skill he would later need in running for public office.

Then Jimmy took up where his father left off on various town boards—the hospital board, the school board, the library board. He also became a church deacon.

Uncle Earl seemed to have looked after everyone in town like a benevolent patriarch. For example, he secretly supplied graduation dresses for high school girls whose families couldn't afford new white dresses. They never knew where they came from.

Jimmy followed in his father's footsteps, seeming compelled to carry on exactly as his father would have wanted. Even when Jimmy himself was very hard up for money he secretly provided those long white dresses, arranging it through the teachers.

There is some confusion about how Uncle Earl had made his money. It was principally from farming and real estate. He would buy and sell farms and would make a nice profit.

He had also recently—not too long before his death—started buying peanuts and selling fertilizer and related farming supplies, but this business had not grown large as yet. Thus, the peanut business was largely built by Jimmy and his wife, and later, Billy and his wife.

Both Uncle Earl and Jimmy farmed by sharecropping. They would furnish the land, seed, and fertilizer. The tenant, who lived on the farm, furnished all the labor and the landowner and tenant divided the profits.

When Jimmy was just getting started in the peanut business, it was very hard for him. He had never been in business. He didn't know how easy it was to lose money through bad judgments.

I remember going to Jimmy and telling him I would be glad to offer any credit advice I could about people to save him trouble. I had acquired a great fund of credit experience for that area from working at my father's store. I had learned whom you could safely extend credit to and whom you should insist deal in cash.

Jimmy did more bookwork and thinking and bargaining than he did manual labor in those early years after he came home to take over the business. But when it was peanut harvesting time, if there was a shortage of help, he would pitch right in and help unload peanuts.

He made his sons help, too. It was only after he was running for President that anyone cared what kind of worker he had been during the hard years and it was heartening to hear Ernest Turner, the owner of the hardware store down the street from my antique shop and a deacon of the Plains Baptist Church where we all used to attend, say, "Jimmy could do more work than any other three men put together. And he was not a mean man. As long as everyone else did their share and did what was expected of them, he was easy to get along with."

Ernest Turner had been in the liquid fertilizer business with Jimmy.

Both Jimmy and I learned the bitter taste of death of a parent at a relatively young age. My experience came first. I loved my mother very much.

Mother, Annie Laurie, was very kind and sweet and loved her two sons very dearly. I can't remember being disciplined by her. She was never too busy to look after us or answer a question. I did not realize her days were numbered. It was in 1940 when I was nineteen and she was only forty-six that God called her away. Her illness was diagnosed as reverse-leukemia.

Because I had met with death, I had greater compassion and understanding when Jimmy experienced his great loss—his father's death in 1953.

Uncle Earl had just struck his stride and had everything going for him when his fatal illness cut him down. His business was going well. He owned a tremendous amount of land. He was respected by the town. He was still running his store, or commissary, as it was called. He had expanded and was beginning to buy the peanut crops from other farmers to process and resell.

Plus that, he had gone into the insurance business and the fertilizer business.

To top all this, he had been elected a representative to the Georgia State Legislature and had started his first term in January of that year. But though he wasn't ready for it, death came anyway in July, and it was a great blow to his family, especially Jimmy, who was in the Navy.

When Uncle Earl died, it was estimated that he was worth well over a quarter million dollars.

I do not believe that Uncle Earl, Jimmy's father, knew that he had cancer. It actually was diagnosed as cancer of the pancreas. He knew that his health was getting worse but he did not know the cause.

After the doctors determined that his illness was fatal and there was no hope for him, they brought him home to Plains.

I remember going to see Uncle Earl a short while before he died—though I didn't know his days were numbered—and we talked about many things in general. He seemed to be depressed and I was doing my best to cheer him up, when he said one thing that I will never forget.

"Beedie, take advantage of *each* day of your life and *live it to the fullest*. Live it as if it's your *last*."

I knew then that he was telling me he was going to die and that he felt too young to die.

When Uncle Earl died, Aunt Lillian turned down an offer to succeed him in the Georgia legislature. She did not want to be appointed to fill out his term. It was hard for me to understand this. I think she would have made a good state legislator and she certainly would have been fearless in speaking her mind.

If she had accepted the legislative post, I think she would have been much better off. As it was, she was deeply troubled for a long time.

It is not a case of the Hatfields and McCoys, but there is sort of a family feud that has involved the Carter family for as long as I can remember. It's too bad that when a man is nominated for President of the United States, the whole town does not back him solidly, but to be truthful, such solidarity would have been too much to expect for Cousin Jimmy.

Plains has always been a two-family town with all the townspeople lining up about evenly between the two family leaders. About half are followers of Jimmy Carter and the other half are followers of Albert Williams.

It was almost automatic that the Williams family and their bunch would not be in Cousin Jimmy's camp. It creates a bit of an uncomfortable feeling in Plains to have two large families cold to one another, but both sides have learned to live with it.

The feud, if that's the right term for it, was really inherited from the fathers of the two current heads of the family. They were competitors in the peanut and cotton business and each had a warehouse.

The Carters are the Johnny-come-latelies in the field of warehousing. The Williams family had its warehouse first, but then Jimmy's father started a competing warehouse and it became very successful.

The reason it prospered was that the Carter Warehouse put in modern equipment, which pleased the farmers and made it easy for them to do business with the Carters.

However, the Williams family has also been very successful and owns much property in Plains.

The rivalry between the Carter and Williams families has been a source of humor around Plains for years. There was a joke that if Rosalynn got pregnant, a Williams wife would have to get pregnant, too. What this said to me, a Carter, is that Jimmy was the front-runner and the Williams were always running to catch up! I guess the thing that annoyed the Williams clan was that they had been the peanut kings first and then the Carters had entered the field and had scored at their own game.

After Jimmy modernized his peanut operation, the Williamses followed suit to some extent. The mini-feud surfaces in little ways and always has.

When Jimmy wanted to open the Plains Baptist Church to blacks for worship services and membership, and argued for it, Albert Williams argued the other side and won.

All of Plains was proud early in 1970 when Jimmy Carter was named "Georgia's Young Businessman of the Year." In February he was presented with a plaque by Mayor Sam Massell of Atlanta for being an outstanding example of what a young man can do under the American free-enterprise system.

Speaking for the sponsor of the award, the *Georgia Business News*, Mayor Massell said, "Carter has taken advantage of the opportunities and faced up to the challenges in the world of business with innovations which have proved both profitable and of great service to the agricultural economy of the area he serves."

The award had not been lightly bestowed. Jimmy had been selected by a team of judges from all over the state which included professors of business and technology, business and industry associations, and the Chamber of Commerce.

Just to show what Jimmy had done to earn the accolade, let me list his achievements:

He had evolved a system for improving the production, storage processing, and sales of high-quality peanut seed.

He had designed and installed a new peanut-shelling system in his warehouse.

He had helped farmers achieve economic growth and stability in his area.

He had helped organize and became president of the Southern Peanut Warehouseman's Association covering three states—Florida, Alabama, and Georgia.

He had been President of the Georgia Crop Improvement Association.

He had helped small businessmen by arranging business-management seminars on improving efficiency of operations.

He had brought in new business and, again, improved the economic status of the farmers around him by building a manufacturing plant for "suspension fertilizers."

And besides all that, he had served in the Georgia State Senate for four years and had been, at various times, state chairman of the March of Dimes, fund chairman of the Georgia Society for the Prevention of Blindness, district governor of Lions International, state director of the WMCA, and trustee of Norman College.

One thing that the judges pointed out was that Jimmy Carter had built up the Carter Warehouse through sheer grit. Starting in 1953 with only an investment of $500, Jimmy by 1970 had increased it to a capital investment of over $500,000.

In those early years after Jimmy returned to Plains, our wives became very close. Our children shared activities and Ruth and Rosalynn shared community interests, especially in the "beautification of Plains."

Besides being related, they have been good friends through the years. When they belonged to the Garden Club together, their special project was the park across Main Street.

Rosalynn and Ruth also used to be members together in the Stitch 'n' Chat Club.

It's because of Ruth's relationship with Rosalynn Carter and her mother, Allie Smith, that I attend the family reunions of Miss Allie's family. Jimmy and Rosalynn, of course, are also always there.

So are Rosalynn's brothers, Jerry and Murray, and her sister, Alethea, and their children and spouses. Every year it gets bigger and in recent years, there have been about 250 Smiths and Murrays and Carters meeting for a big jamboree at the Methodist Fellowship Hall, the first Sunday of every August.

All the womenfolk bring the food. It is my wife's traditional job, every year, to prepare and bring a huge baked ham and a cheese loaf. This is the same dish that Rosalynn and Jimmy call a cheese-ring. It is made from the same recipe that Rosalynn uses and has been in the family for years.

Made with pecans and cheese, it is delicious spread on crackers.

PLAINS CHEESE RING
    1 pound grated cheese
    1 cup mayonnaise
    1 cup chopped pecans
    1 medium-sized grated onion
    ½ teaspoon black pepper
    ¼ teaspoon cayenne

Combine above ingredients. Place in a circular mold and refrigerate. Just before serving, remove from mold and serve with the center filled with strawberry or other preserves.

One of the things Jimmy said he was glad to get back to was our good old southern cooking.

Southern cooking is mighty good. Jimmy and I would eat blackberry pie. It's made with biscuit dough and covered with sugar. Then we would pour rich milk or cream over it. We would eat it in a deep bowl.

Jimmy and I grew up on such things as Brunswick stew made from a hog's head. A good cook can make the most delicious Brunswick stew from a pig's or hog's head and various vegetables.

We also would have a dish we called graveyard stew. It is made of beef and potatoes and other vegetables, simmered in gravy and served on grits or rice.

Barbecued pork is one of our favorite dishes in the South. You can take the hams or sides of a pig—put them on a wire or metal frame and cook them over hot oak wood coals. About twelve hours of slow cooking is required for the best barbecue. With it is served a sauce made of hot peppers, hot sauce, vinegar, and lemon juice.

Most southerners like the barbecue cut up fine or chipped and covered with the barbecue sauce. The skin is also cut up and makes a delicious crisp snack.

Through the years, whenever Jimmy and Rosalynn would come to dinner at our house, there was one thing Ruth had to fix for Jimmy—hot artichoke hearts. Jimmy would be so anxious for them that he would come out to the kitchen and get them hot out of the oven, popping some on a cracker before they were even brought to the living room to be served with drinks.

It was difficult for Ruth to know what to serve for dessert. If she was trying to please Jimmy or help him celebrate some triumph, she made a pecan pie. If she was trying to please me, she made the greatest carrot cake in the world.

Jimmy liked Ruth's recipe for carrot cake almost as much as I did and I'm very fond of pecan pie—made with local pecans—and of artichoke casserole— so we were never too unhappy. I'm going to share these recipes with the reader because I want to share special treats and because people are always asking what the President likes to eat.

These recipes definitely have the Carter stamp of approval.

Carrot Cake
   2 cups grated carrots
   2 cups all purpose flour
   2 cups sugar
   ¼ teaspoon salt
   1 teaspoon baking soda
   1 teaspoon baking powder

1 teaspoon cinnamon

1½ cups cooking oil

4 eggs

Combine above ingredients. Bake in 2 layers for 25 minutes at 375°.

Filling

½ stick margarine

1 box powdered sugar

1 8-ounce package cream cheese

1 cup chopped nuts (pecans)

2 teaspoons vanilla

Combine above ingredients. Place between the 2 layers of the cake.

Pecan Pie

⅔ cup sugar

¼ teaspoon salt

1 cup pecans, chopped

1 cup light corn syrup

3 eggs

½ cup melted butter (*not* margarine)

Combine and pour into unbaked deep-pie shell. Bake at 350° for 50 minutes.

Use this same syrup recipe for 2 shallow-dish pies. Put 1 cup of pecans in each shallow 8-inch pie shell and then divide the syrup mixture between the two. Bake at 300° for 40 minutes.

Artichoke Casserole

1 8-ounce can artichoke hearts

1 cup mayonnaise

1 cup grated Parmesan cheese

Dash garlic salt

Dash salt

Chop and drain artichokes. Mix with remaining ingredients. Bake 30–35 minutes at 325°. Broil the last few minutes to brown the top. Serve hot to be eaten on crackers.

Though Cousin Jimmy and Rosalynn have always had a traditional sit-down turkey and corn-bread stuffing dinner for Thanksgiving, their Christmas eating is not at all what you would expect. You might call it catch-as-catch-can.

What happens is that Jimmy and his immediate family sit down with Miz Lillian for a big Christmas breakfast and then run around visiting and eating a little here and there.

The tradition is for everyone to start the day with the matriarch of the family. Jimmy comes to Miz Lillian's house with Rosalynn and Amy and all the children and grandchildren he can muster.

The menu might surprise a northerner. We Carters think it fairly standard to have this Christmas breakfast: sausage, grits with cheese, bacon, orange juice, and coffee.

I'm going to tell how my wife makes the Carter-style grits. I'll also give the other Carter Christmas traditional treat—the Lane cake. All of us have it in our homes during the holiday season. It was first made by a woman in Americus with that name. First, for the benefit of northerners, a word about grits.

I recall how the farmers at Plains used to take shelled corn to the water mill and swap it for meal. Meal is corn ground to almost a powder consistency. It is used for making corn bread.

When it is not ground so fine, it is called grits—a great southern dish. I have eaten grits and butter all my life. Grits are also good with gravy.

GRITS WITH CHEESE

Combine 1 cup grated cheese with 1 cup grits and boil in 4 cups water until the mixture is smooth, stirring constantly.

Serve with melted butter on top.

What makes the Lane Cake so good, and may surprise some people, is that it has a filling between the layers that is made with whiskey.

THE LANE CAKE
2 cups sugar
1¼ sticks butter
3 cups flour
2 teaspoons baking powder
½ cup milk
7 egg whites, beaten stiff
1 teaspoon vanilla

Blend sugar and butter until creamy. Sift flour with baking powder. Gradually add flour and milk to butter mixture, alternating until it all has been used. Fold in egg whites and vanilla.

This makes a 3-layer cake. Bake the cake in greased pans, lightly floured, for about 35 minutes at 375°.

Whiskey Filling
7 egg yolks
1 cup sugar
1 stick butter
1 cup pecans
1 cup raisins
1 cup grated coconut
½ cup whiskey

Combine yolks, sugar, and butter and heat in a double boiler until mixture thickens.

Remove from stove and add pecans, raisins, coconut and whiskey. Stir thoroughly and you are ready to fill in the layers to make your 3-layer cake. Any frosting can be used but usually the Carters make a boiled white icing.

No Thanksgiving is complete without this Carter recipe of corn bread dressing for the turkey.

Corn Bread Dressing

Mix enough chicken stock in broken-up egg bread (recipe below) to make very soupy mixture. Add:

> 2 eggs
> 2 cups chopped celery
> 1 cup chopped onion

Pour into baking dish and cook at 350° for about 45 minutes or until celery and onions are tender, stirring several times. Let brown on top. Serve with chicken or turkey. And here's how to make the corn bread for it:

Egg Bread (Corn Bread)

> 1 tablespoon shortening
> 2 cups cornmeal
> 1 tablespoon baking powder
> Dash salt
> 2 eggs
> 2 cups buttermilk

Put shortening in iron skillet and heat. Combine ingredients into a batter, pour in hot grease and bake in 400° oven for 20 to 30 minutes. Break bread up into small pieces in large bowl and mix for dressing.

A tradition at the Jimmy Carter house in Plains through the years was to have the little boys help their mother make decorations for the family Christmas tree. Homemade Christmas decorations are popular in Georgia.

Strings of peanuts are just as pretty as strings of popcorn and they can be dipped in color for a cheerful note. Carter women are great for making Christmas cookies.

On Thanksgiving and Christmas holidays it is the Carter tradition to go hunting. Since Jimmy did not spend his Thanksgiving 1977 in Plains, but went instead to Camp David, I don't suppose he went hunting. However, I did.

In Plains on Thanksgiving, we would go squirrel hunting in the morning, come home to a 12:00 or 12:30 Thanksgiving dinner, and then go quail hunting in the afternoon.

Jimmy did go hunting when he came for Christmas holiday 1977 but I don't know whether he bagged anything.

10 · WORM KING

I was not surprised when I learned that Amy's favorite Christmas tree decoration her first year in the White House was the one she had put on the tree herself at the White House, before the family returned to Plains for their Christmas celebration.

The ornament was a long green worm made of pipe cleaners. Amy has had a standing fascination about worms all her little life.

So worms on a Christmas tree—even at the White House—is a perfectly logical thing.

During the campaign, Billy Carter had a line that was always sure to make everyone laugh: "I've got a mamma who joined the Peace Corps when she was sixty-eight. I've got one sister who's a holy-roller preacher. I've got another sister who wears a helmet and rides around on a motorcycle.

"And I've got a brother who thinks he's going to be the President of the United States. So that makes me the only sane one in the family."

Billy could have added one sentence to his family lineup of family kooks: "And I've got a cousin who goes around saying, he's the Worm King of America."

Jimmy had to take a lot of ribbing about the fact that he had a cousin who raised worms. In fact, as late as October 10, 1976, less than a month before the election, the Florida *Times-Union* of Jacksonville did a big article with the headline "Fishermen Prefer Hugh to Cousin Jimmy Carter."

The lead of the story, by Cary Cameron, said:

There may be some fishermen and bait dealers left in this world who still think of Jimmy Carter as "that politician cousin of Hugh's." Hugh Carter was building a national reputation as the king of worm raisers before his younger cousin Jimmy was known outside Sumter County and Navy circles.

Every business that I have been in has come about in an offhand way. Buying bait turned into selling bait, and getting into the antique business was just as casual. It started with the heart attack my daddy suffered in October of 1969. Because of it, he had to go to Emory University Hospital in Atlanta to have a pacemaker installed.

Because of that heart attack, he decided to close out his general merchandise store and I bought him out. I was cleaning out the store, selling everything, when I discovered that what people really wanted most were the antique fixtures—the lights, the fans, the doorknobs. Just anything that was antique.

The idea struck me right between the eyes—why not operate an antique business? And that was when the "Hugh Carter's Antiques" came into being.

Jimmy has heard many times of how Ruth and I got into the antique business and how we would scout the country looking for choice antiques to haul back to Plains. One incident that amused Jimmy was the story of Ruth and me on an antique scouting trip in north Alabama.

We went into a little old store, in a small town in the backside of nowhere. This is where you find your best antiques. We looked all over the man's two-story store and couldn't find a thing that we really wanted.

Finally, I looked over in one corner and saw a cat drinking milk out of a rare carnival glass bowl which I immediately valued at a hundred dollars or more.

Carnival glass is one of my favorite types of glass. I sell it in my own store, all that I can get. Since this store was such an out-of-the-way place, I figured the old man wouldn't know what the bowl was worth and that I could probably buy the bowl cheaply.

I didn't want to arouse his suspicion as to the bowl's value. So I asked the man if he would take twenty-five dollars for the cat. He said yes, but the price was too high, though he would take the money if I wanted to pay it. He got a burlap sack and put the cat in the sack.

Then I said to the old man, "Won't you just throw in that old bowl that the cat is drinking milk out of?" The man said, "Oh no, no, Mr. Carter. That bowl is not part of the deal. That bowl is the best cat seller that I have ever had."

We filled the store with as many antiques as we could find and sold both retail and wholesale. We also held an auction once a month and people and dealers came from far and wide. The auctions stopped in September 1976 when our warehouse burned down. But the retail store continued.

I soon became so busy selling souvenirs that there wasn't time for auctions, even had I wanted to hold them. Since our store is the only one with the name Carter on it, tourists flock in to buy knickknacks and gifts from a Carter. They buy chamber pots, chairs, mirrors, and weather vanes of the past, and they also buy every kind of Jimmy Carter souvenir of the present.

The most popular Cousin Jimmy souvenir, aside from postcards, is a can opener in the shape of Jimmy's head, which makes it seem like you are opening your bottle with Jimmy's teeth.

I believe the whole country got to know that Jimmy's first cousin was an antique dealer from newspaper stories and TV shows. But what they don't know is the effect a TV show can have.

For example, the *Mike Douglas Show*, which was filmed in our store. Mike interviewed Daddy Alton, little Amy Carter, Miss Allie, Rosalynn's mother, and me. As soon as the show was over, the phone started ringing and it was people from all over the United States wanting to buy the antiques they had seen in the background while he was interviewing us.

We also had mail orders from everywhere and could have sold some items ten times, if we had had duplicates. Not only do people collect antiques, but, I have learned, some collect items seen in the background of photographs in books and on TV.

The Worm Farm did not start as a whim. I knew that we could not rear a family, build Ruth's dream house, and educate our children on what I made working at my father's store. On Wednesday afternoons, Dad's store was closed and Ruth and I would spend a lazy afternoon fishing and talking about what we could do to earn extra money to make all our dreams come true.

We always had trouble finding enough worms for bait. Sometimes I would go fishing with Robert Ratliff near Americus in the Flint River. On those occasions we would stop to buy crickets from a friend of mine who was in the insurance business but sold bait as a sideline.

One afternoon as we waited to buy crickets from my friend, there were so many people in line that I thought to myself, this must be a good moneymaking business. Mr. Ramsey, my friend, could hardly fill the orders, there was such a demand.

That afternoon while I fished, all I could think about was those dollars I could make in the cricket business if I could learn how to raise and sell them.

We had good luck that afternoon with the crickets we bought. We must have caught twenty or thirty nice bluegill, a few catfish, and a couple of bass, using the crickets as bait most of the time. It seemed like a good omen.

The next morning I went upstairs in our general store and found an old wooden coffin that had been pushed aside and never sold. One of the buildings our store occupied used to be an undertaking parlor where people were embalmed.

I took this old coffin and put legs on it so that I could sit them in cans of oil to keep the ants from crawling up the legs and getting in the box.

I then put some sand in the bottom of the coffin about three inches deep, and hung a hundred-watt light bulb over the sand for heat. I used some pieces of ceiling board for a top. I then put a chicken water fount in the coffin on the sand with cotton stuffed in the fount to keep the smaller crickets from drowning.

I kept the heat adjusted to about 85° and ordered five hundred crickets from Troy, Alabama, for my starter or breeder stock. The crickets came in a few days and that was the birth of the largest fish-bait industry in the world.

It takes ten days for a cricket egg to hatch under the proper conditions. A cricket lays about ten eggs per day. An adult cricket lays only about ten to fifteen days before she dies. The males live a bit longer.

Anyway, in about twelve days I had a box full of small crickets. It takes about eight weeks for them to grow to selling size.

My box or coffin of crickets developed nicely and I sold about seven thousand crickets from the original five hundred that I had purchased. At that time, very few people around Plains were raising crickets, so I was able to sell most of them to the local fishermen. However, I kept a good many of them to reuse as breeder stock as I had big plans to expand the operation.

I moved the coffin box out to a storehouse behind our store and built about ten more large brooder boxes, three partitions to the box, each partition about thirty inches square.

My production increased and I constantly built more brooder boxes. I sold my crickets by the thousand—ten dollars per thousand—or I cupped them and sold them locally or to other dealers or bait shops who wanted to sell them at a profit.

I could only supply about two towns, Columbus and Macon. I sold so many crickets that I couldn't raise all that was being demanded, so I began to order from another grower in south Georgia at a cheaper price and sold them at a profit to my customers.

I soon had such volume that I decided to build a modern cricket hatchery out of concrete blocks behind my home in Plains, which was a modest house on Bond Street. This is the same street that Rosalynn, Jimmy's wife, lived on until they were married.

In fact, Jimmy and Rosalynn would come to get crickets and worms to go fishing, and they still do, even as President and First Lady.

I continued to do well in my cricket business for several years. All during this time I had repeated calls for worms, but no one anywhere seemed to know how to raise worms.

I began to experiment with them. I built a bed up off the ground—this was a mistake—and ordered five thousand worms from Tennessee.

They soon all crawled out or disappeared so I had to try other methods. I tried raising them in boxes and in tubs sitting on the ground.

This method was partially successful but still wasn't perfect. I finally built beds about five feet wide and thirty feet long, on the ground, with gravel in the bottom covered by boards spaced one inch apart.

The gravel was about four inches deep and served as drainage for the beds. Worms, I learned, need a lot of water but the water must wet the bedding and drain out immediately, washing the acidity from the bed. Otherwise the worms will come to the surface and die.

You immediately know that if this condition occurs—worms dying—your bed has an overacid condition, too much protein in the bedding. Bedding is made out of aged cow or horse manure mixed with hay and Canadian peat moss and leaf mold. Lights have to be burned over the beds on rainy nights so that the worms will not crawl out.

We have always believed that the worms felt they would drown and their natural instinct was to crawl out when a hard rain came. If it is in the daytime, they are sensitive to light and will not come out but stay near the surface of the bed. Burning lights after darkness had fallen had the same effect and gave the worms the idea that "they wouldn't drown so long as they could see the light."

Well, as time progressed, I mastered the art of worm raising and began to ship worms through the mails from a small ad that I was running in *Field and Stream* magazine. I shipped worms in specially made cardboard boxes, packed in damp peat moss. These boxes can be shipped anywhere in the United States like this through the regular mail, if they are marked *Outside Mail*.

My ad in *Field and Stream* was paying off, but still I was not getting the volume of business that I knew was out there somewhere. We were selling about fifteen thousand worms per week and about thirty to fifty thousand crickets.

My wife may have raised an eyebrow at first but she quickly adjusted to the reality of being surrounded by worms. Whenever I was at the store, she would have to stop whatever she was doing and get someone a cup of worms. She got so she could laugh about it and she would kid the family saying, "One day I'm going to get so busy and mixed-up, that I might measure the cup of worms into a chocolate pie." Her neighbors always called her "the worm lady."

She would also tell me, half humorously, that she couldn't see why worms couldn't be cooked because they were so red that when they are all balled up together, they look a lot like a chunk of meat.

We had reason to recall this last winter when a man called from New York wanting to know if I would be interested in commenting on recipes that have been made up to utilize the proteins of earthworms.

Not only that, but in Ontario, California, a worm farmer held a nationwide worm recipe contest in the summer of 1977 and about two thousand recipes were submitted.

The winner was a New Jersey schoolteacher who came up with *quiche Lorraine avec ver de terre*.

The worm farmer holding the contest was trying to show how earthworms, with their 70 percent protein and ease of growing, could help solve the problem of starvation in underdeveloped countries. He claims to keep earthworm oatmeal cookies in his office as an afternoon snack for all to try.

To make worms more acceptable, the grower marinates the worms with lemon juice and boils them three times in fresh water.

It was my wife, Ruth, who came up with one of the best ideas of my worm business. One night she said, "Honey, if it has been so long and difficult for you to learn how to raise worms and crickets, since you have mastered the art, why not write a book on how to do it and sell the book?

"Then you can sell breeder stock for people to get started. This should increase your volume and keep both worms and crickets selling the year round, not just during the fishing season."

I immediately responded that if I did that I would be inviting competition and everyone in the country would be raising worms and crickets in competition with me. But this was not true. My wife was right.

I have never been bothered with the competition and I've sold thousands of copies of the instruction books. I wrote the book *Raising the Gray Cricket, and How to Raise and Sell the Hybrid Redworm,* and began advertising it for one dollar.

The book sold like hot cakes and as I sold it, my volume of worm and cricket sales began to pick up and people rushed to get into the business. It's a great business. You can start either large or small, or you can raise them just as a hobby in your backyard, perhaps like your or your wife's gardening.

I don't know of any new business that takes so small an investment, and yet the market is everywhere. After all, fishing is everywhere and interest in fishing continues to double almost yearly with the construction of more dams, lakes, and private ponds. As fishing increases, the demand for worms and crickets also increases.

We sold so many instruction books at $1.00 I felt that I could hike the price of my book to $2.95, and believe it or not, I sold ten times as many books at the higher price than at the $1.00 price.

I found that a man was more apt to carry through with his worm or cricket raising project if he paid $2.95 for his instructions rather than the $1.00. Buying his breeder stock and equipment from me was the moneymaking end of the business and most people I sold instruction books to also bought their breeder stock and equipment to start from me.

My volume on worms immediately rose from selling 30,000 a week to 100,000 per week and I have shown an increase in sales of worms almost every year since. The competition is nil. There still are not nearly enough worm farmers and cricket farmers to supply the vast expanding market. In fact, there are not many more big producers in the bait business now than when I started shipping in quantity some twenty-five years ago.

I have written a total of seven books on worm and cricket raising. This is all the information a person needs to be successful in the business. We placed a price of $18.95 for all seven of the books along with one thousand red wiggler worms free with the order for the seven books.

When I first went into the worm and cricket business and started building the modern cricket hatchery, many people around Plains laughed at me and thought I was crazy to spend so much money on such a foolish idea. I let them laugh.

When I began to haul worms and crickets to the post office by the truckloads to send off in the mail, people stopped laughing and many of them then came around wanting to learn how I operated the business. Of course, I had the last laugh on them then, as I pointed out the answer was in a $2.95 book I had on sale.

I began to be called on to make speeches to various civic groups and tell my success story about worms. I would tell true incidents to add a little humor to my speech. For example, about the newspaperman who came to interview me about the worm business.

I was telling the reporter how important worms were as bait and as food used in laboratories at universities. "In fact," I said to the reporter, "do you know that a doctor told me the first operation he ever performed was on a worm."

The reporter looked at me and said, "What was wrong with the worm?"

Reporters have been pretty humorous in the headings they gave the many stories about me, "He Wormed His Way to Success," "Sen. Carter's Success Story 'Down-to-Earth,'" and "Low-Down Crawling Subject." My favorite, however, was a fanciful story in the magazine section of the Columbus *Enquirer*— "He Feeds 10 Billion Mouths Daily."

When *Life* magazine did a story on me that came out in December 1959, it almost turned my life around. In six weeks' time after this story came out, I had received over six thousand letters from people who had read the article and they wanted to know how to raise worms, or had some question about the worm business.

Most of these people ended up buying the $2.95 instruction book and many went into the worm and cricket business as a full-time business or a hobby.

Strangely enough, nineteen years later, I still get letters from people who see that article in libraries around the country.

In tribute to the lowly worm, I must say that worms built a new home for my family about a mile and half from Plains. And the worm and cricket farm is out behind my house, which sits on a thirty-acre plot of woods. Only several acres are used in worm raising of course. The worms also paid for a three-acre pond on my farm which is stocked with bluegill and bass.

Many newspapers mentioned, when Jimmy was home one weekend, that he and Rosalynn got worms from me because they were going fishing.

From my bedroom, I can control the amount of light over the worm beds. Big floodlights light up the worm beds when it rains at night so they won't leave home. I have branched into another phase of the business, supplying equipment for cricket raising, such as heaters and thermostats, graders, electric cricket brooders, etc.

Fishermen will also be interested in knowing that I also drop-ship the African worm from an associate shipper in Palatka, Florida. This is a purplish-red worm, larger than the red wiggler, which is available only during the late spring, summer, and early fall months. This worm cannot stand cold and will die at 50° or lower. It has to be put inside with controlled heat in the winter.

I am happy to say that my worm business has upgraded the class of the Plains post office to second class because of our volume of shipping. I have been told that Plains is the smallest town with a second-class post office.

We sell a lot of worms to movie stars who use them for fishing, food for exotic pets, and for improving their lawns.

Worms eat their weight three times a day and food which passes through the worm is called by many the richest material known for growing plants, grass, and flowers. The name for this material is worm castings.

My wife mixes the castings 50-50 with sand and grows the most beautiful African violets and geraniums that you have ever seen. Some plants grow almost twice as large when enriched with worm castings.

A man was kidding me about raising the price of my booklet from $1.00 to $2.95 and my having said in a speech that I sold ten times as many because of the price increase. He asked me if I could explain that a little more.

I used this illustration. I asked him if his wife saw a hat for $5 and one down the street for $15, which did she usually want him to buy for her? He had to admit the $15 hat. He said she would never have been satisfied with the cheaper $5 hat.

Another thing I get kidded about is my master light panel in the bedroom for the convenience of the worms. It was no joke when I lost $15,000 worth of worms one night because it had rained and there were no lights burning over their beds. The next morning I discovered they had escaped and had climbed up into trees and bushes and buildings.

My most favorite packer is Mr. Guy Dominick. He also makes all of our Crickubators, which are the only electric cricket brooders on the United States market that we know of.

All worms are hand-counted. There are no estimates. A customer buying one thousand worms gets fifty extra for good measure. They are counted by the hundreds in a small tin cup.

The most common question that I am asked at civic clubs is about the sex life of the worm. I tell them what I told a reporter who was doing a story for *Business Horizons* which appeared under the title "Hercules of the Soil—the Earthworm."

As Jean F. Farmer quoted me, the lovelife of the earthworm "would make rabbits twitch." Under normal conditions 2,000 worms reproduce into more than 1,000,000 in a year. Though they are hermaphrodites that can fertilize themselves, when they are around other worms they prefer variety!

But it is true that each worm has a male and a female end. As men's clubs chuckle to hear, the worm is one of the few creatures that God has put on earth which can perform the impossible act.

Part Three

INTO THE ARENA

11 · WHAT MAKES JIMMY RUN?

Jimmy had succeeded in becoming almost a reincarnation of his daddy and had continued all his charities, his work, and joined all the right organizations. There was only one thing his father had done that Jimmy hadn't—become a·member of the State Legislature.

It was nine years after his father had died, in 1962, that Jimmy told Rosalynn and then me that he wanted to try for the State Senate. I gave him encouragement. When he told his mother what he wanted to do, she invited a visiting revival minister to come have coffee and talk to Jimmy about it.

The minister was impressed with Jimmy but horrified at his choice of vocation. Calling politics "a discredited profession," the revivalist preacher urged Jimmy to go into "the ministry or some other honorable service."

I liked Jimmy's answer to that. He explained to the preacher that politics and the ministry were somewhat alike, and for ability to do good, winning the senatorship would give him a chance to be "the pastor of a church with eighty thousand members."

Jimmy was thirty-eight then and I was forty-one and I helped him a lot. When Jimmy was speaking in Americus and bragging a little about how his ancestors had been in Georgia for two hundred years, someone in the audience commented, "If the Carters have been in Georgia two hundred years and haven't gotten any further than Plains, it's time one of them did something." Jimmy still enjoys telling that story.

No one can accuse Jimmy of having had an easy time in politics. His first political race in 1962 for the Georgia Senate turned into a nightmare before it was over.

He was running in the Democratic primary against Homer Moore, a prominent and well-liked Georgian from Richland. The race was over the Fourteenth District—a multi-county area at that time. It was close, and when the vote came in, Jimmy had lost.

But John Pope of Americus, a very good friend of Jimmy's, was a poll watcher at Georgetown, Georgia, in Quitman County and he reported that all kinds of irregularities had taken place at the polls there.

John said that a man in charge of the polls instructed people while they were voting to vote for Moore. This was, of course, in violation of Georgia election laws.

Pope said, "During the day I heard the poll manager make these remarks to at least a hundred voters. When the votes were counted, there were 333 ballots issued to voters but there were 420 ballots in the ballot box—a bad discrepancy."

The ballot box was supposed to be sealed and properly cared for as per election rules after the votes were counted. Jimmy contested the election because of the Georgetown ballot box and requested a hearing investigation before a judge.

His request was honored and the hearing was scheduled in the courthouse in Georgetown a few days later.

In the meantime, Jimmy, John Pope, and I went to Georgetown and other points in Quitman County and secured all of the affidavits that we could concerning other irregularities that had occurred in the Georgetown election precinct that day.

Jimmy hired two lawyers—Warren Fortson, a young lawyer from Americus, and a highly recommended lawyer from Atlanta, Charles Kirbo. That was his first contact with Kirbo. Kirbo quickly became his close friend and confidant, and remains so today.

While we were securing affidavits, it often became dangerous and frustrating. One man offered to loan me a pistol because of the danger but I refused to take a weapon. Some people we approached were afraid to talk. Some said they were afraid their houses would be burned if they talked; others feared bodily harm.

In spite of the general reluctance to give statements, we secured about thirty and had them ready for Kirbo and Fortson. I often think back about those days and how we could have been killed or severely beaten.

When the ballot box was opened before the judge—Judge Carl Crowe of Camilla, Georgia—all the ballots had vanished. There were no ballots in the box.

Judge Crowe ruled that the Georgetown ballot box was so shot through with fraud that there was no way to determine the intention of the voters in that precinct and he ordered the election be decided by the returns from the other precincts in the senatorial district.

Jimmy was declared the winner since he led in the total of all the other precincts. I remember how Judge Crowe chewed his tobacco as he listened to lawyer Kirbo compare what had happened to the ballot box to a hen house and chicken thieves who casually drag a brush behind them to wipe out their own tracks.

It is my own feeling, and there is no evidence to the contrary either, that Homer Moore was not aware of the skulduggery of some of his supporters in that precinct.

Though he won over Moore, Jimmy still was not certified. This was an ordeal in itself. Mr. Fuqua, the chairman of the Democratic party, was off hunting pheasant on the Canadian border at the time of the Georgetown ruling. Charles Kirbo had to find him and get him to certify Jimmy's name on the general election ballot.

With three days to go before Election Day, the Secretary of State directed that Jimmy's name be substituted on the ballot for Moore's. But we weren't in the clear yet. We still had the job of hand-stamping all the ballots with Jimmy's name in preparation for Tuesday's election.

Several of us spent all day Sunday finding county voting officials and hand-stamping all the ballots.

Then another crisis occurred. Seven hours before the polls opened, the Superior Court Judge in Sumter County ordered the ordinaries in all counties to strike all names from the ballots and have a complete new write-in election in the Fourteenth Senatorial District race.

Although threatened with contempt of court, two of the county election officials refused to obey the court order, maintaining that their orders concerning elections had to come from the Secretary of State.

That night was hectic. John Pennington, the Atlanta *Journal* political writer, who had reported the entire Georgetown incident statewide, almost came to blows in the Sumter County Courthouse with one of the leading political bosses from Georgetown.

The day of the election was frantic. We were all trying to explain to the voters with handbills and on radio what was happening and how to mark their ballots.

Jimmy won by fifteen hundred votes, at least we thought he did, but now Moore announced that he was challenging the election results because of the two counties that left Jimmy's name on the ballot. Jimmy prepared to carry the case to the Georgia Senate for final judgment but after two or three weeks the challenge was withdrawn and Jimmy had finally and unequivocally won.

The local political leader from Georgetown had been soundly defeated as well. He was later convicted in federal court for vote fraud in an earlier election for Congress and he was given a three-year suspended sentence. Later, he served time for running an illegal liquor distribution in Quitman County.

When Jimmy entered the Senate in 1963, one of the first speeches he made was in opposition to the infamous "30 Question Test," which was given to almost any black who tried to register to vote. This test was absurdly difficult and could hardly be passed by anyone.

One of Jimmy Carter's greatest accomplishments while state senator was the Minimum Foundation Program for Education. He and one or two other legislators authored this bill and this was one of the greatest steps forward for education in Georgia. The program is now called APEG (Adequate Program for Education in Georgia).

Jimmy always felt—and didn't hesitate to say—that the poorest families are the ones who are cheated and mistreated. He disliked most lobbyists of special-interest groups. He felt that they seldom represented the people.

His term as state senator was very successful and he was chosen by his fellow senators as "the Most Outstanding Senator."

In 1964 presidential candidate Barry Goldwater carried Georgia and Bo Callaway, a Republican, was elected congressman from the Third District. In 1966 Jimmy had decided to run for Congress against the incumbent and had already launched a vigorous campaign.

When he announced that year that he was giving up his job in the Georgia State Senate, I decided to run for his Senate seat. I won easily and have been serving in the Senate ever since. I am now in my twelfth year—my sixth term.

I am now serving my second term as chairman of the Senate Education Committee. I enjoy this position, as it is rewarding to try to improve the educational system for the children of our state. I also serve on the Appropriations Committee, Rules Committee, and Fiscal Affairs Committee.

The first time Jimmy ran for governor—1966—I was too busy to do much for him. I was busy running my own race.

It is most unusual that a man try for a State Senate seat as his first elected office, but I was doing just that. Usually a man runs first for county or district office—county commissioner or councilman—but I was determined to capture the seat that Jimmy had held for two terms.

There were five counties in my district then. My wife and I campaigned shoulder to shoulder and covered every town.

There must have been over 75,000 people that we reached, singly or together. Now there are 85,000 in my district, which, because of redistricting, comprises eight counties.

I won't deny that the Carter connection helped me. It was good that people knew I was Jimmy's cousin. However, sharing the same name means you also inherit old enemies and have to win them over and make friends by proving you are your own man.

It was a pity that I won my race, helped by Jimmy's good state record, while Jimmy lost his tougher race for the governorship.

Had he run for the U. S. Congress he would have had no trouble in winning. That was the opinion of almost every political pundit. He would have been a shoo-in. However, early in June 1966, after he had already announced his candidacy for the United States Congress, he had a change of heart.

He wanted to become governor of Georgia instead so that he could stay near his family and roots. The switch did not come easy. He agonized over the decision before announcing it.

The reason there was a chance that Jimmy could win the governorship is that the leading Democratic candidate for governor had had a slight heart attack and had withdrawn from the gubernatorial race. But it seemed that everyone wanted the governorship that year. Congressman Bo Callaway pulled out of the congressional race against Jimmy and announced that he would run for governor.

Even Senator Herman Talmadge started to return to Georgia to run for governor.

It was then the phrase "Jimmy who?" came into being.

Jimmy lost the Democratic primary race by 20,000 votes. Former Governor Ellis Arnall came in first, segregationist Lester Maddox second. Maddox won the Democratic primary runoff election, but trailed Republican Bo Callaway in the following general election. But because of write-in votes for Arnall, neither Maddox nor Callaway got a majority. So the governorship was decided by a vote of the Legislature, which was heavily Democratic, and Maddox won.

Incidentally, several years later Jimmy Carter, after being elected governor of Georgia in a later contest, recommended to Nixon that Callaway be named Secretary of the Army. It was typical of Jimmy to rise above his personal and party feelings and push for the best man. Though Callaway was an old political enemy, and fierce competitor, Jimmy respected his talents.

I'll never forget how depressed and sad Jimmy seemed after he lost the gubernatorial primary race in 1966. He would walk around by himself across his peanut fields, shoulders hunched, looking down at the ground or up at the sky. It was as if he were looking for some answer but there was none.

He had lost to his arch enemy, Lester Maddox, and that made it harder to bear. He knew he had much more to offer the state as a moderate, and yet the people had chosen a reactionary. Jimmy had wanted to help Georgia take its place among more enlightened states and now the state would be dragged down again into bigotry.

What would become of the state and what would become of him? Was he going to let the Maddox mentality prevail for as far into the future as he could see?

He supposed so. What could he do about it? One man. A man who had failed. Jimmy did not encourage any of us to come around during that period.

But no one stops Ruth Carter Stapleton when she makes up her mind and she made up her mind to walk with Jimmy.

One of the things that resulted from his spiritual rejuvenation at the hands of his sister Ruth Stapleton was that Jimmy became a lay missionary. He led a Billy Graham crusade in Sumter County. He also "witnessed his faith" going into homes where the Lord was not well known and got many of his neighbors and townsmen to start coming to church more often.

Yet Jimmy was never satisfied with his religious performance. He was forever weighing himself and finding himself wanting. In one speech, later after he was eventually elected governor, he seemed to be scolding himself, admitting that "I have a tendency to exalt myself," and adding, "I am a much better father and businessman and farmer and politician and governor than I am a Christian.

" . . . If I were as mediocre a governor as I am a Christian, I would be living in political disgrace."

Explaining further, Governor Jimmy said, "Like many other Christians, I tend to feel that I am serving Christ to the best of my ability. Actually, what happens is that we lower our standards to accommodate our character, our accomplishments, and our degree of dedication."

After defeat, and his much reported spiritual rebirth, Jimmy's spirits rallied and he began almost immediately to run for governor again, for the race to take place in 1970. He would work most of the day in his peanut business and drive somewhere in Georgia to make a speech that night. He dictated names and information into a small tape recorder wherever he went.

Rosalynn and his sister Gloria took the names and wrote thank-you notes the next day. Jimmy Carter was building an unbeatable base for his next race.

He constantly studied issues and prepared speech notes and continued to read three or four books per week. He always wrote his own speeches even while he was governor. I often asked him why he didn't use a speech writer when he was governor. He told me he preferred to write or compile his own speeches.

He said he had had so much experience while running for governor two times and making speeches that he did not need a speech writer. In fact, I have very seldom seen him use more than a few brief notes on a small card or piece of paper even when making very important speeches. He has an excellent memory.

While running for governor the first time, he prepared notes on health, crime control, criminal justice, and education. In 1970 some advised Jimmy not to try again—not to run against Carl Sanders. They told him it would be better for him to run for lieutenant governor and then for governor later. Some even suggested that he run for commissioner of agriculture.

Jimmy chose me to introduce him to open his campaign for governor of Georgia in Plains. Thousands had come to town on that day of April 4, 1970. I stood before them, little realizing that I was introducing a future U. S. President. If I had known, I might have been more nervous as I said:

Ladies and gentlemen:
    It gives me a lot of pride and satisfaction to stand here today and introduce a man who I am sure will be the next governor of the great state of Georgia.
    The pride and admiration that I have for this young man are based on a lot of things:
    First of all, he is my first cousin and I have grown up with him here in this small town of Plains. His business is down on that corner and mine is here in the center of the block. As small boys we sold ice cream three dips for a nickel and hot dogs for a nickel

out of those two windows over there.

Jimmy served four outstanding years in the Georgia State Senate. This was valuable legislative experience necessary for any gubernatorial candidate.

He has always been active in various civic, professional, and benevolent organizations including service as district governor, Lions International, president of Georgia Planning Association, state chairman of the March of Dimes, state fund chairman of the Georgia Society of the Prevention of Blindness, trustee of Norman College, state director of YMCA, former chairman of Sumter County Board of Education, and is presently serving on the Hospital Authority Board of the Americus and Sumter County Hospital. This is only a few of the many offices that he has held.

He has only recently been named Georgia's Young Business Man of the Year—a tremendous honor with the award plaque being presented to him by the mayor of Atlanta.

I could go on for some time pointing out many more of his accomplishments but I will stop and sum it up with these words—he's a great guy with a wonderful smile and outstanding determination, and with your help and cooperation, and with God's guidance he will bring out the best in Georgia.

Ladies and gentlemen—I present to you the next governor of Georgia—Jimmy Carter!

It was my big moment. I had launched a star that would not be just a meteorite, flashing briefly across the heavens, but one that was destined to cast its light for years to come.

Most people do not know that I had anything to do with Jimmy Carter's campaign for governor. In fact, I'm not sure that most people even know Jimmy has a first cousin named Hugh. I have read many newspaper articles telling of the people who helped Jimmy get elected to the top post in the state and they do not mention Hugh Carter.

I suppose I should be content that at least my wife, Ruth, remembers and often comments on how I helped, if only to needle me because I do not seem to have presented a big enough image to come to the attention of the newspapers—except as the antique store owner Jimmy visits when he comes home to visit Plains.

I am human enough to want to be acknowledged for whatever part I did have in the campaign of this famous relative—just for what I did and no more.

I remember the day early in 1970 when Hot asked me to help him with his second campaign for the governorship. I was in the Georgia Senate, and in this position I knew I could be of tremendous help to Jimmy.

I knew Jimmy and his fine qualities and I pledged my complete and total support. And I did throw myself into his campaign totally.

We decided after much discussion that it would be best for me to operate principally from my worm farm office in Plains. We had a statewide WATS line installed.

I was to serve as his statewide coordinator, working with Rosalynn and Hamilton Jordan, in setting up county organizations in every county in Georgia and maintaining harmony and smoothness in each of these organizations.

Also, I was to make calls to prominent people all over the state, especially legislators, state officials, and influential businessmen, seeking their support for Jimmy in the various sections of Georgia.

Finally, I was to be a troubleshooter.

I had no idea what I was getting into. When I was home, the phone would ring every two to five minutes even through the middle of the night. I spent so much time on the campaign that I had to let my business run itself.

Every time Jimmy would make a statement to the press or public, he would make a few enemies among his campaign workers and leaders, and the angry ones would call me to say they were quitting. Being troubleshooter meant I had to talk and talk and talk until they promised to stay on the job. Sometimes they would say, "All right. But you tell him I'm doing it for you, not Jimmy." That went on for months.

Sometimes angry campaign workers would storm over to my house and my wife would have to soothe their ruffled feathers if I was not there.

I worked closely with Rosalynn and Hamilton Jordan on the organizational problems and I worked closely with Cecil McCall and Dave Gambrell and Charles Kirbo in soliciting funds for the campaign. They would feed me names of possible contributors and I would get to work on them on the WATS line.

What did Jimmy promise me if he won the governorship? One thing. He said if he won, he wanted me to be his Senate floor leader. I looked forward to this assignment and he kept his promise.

Hamilton Jordan and I had good teamwork going. We broke up the state into sets of ten counties each. Ham would visit the counties if necessary and interest important people in joining the county organization while I tackled people by phone with the names he furnished.

After the first ten counties were completely organized we went on to the next set of ten.

We always selected a county chairman, an assistant, and a treasurer in each county, who could take it from there, with our continued help. We soon had the whole state organized, county by county, with the exception of a few small counties which we united for better efficiency.

Hamilton Jordan stayed at the Atlanta headquarters to oversee the entire campaign. I found myself working on the phone about fourteen hours a day. Rosalynn was traveling a lot and shaking hands and speaking—as was Jimmy. But in between campaign swings, she furnished invaluable help on the phone.

One of the big jobs, after having the state completely organized, was to call—at least weekly—each county chairman to see if he had any problems that we could help him with, any names for soliciting of campaign funds, and if he had run out of campaign literature.

There is no substitute for the personal touch in keeping each county chairman buoyed up and aware that you care about his performance.

Because of these calls, we were able to work out any animosity that arose before the campaign could grow sour in their area. And there were indeed numerous problems to cope with. Volunteers inside of county organizations would get jealous of each other and we would have to talk to each side and stress that we were all working for Jimmy, and as long as we knew and Jimmy knew what they were doing to help, that was all that mattered.

Occasionally, we would have a resignation and if I couldn't locate a replacement by phone, Hamilton Jordan would have to make a quick trip to the county to find a new man or woman with the proper drive and dedication.

In my office in Plains—the worm farm office—we had big charts on the wall with each county listed, its chairman, assistant, and their phone numbers.

We also had a map on the wall—it is still there—showing how well Lester Maddox and Ellis Arnall had done in each county in the 1966 campaign when they had beaten Jimmy. Of course, we worked harder on the counties in which Jimmy did the poorest in the 1966 campaign.

The most important thing in my office headquarters at Plains was our telephone log. Each person that Jimmy, Rosalynn, or I called was recorded in a book with the date the person was called, the time of day called, and a brief summary of the results of the call.

Early in the campaign Jimmy usually came into the worm farm office headquarters at least four or five nights a week. Near the end of the campaign, he was in only about two nights per week. He would immediately consult the telephone logbook to see if Rosalynn or I had left him messages about persons he should call or problems he should handle on the phone himself.

We all used the same phone but at different times. Sometimes, I would go several days without seeing Jimmy but we would be in close touch daily via the telephone log. Jimmy kept a key to my office so that he could get in at any time of the day or night.

I have this log in my possession and I value its historical record. Each telephone call or each message involving a once-defeated candidate trying again for governor was a small step up the ladder to the presidency of the United States.

Down the street from my office in Plains was Jimmy's correspondence and finance office, managed by his sister Gloria Carter Spann. Many volunteers worked in this office under Gloria's direction. Gloria was a tremendous asset throughout the campaign.

Computer equipment and automatic typewriters were used. Cousin Gloria kept accurate card records of all contributions that came in, whether large or small.

Most of the contributions were small, from five to one hundred dollars each. This was good, as a base of many smaller contributions involves more people. We had set a fifteen-cent-per-capita finance goal based on the population of each county.

Jimmy had a good sense of humor about the campaign, in spite of grim determination to win. In a flyer printed up for him, which showed him in his various roles, the headlines said, "Some call him various things—after January 1971 we will all call him *Governor.*"

And under the grinning face of Cousin Hot were the words "Elect Jimmy Carter."

When you read the small print on the flyer, you found that some of the things they called Jimmy weren't too bad. Things like "conservative farmer," "son," "young man," and "fellow citizen."

Jimmy was a tireless campaigner.

I remember helping him shake hands with workers from a factory shift in Atlanta who were getting off from work. We stood just outside the door in the early morning light and, as they came out, asked each tired worker to vote for him, Jimmy giving each a folder which contained a biography and what Jimmy believed in and what he promised to do.

Most of the workers looked skeptical and some commented that they were sorry Jimmy couldn't win because they had heard Carl Sanders had received most of the big endorsements from newspapers and organizations.

Jimmy just smiled and said, "No, you will have a Carter for governor. The individual goes into the voting booth, not an *organization.*"

One of Atlanta's big newspapers fought Jimmy early in the campaign and said Jimmy was an ignorant and bigoted redneck. This kind of talk hurt him with some already committed liberal and idealistic supporters but he overcame it.

It made Jimmy work even harder. He worked hard to get the black vote. He visited a lot of black church leaders, who were a great help to him.

Jimmy told me an interesting story during the campaign. He had gone into a school in Columbus, Georgia, to meet some black teachers. He came to one who was timid and had little to say.

"What is your name?" Jimmy asked. The shy woman blurted out, "I ain't nobody." Jimmy tried to explain to her that she was one of the primary reasons that he was running for office—so that black people could come into their own.

Though I was busy with my telephoning, now and then I would be rushed one place or another to introduce the candidate. One afternoon during the gubernatorial campaign, I was asked to fly to Waycross to introduce Jimmy.

Rudy Hayes, managing editor of the Americus *Times Recorder,* my wife, and two or three others flew down with me. We had a very young pilot whom we didn't know and had never seen before.

We were a little jittery about that. But there was no comparison to how jittery we got as the plane kept bumping on the underside. We learned later it was the wheels being let up and down. What made us especially apprehensive was that an extra person had been permitted to come along, though there was no space for him and he was sitting on the floor.

The pilot had figured out the total weight by asking each of us what we weighed, which convinced us all that the plane was bumping along because it was overloaded. Afterward, Rudy Hayes said he had been so scared his hands had become hot enough to fry eggs on them.

A car met us at the airport and we arrived at the rally just in time to hear on the loudspeaker the announcement "And now Hugh Carter will introduce the next governor of Georgia."

I had to leap from the car and run to the microphone at full speed. As I raced to the platform I happened to look over at Jimmy as I passed by him and asked him if he was ready.

To my astonished eyes, I saw that he was in deep trouble. Someone had brushed up against him and turned his plate of barbecue over on him and also his tea so that his clothes were a mess. I had no time to stop. I reached for the microphone and it was on with the show.

As Jimmy cleaned himself up a bit, I spoke, giving him as much time as I could.

I still have the speech with the many barbs directed at the other candidate. "Let us all join together," I said, "and send Carl Sanders back to his plush social clubs, the big bankers, and special-interest people."

Then I pointed out that Jimmy Carter represented "the working man, the little people of Georgia, and that's the kind of man we need and will have for the next four years as governor of Georgia."

I pictured Jimmy as a fresh breath of air for the stagnating state, untainted and untarnished.

> In this race for governor of Georgia, Jimmy does not have a high-powered and big-financed campaign like his opponent, Carl Sanders. In contrast to Sanders, Jimmy does not have enormous wealth or powerful political ties. He is not backed by big money and special-interest groups. And because of this, he is a free man and can speak out for you as your governor with a great degree of honesty and sincerity.
>
> The big, smooth-sailing, high-powered, rich, well-financed Carl Sanders' campaign has been torpedoed by the former Navy submarine officer—Jimmy Carter—and Carl's rich boat is sinking deeper and deeper every day as he slings his mud all over Georgia after years of wheeling and dealing in plush social clubs with the big bankers and special-interest groups. Carl Sanders is losing and is a desperate man.

The crowd was with me and someone yelled, "Yeah, man." I turned then to what Jimmy had to offer.

Jimmy Carter's platform is realistic, designed for you and for all of Georgia and designed to move Georgia forward. His goal is, and I quote, "To bind all of our people together in a spirit of cooperation, confidence, and determination to bring out the best of Georgia."

Jimmy offers a freshness and warmth that is more identifiable with you, the people. I consider these as Jimmy's most powerful words and I believe that these words will go down in Georgia history—I quote—"I shall speak up for the Georgian who wants nothing selfish from government, who cherishes the fundamental principles of fairness and honesty, and who wants to stand up anywhere in the world and say, 'I'm a Georgian,' and be proud of it."

That's your Jimmy Carter and here he is tonight!

In spite of his messy attire, which made him look a bit like the redneck the Atlanta newspaper had called him, Jimmy went on to make one of the best speeches I've ever heard him make.

For the last three months before the primary—which was held on September 23—Hamilton Jordan scheduled Sunday afternoon gatherings at our headquarters in Atlanta, the Quality Central Hotel. These meetings were a free-for-all with county chairmen and workers from all over the state as well as anyone else who wanted to come.

The meetings would last about two hours and at the end we would have Jimmy come in for a hero's welcome and he would give a little pep talk.

I served as master of ceremonies. At the end, we would have a little fun raising money by auctioning off unusual items.

I remember one afternoon we auctioned off a small dog contributed by Mrs. Connie Plunkett of Carrollton, Georgia. It brought six hundred dollars and was bought by Jim Barbre of Dalton, Georgia, amid much merriment. The spunky little dog was treated as a hero because we were desperate for funds.

As the primary date neared, the meetings grew larger as the word got around that politics with Jimmy Carter was fun. Finally, we were having about five thousand in attendance—too many to get into the hotel ballroom.

I presided again as master of ceremonies on election night in the state headquarters. Pandemonium broke loose as precinct after precinct, county after county, came in with Jimmy leading. We had won at last!

12 · GOVERNOR JIMMY

I think the Carter gubernatorial administration in Georgia will go down in history as one of the most highly controversial, aggressive, and combative—but also very productive.

When Jimmy could not buck the power of Lester Maddox and his crowd in the Legislature, he made direct appeals to the people of Georgia and this was an important channel of strength. I notice that as President, he still does not hesitate to go over the heads of Congress to the people when he thinks the cause is just.

As his floor leader, I would get to see him every morning at 8:00 to go over all the bills that would appear on the Senate and House calendar for that day. He held this daily meeting for his floor leaders from both sides of the Capitol.

By the time we got there at 8:00 A.M., he would already have become familiar with the bills. He could read and absorb very rapidly, even then, before the speed-reading course he took at the White House.

Governor Jimmy would ask our opinion on the various bills and then all of us together would make a decision whether to fight or support the bill in question on the floor of the Senate or House. We were encouraged to argue and stick to our guns on why we were for or against a measure. But then, somehow we would resolve it so that we would be a unified front to fight for or against, as a group.

His special interests were government efficiency and the reorganization of the state government, budget reform, health care, education, and prison reform.

Jimmy always felt that crime and punishment were especially cruel to the poor and those unable to help themselves.

I remember that day in January 1971 when Jimmy Carter was sworn in as governor at last. The day was bitterly cold but Jimmy was radiantly warm—he had come in from the cold of emotional upheaval.

He stood secure and strangely calm, with that little smile on his face, on the platform on the front steps of the Georgia Capitol in Atlanta with his old rival, Lester Maddox, standing grimly near him. I stood only a few feet from the governor-elect and watched the faces of both men.

The grim look on Maddox' face did not change as the newly sworn Governor Jimmy proclaimed:

"I say to you . . . that the time for racial discrimination is over."

Jimmy went on to promise that the law would be enforced in Georgia. And it was. No more would school doors be barred to black children.

Jimmy had a state to govern but he still had to fight for the right to govern it. Maddox had his henchmen everywhere and he did his best to trip Governor Carter so that he would fall on his face.

Lester Maddox had maintained a stranglehold on the state and he still was trying to retain the power he had had as governor by coming back as lieutenant governor.

Maddox had maintained a strong influence by dispensing patronage through some three hundred boards and commissions. Jimmy was determined to get rid of many useless state agencies. And he did.

Jimmy managed to cut in half the administrative costs of the state government. He deserves a lot of credit for that because he came into the state government at a very difficult time.

Jimmy was shocked at the corruption he found. He took time to help people personally. Once he told this story:

I was in the Governor's Mansion for two years, enjoying the services of a very fine cook, who was a prisoner—a woman. One day she came to me, after she got over her two years of timidity and said, "Governor, I would like to borrow $250 from you."

I said, "I'm not sure that a lawyer would be worth that much."

She said, "I don't want to hire a lawyer, I want to pay the judge."

I thought it was a ridiculous statement for her; I felt that she was ignorant. But I found out she wasn't. She had been sentenced by a superior court judge in the state, who still serves, to seven years or $750. She had raised, early in her prison career, $500.

I didn't lend her the money, but I had Bill Harper, my legal aide, look into it. He found the circumstances were true. She was quickly released under a recent court ruling that had come down in the last few years.

The new governor believed in fair trials and fair punishment for people who break the laws. Rehabilitation of our prisoners was uppermost in his mind and throughout his administration he worked to improve the status quo in our prisons. Education programs for our prisoners and recreation programs were always given priority.

There was one case that comes to mind, which shows how big a heart Governor Jimmy had. One of the black children who had been his playmate as an adult was sent to prison on a voluntary manslaughter charge and sentenced to five years. As the man himself tells it, "What happened is a boy tried to kill me and I shot and killed him in self-defense."

Even before this man was sent to prison in January 1970, the same month Jimmy became governor, Jimmy went to the jail to see him and pray with him. Then when he was in prison, Jimmy would send someone to the man's home regularly with bags of groceries. Eventually, he helped him be released on parole in July of 1971 and helped the man get a job driving a truck.

Jimmy had faith in his former playmate and knew the good that was in him. As children they had boxed and wrestled together, and when Miz Lillian took Jimmy to shows in Americus, this playmate was one invited to come along. He would go but had suffered the humiliation of not being able to stay with Jimmy and his mother because of segregation and had to see performances from a different section.

Jimmy made great strides during his administration to give the black man his rightful place in society.

But it was in spite of archsegregationist Maddox. Maddox' grim look at Jimmy's swearing-in portended the future.

About anything that Jimmy Carter wanted to do, Lieutenant Governor Lester Maddox didn't want to do—even such a simple thing as wanting a special fine arts committee to oversee furnishings in the Governor's Mansion. Jimmy had wanted it to make sure that the historic quality of the mansion be preserved.

Lester Maddox killed the bill by refusing to call it up. I was for the bill and agreed that it was important to prevent someone from going into the Governor's Mansion and throwing out fine historic pieces to put in a lot of modern furniture.

Maddox sent word through a henchman that he didn't want such bills clogging up the calendar.

Maddox' trusted lieutenant was Culver Kidd of Milledgeville, who was chairman of the Senate Committee on Economy, Reorganization, and Efficiency in Government. Through "Captain Kidd," as we called him, Maddox was able to bottle up a lot of Jimmy's pet legislation for improving state government.

Jimmy is a very forthright person so as soon as he took office, he called in his lieutenant governor and made it clear that he—Jimmy—was going to run the state and was not going to let Maddox ruin his programs. He would do what he had to with or without Maddox' help. And as it turned out, everything Jimmy managed to get done was without the help of Lester Maddox—except for the times I was able to prevail on Maddox not to fight certain bills.

Even the newspapers were aghast at the constant fighting that was going on between the two men—the old leader still hanging on, and the new warrior. Headlines appeared like, "Jimmy and Lester Slug It Out."

One of the things Jimmy instituted against great opposition was "zero-based budgeting." What this meant was that government agencies would not automatically get their funds from year to year, but would have to justify their programs on the basis of need before the money was allocated each year.

This way needless programs were not continued.

Another much publicized Carter decision was to kill plans to dam the Flint River in the Sprewell Bluff area. I was in on this fight and know how hard Cousin Jimmy worked to be sure he was absolutely right in bucking a lot of big people.

After he studied what everyone had to say, Jimmy vetoed the plan, later explaining, "This dam would have only benefited a few landowners; it would not have helped a huge section of west-central Georgia and would have hurt the environment."

Jim Morrison, the executive director of the Georgia Wildlife Federation, echoed what Jimmy said about the environment and labeled Jimmy's decision as "courageous and proper."

But the veto did not halt the fight. It only intensified it. Fortunately, the opposition was not able to muster the votes needed to overthrow the veto.

Jimmy had other experience with trying to bring about a reform only to have landowners become the recipients of any benefit. That's what happened in 1973 when he proposed a $50 million property tax relief bill. The Carter plan was rewritten in the House and as it turned out big landowners and big corporations ended up with thousands or even, in one case, over a million dollars in tax relief, while the average property owner got thirty to forty dollars tax relief.

Jimmy was determined to keep such a disaster from happening again.

Jimmy was a different kind of governor from the kind Georgia was used to. He wasn't a socializer or mint-julep fellow; he was a worker right from the start. And he was also a man with a talking relationship to the Lord.

The South is full of "born-again" Christians who do a lot of talking about it. Jimmy didn't just talk. He actually had a little room off the governor's office that he made into a prayer room. He would go in there several times a day to pray and commune with God.

I was a frequent guest at the Governor's Mansion, and so was my wife, Ruth. In fact, when I injured my back and was in the hospital, the governor and Rosalynn did not want Ruth to stay all alone in the motel where we stayed during legislative sessions, and insisted that she come live at the Governor's Mansion.

I would say that of all the governors' mansions in the United States, Georgia's is the prettiest. It is traditionally southern, gracious, and inviting.

I can remember the dinners that Rosalynn would serve there at the mansion and they were very wholesome meals. Let me give you just one menu that comes to mind because I remember how much I enjoyed it: pork chops, butter beans, string beans (yes, we had both), corn cut from the cob, biscuits, two kinds of pickles—dill and sweet—iced tea or milk, and any flavor ice cream we wanted.

While Jimmy was governor, my daughter Connie worked for a time with the governor's intern program and wrote a brochure on foster care of children. She was also working with the child abuse office of the Welfare Department.

Now and then she would visit Uncle Jimmy and Aunt Rosalynn in the Governor's Mansion and would have dinner with them. She would report that Uncle Jimmy ate supper with his blue jeans on.

Most of the time Jimmy and I would try to forget our close relationship in the interest of working on legislation in a businesslike and professional way. However, every now and then we would be suddenly yanked back to the realization that we shared a common heritage. Once was when we received the sad news through a telephone call from Dad that our eighty-seven year old Aunt Ethel, Dad's sister, had died.

The funeral was to be in Plains, Georgia, at the Plains Baptist Church, where she was a member. I had just gotten out of the hospital and was recuperating from a back operation for a ruptured disk. Governor Jimmy called and asked if I would be able to travel with Rosalynn and him in a plane so soon after my operation.

I told him I would have to call my doctor and see but that I hoped I could. The neurosurgeon who had operated suggested that I try to lie down on the plane on something hard, if possible.

I called Jimmy back and told him that Ruth and I would like to fly down with him so we all planned the trip together.

Knowing how the governor felt about people who were late—he once flew off leaving a guest on the runway because he had arrived at the airport a few minutes late—I was relieved that the governor had a state patrolman come to our hotel to pick us up. But for some reason, the patrolman got confused and took us to the wrong airport.

Only at the airport did he realize there must be something wrong, because the governor's plane was not there, and made a hurried call to the governor's office.

Then it was all systems go as we blazed our way to the other airport, sirens wailing. The governor and Rosalynn were already waiting for us and Jimmy was at the toe-tapping stage. I'm sure if it had been anyone else, or an event less important than a funeral, he would have been up in the sky by then.

More trouble. The plane would not crank so we had to transfer to two smaller planes and secure a pilot and copilot for the second small chartered plane that I would use.

Jimmy was as gentle as a nurse as he helped me into the plane. We turned down two seats and spread a plywood board that my dad had made for my back—a very hard couch to lie on for the three-hundred-mile round trip.

After Cousin Hot and one of the security men got me situated, Jimmy flew off in the other plane with his security man and Rosalynn. A second security man rode in my plane with Ruth and me.

Both planes flew along together, and we landed forty minutes later, one behind the other. Two patrol cars were already at the airport ready to take us to the church and we made it just in time. Another fifteen minutes and we would have been too late.

Aunt Ethel had been very close to all of us, as were her sons, our first cousins, Willard and Linton Slappey. After the church service we went to the Lebanon Cemetery for the burial of Aunt Ethel, next to her husband, Uncle Jack.

When it was over, we didn't even have time to go to our own houses to see that everything was all right because bad weather was closing in. It was a rough flight back to Atlanta and to the embarrassment of our security man, *he* was the one who was airsick all the way. As Jimmy greeted me back on the ground, he said he didn't see how I stood the trip in my condition. I guess I looked worse than I felt.

There was another important occasion we participated in as a family and that was the second Nixon inaugural in January 1973.

We did not know that the President we were honoring was on his way out of office in disgrace. Jimmy had asked Ruth and me to go with him and his family, Caron and Chip, Jack and Judy, and Jeff and Annette.

Senator Frank Eldridge of Waycross, Georgia, and his wife, Leland, had also been invited to go along. We left early in the morning on a large plane, and when we arrived in Washington, a couple of hotel rooms had been reserved for us just for the day.

Then we made a sad discovery. Though the Inaugural Committee knew we were coming, they failed to provide enough seats. Of course, Jimmy and Rosalynn got close enough to see the swearing-in ceremony but we had to listen to it on a car radio while riding to the Pentagon for a tour.

Since no tickets had been provided for us, we had been assigned a car and a driver-guide to tour the sights of Washington instead.

What a difference it makes to attend a Democratic inauguration—Jimmy's inauguration—rather than a Republican inauguration. We had been left out in the cold even though we were close family members of the governor of the state of Georgia.

Nixon had not yet finished his inaugural speech when we arrived at the Pentagon. We didn't stay in the car to hear the rest of it. Instead, we just went into the Pentagon and enjoyed the tour.

We did have good seats for the inaugural parade reserved for us. It was an unusually cold day. I remember how Nixon passed by in the parade in an open convertible waving to the crowd like a monarch—so different from Cousin Jimmy's walk down Pennsylvania Avenue four years later.

Jimmy had told us to meet him and Rosalynn that night at the

Watergate complex for a cocktail party given by Dillard Munford of Atlanta. Munford owned a chain of food stores.

I remember seeing my good friend former State Senator Bill Flowers, now president of the famous Flowers Baking Company. Jimmy and I had both served in the Georgia State Senate with Bill.

We all had a great time at the party and met a lot of old political friends whom we hadn't seen since the gubernatorial campaign in 1970.

After the cocktail party, Senator Frank Eldridge and Leland, Jimmy and Rosalynn, and Ruth and I went down to the restaurant level in the Watergate building for dinner. We ordered, but they were so long in bringing our food that Rosalynn and Jimmy had to leave before having an opportunity to eat.

They attended one of the inaugural balls. Thanks to Nixon, we didn't have tickets for any of the balls. Our waitress kept crying for some reason. We didn't find out why, but she was so upset over something that I thought we would never get our food. Later, when "Watergate" became a household word for corruption, which reached into Nixon's Oval Office, I would remember our night there and the crying waitress.

We finally departed Washington by plane for Atlanta about midnight and got back to Atlanta about 2:00 A.M. We were all tired out and most of us slept all the way in to Atlanta.

It had been a long but enjoyable day. Jimmy and his family, upon arrival in Atlanta, were hustled back to the Governor's Mansion and Ruth and I back to the Marriott.

As a footnote to history, it seems almost unbelievable that a governor's party to Nixon's inauguration would be given only two tickets close enough to see and hear the inauguration and two tickets to attend the ball.

Jimmy felt very bad about the whole affair. As I look back on the Nixon inauguration in 1973, and compare it to Jimmy Carter's in 1977, there was no comparison in the concern for the welfare of honored guests or in enthusiasm, beauty, organization, and participation. Cousin Jimmy's excelled in every way.

Jimmy had always conducted his own peanut business honestly and efficiently and he approached the business of state government with the same honesty and efficiency. I felt confidence and pride in his actions.

It is very difficult at times in politics to do what is best for the majority of people and the state. Special-interest groups and close friends try to influence you to do the things *they* want most, regardless of how it affects the other people or the majority of citizens.

In my senatorship, I try to vote the convictions of the majority of the people of the district I represent and not always the wishes of minority groups. And also, not just what *I* want done. In my opinion, Jimmy used the same principle as governor. He operated on prearranged long-term plans and not spur-of-the-moment decisions, tempering those decisions with wisdom and justice.

Because he was not a team worker or pawn of special interests, Jimmy did not always get along with the legislators, but most of them respected him and this was proven by the amount of his recommended legislation that was passed.

But in one thing, he and the Senate failed. That was in trying to pass legislation to permit the Senate to elect its own president—presiding officer—and to let Senate Committees be chosen by a committee rather than the lieutenant governor.

The importance of this cannot be overestimated. In Jimmy's term in office, it meant that Lieutenant Governor Maddox still wielded great power in being able to name the committees of the Senate, as he presided over the Senate.

Now for what Governor Carter did do. I remember that one of the important things Jimmy did while governor was to form a biracial civil disorder unit, consisting of three persons.

Well trained, dressed in civilian clothes, they used no force but used maximum communication and persuasion. They had a minimum of publicity. Yet so effective was their gentle persuasion that by 1973, only 177 hours of state patrol time had to be spent in civil disorders.

In comparison to this, from 1968 through 1970, thousands of hours had to be spent on this problem.

The long struggle for the Human Resources Bill showed how hard it was to get anything done in the State Legislature while Maddox fought Jimmy's reform movement tooth and nail.

Eventually, we won and I was heartened to read what columnist Beryl Sellers had to say about the passage of the Human Resources Bill: "Much credit for the uphill victory achieved . . . on his human resources legislation must go to his first cousin, Sen. Hugh Carter of Plains."

I am proud that I was able to help bring about the establishment of the department that has helped rehabilitate thousands of drug addicts, instituted a much needed program to discover sickle-cell anemia victims, and brought about local community treatment instead of incarceration for nondestructive mental patients.

Jimmy and I have often talked of how difficult it is to accomplish a piece of legislation, even though it is going to be of great service to a state. My own accomplishment, which I am most proud of, and which Jimmy, too, applauded, is the bringing about of the Providence Canyon State Park in Stewart County, Georgia, nicknamed "The Little Grand Canyon," about thirty-six miles west of Plains.

All the time that Jimmy and Maddox were feuding, I tried hard to maintain a working relationship with Maddox so that I could maintain communication between the two and at least have a good chance of getting some of Jimmy's proposed legislative program through the Senate.

In spite of many fierce and heated battles in the Senate we were successful in passing better than 90 percent of Jimmy's reorganization legislation, reducing three hundred agencies down to twenty-two. One of the big fights we lost to the Maddox forces, however, was the proposed placing of the Forestry Department under the Department of Natural Resources.

Jimmy's reorganization program saved much money for the Georgia taxpayers. One of the more outstanding things that Jimmy accomplished during his administration was to invest the money belonging to the state so that it would bring in the maximum income, or interest.

The state had kept $300 million in tax money in the treasury, not yet spent. It had previously been parceled out to friendly banks as political favors, and the taxpayers lost enormous amounts in the uncollected interest that could have been acquired with proper management.

When Jimmy activated a Depository Board, sealed competitive bids were required to be submitted by banks to secure the state money. Interest income increased 244 percent to the State Treasury in four years' time.

All agreed that finally the state's banking business was being conducted openly, decently, and free of political influence.

When Jimmy left office in January 1976, our Georgia state surplus was almost $200 million. The 1975 budget was actually $10 million lower than the 1974 budget because of an underestimating of savings because of reorganization. For many years to come, the state will benefit from Jimmy's clever management of state finances.

Next to reorganization, Governor Jimmy Carter spent the most time planning the preservation of the state's natural resources. He was successful in passing many environmental protection laws. Some of these programs had tough sledding getting through the Legislature.

Jimmy is to be credited with the Heritage Trust Program. During his administration, two thousand historical sites in Georgia were inventoried and assessed. Many historic sites were purchased under his guidance.

I remember how personally involved he became when the U. S. Army Corps of Engineers wanted to build a major dam on the Flint River, fifty miles southeast of Atlanta. It was reported the the claims of the corps to justify the dam were not true.

Jimmy was deeply concerned because he had supported the project on the basis of engineering reports that the dam would generate large amounts of electric power, control floods, purify the river waters, and provide financial benefits over a period of one hundred years.

Jimmy was determined to find the truth. He inspected the proposed Sprewell Bluff Dam project and lake site several times by air and actually went down the Flint River twice in a canoe to look over the proposed project area.

Public hearings were held. Senator Herman Talmadge shared Governor Carter's concern. They jointly asked the General Accounting Office of Congress to substantiate the claims of the Corps of Engineers. There were numerous delays in furnishing this requested information.

The report was finally delivered to the governor in August of 1973. The claims indeed had been exaggerated. The major benefit appeared to be simply recreation.

Furthermore, all the state and federal recreation agencies opposed the building of the Sprewell Bluff Dam.

Jimmy Carter vetoed the dam project.

Now came high drama. The House of Representatives voted to recommend to build the dam in spite of the objection of the governor.

The House resolution came to the Senate, where it cleared the Maddox-selected committee and arrived on the floor of the Senate.

The governor called me down to his office and impressed on me the importance of defeating this resolution. He explained to me, his floor leader, why he opposed the dam project and I agreed 100 percent with his assessment and stand.

The governor then assigned Frank Moore of his office—he now holds an important job in the White House—to assist me in somehow defeating the resolution.

Unfortunately, the job was made harder by the fact that my colleague, Senator Al Holloway, the other floor leader for the governor in the Senate, was committed to vote *for* the project.

It was an almost unprecedented situation for the governor's two floor leaders to oppose each other on an issue. It was one of the toughest fights of my career. Nip and tuck all the way. I had to repair whatever damage to my cause Senator Holloway was causing as well as win members to my side.

In a nonstop marathon I talked to all the senators, and after much work and politicking on the part of Frank Moore as well, the resolution failed to pass, although the vote was dangerously close.

It was a great victory for the governor and he sent for me to come to the governor's office for a pat on the back and a word of congratulations. I don't remember ever seeing him any happier during his entire term as governor than he was after that vote in the Senate.

The visit in his office was doubly felt because Jimmy very seldom ever thanks anyone profusely. I think this is one of his minor faults. If he would express a little bit more thanks and appreciation as President, he could accomplish even more than he does.

One way in which Jimmy Carter was different from most governors is that he tried to establish a closer relationship with foreign governments on a state level. I don't know how many times I have heard him say, "There is only one nation in the world which is capable of true leadership among the community of nations and that is the United States."

Still, he was very conscious of what the United States could learn from other nations. For example, he feels that if Switzerland and Israel can eliminate illiteracy so can the United States.

As governor, Jimmy visited ten foreign nations, including Germany and Japan. His goal was to promote friendship and trade. He often invited foreign dignitaries to visit him at the Georgia Capitol.

Thanks to Jimmy, Atlanta now has a large and rapidly growing consular corps and Georgia has established offices all over the world to continue Jimmy's program of promoting Georgia trade and goodwill.

When I read in the newspapers that Cousin Hot is not getting along well with the Congress of the United States—that he is displeased with them or that they are displeased with him—I smile.

Jimmy has always hated to apologize or admit he was wrong and he has not changed. I remember when he made the serious faux pas, politically, of calling the 1974 Georgia Legislature "the worst in the history of the state" and then expecting it to still pass his bill.

Naturally, it had the opposite effect and the legislators staged a sit-down strike for several days, demanding a full apology. I was one who felt Cousin Jimmy should diplomatically retract his statement completely.

But he stubbornly refused to apologize. Instead, he softened his original insult just a little bit by saying that he hadn't meant that *all* the legislators were the worst in the history of the state.

There were many times that Jimmy could have made deals, but he had too much integrity to compromise. I remember once when Jimmy was trying to get one of his reorganization bills passed, in the State Legislature, one of the state senators hinted that he might change his vote to be on Jimmy's side if the man's father received a promotion in his state government job.

The word was passed to the governor and he simply refused to recommend that the fellow's relative be promoted. He didn't do business that way. He wanted his programs to win on their own merits.

One of the best things that Governor Carter did was to change the way judges were selected. Instead of practicing cronyism, using judge-ships as payoffs for favors that had been done to help him or other party members, he set up a ten-member commission of selection.

The commission screened potential judges to find the best men, and true to his word, Governor Jimmy would appoint one of the five men the commission had recommended.

Heading the selection commission was Henry Bowden, a highly respected Atlanta lawyer who recalled during the presidential campaign that "never did Jimmy Carter tell us to put someone on the bench because he was a friend. He would just say to be sure and find him the five best people."

But at the time, the governor was not applauded by some of his own party members who deplored the fact that they could not get jobs for their loyal followers, not to mention his.

That is the kind of man Jimmy is. He will surely pepper the Congress in the same way he did the State Legislature, if the spirit so moves.

As for how he treated his own hometown of Plains, it is safe to say that he bent over backward to avoid doing anything for the town that could be construed as favoritism. I remember how hard it was for me to get some simple road improvements because of his stiff-nosed attitude.

Let me tell you about it. Tom Moreland, who was commissioner of transportation, Craig Brach, and I came to Plains to see what the town needed in the way of roads and sidewalks.

We had already paved most of the streets in the town but the main street in front of the stores was badly in need of curb and guttering and a new sidewalk in front of the strip of stores.

It really was disgraceful the way the governor's hometown looked. The old sidewalk had been in service since about 1925 and was full of holes and worn out.

When the governor was approached, he was reluctant to spend highway money in Plains, not wanting to be criticized for spending more on his hometown than other towns in Georgia.

Still Tom and Craig and I decided that the work needed to be done. And Tom came up with the solution that if I, as senator, requested the improvements, he could go ahead and authorize it. I did. He did. The work was begun.

A few days after the work was begun, Tom got a stern note from the governor questioning his authority to do the work. Tom replied that the job had been requested by the senator who lived in that district and that he, the commissioner of transportation, thought it was justified and had proceeded with the work.

There was silence after that, but when it was all done, the governor wrote another note to the commissioner in a much friendlier vein, telling him what a great job he had done and how much his work had improved the town.

I also learned, to my personal sorrow on another occasion, how Governor Carter would bend over backward to keep from seeming to show favoritism.

That was when U. S. Senator Richard B. Russell of Georgia died in January 1971 and Jimmy as governor of Georgia was required to appoint a successor.

Governor Carter was in no hurry to name a successor to Russell. It was an important appointment and he didn't want to make a mistake. It was very definitely a political advantage to be appointed to serve over a year in the office before having to run for the office in the primary and general election in 1972.

I never asked Jimmy about the possibility of his appointing me, nor did I ever discuss or mention the appointment to him, or express to him that I would like to be given the appointment. I was sure that he knew, without my having to ask him.

The rumors flew thick and fast about who would be named by Governor Carter to fill the unexpired term. Though many were mentioned, almost all the Democratic leaders placed my chances among the top three contenders.

As Bill Shipp, the political editor of the *Constitution,* put it, "Anybody who got rich off of worms ought to be smart enough to be a U. S. Senator." But he gave my chances of getting the appointment a rating of "fair to middling," because, as he put it, "Governor Carter needs Hugh to help him in the State Senate to get the administration program passed."

There were those who suggested that the governor get Lester Maddox out of his hair by sending him to Washington for two years, but they were laughing as they said it. Bill Shipp commented that the appointment of Maddox would certainly mean that Carter would have clearer sailing with his reform legislative program "but why reward someone for being a nuisance."

In the serious running, along with me, were former Governor Ernest Vandiver, David Gambrell, and Charles Kirbo.

Vandiver was probably the person Senator Russell would have wanted to succeed him. He was a nephew by marriage to Senator Russell and there was a rumor that Jimmy Carter had promised him the Senate seat in return for his support during the campaign.

But Jimmy denied this and I believe him. One thing that marred his chances for getting the seat was a medical matter—heart condition.

David Gambrell was chairman of the State Democratic party and he had shown loyalty by backing all the Carter reforms, so his chances seemed very good. Also, he had worked very hard all during the gubernatorial campaign.

Based on friendship outside the family, Charles Kirbo had the inside track. He was a fine lawyer with a large law firm in Atlanta and was just about Jimmy's best friend. In fact, Kirbo was Jimmy's chief strategist during his winning campaign and certainly would be able to make a lot of friends for Jimmy in Washington—looking forward to that future presidential try.

But again, would Jimmy want to do without his close adviser for two years? And would Kirbo want to leave his firm?

Senator Floyd Hudgins of Columbus and Senator Martin Young of Rebecca, Georgia, told me that they took about half of the Georgia State Senate down to the governor's office on the second floor of the Capitol to urge the governor to appoint me. They told me that the governor was very polite to them but made no commitment.

A friend from Columbus and another close friend from Macon urged citizens from all over the state to write the governor on my behalf and they responded.

With hindsight, I believe this was unfortunate. I heard that the governor told the press that no amount of pressure of this kind would have any bearing on whom he would appoint.

As each day passed by and he didn't make the appointment, the tension built, fanned by the press. Practically every newspaper in Georgia was speculating on who would be named.

I really wanted the appointment, and frankly, it is the only appointment that I have *ever even been interested in* for myself. I was qualified and I felt that I had been loyal and faithful to Jimmy in helping him to get elected and I felt that I deserved his careful consideration for this most important position.

I felt comfortable in hoping that he would give me the appointment. I knew that if he sent me to Washington as a U. S. Senator, I could be a big help to him as governor and also to the state of Georgia.

As a further footnote, as I look back on the situation, I know now what a tremendous help I could have been to him serving in the U. S. Senate while he was running for President, and even now while he is President.

Jimmy had promised the people of Georgia that he was not going to appoint a bench warmer. This indicated to me that he was going to appoint a man who could win in 1972. I felt I was that man. I had the experience, I had the respect of the people of Georgia, and I had a good political record.

Although Gambrell was a splendid person and a very intelligent lawyer and a good friend of mine, I didn't feel that he was a particularly skilled politician. I felt strongly, even though I didn't say so, that he would be a bench warmer and could not be elected in 1972.

Late on the Sunday night before Jimmy made known his choice for the Senate seat, he called me at the Marriott, where my wife and I were living during the legislative session, and asked me to see him early the next morning.

He said he had something to tell me.

I knew that *this was it* and I would soon know my fate. I am sure he knew how anxious I was to get the appointment.

I didn't feel at that time that nepotism should enter into consideration since I had my own years of service in the Georgia State Senate and Jimmy knew well my ability as a politician and my capabilities to serve as not only a Georgia state senator, but a U. S. senator.

I kept hoping that he would remember when John Kennedy appointed Robert Kennedy, his brother, as U. S. Attorney General. At that time, President Kennedy didn't let the possible theory of nepotism stop him from appointing the person he felt to be the best candidate, his brother, as Attorney General.

When I went in, Jimmy shook hands with me, told me he was glad to see me, and asked me to sit down.

Then he sat down, too, in the governor's chair. The suspense was painful. Jimmy said that it had been a very difficult decision for him to make and that he had decided to appoint David Gambrell to the U. S. Senate to fill the vacancy created by Russell's death.

He said he knew that I would be disappointed and he knew that many others would also be disappointed. But he gave me no reason for not appointing me. Some told me later that they felt he didn't appoint me for fear of being accused of nepotism, but I don't know this to be so.

Jimmy told me that in appointing Gambrell there would be a vacancy for the chairmanship of the Democratic party in Georgia and that he was asking me to accept it. I immediately declined the offer, explaining to him that I was not interested in that appointment and preferred to remain a state senator.

He asked me not to give him a definite answer at that time but to think about it for a few days and let him know. I told him there was no need to wait—my decision was final. I would not accept the chairmanship of the Democratic party.

I left the governor's office very disappointed, but knowing that it had been possibly one of the greatest and toughest decisions Jimmy Carter had ever had to make and I admired him for having had the courage to stick to his choice in face of the support and pressure that had been presented to him on my behalf.

Jimmy had had the courage to let me know in advance, so I could conduct myself accordingly. Still, why it was Gambrell and not me, *I will never really know.*

The announcement was made public that afternoon in the House of Representatives' chamber, which was packed to capacity. Hundreds of my friends were there and quietly expressed to me their regrets that I did not get the appointment, especially members of the Georgia Legislature, most of whom had been supporting and pulling for me.

I was heartsick but tried to hide it and put on a cheerful smile.

There was one more duty I had to perform to show I was a good sport. I was invited to fly to Washington with Jimmy, Gambrell, Kirbo, and many other Gambrell well-wishers to attend the swearing-in ceremonies for David Gambrell.

I went to prove that I could take disappointment with a smile, even though I was sure everyone who knew me knew that I was extremely disappointed.

Time went by. Charles Kirbo accepted the party chairmanship that I had declined, and I must admit he did an excellent job with it.

I think that my wife, son, and brother, Donnel, were even more disappointed than I when Jimmy did not appoint me to fill Russell's place. Ruth cried several times, saying that I had taken several years from my life to get Jimmy into the governor's chair.

She was overestimating my importance in the scheme of things. And the fact is that I had wanted Jimmy for governor because he was the best candidate, and he owed me no special favors, not even free peanuts.

But I do believe I was a man for the job of U. S. senator because I had worked very hard in politics and had the best background for it.

My judgment later proved to be correct when Gambrell did not succeed in winning the Senate seat under his own power two years later and was defeated by Sam Nunn. Gambrell also lost in a later try for governor.

I will always wonder what the course of events in my life would have been had I been the appointee rather than David Gambrell.

I will never forget one of Jimmy's last gestures before leaving office. He installed a portrait of Martin Luther King, Jr., in the halls of the Georgia State Capitol.

During the time the King portrait was being installed, the Ku Klux Klan was parading outside.

Cousin Jimmy had shown courage to make this symbolic move.

13 · "YOU SHOULD RUN FOR PRESIDENT"

When a man becomes President, everyone wonders who deserves credit.

In a way, I'd give Admiral Hyman Rickover a lot of credit for the fact that Jimmy won the presidency. It was because Rickover pulled him up sharply and made him feel guilty that Jimmy decided to use a strategy of "total effort all over the nation" instead of the spotty approach, which had been traditional in presidential campaigns.

That was the lasting effect of the now famous story when Jimmy was being interrogated by the admiral as a candidate for his nuclear submarine program.

I have heard Jimmy talk of that interview many times—how impressive the admiral looked and how he never smiled. And how Jimmy felt himself becoming saturated with cold sweat.

Jimmy had been proud that he had finished 59th in his class of 820 at Annapolis. But instead of complimenting him when he found out Jimmy's standing, the admiral had looked even more disapproving.

"Did you do your best?" Rickover had asked sternly.

Jimmy had gulped and admitted, "No, sir, I didn't *always* do my best."

Jimmy had been thrilled and grateful that apparently in spite of not having done his best, Rickover had chosen him anyway and he had determined that from then on he would be able to say he had done his best.

When he returned to Plains to run the peanut business, he wanted to be the best in the business and he read every book he could find on the subject of warehouses and peanut farming.

"Why not the best?" became a phrase that haunted him and he chose it as his theme for his presidential campaign. He also chose it as the title of his own book which came out during the campaign and told the nation what Jimmy was all about.

Maybe it was September 5, 1974, when the idea popped into Jimmy's mind to become President. That was the day when, as governor of Georgia, he met with the other twelve governors of the thirteen original colonies. As he told it later, he could hardly concentrate on what was going on because he was thinking about those leaders of two hundred years before who had met during that first Continental Congress and what they faced.

They had been as confused and disillusioned about events then as politicians were in 1974 over Nixon's disgraceful behavior. And then he thought how they had been angry enough to get to work and straighten out their troubles and manage their own affairs.

The thought came to him that in 1974 again there was a need for bold inspired leadership to handle our own affairs and restore the country to its self-respect. He looked around and then appointed himself to start furnishing that bold leadership.

Looking back still further, it is clear that some of the things Jimmy was saying as governor in 1973 drew attention to himself as possible presidential timber. He held a press conference every week as governor, and on one occasion he openly charged President Richard Nixon with being "the worst President of my lifetime."

Of course, he knew that this attack on an incumbent President would make headlines outside of the state of Georgia and it certainly did. It started Nixon defenders demanding that Governor Jimmy Carter prove his charge. Jimmy said, "I don't have to—the facts are coming out every day in the newspapers."

It turned out that Jimmy was right and Nixon became the first President in the history of the nation to resign, due to the Watergate scandal involving him.

Many people deserve credit for getting Jimmy where he is today. One member of the family whom I haven't seen mentioned as contributing to Jimmy's success is our cousin Jimmy Deriso. Jimmy Deriso died in 1977 but he was a pillar of strength when Jimmy needed him in the gubernatorial race of 1970.

Deriso raised fifteen thousand dollars for Jimmy's campaign when he was chairman of the Sumter County for Carter Financial Committee and I have a picture taken in the summer of 1970 showing the presentation of that check at a time when it was desperately needed. I am in the picture with Jimmy to receive the contribution and I am quoted as saying in the newspaper caption, "The tremendous response from Sumter Countians has been humbling and I shall never forget it."

146

Jimmy Deriso was made treasurer of the state Democratic party while Jimmy was governor. He was a very wealthy man—a big stockholder in the Winn-Dixie Stores.

I remember once Jimmy Carter commented that to the best of his recollection it was a Thomasville heating and air-conditioning contractor, Frank H. Neel, who probably was the first man to urge him to run for the presidency.

Jimmy was not even governor yet, but only running for the governorship. It was in 1970 and Jimmy was speaking to the Kiwanis Club. So impressed was Neel that he got carried away. He predicted that not only would Jimmy win the governor's race, but he thought Carter ought then to start immediately to run for President.

Jimmy was amused that these successful businessmen in the town where Republican President Eisenhower used to come to hunt quail would recognize a future President in him so early and he just filed it away in his mind.

But I'm sure that things like this kept adding up to make Jimmy feel that he *was* presidential timber.

Cousin Hot was not extremely popular when he left the Governor's Mansion in January of 1975. But he knew in his heart he had done a good job and I and his intimates knew he was thinking presidency.

Like a Crusader, he felt that God was on his side. It may have been after the Nixon landslide in 1972 that Jimmy began to consider running for President. I know that many people are taking credit for being "the first" to urge him to run.

But I think that maybe it was the other way around and such an astute politician had Cousin Hot become that he was able to plant the little germ of an idea in their minds and let them tell him that he should run for President.

I think it's great that a lot of people share the credit for his running for the highest office. It took a lot of people wanting desperately for him to make the try for such a gigantic enterprise to be carried out—and to success, no less.

In 1970 when Jimmy was running for governor I recall an incident now which stands out vividly in my mind. State Senator and Mrs. Brooks Pennington were entertaining in their home for Jimmy and Rosalynn near Madison, Georgia.

My wife, Aunt Lillian, and I drove to Madison together in my car. It was a great political get-together on Jimmy's behalf—several hundred attended.

The thing I remember most was a conversation I had that night with Charles Kirbo, Jimmy's closest personal friend. He told me he felt Jimmy would certainly be elected governor and we all needed to exert our maximum effort to make this a reality.

He then intimated to me that he believed Jimmy would go to even greater heights after the governorship—and I realized that he was referring to the presidency. This indicates to me now that as early as 1970 some of Jimmy's closest friends and advisers were aware that someday he would run for the presidency.

There are several memos that have been very important in Jimmy Carter's career. They indicate to me that maybe Cousin Jimmy really started thinking about the presidency quite seriously at the time of or right after the Democratic presidential convention in Miami in July 1972.

And certainly in November of the same year. The first memo was written July 25 by Peter Bourne, whom Rosalynn much admired because of very impressive work he was doing with depressed patients, drug addicts, and alcoholics as director of the Mental Health Services in Atlanta.

Bourne had become Rosalynn's adviser in her effort to improve the quality of mental health care in Georgia as her contribution as governor's wife. Bourne had become very close to Hamilton Jordan as well.

Bourne sent Cousin Jimmy a most encouraging pep talk on why he could become "a major contender for the Presidency in 1976." One of the things that impressed Jimmy was his analysis of why Senator Scoop Jackson, one of Jimmy's heroes, failed to get the 1972 nomination—"because he never made a full commitment and never had the real *will to win.*"

When Jimmy decided to go for the presidency, he went all the way and never let himself deviate from his goal for more than a few hours at a time.

The second memo, written November 4, 1972, was a seventy-two-page blueprint for victory. Written by Hamilton Jordan, Jimmy's executive secretary in the State House, the memo is filled with page after page of things that Jimmy would have to do if he wanted to be President.

I was amused that one of the things was to get my brother, Donnel, vice-president of Knight Newspapers, to invite some of the top political writers for a weekend of fishing. That was to be part of his concerted effort to get acquainted with eastern journalists such as Tom Wicker and Scotty Reston because it was most important for such political columnists to take Jimmy's candidacy seriously.

The things that Ham told Jimmy are really a blueprint for anyone getting ready to embark on a serious candidacy for President—such things as find a very wealthy man and cultivate him, improve your speaking ability, get a speech writer who will get cracking immediately, work like the devil to win the early primaries, especially New Hampshire and Florida.

My favorite from among the overwhelming amount of advice Jordan threw at Jimmy was a very simple one—to work on developing a "Kennedy smile." Jimmy didn't have to work at it hard. He already had it and he added to it the mannerism of jabbing the air with a forefinger, the way Jack Kennedy had done.

I remember Ham very well from the 1970 governor's race, but actually his friendship with Cousin Jimmy goes back to 1966, right after Jimmy announced that he would seek the governorship.

Hamilton liked Jimmy enough to sign up as a campaign volunteer. He was only twenty-two years old and still in college, studying political science at the University of Georgia.

Every day Hamilton would come from Albany to work on the campaign at the Carter Peanut Warehouse. Ham and Rosalynn handled it all themselves, contacting people and writing persuasive letters.

There was so little competition that Ham Jordan ended up as Jimmy's campaign manager. Though Jimmy lost, Hamilton still had faith in him, and in 1970 he was back again for more.

A third person who had a great influence on Cousin Jimmy and his ambitions was Jerry Rafshoon, an advertising expert from Atlanta. He, too, discovered Jimmy in 1966.

I'm very impressed by Jerry and also his brother, Charles, an excellent photographer who did many of the fine photos of Jimmy Carter used during the presidential election.

But getting back to 1966, Jerry Rafshoon had just opened a new ad agency, modestly calling it Gerald Rafshoon Advertising, Inc. He didn't have much business and his background was that he'd worked at Lyndon Johnson's radio station, KTBC, for fifty dollars a week.

Jerry may not have been affluent yet but he knew a lousy campaign ad when he heard one and he was hearing one on the radio that kept repeating, "Jimmy Carter is his name—Jimmy Carter is his name."

Who cared? Nobody. There was nothing that made the listener want to know the man behind the name. Jerry gave his opinion to a reporter who was covering the Carter campaign and that reporter, Hal Gulliver, passed the opinion along to the candidate.

Carter asked Jerry if he could think of something better and Jerry worked furiously and came up with over a hundred pages of ideas and presentations.

Though Jimmy lost, he stuck with Jerry, and Jerry was one of the few people Jimmy would relax and drink beer with. In fact, Jerry can tell of the days when Jimmy still drank beer and threw darts in a little tavern and walked around like an average man.

There were so many hurdles in Jimmy's path to the White House that had to be leaped over. Money, campaign workers, and the challenge of many contenders in the primaries.

Another southerner, George Wallace, was definitely a major factor in the 1976 presidential race. Wallace got 381.7 delegates in 1972, and he had a tremendous amount of nationwide support before he was shot in Laurel, Maryland.

It is said that Wallace collected close to $8 million in the following years after the attempt on his life to run again for President. When the race started in 1976, wheelchair or not, he had to be considered a major factor.

The Democrats, in order to regain the White House, had to defeat Wallace. The Democrats figured Jimmy Carter could stop him. Of course, Jimmy would be helped by Wallace's bad health, though that seems a callous thing to say. But it is true.

Wallace began his campaign fairly strong, but it was clear his perception of what was going on was not what it used to be. He had grown quite deaf and this, along with his paralysis, meant a double handicap.

Wallace had to win in Florida to stay in the race and he was beaten badly there. After that, he seemed to be a beaten and lonely man. I am sure his aides were advising him to quit the race.

It's hard to remember at this late date what Jimmy was up against when he was making up his mind to run. Everyone was saying—in early 1974—that Ted Kennedy, who was only in his early forties, could have the Democratic nomination simply by lifting a finger to indicate yes.

To get that kind of response, Jimmy had to walk, run, fly, and battle his way to recognition from state to state, all over the country. It really did seem a ridiculous undertaking for Jimmy, at first. Few men would be willing to risk so much time, energy, and money on such a slim chance.

And besides the specter of a Kennedy shoo-in at the 1976 Democratic Convention, Jimmy had to consider all the other contenders. They numbered thirteen—but fortunately the unluckiness of that number was on their part, not Jimmy's.

There were Senators Henry Jackson of Washington, Frank Church of Idaho, George McGovern of South Dakota, Hubert Humphrey of Minnesota, Birch Bayh of Indiana, Lloyd Bentsen of Texas, and Walter Mondale of Minnesota, as well as ex-Senator Fred Harris of Oklahoma.

Then there was Representative Morris Udall of Arizona, the only candidate from the U. S. House of Representatives, but a potential winner. Then came the governors—George Wallace of Alabama, who still had a great following, Milton Shapp of Pennsylvania, a powerful state, and Jerry Brown of California, who appealed to a great majority of young voters.

And finally there was Sargent Shriver of Maryland, who had two pluses. He had experience as a vice-presidential candidate, in the '76 campaign, and he had the glamour of the Kennedy name since he was married to one of President Jack Kennedy's sisters. If Teddy Kennedy got behind Shriver, there was no telling what could happen.

Also, some felt that Shriver was simply holding Senator Kennedy's place for him.

Jimmy's advisers were urging him to go see Ted Kennedy to make sure he was not wasting his time in running if Ted was going to enter late and walk away with the nomination. But this was one bit of advice that Jimmy didn't take and he went ahead laying the groundwork for his own campaign and did not bother to see the senator until he himself announced his candidacy.

Jimmy came away from that meeting feeling confident that Ted was not one of the candidates he need fear in the '76 go-around.

It was surprising how jealous some of the old-line Democrats were of the upstart Jimmy Carter. Robert Strauss, the Democratic national chairman, for whom Jimmy had worked, when governor, as campaign chairman, had little good to say about Carter.

Eugene McCarthy, the glorified liberal, blasted Jimmy in

speeches on college campuses calling him as much or more of a "demagogue" than Gerald Ford and "just as militaristic."

President Ford's campaign manager and the Republican party were so delighted with McCarthy's attacks, they did not deny that they were considering giving McCarthy money to keep him traveling and spreading his hate-Carter message.

Of course, Jimmy liked to hear little stories that poked fun at Gerald Ford and hinted that Carter had a good chance to win. Like when it was reported that Washington nightclub comedian Mark Russell had said, "I think the light that Ford sees at the end of the tunnel is the front end of a train."

But he also had to hear the jokes the candidates were making about him, and these were not always so funny, for Jimmy, though he always managed to smile. I remember when Mo Udall was quoted during the primaries as quipping, "If President Ford and Jimmy Carter are the two nominees, all sides of the abortion issue will be represented. Ford will be in the middle and Carter will be on both sides."

Jimmy himself liked to poke fun at Ford and his predecessors in the Republican party. "Jerry Ford," he said, "serves in the great tradition of Warren Harding, Herbert Hoover, and Richard Nixon."

Another Carter gambit aimed at his opponents was this:

"He's a true leader representing accurately what his party is. When he became President, he said he was not a Lincoln, but a Ford, and he told the truth. I have to give him credit for that.

"Ford's a good automobile, but it's not doing too well in the White House. It's stuck in the mud, four flat tires, out of gas, gears locked in reverse, if it ever does move again which I doubt, I'm sure we're going to try to back it into the future."

The campaign itself was no easy matter for Carter or his staff. The incumbent, with rare exception, is reelected. Jimmy was the unknown and he had to act quickly in his bid for the presidency. His aides admitted their concern over Ford's aggressive approach to the campaign and even Jimmy's campaign manager, Hamilton Jordan, was concerned that "everything we've worked for could disappear in a few short weeks."

Another of Jimmy's firm supporters as well as his Democratic county chairman in Des Moines, Harry Baxter, had a feeling of doom when he said, "He's going to lose. I feel it in my bones as I did when he was trying for the nomination."

I sometimes wonder what would have happened if Jimmy had run for Congress and gone to Washington. Would he still have become President? Would he still have become governor? Would he have stayed on as congressman and still be in Washington today, in the legislative division in government?

I think that Jimmy would have tried to become President by the same route Jack Kennedy used—first, congressman, then senator, and then race for the presidency.

When Jimmy became a serious candidate, everyone started comparing him with Jack Kennedy. There really is quite a resemblance between the two, even with the color of their hair and their boyish grins that helped put each into the White House.

Silly as it seems at first glance, maybe it was that certain resemblance to Kennedy that brought Jimmy the presidency—and amusingly, looking back, by the same kind of Kennedy-small margin.

I'm sure that Jimmy worked at helping this comparison along. He was advised to do so by those closest to him in shaping his campaign. John Fitzgerald Kennedy used a nickname. James Earl Carter, Jr., used a nickname.

Jack Kennedy stabbed the air with his finger as he talked. Jack smiled at all the pretty girls. Jimmy smiled at all the pretty girls. But there, that particular comparison ended. Though Jimmy admitted he "lusted" occasionally, no one, including me, can find any evidence that he strayed from his true love, Rosalynn.

Both, however, are found particularly attractive by females and many have told me that they find Jimmy sexy in the same way that JFK was, and wish they could get closer to him. Kennedy bragged about his girl-chasing. Jimmy was basically shy with girls.

Both had brilliant minds. John Kennedy was graduated from Harvard in 1940 *cum laude*. Jimmy was graduated from the Naval Academy at Annapolis in the upper reaches of his huge class.

Both were considered a little scrawny—Jack eventually got his weight up to about 160 pounds by working at it, and Jimmy, who was about 132 at Annapolis, eventually got his weight up to about 140.

Both were restless and determined and set a pace of work that others considered almost unbelievable. Jack, when he wanted something badly, did not let his bad back injury and other physical problems stop him.

Both liked to walk around with a minimum of clothes in the privacy of their own homes. Jack would wear only a towel around his waist; Jimmy wore a little more but stayed barefoot.

In one personal mannerism, Jimmy and Jack are completely op-posite. Jack was known for his sloppiness and the way he dropped his clothes wherever he stepped out of them. I can attest to Jimmy's extreme neatness. It is almost an obsession with him to put his clothes away as he takes them off. His room is always immaculate and he makes a point of making his bed in the morning the moment he gets out of it.

I don't know whether he still does that at the White House, but if he has changed, I'll bet it was because the maids encouraged him to leave something for them to do.

Whenever Jack Kennedy made a speech, the girls sat up on the edge of their chairs, similar to the way Elvis Presley attracted them. Jimmy has a lot of this same magnetism. The girls think he is hand-some and like to rave about his looks.

Both loved the water. Jack Kennedy entered the U.S. Navy in 1941 and served in PT boats. Jimmy had a great Navy career and served principally in submarines.

Both liked showers and would stay in the shower a long time. Both liked to swim.

Each had overwhelming confidence in himself. Both were speed readers. Both were trigger-quick in responding to questions of the press and both knew how to turn a heckler's diatribe into a bit of humor.

Both entered politics as legislators—Jack as United States repre-sentative of Massachusetts and Jimmy as Georgia state senator. Both men had a faculty of making people curious about them and always remained somewhat of a mystery even while they were trying hard to be open.

There really wasn't a great difference in their ages. Jack Kennedy was born May 29, 1917. Jimmy was born only seven years later, on October 1, 1924. Both were born of fathers who were overachievers and prominent men in the community.

Joe Kennedy was known to be terribly generous to his friends and Earl Carter was the same way. Many times he would loan people money knowing that he would probably never get it back, just to be a good Samaritan.

Both their mothers also had something in common. Jimmy's mother, Lillian, nursed the sick in her community, whether they were black or white, had money or not. Jack's mother, Rose, was also known to be community-oriented and to help those who were physically sick.

Also, both mothers encouraged the religious upbringing of their children, taking them to church from an early age. As a third similarity, both mothers were the daughters of politicians, who were known to be especially good at wheeling and dealing.

Jack's maternal grandfather was John Francis Fitzgerald, mayor of Boston and a U.S. congressman. He was a powerful influence on Jack. Jim-Jack Gordy, Jimmy's maternal grandfather, though not a legislator himself, was a great influence on the State Legislature and was a man you saw to get things done.

It all added up to quite a resemblance. But resemblance doesn't win a race—that takes work. Unlike the "silver spoon," nobody is born with a "presidency" in his mouth.

A lesser man than Cousin Hot might have been discouraged that the vast multitudes of people had no notion of who he was—and couldn't have cared less—but Jimmy saw the humor of it.

As Jimmy once described those early morning sessions outside a factory when the shift was changing, "It was a little disheartening. I would shake hands as the workers came by and I would say, 'I'm Jimmy Carter, I've been governor of Georgia, I'd like to have your vote, I'm running for President,' and by that time they would be almost out of sight. I'd be talking to their back.

"Then they'd stop and they'd come back and they'd say—'President of what?'"

We had all had a taste of state politics but nothing could prepare us for the gigantic size of the Democratic National Convention in July. Naturally, all our family zeroed in on New York from all directions, and it was a colorful place to be.

Mayor Beame had said that he would clean up the city and get all the prostitutes off the street before the convention opened. But from how it looked on our arrival, he must have missed a few ladies of the night.

Our plane was struck by lightning as it approached New York during a terrible storm. The women were crying and one of the stewardesses, seeing fire coming from the cockpit, screamed, "Oh my God, we're going to die."

155

Fortunately, the pilot came in safely since he had excellent ground control and the passengers were all hustled out.

My wife and I stayed at the Americana and Connie stayed at the Holiday Inn on Fifty-seventh Street. Connie, our younger daughter who had just married her fiancé, Leon Collins, had only recently returned from the Bahamas, where she had been honeymooning. It was amusing that one night the cabbie trying to get from her hotel to ours got lost and my little old country girl daughter had to act as copilot. She did not tip him for that performance.

The night Jimmy was nominated, a crowd of us were taken to a fun spot to celebrate. There was quite a crowd in our cab—a New York lawyer who was our host, Bernie Wilson; my daddy; my brother-in-law Pete Godwin and his wife, Dot; Connie and her husband, Leon; and of course, me and my wife, Ruth.

Bernie took us to the Monkey Bar, where a musical genius sat at the piano making up songs. He would ask for ten or fifteen words and then compose on the spot. We said, "Peanuts, Jimmy Carter, White House, worms," and so forth, and he made up a song that had us roaring with laughter.

He had a hard time fitting worms into the story of a man named Jimmy Carter who was headed for the White House but he had a vivid imagination. Connie did get a chance to talk worm farming one night with Coretta King, Martin Luther King, Jr.'s, widow, who sat behind her once during the convention.

She had never heard of a worm farm and said she was coming down to see it with her own eyes.

The family, especially Connie, were thrilled to rub elbows with all the Democratic movie stars and other celebrities. Connie almost swooned over Paul Newman, and Aunt Dot sat next to E. G. Marshall, truly enjoying their conversation. I had conversations with two celebrities whose names were quite similar, Lorne Greene of *Bonanza* and the glamorous stage star Lauren Bacall.

I also chatted with Telly Savalas of *Kojak*, Danny Kaye, and Lynda Robb, LBJ's daughter, and her husband, Chuck.

We were astounded at the reaction of the crowd when Jackie Kennedy Onassis came in. She sat down across the aisle from us. She was with her sister and some other family members. Hubert Humphrey was speaking at the time but all eyes turned to Jackie and all the cameras ninety-to-nothing.

I don't believe anyone heard a word that HHH was saying.

In order to get into the convention hall, we had to wear big cardboard passes around our necks. We had green passes which entitled us to sit in the family section. But we also had to have a card that said *Honored Guest.*

The security was tight. There were ticket checkers and guards everywhere. Still, this did not stop Leon, my new son-in-law, when he decided he wanted to go speak to my son, Hugh, Jr., who was a floor leader for the Georgia delegation.

Leon did not have a pass to get on the convention floor but he said, "Don't worry, I'll make it."

He turned his pass over, stuck it in his coat, and walked onto the floor through the security guards as if he had every right to be there. When he finally walked up to Sonny, my son gasped and said, "How in the world did you get down here?"

When Leon told him, Sonny was most amazed but more than that, fearful about the lack of security should some nut try to walk through.

When Leon finished frolicking on the convention floor, he headed back to our section and was immediately challenged by a guard who asked him how he had gotten down to the floor. Leon replied, "I walked, how else?" And walked past the stunned guard.

Usually, a bus would be waiting to take the family members to the various Jimmy Carter parties going on around town. It was nip and tuck getting to the parties in time to see Jimmy Carter, who would make an appearance, say a few words, and dash off to the next party. Once, I tipped our bus driver ten dollars for getting us to a party on time.

My comedian son-in-law, Leon, said, "Give me your hat and coat, man, and let me drive this bus." But even though we were on time, Cousin Hot had already come and gone and people were grabbing souvenirs and wolfing down fried chicken faster than the waiters could fill the platters.

Somewhere along the line, Leon and Connie had their first celebrity experiences of a reporter wanting to see the convention through their eyes. He made an appointment to take them to breakfast the next morning to get his story. Connie and Leon had been so schooled in not talking about family matters that they were very disappointing sources and were sure that the poor reporter had not gotten back his investment.

Connie and her husband collect matchbox covers and all of us were on the lookout for all the interesting matchbooks we could find for them. It always makes a trip just a little bit more exciting to be on the lookout for something that you or someone near to you is collecting.

We were also collecting memories and we certainly added to that collection one night when we were standing outside the Holiday Inn to witness the arrival of two conventioneers from North Carolina. They had driven all the way with a *donkey* in the back seat.

They had also cut a record about Jimmy Carter and the White House and were giving away free copies.

Later, back at the Americana, there they were again with the donkey. It had a beautiful blanket on its back that read: JIMMY CARTER FOR PRESIDENT.

The inside story is that it was Rosalynn Carter who tipped the scales in the choosing of Walter Mondale to be Vice-President. Several of the men that Jimmy was considering as his running mate had fine qualifications but Rosalynn took a liking to Joan Mondale.

She liked Joan's quiet, gentle manner and the fact that she was the daughter of a Methodist minister. Rosalynn had grown up a Methodist, too, and been very close to the church.

The one I felt sorry for in New York was Senator John Glenn because it was my impression that he was just a hair's breadth from getting the vice-presidential nod.

It looked even more as if John Glenn was getting the nod when Cousin Jimmy went to great trouble to get the former astronaut on the phone. For some reason, the switchboard operator at the Sheraton Hotel where Glenn was staying would not give out Glenn's room number even though Greg Schneiders, one of Jimmy's top aides, kept telling her that the presidential candidate, Jimmy Carter, was trying to reach him.

The operator also refused Schneiders' plea that she send someone to Glenn's room to tell him to call Jimmy Carter back. Cousin Jimmy suggested that Greg cab over to the Sheraton and alert Glenn. Somehow Schneiders finally got through without having to take a cab, and just as he was getting Glenn on the phone, Jimmy was unable to come on the line because President Ford was calling him on another telephone to congratulate Carter on having been nominated.

So by the time Carter finally spoke to Glenn, Glenn had every reason to think he must be the one. But when Carter finally came on the line, it was not that message at all. He told John that he wanted him to be a good friend and he wanted to count on him in the campaign but that he had picked someone else to be his running mate.

As I got the story later, Glenn met defeat with a touch of humor. He looked at his wife, who was waiting with bated breath to hear the news, and said, "Well, Annie, you were wondering who was going to cut the grass this weekend. It's going to be me."

Rosalynn Carter had wanted Joan Mondale to work with and to show her the ropes in Washington, but when the moment of truth came, and the press turned to Joan Mondale asking her what her plans were for working projects, Rosalynn suddenly reacted as if she was still competing with Miz Lillian and Miz Lillian was trying to steal the show.

Joan Mondale started to say that she was going to work for the retarded and other unfortunate people, but Rosalynn, obviously annoyed, brushed her away and continued the briefing of the press herself. No one was going to run Rosalynn's show, and she made that clear.

It has been interesting to me to see that the First and Second Ladies of the land have not competed in the same field of endeavors but have gone separate ways. Rosalynn has become the leader in the field of aging, the handicapped, and mentally retarded. Joan Mondale has concentrated on improving the state of art in the United States, encouraging the development of artistic talent and finding ways for artists to display their works. Her home, the official vice-presidential residence, is a veritable art museum.

Art was used, incidentally, to earn about $150,000 from the sale of a portfolio of artists' works called "Inaugural Impressions." They were lithographs and silk screens showing impressions of Jimmy Carter's inauguration and they sold for $2,500 a portfolio. The artist whose work got the most publicity hadn't even come to the inaugural.

That was Andy Warhol, who did, I thought, a sketch of Jimmy that any schoolchild could do by holding a picture of him to a window and tracing on tissue paper.

But because the name has come to mean great showmanship, his picture was the one all reporters and guests were most curious to see when the President invited the artists to the White House to exhibit their impressions and unveil the portfolio.

Among the artists who didn't get the attention they merited—though each one got a $10,000 honorarium—was Robert Rauschenberg, who had executed a lithograph combining the statue of Lincoln at the Lincoln Memorial, the inaugural crowd at Lincoln's inauguration, some Confederate soldiers, and the new President of the United States, Jimmy Carter with his daughter, Amy.

To me this lithograph had a deep meaning, a message to the American people, saying that the Old South had become the New South in the symbol of the child and that the whole nation was now united.

Part Four

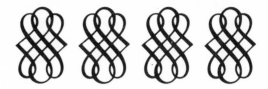

THE
CARTER
CLAN

14 · CARTER GENEALOGY– SAINTS AND SINNERS

I haven't found any horse thieves in our genealogy but we have had our share of skeletons and bloodshed. At times we have been more sinned against than guilty of wrongdoing against our neighbor.

The Carters have always been a family of high emotions, and violent things have happened. Even President Jimmy showed a little trend toward violence as a child when he filled his sister Gloria's backside with a little buckshot in a fit of extreme irritation.

The British, who love the study of genealogy even better than my daddy, Alton, have worked very hard at tracing our roots in the British Isles. One genealogist, Noel Currer-Briggs, claims to have traced us back to a wine merchant named Thomas Carter, who was born in London in 1610 and set sail for America in 1635, landing in Virginia in the Isle of Wight County along the James River.

Currer-Briggs also has traced our distant cousins, and discovered we are related to the past owners of Chequers, the historic country estate outside of London which is used as a retreat for British prime ministers, the way Camp David is used for the current head of the Carter family.

It is kind of thrilling to realize this historic place was owned by Carters of my blood from approximately the year 1300 to 1700.

An American genealogist, however, James M. Black, senior researcher at the Mormon Genealogical Library, has traced the Carters back to a still earlier date. He claims Jimmy's and my roots go back to John Carter, who was born in 1575 in London. He still has the first Carter, John's son, Thomas, coming to the New World in 1635.

The record of John Carter's birth was recorded in 1575 in Christ's Church, in London.

According to *English Surnames*, by Mark A. Lower, London, 1849, Carter is an old occupational name like Baker, Smith, Taylor, and others.

It was sometimes spelled Carteer. According to the book, many cart drivers took the name without being related. For example, when the gypsies came to England, they took various English surnames, including Carter.

Sometime before writing his book, Lower had counted the number of Carters in the English register of births, deaths, and marriages in the period 1837–38. It showed Carter to be among the sixty most numerous names.

The Carters have been a part of the history of Georgia's Plains area since the Indians were moved out of it in 1830. But the first of our ancestors to set foot in America came to Virginia from England as an indentured servant or "white slave."

I was fortunate in that the chief family historian for the Plains Carters was always my own daddy, whom Jimmy called "Uncle Buddy." When Jimmy was bragging about his roots in Georgia history, during the presidential campaign, he suddenly realized that he did not have all the answers and so he came to see Daddy.

He brought along a tape recorder and took down everything Uncle Buddy had to say about the history of the Carter family.

This was not the first time he had consulted Daddy about our background. After his defeat, in his first race for the governorship, when he was healing his emotional wounds and girding himself for his second try, he had taken Uncle Buddy to inspect the historic Rock House, in McDuffie County, the oldest house belonging to an ancestor in this area.

I have some snapshots of Jimmy and Daddy taken in front of the run-down, decrepit structure in 1968. It does not look like that anymore. It has been restored and labeled a historical landmark.

The Rock House was built around 1785, twenty-inch thick walls as protection against the Indians. It also had something else as insurance against Indian attacks. It originally had no windows on the main-floor level but only windows high under the sloping roof where no Indian could climb through. Later residents chopped out window areas in the stone.

The house was first built by Thomas Ansley, Jimmy's great-great-great-great-grandfather—and mine.

As mentioned, Thomas Carter, Sr., is the first Carter ancestor who can be traced. After landing in Virginia in 1635, he worked as an indentured servant for five years, as was the custom, to pay for his passage on a ship that was probably no better than the African slave ships. Some passengers had sold themselves into bondage for seven years, so at that, Thomas was lucky.

The way the family history goes, Thomas arrived at the age of twenty-five and after he had worked off his indenture, went to the West Indies because he saw no way of becoming wealthy in America. With the usual family luck for adventure, Thomas Carter got involved in the British maneuvers to clear the Spaniards out of the Caribbean area.

Thomas was taken prisoner by the Spaniards and escaped about two years later, getting back to London on a Dutch ship.

But he didn't stay in England. Back he came to Virginia, where he became a wealthy man with four indentured servants of his own.

Thomas Carter's only known son, Thomas Carter, Jr., also had a colorful life. He was a revolutionary and in danger of losing his head a full century before the Revolutionary War. Born in 1648, Thomas, Jr., joined Bacon's Rebellion in 1676, part of a group who were agitating for "self-determination," considered treasonous by the British King as well as by the governor of Virginia.

In fact, the governor executed some of Bacon's followers, and Thomas and some of his comrades escaped execution, after Nathaniel Bacon died, by signing pledges of allegiance to the King.

The Virginia governor pardoned him, and Thomas, Jr., went on to fame and fortune through a most advantageous marriage. In 1673 he received four hundred acres of land as a wedding dowry from his new father-in-law, George Moore, the wealthy Justice of the Court of Isle of Wight County, Virginia, for marrying his daughter Magdalen.

It must have been a fairly happy marriage. The couple had nine children including Moore Carter, who was Jimmy's and my great-grandfather, seven generations removed.

Moore Carter was also a lover of freedom. Born in 1680, he, too, revolted against King George II of England. In 1735—again, well before the Declaration of Independence—he moved to North Carolina, where he refused to pay his tribute when King George II doubled taxes on land holdings.

Eventually, Moore Carter and his neighbors prevailed and the amount of tax was lowered. That's the good part of the story—Moore forced a king to back down. But the bad part is that Moore, who owned a large plantation, also owned slaves, some of whose names are known.

One of Moore's six children was Isaac, the President's and my sixth-generation ancestor. Isaac Carter, born in 1730, took part in the American Revolution in several important ways. He had three sons who fought with the colonists against the British, and he personally supplied a tremendous amount of provisions to the Continental Army and North Carolina militia from his estate of over seven hundred acres.

Now we come to a bit of confusion. There were two fifth-generation ancestors who came to Georgia from North Carolina—James and Kindred Carter. Daddy had always assumed that we were descended from James but genealogists say we were descended from Kindred, born in 1750, who was one of the Carters who did not fight in the American Revolution.

Kindred was probably a Quaker and that could explain why he did not take part in the war. His name is a Quaker name and there was a large Quaker colony in the northeastern part of North Carolina, where he lived.

In spite of being a Quaker, the records show that Kindred did own ten slaves. The reason for the exodus of the Carter ancestors was economic—a depressed economic condition. Kindred abandoned his six-hundred-acre farm and came to a plantation half the size in the part of Richmond County which is now McDuffie County, Georgia.

But we get back to a James Carter anyway because one of Kindred's sons was James Carter, who was Jimmy's and my great-great-great-grandfather. James Carter seems to have been the first Baptist in the Carter family. He was also a very lucky man.

Born in 1773, he lived to be eighty-four years old and died as a wealthy landowner because of land lotteries. James Carter won two tracts of land totaling around seven hundred acres in the Georgian lotteries, which were held to redistribute land taken from the Indians.

Among James Carter's nine children was a son named Wiley Carter, who was the President's and my great-great-grandfather.

With the story of Wiley, violence crops out on the Carter family tree—a murder that was the result of a dispute over stolen property. That particular kinfolk, who was born in 1798, was a wealthy plantation owner in Warren County, Georgia, with twenty-nine slaves.

According to court records, in the winter of 1841, a neighbor whose last name was Usry—no first name was given—allegedly stole one of Wiley's slaves. As the story goes, Wiley got the sheriff and a posse of men and went to get his property.

The sheriff took along a warrant but Usry refused to come out of his house and discuss the matter. Instead he shouted curses and threats and even cast aspersions at Carter's wife. This alone would have been grounds for a pistol duel since it was still the age of gallantry.

At this point, the sheriff was ready to break down the door but Wiley said he didn't want to take a chance of hurting Usry's wife, who was also inside, and he suggested that they wait until Usry sobered up a little.

They waited, and about dawn, Usry's son ran from the house and warned that his father was going to kill Wiley Carter unless he left. But Wiley stood firm and suddenly Usry came through the door.

Exactly what happened is not clear but witnesses said that both men had raised guns while cursing each other and Wiley Carter fired first, killing Usry. Wiley Carter was charged with murder but the case did not come to trial until the next spring.

Then at a day-long trial in April 1842 Wiley was found not guilty. However, Wiley eventually moved his family away from the scene of violence.

He settled near Plains in Schley County and died so wealthy that he left about twenty thousand dollars to each of his twelve children. One of those children was Littleberry Walker Carter, who was our great-grandfather.

Incidentally, the Wiley Carter we have been talking about was the man who married another Carter ancestor, Thomas Ansley's granddaughter, Ann Ansley, and lived in the Rock House.

Littleberry Walker Carter, born 1832, added another violent episode to the Carter family tree. During the Civil War, Littleberry served in the Confederate Army's famous Sumter Flying Artillery, which was headquartered in Virginia.

There is some evidence that Littleberry was present at Lee's surrender at Appomattox. Some accounts say that Littleberry was killed in a fight over a merry-go-round by a man with whom he was in business. My father said that this is wrong; according to the account told by his father, William Archibald Carter, Littleberry Walker had a big fight at a carnival over a gambling device operated by a foot pedal.

The use of the word "flying jenny" seems to be confusing. A merry-go-round was called a flying jenny. According to some versions of the story, Walker was knifed to death and the man against whom a murder indictment was issued, D. P. McCann, fled to South America and was never heard from again.

According to the story, the day that Littleberry died, his wife did, too—from shock and grief.

But that isn't true. The fight didn't kill Littleberry.

As a matter of fact, according to our family records, Littleberry died the day after his wife died, of the same disease. They were buried in a family cemetery near Souther Field, which is near Americus and where Charles Lindbergh made his first solo flight.

In 1926 Nina Pratt Carter—Daddy's mother and my grandmother—and Aunt Nannie Jenkins went over to the family cemetery at Souther Field and some farmer had fenced in the acreage where the cemetery was located and hogs were being kept in the area.

They were afraid the hogs were going to root up the graves, so they immediately got hold of Uncle Callie—Calvin Carter—and employed an undertaker. The undertaker took up the caskets and moved Littleberry and his wife to the Americus cemetery.

They were buried in sealed metallic caskets and the undertaker was very careful not to let the caskets be opened because he was afraid germs might escape and spread diphtheria, even though Littleberry Walker and his wife had been dead for about forty-three years.

In our records, Littleberry's wife is called Diligence. In other accounts I have read quoting genealogists, Littleberry's wife is named Mary Ann Carter.

Littleberry left four children, among whom was William Archibold, the President's and my grandfather.

William Archibald Carter, who was born in 1858, was nicknamed Billy. He was a very successful man who owned several sawmills and much land in Early County, Georgia. He had five children, including my father, Alton, and President Jimmy Carter's father, James Earl.

A great family tragedy that my daddy, the President's uncle, witnessed was the senseless murder of his father in a trivial dispute, the third incidence of violence in our family tree. Before I tell you how it came about, let me tell you about the family and early life of Uncle Buddy, as the President called my father.

An interesting sidelight about Grandfather Billy Carter, who was shot and killed, is that he and his cousin, Uncle Dave Carter, were first cousins, married to sisters. Uncle Dave married Lula Pratt and Grandpa Billy married Nina Pratt, my grandmother.

The way it happened is that Lula came from Abbeville, South Carolina, to Friendship, a community about eight miles north of

Plains, to visit Dr. Holloway, who was married to the girl's aunt. On the visit, she met Uncle Dave and married him. Then Nina came to see Lula, met Billy, and they got married.

They started a whole string of marriages. Nina's half sister Mary Pratt came to visit Nina and met Hall Calhoun and married him. Then Carrie Pratt came to visit Mary Calhoun and married the local doctor, Cleve Jowers. And finally, bringing most of the family to the Plains area, Jeff Pratt, a half brother of Nina, came to visit her from Abbeville and married Nell Hightower.

Nina and her sister really started something. Perhaps what this story really shows, however, is that the people around Plains are very persuasive when they are courting—especially the Carters!

Out of the marriage of Billy Carter and Nina Pratt came my daddy, William Alton Carter, who died in January 1978 when eighty-nine years old.

He was born August 17, 1888, in Arlington, Georgia.

Jimmy and I both enjoyed hearing my daddy talk of his childhood. Both boys and girls wore dresses in their early childhood back in those days and Daddy remembered that he wore a dress until 1893, when he was five years old.

One of the stories we found hilarious was of Uncle Buddy's first speech in school. His home was only a hundred yards from the schoolhouse at Arlington and every Friday afternoon the children would make speeches before leaving for the weekend—the forerunner of Show 'n' Tell.

Since he was a little busybody outside his house, talking to all the teachers and children who went by, he was invited to come to the schoolhouse one Friday and make his own speech.

He got up before the class with his little dress on. He remembered every word of the speech he made as if it hadn't been eighty-four years ago:

"Monkey sitting on the end of a rail, picking his tooth with the end of his tail. Mulberry leaves and calico sleeves—all schoolteachers are hard to please."

Daddy says a black boy about ten years old baby-sat him when he was two to five years of age and probably taught him this rhyme. In those days, there were no wire fences and all fences were made of split wooden rails. The monkey he was referring to in his speech must have been sitting on the end of a fence rail.

Uncle Buddy seemed to have a charmed life. When he was eight years old, his life was spared in a bizarre incident. On Sunday, March

21, 1897, Alton and his sister Ethel had ridden to church in a new buggy that his daddy, Billy Carter, had bought. The horse he drove was blind and on the way home from Sunday School the blind horse ran into something and broke the double-tree and they had to leave the buggy right in front of the schoolhouse and walk home four miles.

The following morning, his daddy brought him and his sister to school on a load of lumber he was delivering. He noticed that a storm was coming up and sometime during the morning, he and two other boys went out to the broken buggy to rescue the cushion before it was ruined by rain and wind. The wind was already blowing hard.

This action saved their lives. They were just running back into the schoolhouse when a violent tornado struck and collapsed the building, killing eight children who were inside instantly and causing one to die a little later.

Alton was pinned down by a board which broke his arm, leg, and nose. The second boy was blown across the school yard and into a field and was completely unhurt. The third, like Daddy Alton, was pinned down. A nail was stuck in his back and Daddy could still remember the poor boy hollering with pain until he was rescued.

The President's daddy, Earl, was spared because he was only a two-year-old toddler at home.

Ethel, too, was spared, though she was badly bruised.

It was Daddy's father who rushed back to the schoolhouse after the storm, took an ax, and cut the fallen timber from Alton's body to free him.

The school was destroyed and the next school Daddy attended was built by his own father, Billy. A relative taught at the school until 1900 when the family moved to Cuthbert. Hardworking Billy Carter, President Jimmy's grandfather and mine, commuted to Cuthbert on weekends and during the week stayed in Rowena, the country community where he ran a sawmill and cotton gin.

Grandfather Billy Carter also operated a commissary store, mainly for his employees. But after a few years he gave up running the commissary and rented the store to a man named Will Talaferro.

And now we get to a very dramatic moment in our family history. As background for what happened, it should be explained that Grandpa Billy had learned that every Sunday gambling and liquor drinking went on in the store. Grandpa Billy was furious and told Will Talaferro to move out.

So Will did move and he built a store of his own but he took along a desk made out of a thread case which belonged to Billy.

Grandpa Billy stewed about the matter and finally on September 3, 1903, told my daddy, who was then only fifteen, to go down to Will Talaferro's new store and tell him to return the desk that he had taken. Daddy Alton was to ask for immediate possession of the desk because Grandpa needed it at the cotton gin office to work on.

My daddy went down there and told Talaferro what his daddy had said. Talaferro told him that he had bought the desk and that it didn't belong to his daddy. However, Talaferro let Daddy have the desk and Daddy took it down to the gin.

Daddy and Grandpa Billy were living in a house between the gin and Will Talaferro's new store. That evening after they got home from the gin about 7:00, Billy and his son Alton were sitting on the porch and Billy decided to walk up to the store and and talk to Will about the desk.

My Daddy watched him walk up there and put his two hands on the window and start talking to Talaferro. They began a violent argument.

Billy went into the store and they began to fight with bottles and fists. Then Billy came out of the store and started home but Talaferro ran out with a pistol.

Daddy thinks it was a Smith and Wesson, .32 caliber. Talaferro fired three times at Billy and one of the bullets hit him behind the ear. Grandpa Billy did not have a gun but he did have a twenty-five-cent barlow knife—a very small knife—in his hand.

My Daddy Alton witnessed the shooting. Daddy's mother rented a horse and buggy and hired a man at the stable to bring her from Cuthbert thirty miles away that night.

They put Billy on the train and took him to Cuthbert to the doctor and home. There were few hospitals in those days. Billy died the next day. He was only forty-five years old. He was buried at Cuthbert and I visit his grave occasionally.

They tried Talaferro three times for murder. The first two times mistrials were declared. The third time, Talaferro was cleared of the charges. Now, little Alton, as head of the family at only fifteen years of age, decided that he must move away from the scene of the violence to avoid further violence.

He moved his family, including Earl, President Jimmy's daddy, who was only nine years old, to Plains to make a new start.

Daddy's uncle, Calvin Carter, of Americus helped Daddy sell out Grandpa Billy's gin, farm, and sawmill. With this money the family was able to buy a house in Plains—the one that still stands just behind the Methodist Church and only about four hundred yards from the now famous train depot, which was used as Jimmy Carter's presidential campaign headquarters.

They also had enough money to buy thirteen hundred acres of land. The family still owns five hundred acres of this land. The other eight hundred acres have been sold.

The first year in Plains, Daddy attended the eighth grade. This was the last schooling he had. He could not handle the responsibilities of earning a living for his mother, brothers, and sisters and still go to school.

In 1905 he went to work as a store clerk for Oliver McDonald Company, the biggest merchant in town. Daddy's starting salary was twenty-five dollars per month.

In 1909, after four years of clerking, several leading citizens of Plains were impressed enough with his industry to finance him in setting up his own store—Plains Mercantile Company, Inc. He was twenty-one.

Seven years later, the town of Cuthbert again entered my daddy's life when a girl from that town came to Plains to teach and Daddy fell in love with her. Her name was Annie Laurie Gay and they were married in September 1916.

My brother, Donnel, was born the following year. I was born in 1920, which was important to Daddy for another reason as well. That was the year he was elected mayor of Plains, a post he held for twenty-eight years.

Someone in the Carter clan wrote "Battle Hymn of the Carters," a song to be sung to the tune of "Battle Hymn of the Republic." The chorus:

> Glory to our grand ol' family
> Virile, worthy, brave and loyal
> Glory to the name of Carter!
> The clan goes marching on!

15 · THE REAL JIMMY

The President sleeps in jockey shorts, doesn't like his shirts starched too much, likes polyester suits—they are easy to care for.

During the campaign he washed his own socks in his hotel room each night, or wherever he happened to be a guest, and people thought that was pretty amazing.

It's the same as when he carries his suit-carrier over his arm when boarding flights.

Jimmy likes to get out of bed very early in the morning when no one is up and paddle around the kitchen in his bare feet, fixing his own coffee.

Then he likes to sit with it sipping as he looks out the window at the landscape.

That's the real Jimmy. And so is the Jimmy who visited my pond in August 1976, soon after he had won the Democratic nomination.

I said, "I'm getting it ready for you to bring some of your big shots down here to go fishing."

He said, "Big shots! I want to fish in that pond myself." And he intends to—he wants to use it as a place to relax and meditate and get away from crowds.

That's the real Jimmy, too, who wants to meditate quietly as he fishes or hunts for arrowheads. The real Jimmy spends a lot of time thinking about values and the artificial setting of values.

Once when Jimmy was given a beautiful blanket as a gift, he told this story:

This reminds me of an old gentleman who ran a little country store in south Georgia.

He was a shrewd merchant, but he was also very devout. And he tried to put on an aura of being deeply religious whenever he dealt with his customers to give a good image and for public relations. Whenever he rang up a sale he would always say a Bible verse.

One day, his grandson was there in the store visiting and he wanted to make a good impression. So a lady came in—it was drizzling rain—and she bought some cheese and some bread. It was about a thirty-cent sale and he thought awhile and he said, "The Lord will provide." And rang up the sale and put the money in the cash register.

In about twenty minutes, she came back and she threw the cheese and bread on the counter and she said, "The cheese is too hard and the bread is stale. I want my money back."

So the old gentleman reluctantly put the produce back on the counter and went to the cash register. He thought for a little while, and finally he hit the key and he said, "The Lord giveth and the Lord taketh away."

About that time it began to rain a little harder and a Cadillac automobile drew up in front—a beautiful car—and a nice trailer behind with a racehorse inside. A gentleman came running in and he said, "I've got to have a blanket for my horse."

And the old gentleman had three very cheap blankets on the counter, all the same quality but different colors. And he put a blue blanket on the counter and the gentleman said, "How much is it?" And he said, "Five dollars." He said, "That's too cheap. Do you have a nicer blanket?"

And the old gentleman put the blue blanket back under the counter and he picked up a yellow blanket and he said, "How about this one?" And the traveler said, "How much do you want for it?" He said, "It's only twenty dollars." And the fellow said, "I've got a horse outside that's worth about a half a million dollars. And I can't afford to put a twenty-dollar blanket on a half-a-million-dollar horse." He said, "Is that all you've got?"

He said, "No, sir, I've got one more blanket. I've got a nice red blanket." He said, "Well, how much for this?" He said, "I can let you have this blanket for a hundred dollars." And the guy said, "Okay. I'll take it."

So he gave him a hundred dollars, went outside, put the blanket on the horse, and drove off. And his grandson knew that all three blankets ordinarily sold for about three dollars. And so the old gentleman went over to the cash register and his grandson watched him very closely, and he finally hit the cash register, his face brightened up, and he said, "He was a stranger, and we took him in."

Jimmy has never been impressed with the dollar signs on things. He has never been ostentatious and bought big cars for himself—although he did buy them for his mother—and he has always been more interested in the intrinsic value of a thing.

Jimmy's first car was a Studebaker that he bought in 1948. Cars have never meant too much to him and it seems to me he was always driving a modestly priced car.

I think this accounts for his lack of interest at the White House in keeping up a good show by having the top aides ride around in fancy limousines as all recent presidents did.

I seemed to remember that Jimmy was usually riding around in a Chevy of some sort. And it seems to me that he had periods when he didn't even own a car but borrowed cars or maybe rented them. He was very disinterested in a car, except as a means of getting somewhere.

It is touching, to me, that when we were children together, some of the simple things we did influenced the thinking of a future President.

Our idea of wealth was a pocket full of good stones for our slingshots. Once Jimmy referred to it in a serious speech about decisions one has to make. It gave me a kind of thrill to realize I was part of the making of a President:

"One day I was leaving the railroad track with my pockets full of rocks and hands full of rocks, and my mother came out on the front porch—this is not a very interesting story but it illustrates a point—and she had in her hands a plate full of cookies that she had just baked for me. She called me, I am sure with love in her heart, and said, 'Jimmy, I've baked some cookies for you.' I remember very distinctly walking up to her and standing there for fifteen or twenty seconds, in honest doubt about whether I should drop those rocks which were worthless and take the cookies that my mother had prepared for me, which were very valuable."

Quite often, we have the same inclination in our everyday lives. We don't recognize that change can sometimes be very beneficial, although we fear it.

Jimmy Carter is said by some to be mysterious. The members of the public who feel this way do so because they hardly knew him until a few months before election. I have known him throughout his political career and life and I would never call him mysterious.

I would say that he is original and stubborn. He has his own ideas about what should be done. He is a good listener and weighs all advice, but the decision he makes is his own.

His eyes can be cold or warm depending upon the question or the subject or whether he approves or disapproves.

People have asked me how one could tell if Jimmy is angry, because he never seems to raise his voice. I tell them that he doesn't have to. You still know when he is angry. He just turns cold and he will turn eyes on you that are like a couple of pale blue ice cubes.

But he doesn't sulk. He just starts working very hard at something else till it's out of his system.

Yet he is capable of great warmth.

In Jimmy's home, as in ours, members of the family and their friends hold hands and ask the blessing before every meal.

But that is only the beginning of Jimmy's prayers. It seems like he is always pausing to commune with God. Many times he will say a little prayer for some other person who is in trouble. I think there are many days he pauses a half-dozen times for a few words of prayer. Jimmy has said that he did not ask the Lord to make him win the election and I believe him.

What he did pray for was that he would be worthy and able to make proper decisions.

I have heard some say that Jimmy exaggerates. I think everyone does this at one time or another. I remember one time Jimmy said, "No powerful politicians endorsed me." Many endorsed him. Perhaps he was just hurt that they weren't getting up on platforms to proclaim their endorsement. Or maybe he was distressed about the important one who got away.

I can say this, however: I certainly don't think that Jimmy exaggerates any more than any other politician that I know.

I can also say this; in all the years that I have worked closely with him politically, I have never seen him press for anything that wasn't 100 percent right and honorable.

Jimmy is competitive. He doesn't like to lose a softball game. He doesn't like to go hunting and let his hunting partner outshoot him. He doesn't like to lose at tennis, one of his favorite sports.

And he doesn't like to lose a legislative battle. Many times when I served as a floor leader in the Georgia State Senate, he would send for me and say, "Beedie, we've got to win this one. What can I do?"

And we usually entered the fight with such determination that we got the bill passed. Sometimes by only one or two votes, but it passed, and that's what counts.

Jimmy and Rosalynn are different types in that Jimmy likes to get to bed about 11:00 P.M. and be up at 6:00 A.M., if not earlier, and Rosalynn likes to stay up half the night. She loves the quiet mystery of the night and she reads or listens to music when everything is quiet.

As a guest, Jimmy is just about perfect. He doesn't keep his host up half the night and he doesn't get drunk. He likes to munch on mixed nuts in the evening and before he goes to bed he likes a glass of buttermilk. With the buttermilk he enjoys a cheese dip or chunks of cheese and crackers. You might call him a dairy freak.

In the morning, if he has been an overnight guest, he always makes his own bed and leaves the room just the way it was when he arrived. On the plane ride home, he will already have finished a thank-you note by the time the plane lands. He always writes a handwritten thank-you note.

When I heard that Jimmy was taking a speed-reading course at the White House, with Rosalynn, I couldn't understand why Jimmy needed it. He had already taken one in Georgia and learned to read at the speed of about one thousand words a minute.

Rosalynn was almost as fast as he when they took the course at the college in Americus—Georgia Southwestern.

Jimmy is the kind of person who doesn't have to diet to keep his weight down. He uses up a lot of energy just in being always on the move. Even when he is meditating, he frequently walks as he thinks. But early in the morning on a weekend, he likes to just sit and gaze off into the distance at trees or clouds or other things of nature. That, to him, is luxury.

Even though he works long, hard hours, Jimmy has always been in fine health and I've never known him to take medicine or anything of that sort except vitamins.

His diet is still the simple diet of a farmer. If he has what he really wants, it is lots of vegetables, especially the sort that northerners do not appreciate—butter beans and collard greens—plus zucchini and every other kind of squash. His favorite meat is chicken and his favorite luncheon beverage is buttermilk. Lunch is just a sandwich and buttermilk or tea. He'll have a cheese or steak sandwich or a hamburger.

Jimmy was the kind of husband any woman would thank her lucky stars to have because he actually enjoyed helping Rosalynn cook. In fact, after they would come back from campaigning, Jimmy would use it as a form of relaxation and to recover from the tension he had been under. He'd be happy just puttering around the kitchen.

Brother Billy would send over some eggplant and Jimmy would fix one of his favorite dishes that he called goulash. An eggplant goulash would be made of tomatoes, peppers, and eggplant, along with his favorite spices, baked in a casserole.

Rosalynn has always had a great influence on what Jimmy ate, and to show what respect he had for her opinions, he always used to eat a good big breakfast because she thought it was necessary to start the day.

Jimmy never disputed it and ate big breakfasts until he was elected governor. Then he made his Declaration of Independence from big breakfasts. He said he had never enjoyed them and had just been eating them to please her, but would eat them no longer.

From then on all he had for breakfast was orange juice and black coffee. Only on weekends, when he was more relaxed, would he have the traditional grits and eggs.

Another of Jimmy's Declarations of Independence had to do with Rosalynn's desire to have a house always immaculate. Because Georgia is very dusty with its thick red clay, Rosalynn was always worrying about Jimmy and the rest of the family tracking in dirt on the beautiful carpets of their new house.

Jimmy got tired of hearing Rosalynn talk about how the carpet was changing color from the dust that was being tracked in. Finally, one day he took her by the shoulders and looked meaningfully into her eyes and said, "Rosalynn, it's because *people* live here that it looks that way. Would you want it otherwise?"

Rosalynn never complained about the carpets again.

Jimmy has been meticulous in treating his own mother and his mother-in-law equally. It isn't easy.

On Christmas, for example, he always has breakfast with his own mother and an informal buffet dinner with Rosalynn's mother.

After her daughter became First Lady, Miss Allie, at age seventy-one, took her first trip abroad. She was among 381 people from Georgia who went on a people-to-people exchange in July 1977, with 381 Britons. In fact, Allie was on the first "Friendship Flight" out, headed for New Castle. The program was one that Jimmy began when he was governor, to make the people of Georgia more aware of the brotherhood of nations.

A little later Lillian Carter arrived in Dublin, Ireland, all dressed in green and was grandly received by the lord mayor while the band played "When Irish Eyes Are Smiling." She was part of a 254-member Friendship Force exchange visit to Ireland.

Jimmy always bends over backward to be fair and see to it that whenever something nice is done for his mother, something nice is done for Rosalynn's mother, and vice versa.

Of course, Miz Lillian's trip to India as the emissary of the President belongs in a different class. She was qualified to go because she had gone to India and worked in India on her own, and had won the gratitude of the Indian people as a Peace Corps volunteer.

It was Miss Allie who had the honor of being invited by the Carters to sleep in the Lincoln bed at the White House when she stayed there during the inaugural festivities.

Whenever the First Family goes to Plains, Rosalynn spends as much time with her mother as she can, still sitting and sewing with her, although Miz Allie no longer needs to sew for a living. Instead, the First Lady's mother spends spare time clerking in a Plains gift shop, to give her something to do.

She used to be content to just sit on her porch and sew or read, after she retired from the post office, but tourist buses stopping to gawk at her or pointing out the bus windows at her made her too uncomfortable to use her porch anymore. I pass that porch often and it seems lonely without that pleasant and familiar figure rocking there.

I think Allie has one of the sweetest expressions a face can have and mother and daughter look quite alike. In fact, if you look at Allie Smith you can see what Rosalynn will look like years from now.

Since she never remarried, Jimmy has always looked out for Rosalynn's mother.

The family always thought that Miss Allie would end up marrying Postmaster Robert McGarrah for whom she used to work. They were neighbors and co-workers for many years. Robert, as he is called, used to be a pharmacist, working for my wife's daddy, before he became postmaster, the position he still has at this writing, though he is nearing retirement age.

Then there's Jimmy's relationship with his brother, Billy.

Jimmy always turns any comment about Billy into a joke. He simply refuses to criticize his younger brother. When people ask him about Billy's beer drinking, the President says, "Billy's doing his

179

share for the economy. He is helping to put the beer industry back on its feet."

And if they hint that it is a little shocking for Billy to be charging for personal appearances, Jimmy will say something like, "I'm hoping to have enough money to afford him, maybe get him to put in an appearance for me."

It's not just Billy Beer that is making Billy rich. From what I heard, he turns down more chances to endorse products than he accepts.

No wonder Jimmy doesn't complain about his brother. Jimmy's a realist—would you complain about someone who had earned you $40,000 or $50,000 a year while you busied yourself with things more to your liking?

That was the situation between Jimmy and Billy. Billy slaved away at the warehouse, building up the business until it grossed about $2½ million dollars a year, and made it possible for Jimmy to have an outside income of around $50,000 even while Jimmy was governor. Jimmy feels he owes Billy a debt of gratitude that he can never fully repay.

That's why Billy can clown around, cash in on Jimmy's fame, or pretty much do what he wants and fly in the face of convention yet still not be scolded by Jimmy or even suffer a raised eyebrow.

I think that Billy's business sense, which is making him a richer man than the man in the White House, is finally coming in for a lot of new respect, though some of it is given grudgingly.

Though the brothers seem so very different, both are alike in a certain way. That is in being thick-skinned. Jimmy was able to take any amount of abuse and putdowns in his hard drive for the presidency. Nothing could stop him. Billy had the same tough hide in taking the ridicule and abuse of people who said he was making a fool of himself in his public appearances wearing outlandish costumes and doing outlandish things.

Billy would stand it because he was every bit as determined as Jimmy in achieving his own goals. What is Billy's goal? To earn enough money to assure a bright future for his six children.

He knows the public is fickle and he is taking advantage of his current popularity, which could peak and recede at any time.

Even if his popularity fades away—which I doubt will happen— Billy will be left with a lot of memories of life in the limelight. How many other people can say that when their baby son was born, they received a gift of a set of diapers monogrammed with dainty Pabst emblems, as Billy received from Shirley MacLaine, the movie star.

I was very amused to read an article on why Jimmy Carter had not made the 1977 Men's Best Dressed List as other recent presidents had. Jimmy was always loyal to his friend Lamar Plunkett, a former Georgia senator who owns a suit manufacturing company. He would buy his suits from Lamar.

I'm sure it is not Lamar's fault that, as the experts pointed out, Jimmy's shirt sleeves did not hang below the suit coat the exact distance approved by the arbiters of men's fashions.

When Jimmy gets dressed up I think he looks very nice and I have complimented him on how nice he looked in some new suit. I don't know where he is buying his suits now, but I wouldn't be surprised if he is still faithful to his friend—it would be typical of Jimmy.

I believe the fashion powers that be also complain about Jimmy's rumpled look. I would call it casual. I know that Cousin Hot is happiest when he is wearing corduroy pants or blue jeans and a corduroy jacket with open plaid shirt and his hiking boots. And I'm also sure that the only list he wants to be on is that of the ten best presidents or ten most faithful followers of the Lord.

That's the real Jimmy.

16 · ROSALYNN– THE UNKNOWN CARTER

Rosalynn is the unknown Carter. Everyone is so busy talking about the exuberant, colorful members of the family—Lillian, Jimmy, and Billy, not to mention religious healer Ruth and motorcyclist Gloria—that Rosalynn gets preempted.

Even little Amy, with her tree house and lemonade stand and her bringing of a book to a formal dinner, gets more attention than her more low-key mother.

But Rosalynn Carter is one of my favorite people—a person who exudes sweetness from within and a shyness that is sometimes mistaken for coldness. But around people she knows well, Rosalynn is far from shy.

She can handle any situation, but then if she is hurt, she will go off alone somewhere and cry. During the presidential campaign something said about her had hurt her very much and she came home to Plains and cried for three days. I never did find out exactly why but I wished the people who called her "the Iron Butterfly" and also "the Steel Magnolia" could see her then.

I have never known anybody to work more strenuously at projects for self-improvement than Rosalynn. One of the first things she did, in order to keep up with Jimmy, was to read *War and Peace*, because Jimmy was always referring to it. Then she memorized a lot of Shakespearean passages because Jimmy had done the same and they would walk along hand in hand, quoting passages at each other and mulling over the meaning.

Early in their marriage, Rosalynn took a course on the great books. And when she was through that, she took a course on art appreciation. It's a family story that Rosalynn had a taste of real art. Jimmy was stuck with an art lesson kit inherited from a fellow officer in the Navy.

Since Jimmy was far too busy to fool around with it, Rosalynn decided she would study art and she actually completed one painting. It was a still-life with a very unusual arrangement of a tomato, a teapot, a stick of celery, and a hazy background.

That was the end of her art self-taught, but the beginning of her deeper appreciation of paintings she saw in galleries and of the subtle techniques employed by polished artists.

When Rosalynn studied Spanish, following Jimmy's lead, she did it wholeheartedly, using tapes to get the proper pronunciation and she got Jimmy to go to Mexico on vacation so that she could practice and enjoy her new talent.

Almost everyone knows that Jimmy took another speed-reading course in the White House to help him keep up with the mountain of reading he wanted to do. But Rosalynn, too, took a speed-reading course.

Also, as many people know, Rosalynn took a course in bookkeeping and worked long hours in the peanut warehouse office taking care of the books. In fact, her little boys would go right to the warehouse after school, because that was where their mother was.

Even when relaxing and listening to music, Rosalynn made a self-improvement task out of it. She studied operas by listening to them on records, and also symphonies. She and Jimmy would sit contentedly listening to Rachmaninov, their favorite.

The same went for dancing. Rosalynn, who was an excellent dancer to begin with, talked Jimmy into taking professional lessons in ballroom dancing, jitterbugging, and most particularly, square dancing, which became their favorite.

I was very amused to learn that because of the presidential couple's interest in good music and ballet and attendance at the Kennedy Center at least once a month, Jimmy is known as the "First Culture Freak President."

Not only do Jimmy and Rosalynn attend the theater, for the more highly cultural performances, but they strive to give their own guests more cultural entertainment mixed in with homespun things such as the Georgia Cloggers.

The high spot for Rosalynn was when Leonard Bernstein asked her to perform as narrator Aaron Copland's *A Lincoln Portrait*. Rosalynn's performance at Constitution Hall went off without an error, to the proud appreciation of Jimmy.

Maybe because of the undercurrent of disapproval of Miz Lillian, or maybe because it was just her way, Rosalynn tried to be the most perfect wife and housekeeper in the world and was never completely satisfied with anything.

She had a great interest in interior decorating and her house was always immaculate and litter-free and the furniture carefully placed. She was just as precise about her own appearance and wore very conservative clothes. In fact, the press took her to task for being too severe in her plain suits and blouses.

She always looked good to me, very soft and pretty, but somewhere along the line, she suddenly looked much more rested, and the years of hard work were erased from her face by plastic surgery.

Jody Powell, the President's press secretary, admitted that Rosalynn had had what was called a blepharoplasty, which was a little operation around the eyes to remove any puffiness or sagging in the lids.

It was just one more thing that Rosalynn did in her eternal quest for self-improvement, like studying Spanish or violin.

Or going to cooking school. As the governor's wife, she took the time to study gourmet cooking.

But she also worked at things which weren't so pleasant. For example, as the governor's wife, she worked at a mental institution to learn firsthand the emotional problems of the patients. It was the Georgia Regional Hospital and she was, of course, an unpaid volunteer. This gave her the background to serve on the Governor's Commission to Improve Services for the Mentally and Emotionally Handicapped.

Rosalynn's life had not been easy.

If there is anyone who is a hero or heroine in the Carter family, I would choose Rosalynn. She had done the most adventurous campaigning, been the most self-effacing and modest, and taken the most abuse from her mother-in-law, Miz Lillian.

For her handling of Miz Lillian alone, she deserves a medal. For her modesty, she deserves another medal because I am not sure that without her Jimmy could have won. Yet I have never heard Miz Lillian acknowledge her daughter-in-law's true part in the campaign.

The general public does not know that it was gentle Rosalynn who went into neighborhoods seeking the black vote. And the vote of the underprivileged. She walked unafraid because she felt in her heart that God was protecting her because Jimmy had a mission to perform as President. She really felt part of a divine plan.

She went about accompanied only by another female much of the time. And I'm sure that it was the sweetness and purity of her expression that was her greatest protection. It would take some kind of a monster not to have appreciated her visits to some neighborhoods.

In spite of Miz Lillian's high-handed manner with her daughter-in-law, I have never heard Rosalynn say one mean thing about her mother-in-law or complain in public. In that way, she is exactly like her own mother, Allie Smith, who has never been heard to say anything disparaging about anyone.

Even when her son, Murray, Rosalynn's brother, was getting a divorce, she said not one bad word about Frances, his wife. In fact, Frances continued to come to Allie's house as if nothing had happened. She would go there for dinner. She would call her ex-mother-in-law to get her advice on anything, just as before, and Frances continued to call her "Mother."

That was the kind of loving person that Allie was and is. And that's the example that Rosalynn learned from.

However, there has always been a slightly tense situation when the two women who must share Jimmy come together.

I was especially interested when I read that something of the same situation existed in the White House and even before the White House in the life of President Franklin Delano Roosevelt. He, too, had a mother who could not bow out gracefully, but wanted to be a part of his public and private life.

Mrs. Delano Roosevelt moved into the White House and was finally told by First Lady Eleanor that *she*, not Mother Delano, was the First Lady.

According to the story that circulated around our family, Rosalynn and her mother-in-law had their showdown at the Governor's Mansion back in 1971. When Jimmy and Rosalynn were moving into the beautiful and spacious governor's home Miz Lillian simply went along, too, and cheerfully announced that she would be the Acting First Lady because Rosalynn wasn't sophisticated or knowledgeable enough to handle it.

To Rosalynn's credit, she did not cry and carry on or make Jimmy do her fighting for her. She waited until they both were in the kitchen out of Jimmy's earshot and with voice that was as steady as she could muster, she told her mother-in-law that she fully intended to run her own household but that Miz Lillian could always "come and visit."

She even dared to tell her that it would be better if she packed and left and came back when things were in better order.

Miz Lillian was stunned but she did pack her bags and leave. And Rosalynn became a marvelous hostess and homemaker, even branching out in projects outside the home.

185

The family feud between Rosalynn and Lillian extends also to Rosalynn's mother, Allie, and her brother, Jerry. It was the talk of the town when Miz Lillian embarrassed Allie Smith in public by refusing to sign an autograph card during the presidential campaign because Miss Allie had signed it first.

Miz Lillian does not do things quietly and her shriek that she was not going to autograph anything that Miss Allie had autographed came as a shocking blow. But Miss Allie should not have taken it too badly because Aunt Lillian did the same with other members of the family, including me. She refused to sign mementos I had already autographed. I just laughed.

The day that the shocking incident happened, a potential voter—a tourist—had gotten Allie Smith's autograph first and then handed the card to Miz Lillian. Miz Lillian had voiced her rancor and tossed the card back at the chagrined autograph seeker.

"There's only one person's name that I'll sign mine under, and that is Jimmy Carter," she said with finality.

Miz Lillian's slight haughtiness toward her daughter-in-law has had a psychological effect on Rosalynn.

Rosalynn could never feel completely at home with her mother-in-law. She always felt somehow on probation, as if she were being judged worthy or unworthy of the privilege of being a member of Miz Lillian's family.

Because of this, I think, Rosalynn worked much harder than any young wife could be expected to, to be *perfect*. And because it was almost a relationship of judge and humble serf, Rosalynn never felt close enough to her mother-in-law to ever call her anything but Miss Lillian.

I have never heard Rosalynn call her mother-in-law anything but that— "Miss Lillian." Maybe things have changed in the White House, but if so, I don't know it.

My own observation is that the two women—Rosalynn and Lillian—have learned to cope with each other and to accept each other more now than ever before. Because each one has become a star in her own right, neither one needs to work so desperately to be a star with Jimmy.

Aunt Lillian is still the dominating force in almost any company but this has made her, in her new status, a kind of folk hero and beloved curmudgeon.

Rosalynn, on the other hand, has become more relaxed and tactful and sure of herself as the world-traveled and much honored representative of the President.

Still, old habits die hard and Rosalynn is working as hard at self-improvement, even today at the White House, as she did back in Plains, and Atlanta—speed reading, violin, etc.

Rosalynn has added one more beauty aid to her self-improvement list. She now uses contact lenses. They were fitted by a specialist from Savannah, Georgia. She is considering getting contact lenses for Amy so that Amy will not feel different from other children.

Self-improvement is so catchy around Rosalynn that even Amy's nurse, Mary Fitzpatrick, has caught the bug. From what I hear, she is studying piano with the help of Jeff's wife, Annette.

Miz Lillian and her daughter-in-law have always been different in attitudes—take the matter of money.

Rosalynn has always been very thrifty, buying her dresses when she couldn't make them, but paying only a modest amount. Miz Lillian liked to show that she bought expensive clothes and during the campaign announced that she had just paid three hundred dollars for one of her dresses.

During the campaign, when Rosalynn had to spend a lot of time away from Amy, Lillian wanted to take care of Amy. But Lillian seemed to have a deaf ear to any instructions Rosalynn would give her; for example, when she would leave little Amy in the care of Grandmother Lillian, she would ask her to please watch Amy's diet and not to let her eat sweets.

Rosalynn would throw up her hands in horror when she would return and find all kinds of cakes and candies and other sweets stacked in the refrigerator, where Amy could help herself between meals.

So concerned is Rosalynn that Amy eat only fruits and nuts and coconut in place of candy that she invented a fruit candy she makes for Amy of ground dried fruits, nuts, and coconut or sesame seeds.

As the governor's wife, Rosalynn threw herself into projects where she felt she could be of help as the ears and eyes of the governor—particularly mental health and the education of retarded children. She also became very concerned at the neglect of senior citizens and made her own survey of homes for the aged.

At the White House, Rosalynn is almost as much a workaholic as her husband. She gets up at 7:00 A.M., gets Amy off to school, just as if they were still in Plains, and then shows up at her White House office with a briefcase full of work at 9:00 A.M. Then in the afternoon, she takes a briefcase packed with work up to the White House living quarters to study after dinner when Jimmy returns to the Oval Office.

Rosalynn is really striving for ways to help the elderly and the mentally handicapped. One thing that I know she has suggested to Jimmy is a toll-free information center to assist the aged. Senior citizens could simply pick up their phones and get help or answers to their important questions.

Having seen how busy Rosalynn had been with worthwhile projects as the wife of the governor, I wondered what she'd do as First Lady. I didn't have long to wait. Almost as soon as she was settled in she started studying the problems of aging on a national level.

She toured nursing homes, attended a meeting of twenty-three representatives of organizations that deal with the aged, and took notes on their suggestions.

As a special treat for the elderly she entertained two thousand senior citizens at the White House. It's hard to know yet how much influence Rosalynn will have in making a better life for our older population. One thing she pushed for was legislation to abolish mandatory retirement.

Two things I know influenced her. One was how sad her mother was to be forced to retire from the post office at the mandatory age of seventy. The other was seeing how well my daddy functioned as an eighty-nine-year-old salesman in my store.

Another project that Rosalynn wants to tackle is the treatment of the mentally ill. She has told me that she feels many people who are in institutions could be out doing useful jobs in the community. Not only would it save taxpayers' money, she says, but would help the patients gain their self-respect, since there is still a stigma attached to such institutions.

The gal who was once so shy that she would hide out behind the house rather than meet people she didn't want to see has grown into a very poised First Lady who oversees a staff of nineteen people.

Rosalynn is the kind of First Lady material that Eleanor Roosevelt was, daring to go into dangerous areas as the President's "eyes and ears." Eleanor went into coal mines to see conditions under the ground. Rosalynn did not go into mines, but she did rush to flood areas at Toccoa, Georgia, where a dam had burst to see the devastation and report her findings to President Jimmy.

A few days before the flood, Rosalynn had made a speech to the

National Association of Retarded Citizens and called for a concerted effort to get more retarded people into meaningful jobs and normal jobs rather than stashing them in institutions.

Rosalynn talked about a scientific study which indicates that there would only be half the number of mentally retarded persons if parents took proper care of children before and after birth and followed certain health rules.

It touched my heart and made me want to get involved in Rosalynn's program.

I don't know how long Senator Herman Talmadge plans to stay in office but when he does step down, I would say Rosalynn Carter could become one of the most formidable candidates. United States Senator Rosalynn Carter from Plains, Georgia.

Rosalynn may look dainty and feminine—and she is—but she is also one of the most driving, ambitious women I have known and one of the most intelligent.

Almost everything Jimmy knows Rosalynn knows because he has always used her as a sounding board and she has always given him her true opinion. She knows how to be a professional politician and, more than her husband, realizes that politics is the art of compromise.

She knows that political positions are not anchored in concrete and that flexibility is the name of the game. She has had a master teacher in her husband. At the same time, she has had a great part in teaching him. They make a formidable team.

I have seen them disagree but unless one observed closely, no one will ever know it. They get off alone and work it out and come up with a single solution.

I have often heard Jimmy brag about how well Rosalynn can speak and how she can recruit volunteers. She is easy to talk to and can communicate well with the voters. Many of them would tell her things that they would not say to Jimmy.

But the best story is how Jimmy reacted the first time he heard Rosalynn stumping for him during the presidential campaign. She had worked out her own speech and had been giving it by herself for six weeks while each traveled in a different direction. But finally, they were going to share the platform in Trenton, New Jersey.

Jimmy had no idea of what she was going to say and he was not paying too good attention to her as she started because he had other things on his mind—like what *he* was going to say—but suddenly her words were getting to him.

He found himself reacting emotionally as he heard her give a touching account of how they had "scrimped and saved to make the peanut business a success. I worked, the children worked, I kept the books, we worked hard."

Then having softened him and the audience up, Rosalynn launched into what Jimmy had done and tried to do and fought to do as a governor. How he'd abolished several hundred agencies to save money and how he had instituted economies even in the matter of the telephones that had saved the taxpayers almost $800,000 on the telephone bills alone.

And then finally, Rosalynn said the thing that brought tears to his eyes: "There has never been any hint of scandal in Jimmy's business life and Jimmy has never had any hint of scandal in his personal life."

Jimmy went to her side, grabbed her and kissed her, and with tears still in his eyes called to the audience, "How many of you would like to have this woman as First Lady?"

The crowd clapped, roared, and stamped its approval, and Jimmy, with his arm around Rosalynn, shouted, "I agree with you."

The world had a little laugh when Jimmy made a tactical blunder by telling a *Playboy* magazine reporter that he had "lusted for other women." The public did not know how misleading this statement was or how hurt Rosalynn was by it.

She acted very calm and unconcerned but it had been a painful thing for her. I believe Jimmy had not meant that he wanted other women but merely that he was not a holier-than-thou kind of person pretending that he had never looked at another woman and found her attractive. My analysis was that Jimmy had wanted to sound like a "regular" guy and not a saintly or holier-than-thou type.

But actually, the truth is that Jimmy and Rosalynn are one of the greatest love stories that I know. To see them together is an inspiration because even when they had been married thirty years, they were still acting like a couple of kids, touching knees when they sat together at a party in our house or elsewhere, and holding hands as they walked.

Jimmy has told me now and then how wonderful it is to be in love and not to need anyone else. In fact, he and I have both felt ourselves lucky in having found partners right in our own hometown, who have been able to make us love them more as the years go by.

Jimmy's greatest hope for Amy is that she can grow up to be like her mother.

Fashion writers threw a fit when Rosalynn announced that she planned to wear the same gown to the 1977 inauguration in Washington, D.C., that she had worn in 1970 when Jimmy was elected governor. She was doing it for sentimental reasons, she said.

Some industry leaders appealed to President-elect Jimmy to tell his wife that she would ruin the women's apparel business if she did not buy a new gown or have one made for her. Rosalynn didn't say she would change her mind and she didn't say she wouldn't.

I had seen the gown that night in Atlanta in January 1971. I was master of ceremonies at the ball held at the Marriott Hotel. We had several balls that night around Atlanta, though the Marriott one was the biggest.

Jimmy and Rosalynn made the rounds and attended all the balls.

I was in Washington for the 1977 inaugural ball but this time just as a proud relative, and when Jimmy entered the ballroom proudly leading Rosalynn by the hand I applauded loudly, partly for the fact it was the presidency at last, and partly because Rosalynn had done it! She had stuck to her guns and worn her six-year-old blue gown.

She looked truly beautiful and as my wife, Ruth, remarked to me, when that gown is placed in the Smithsonian, along with other First Lady gowns, Georgia will be twice honored.

In Washington, she sought and accepted advice from Margot Hahn on how to dress as First Lady.

Behind the scenes at the White House, Rosalynn still dresses in slacks the way she used to in Plains. In fact, she is apt to wear slacks when she occasionally has a working lunch with the President in his Oval Office.

The newspapers have made a big thing of the fact that the First Lady has serious conversations with the President in his private office, just like any official visitor. People wonder what they talk about.

According to what Rosalynn said, she organizes her material for her talks, just as if he were with a stranger. She may argue in favor of some program that interests her, such as hiring more women to high positions.

Once the briefcase notes were about the feasibility of installing a solar heat system at the White House as an expense reduction and as a model for the nation. Another time, she recalled, she brought her arguments for creating a separate Department of Education, taking educational problems out of HEW.

Rosalynn's best friend is Edna Langford, her son Jack's mother-in-law. They became acquainted in 1966 when Edna Langford, whose husband is a fine Georgia politician, supported Cousin Jimmy in his race for the governorship. The women are so alike that they even wear the same kind of scarves and same style clothing.

Edna Langford has traveled with Rosalynn to Mexico and other places. I think their friendship helped the Jack and Judy romance. In fact, some people were surprised when the couple married in 1971 because the youngsters didn't always seem to get along too well.

Gradually, they got used to each other and from all I hear, have a fine marriage with each maintaining many interests inside and outside the home.

Judy is quite interested in ERA and spoke at the Houston International Women's Year Conference in November of 1977. Unfortunately, nobody was paying attention to the convention because that was the very time the Egyptian President, Sadat, made his historic visit to Israel in the interest of peace.

Next to Edna, the wives of the Carter sons are Rosalynn's best friends.

What kind of mother-in-law does Rosalynn make? I would say a very loving one. There is one family story that shows it clearly.

Jack's wife had a miscarriage and was not in too good health for a time. Jack was moving Judy into a house from their college apartment. Even though she was First Lady of the State, Rosalynn helped Jack get the house in order, washed whatever needed washing, and even painted the closets.

Jimmy and Rosalynn were heartsick when Chip Carter and his wife, Caron, were not getting along as husband and wife. It was a drama played out in public. But the First Family has come through other worrisome experiences with their sons, and it has not diminished the close-knit family ties.

Their firstborn son, Jack, was discharged from the Navy for smoking marijuana and given a "general discharge." This is a discharge which is less than an honorable one.

Today, Jack and his wife lead a happy well-adjusted life and Jimmy is proud that Jack is striking out on his own as a soybean warehouse man in Calhoun, Georgia. When Jimmy became President, son Jack had been a lawyer in Calhoun and was the only Carter offspring who did not go to live at the White House, because he was determined to show his independence.

Chip Carter was the son I got to know best because he worked in his daddy's office when Jimmy was governor. Just as in the early days of Jimmy's presidency, Chip worked without pay in his father's office, when he wasn't working at the National Democratic Headquarters—his eight-thousand-dollar-a-year job.

Not only that but Chip, for a time after the governorship, was the only son living in Plains. He lived in a mobile home right on Main Street near the depot. There were several mobile homes there and we would always give directions to Chip's house by saying it was the third mobile home from the post office.

It might not have been grand, but at least it was paid for and Caron did a good job of making it as much like a house as possible. Caron and Chip would even relax outside on lounge chairs as if they were on their own private patio.

Chip seemed to like his relaxed mobile home life so much that Caron would tease him by saying that if they ever got a divorce, he could have custody of the mobile home and she'd take the dog.

When they were contemplating splitting up, I remembered her joke and thought of the old saying that "a joke is a half-truth."

My feeling is that Chip Carter has never stretched himself to fulfill his great potential. His daddy expected great things of him because he once got the highest score on the national scholastic achievement test, I believe, when he was in high school.

However, he did not apply himself to his studies at Georgia Southwestern and dropped out after his first year. He did try again another year but again dropped out. Perhaps he was trying to do too much at one time because, according to Caron, he had what amounted to a double major—political science and history.

Caron and Chip met when she was working in the governor's office. He had been dating many girls who were more sophisticated than she and she paid no attention to him. Caron maintains that this was the reason Chip finally tried to date her—because she had been aloof.

She has said she didn't want him to think she was just impressed because he was the son of an important man. As a gal with a master's degree in education, she was a much more serious girl than the others he had been dating.

But after his first date with Caron, Chip seemed to have turned a corner and he never dated another girl.

Chip may be the Carter who follows in his father's footsteps yet. Now and then, he has hinted that he might want to run for office one day and wants to be in Georgia for that reason.

I think Jeff is the shiest of the Carter kids. I'm told that on the campus at George Washington University, he looks like any other kid in blue jeans and the young Secret Service men assigned to him wear blue jeans, too, to fade into the crowd.

It was amusing that no reporters followed Jeff his first day at the new college though a crowd of them followed Amy, who was starting school in Washington on the same day. That was the way Jeff wanted it. He just slipped away from the White House and went to school. He told me his major interest is studying about food supply and environmental problems.

Though Jeff is the youngest of the Carter sons—twenty-four at this writing— he seems to be the most relaxed and trouble-free.

17 · MIZ LILLIAN– HAVE SARI, WILL TRAVEL

Aunt Lillian is not shy. When she was in Ireland she told the press, "Jimmy has my brains." She again refused to acknowledge that Jimmy might even have an edge on Billy and insisted that Jimmy and Billy "are equally smart."

I think she came a little closer to the truth when she said, "Billy has my outlook on life," since they are the two most colorful and outspoken members of the Carter family.

I once read an article in which several psychiatrists tried to explain why Billy and Miz Lillian have such powerful appeal to the public. All the psychiatrists agree that it was more than just their relationship with a President of the United States that made them a smash hit wherever they appeared.

In the case of Billy, the appeal was his image as a country boy who outsmarts the city slicker. In the case of Miz Lillian, it was admiration for her stubborn independence and her gutsiness in becoming a Peace Corps nurse in India at the advanced age of sixty-eight. She symbolized the American Dream that life begins at forty, or sixty, or whenever one is ready to embrace a new career.

Reporters didn't know what to make of Miz Lillian during the opening of the campaign, because she wasn't at all your average sweet little candidate's mother saying all the nice things she can think of about her boy.

The family was used to her tendency to downgrade, but even so, I still cringed a little for Cousin Jimmy when Aunt Lillian kept insisting that Jimmy was nothing special. As she told some reporters, Jimmy was "just a little redheaded, freckle-faced boy who lived in the country. There was nothing outstanding about Jimmy at all. He made good grades, but so did the rest of my children. There was nothing special about Jimmy."

I thought to myself that Miz Lillian hadn't really known her little boy after all.

When she was asked if Jimmy had ever gotten into trouble when he was a little boy, instead of saying she was so glad he hadn't, she said, "No, and I wish he had because it's so unfair to the other children."

There is much Aunt Lillian seems to have forgotten.

I'm sure the country wasn't ready for someone as outspoken as Aunt Lillian, but after they got over the shock of it, I think they were happy to hear her say things that proved their own family was pretty normal after all.

There was just nothing she wouldn't say, if she felt it at that moment. About her daughter Ruth, she said, "She's not a very good mother."

About Billy, she said that he drinks too much beer but "if he ever tried to change, he'd be the biggest mess in the world."

She even admitted that Billy, not Jimmy, was her favorite, putting the blame on the fact that "I think Billy needs my love more."

I really don't know what religious denomination Aunt Lillian will end up with. Though she goes to the Baptist Church now and then—though not our new Maranatha Church—she has said, "Being a Baptist doesn't mean too much to me."

I think if she lived closer to Ruth, she would just go to church with Ruth, wherever she went.

Aunt Lillian takes a delight in flaunting the fact that she drinks a bourbon highball or two just about every evening. Other ladies in a church town like Plains would hide it, but Miz Lillian wants the ladies to know that she will smoke and she will drink if she wants to, and she does want to.

She freely says that the secret of her energy and long life is, "I live right—and don't forget that little shot of bourbon." She says, "I'm a bourbon woman."

For contemporary history buffs and White House watchers, it might be interesting to note that Aunt Lillian's favorite brand is Jim Beam—and that is what Jody Powell would pick up for her by the half-pint during the campaign.

Aunt Lillian tells a story about her trip to Ireland. She had gotten thirsty and asked a couple, in Dublin, if she could have a drink. She assumed that they were handing her water. She took a good big gulp and it turned out to be brandy, burning its way down her throat.

Jimmy and I are not the first politicians in the Carter family. Jimmy's maternal grandfather, James Jackson Gordy, Aunt Lillian's father, was a man we both remembered for his colorful politicking.

We knew him as Grandpa Jim-Jack, which he was called around Plains, but around the State Capitol in Atlanta, he was called Uncle Jack. Jim-Jack was as unusual and quaint as Miz Lillian is. And make no mistake about it, Aunt Lillian is every bit the politician her son and father were when she wants to be.

My dad, who was a Lillian-watcher for a long time, always commented, "She is probably the hottest politician of them all."

Aunt Lillian's daddy was born in 1863 at the time of the Civil War, and he spent most of his waking hours hanging around politicians. It paid off in that he was made postmaster of Richland, Georgia, for being the only Democratic friend the party could count on in the area.

He also held other appointive jobs—for example, federal "revenooer" in Prohibition days—but he never put himself in jeopardy by running for an elective office.

Whenever the State Legislature was in session, Jim-Jack was not to be found around Plains or Richland. He would go to Atlanta and stay in a rooming house, spending all his time hobnobbing and doing favors and errands for the men of power. "If it was anything to do with politics, he was in hog heaven," said my daddy.

His top hero was Tom Watson, who ran for President of the United States two times on the Populist Ticket. Grandpa Jim-Jack even named the youngest of Jimmy's maternal uncles Tom Watson Gordy and informed Watson of this honor.

Watson wrote Jimmy's Grandpa Jim-Jack a note saying that he appreciated the honor but he hoped "that the infant who will bear my name through life will find the road onward and upward less rocky than it has been to his namesake."

Jim-Jack did not even make a splash in history for the contribution he probably deserves credit for—the modernization of mail to farmers, "rural free delivery."

Just about everyone close to Lillian has been scarred a little by her branding-iron tongue. Knowing how hard Cousin Jimmy works to appease his mother and keep her happy, I felt badly myself when she said right out on several occasions, statements like "Billy is my favorite" or "Billy is the child I love best."

Yet Billy has put her down in public saying, "The only time she talks to me is when she needs something."

It's the kind of thing Jimmy would never say in a million years.

She shook the press by commenting bluntly, "You people have even less to do than the Secret Service." The hardworking Secret Service men who are forever risking their lives were not too pleased with that statement either.

Every time I clash with Aunt Lillian I regret it and determine that I'll never lose my temper again with her. Unfortunately, since we are both hardheaded—as all members of our family are—it's hard to keep this resolution.

During the presidential campaign it was hard not to snap at Aunt Lillian's bait when she was being particularly high-handed or needling me. I remember one night when all of us were guests for dinner at my brother-in-law's house about a mile south of Plains.

Pete Godwin, my wife's brother, and his wife, Dot, were entertaining both the presidential and vice-presidential candidates. In fact, a friend from New York, Bernie Wilson, an attorney, had flown the lobsters we were having down from New York. The guests were, besides Jimmy and Rosalynn, Walter Mondale, Aunt Lillian, Ruth, my wife, and me and, of course, Bernie Wilson.

When Aunt Lillian walked in, she looked at me and said sharply, as her opening gambit, "Hugh Carter, you are getting rich off Jimmy."

She was referring, of course, to my antique store in town where I had added Jimmy Carter and Plains souvenirs, as had all the other shops on Main Street, no matter what their basic business was.

I knew I should just laugh off this remark and say nothing, but she had struck a raw nerve because she had actually been helping one of my competitors with their souvenir business.

"I am not making any more than Maxine and Buford Reese," I said. "What about them?"

Aunt Lillian for weeks had been visiting their Campaign Headquarters Depot Souvenir Shop every afternoon and greeting tourists and signing autographs for them—something she had never done for me. I had never said a word about it and I had been told that the profits of this business above expenses were going to be used for civic improvements. I was not objecting in any way but I didn't think Miz Lillian had any more right to accuse me of moneymaking than any other merchant in town who was just running his business.

It was a trivial thing and I was almost ready to change the subject to something more pleasant when she snapped, "I don't want to ever speak to you again." Stung again, I bounced right back with, "If that's the way you feel, I don't want to speak to you again, either."

Well, the damage had been done. I was ready to forgive and forget but obviously she wasn't. Aunt Lillian didn't speak to me anymore that night or for several weeks following. She always turned her head or avoided me entirely.

She finally did speak to me on one or two occasions when there were others around and it couldn't be avoided. But it was a reserved, cool hello.

The most obvious and disappointing occasion when she didn't speak to me was when she stood in the receiving line with the President at the White House when the Peanut Brigade Reception was being held on Friday after the inauguration.

After shaking hands with the President and Rosalynn, she saw me and my wife in the line and turned on her heel and left the line to avoid speaking to me. My wife was aware of this snub, too, and I later explained to my son, Hugh, Jr., how it hurt to have her ignore me this way at the White House, expecially over so trivial a matter.

Sometime before the inauguration when I was talking with Jimmy and Rosalynn about another matter, and we were all sitting in their living room in Plains, I told them about the incident at my brother-in-law's house and how sorry I was that it had happened.

Jimmy and Rosalynn told me to forget it. Jimmy said he would talk to his mother and straighten out the matter. I guess he forgot it because even now at the White House, when both of us were there united in our love of the man who had meant so much to us for so many years—Jimmy Carter—she still had time to think of petty things.

Wanting to put an end to the animosity that continued through the spring in Plains, I wrote her a letter on June 8, 1977, and apologized for the incident which had occurred so long ago. I did not receive an answer.

I also discussed the incident with Maxine Reese, who had always been a good friend, and told her everything that was said that night at my brother-in-law's house and what had been in my mind.

Maxine said that I should have just laughed it off when Aunt Lillian made her first remark.

Not wanting to have anything but the friendliest relationship with the mother of my boyhood buddy, I even invited Aunt Lillian to go fishing in my pond, telling her we had been catching bluegill which weighed over a half pound. Much as Aunt Lillian enjoys fishing, she did not respond.

In November of 1977, my son, Hugh, Jr., was sent by the President to give a talk to the State Library Association meeting in Atlanta. I went to hear him and found Aunt Lillian was sitting on the platform with Sonny. I hoped we would have a friendly chat but she merely answered my greeting with a stiff hello and I knew it was hopeless.

When I got home to Plains, I told Daddy Alton about it and he said, "She hasn't spoken to me either for six months."

I said, "But why?"

He said, "It's just Lillian." Daddy just shrugged it off.

He was used to her giving him the cold shoulder for some trivial reason and then eventually getting over it.

In this case, she got over it when my father died; she attended his funeral, and spoke sympathetically to me several times at the house before the funeral. She asked me if it would be all right if she attended a previously scheduled event in Atlanta and I said it would be perfectly all right.

Looking back, Miz Lillian was a different person in the old days. When Ruth and I were getting married, Aunt Lillian filled in for my mother, who had died while I was in college. She entertained, giving the wedding rehearsal dinner at the Pond House. It was a beautiful dinner party.

She and Uncle Earl invited us to many parties and fishing trips during our early married life, and even though they were older, we always had a good time with them.

Uncle Earl died soon after our third child, Connie, was born—she never really knew him. I remember he came to see her one Sunday afternoon when she was a tiny baby and he was getting ready to leave for his term in the Legislature.

My older children loved him. He was a very lovable man and children took to him, even though he was a taskmaster with his own son Jimmy.

To show how close we used to be, I remember one time soon after I came home from the Army in 1946, Aunt Lillian, Uncle Earl, and my wife and I went as a group to Orange Lake, Florida, on a fishing trip. We spent two nights in a fishing camp and had a wonderful time.

I can remember our catching big bluegills and bream about as big as your two hands and weighing over a pound each.

I remember, too, that the ladies were a little disturbed by the water snakes that kept swimming toward the boat while we fished. Uncle Earl and I would have to swing at them with paddles to keep them from crawling into the boat. But in spite of the snakes, we brought home a lot of fish.

Jimmy Carter owes his very life to the fact that a schoolteacher named Maggie Jenkins left town. That was the girl whom Uncle Earl—Jimmy's father—was supposed to marry, and according to my daddy, Earl's brother, the whole town thought they were going to.

For some reason, Miss Jenkins decided to teach for a while at a college in Milledgeville about the year 1921. That romance quickly cooled when Uncle Earl started dating Aunt Lillian. Or to use her complete maiden name, Bessie Lillian Gordy.

The night Hugh, Jr., was born, Jimmy's mother, Miz Lillian, was at the hospital with Ruth, assisting Dr. Bowman Wise. In the middle of the night I had called Aunt Lillian telling her of Ruth's condition and she had advised me to get Ruth to the hospital right away and she would follow soon after, which she did.

I will always be grateful to her for helping us during the birth of my only son.

Aunt Lillian is the real sports fan of the Carter family and gets much more excited over the World Series than she does about politics—other than Jimmy's winning. At that, maybe you can say she is equally as excited about Jimmy's coming to bat for the country as for the first batter in the World Series.

When a player left the New York Mets over a contract dispute, Aunt Lillian was furious and said scornfully, "Some players today don't have loyalty to anything except money."

In the World Series of 1977 she rooted for the Dodgers, as she has since 1947 when the Dodgers were the first major league to hire a black player—Jackie Robinson.

Her pet peeve in sports is ABC announcer Howard Cosell and she is always ranting about him. "I don't want him to die," she said once, "but I wish he'd have a sore throat and they'd take him off the air."

I think Lillian would have been very happy had her son become a great sports figure instead of President. Especially if he had become a wrestler. She is about the biggest wrestling fan I know.

However, if Miz Lillian does not want to do something, she simply refuses and does not worry about disappointing other people. One person who had been led to believe that Aunt Lillian would never turn her back on him was Harley Race, the world's champion wrestler. I believe he won the world title in February of 1977.

He came to Plains especially to see her and he telephoned her to say that he was there. He felt sure she would come uptown to meet him or invite him to her house. She did neither.

I guess Miz Lillian felt the campaign was over or just didn't feel like it or wasn't dressed or something and she simply told him on the telephone that she was happy to have a chance to talk to him but it would be impossible for her to see him.

I have never seen a fellow so disappointed as Harley Race was. He and his wife came into the antique store and talked to me and my dad for a long time. Harley had his world's champion belt with him. He had thought that he would be able to show his belt to his number one fan.

I looked everywhere trying to find some photographers or newsmen to write about his visit to Plains but could find no one. Any other day, photographers would have been all over the place just waiting for a good picture. I told him next time he planned a trip to Plains to let us know in advance and we would roll out the red carpet for him.

It was rather amusing, during the campaign, that Jimmy's mother would act disgusted because Jimmy was helping Rosalynn with housework, as if Rosalynn had forced him into it. Jimmy would explain that he was helping Rosalynn because he wanted to and because things needed doing but Miz Lillian would grump about how Jimmy had time for everything but his mother.

It was just competition between the two women, Jimmy knew, and he would always placate his mother and hug her and make her feel important, too. Aunt Lillian would pass the word around town that if she needed anything, she always knew who to go to—her son Billy.

It's ironic that Lillian should sometimes turn against Rosalynn because Rosalynn had been her daughter Ruth's best friend for years. The girls had stayed at each other's houses frequently. And more important than that, Miz Lillian had taken care of Rosalynn's father when he was dying of leukemia.

In fact, when Rosalynn's daddy died, Aunt Lillian took Rosalynn home with her so that she and Ruth could comfort her and Rosalynn had spent that night at the Carter home.

There can only be one Miz Lillian. I've never met anyone quite like her, and one will do for a family. She was considered the most flamboyant woman of the community doing what she wanted to do even if it was against the tide of public opinion.

The town laughed sometimes and sometimes got angry—and sometimes she lost friends.

I've had many tourists come in my store and tell me that Aunt Lillian would not autograph a book or card or picture or anything that

I or my daddy or Rosalynn's mother had already autographed.

This was back when she was coming down to the old depot every afternoon to autograph for an hour or so. I certainly autographed a lot of them that *she* had already signed. Tourists are always anxious to get the autograph of any of the Carter family—no matter who it is—and I am always glad to accommodate them. So was my daddy. We try to be nice to all visitors coming to Plains.

Don't get me wrong. I admire what Aunt Lillian did—going to India at the age of sixty-eight after volunteering for the Peace Corps, and ministering to the sick. And I think she was very courageous to have nursed and actually embraced leprosy patients. It was a fine Christian act, and one that I am not sure I would have had the faith that passeth all understanding, to put myself in that jeopardy.

But myths have arisen concerning Miz Lillian's India adventure. She was not known throughout India for her work, and visitors from India to this country after Jimmy became President were amazed to learn that the President's mother had ever been in India, let alone worked there.

Nor was Aunt Lillian all that enchanted with India, as one is led to believe now. In fact, her letters home were filled with complaints and she could hardly wait for her term to be over so she could get her transportation home.

She was like a soldier doing her duty but it was no love fest, as it is being turned into now.

There is one touching family Christmas story that involves Aunt Lillian. When she was in the Peace Corps in 1967, she could not bear to see all her lovely Christmas gifts which had arrived through the mail from her family—there was too much suffering all around her. She gave all her presents away to those who needed things more than she did.

I would say that was typical of Aunt Lillian. She could be extremely warmhearted when she saw the suffering of strangers.

When Aunt Lillian returned from the Peace Corps, all her children had a surprise for her. Spearheaded by Jimmy, they had gotten together and built a new Lake House to replace the one that had burned down. Now she had a place to fish whenever she wanted to, and a hammock to lie in beside the water to read to her heart's content.

She spends a lot of time alone at the Lake House when she is in Plains.

There are few pictures of Miz Lillian when she was young. The reason very few pictures exist of her is because she was always the family's photographer and she was always taking the pictures, rather than being taken.

However, she was a very attractive woman, although not beautiful. She wore her hair short with bangs coming down over about half of her forehead. Her hair was parted on one side. She used lipstick which showed her independence and modernity.

Lillian and Earl were engaged to be married when she was still in nurses' training. She says when she started going with Earl she wanted to forget about the nurses' training and get married. But Earl insisted that she finish what she had begun.

She went to Atlanta for six months to complete the course and when she came home to Plains, they were married three months later.

The first thing Earl purchased after they married was seven hundred acres of good farm land. He bought it on credit and I have been told it is the only thing he ever had to buy on credit. He soon paid for it completely.

Earl and Lillian Carter lived in various apartments in town. I can remember visiting with them in the Cook House, and also the house occupied now by Mr. and Mrs. Arthur Maggio, who have recently moved there from Florida. Earl and Lillian had the upstairs apartment in this house. I was only about three years old, Jimmy had not yet been born, but I can remember once spending a night with them there.

Like almost everyone in Plains of my generation, I have much to be grateful for to Aunt Lillian, whom the town calls Miz Lillian. And even though on and off she has become irritated and angry with me, I love her very much.

When I was very small, even before her firstborn, Jimmy, was born, I remember I used to visit with her and Uncle Earl and I will always cherish the attention that she gave me.

She loved my mother, Annie Laurie, her sister-in-law, very much, and was very kind and attentive to her when Mother was ill. I remember when my mother died in 1940, Aunt Lil was right there at her bedside looking after her in a professional way, as she was a registered nurse.

Miz Lillian also attended my wife, Ruth, when all my children were born—Hugh, Jr., Laurie Gay, and Connie.

I will always be grateful to her for the love and consideration she has shown the various members of my family throughout our lives.

Though she took care of the world, she herself came apart at the seams when she lost her husband. There seemed to be no one that she could lean on and I felt very sorry for Aunt Lillian back in 1953. In a way it seemed her life was over when her husband died. We did not know that great things still lay ahead for her.

Aunt Lillian had been born one of eight children about twenty miles west of Plains in 1898. Her daddy was the local character—most famous man in Richland, postmaster for thirty-two years under four presidents, and a regular around the Georgia State House when it was in session.

From "Uncle Jack," as he was called in political circles, Aunt Lillian learned to be very independent. After becoming a registered nurse, in 1923 she went to work for the Wise brothers, who ran the local hospital, the Plains Sanitarium.

It was in this hospital that she gave birth to her son Jimmy —James Earl Carter, Jr., who would become the thirty-ninth President of the United States.

Aunt Lillian actually worked for all three doctors who operated the Wise Sanitarium—Thad, Sam, and Bowman. Bowman was the youngest and it was his daughter Marguerite about whom Lillian had a fond dream that Jimmy would marry her. Bowman's widow still lives in Plains. Thad Wise, incidentally, lived in the same house that Jimmy and Rosalynn had, and died there.

Jimmy moved into that house sometime later—it was a mile from the farm on which Jimmy had grown up. Many outsiders think that the Wise brothers must have been Jewish, because Wise is a common Jewish name. But these doctors were Protestant.

Still another Wise family—P. J. Wise—produced a son Phil, who was of great importance in Jimmy's presidential campaign and deserves much credit for Jimmy's victory in the Florida primary. The Florida primary was the primary that made it obvious that Jimmy would be a serious presidential contender.

It is interesting that the most outspoken and independent female of our family bowed to the wishes of one man—her husband. She was twenty-five years old when they married in September of 1923. She may even have thought that she would have a career as nurse and never marry, when a kindly fate sent her exactly the right kind of husband.

Uncle Earl was tough and independent, too, and he could stand up to her. She leaned heavily on him even though she seemed not to.

He was always the boss and she knew it.

Now and then she exercised her independence by bringing blacks into the home. He humored her and did not forbid it. If he had forbidden her or his son Jimmy to invite blacks into the house, except in a boss and worker relationship, I'm sure Uncle Earl's will would have prevailed.

Uncle Earl and my daddy were both alike in being very strong personalities, and they always were the bosses of their respective families.

My Daddy Alton told me that Uncle Earl had Army service before getting married. He was drafted into the Army in 1916 and reported to Camp Wheeler in Macon, Georgia. Daddy remembers how handsome Uncle Earl looked when he came home on leave in his uniform.

He was headed for combat duty in Europe but World War I ended while he was at home and he never did have to go overseas.

Daddy was not drafted. He was called up for examination several times but because of all his dependents—a wife and baby (Donnel), a mother and sisters—he was not drafted.

After Uncle Earl died, Aunt Lillian was a lost soul. Very depressed. She tried to put on a good face and keep going but it was obvious that she could not stand Plains and all its memories. Still, we were amazed that she actually did leave Plains and became a house mother at the Kappa Alpha Fraternity at Auburn University, in Auburn, Alabama.

She had not only escaped the town, she had fled to another state. It was good for her to be surrounded by young men and I'm sure she was perfect for the job. She always related best to boys even when I was growing up.

Eventually, she needed a new challenge and she quit her job to come back to Georgia to supervise a nursing home at Blakely. The change of locale and people gave her time to heal from her terrible loss, and after two years at the nursing home, she herself decided to return to Plains.

Miz Lillian was never a stay-at-home. When she wasn't nursing someone or working at the Wise Sanitarium, she would be visiting with lady friends. Even though she couldn't sew—or refused to sew,

I'm not sure which—she was for many years a member of the Stitch and Chat Club, which still meets several times a month. But sometime after her son became President, Aunt Lillian simply quit the Stitch and Chatters.

Aunt Lillian and her son Billy are very much alike. They both speak their minds freely and sharply and let the chips fall where they may. Outsiders, such as tourists, are very amused and call it great humor but it doesn't always seem funny to people close to them.

As someone said about Aunt Lillian and Billy, "If they can't knock, they won't say anything."

I believe the trait of speaking bluntly and not bothering to be diplomatic is a Gordy trait and not a Carter trait. Though this trait has made Lillian many new friends around the country, in Plains her circle of friends has narrowed.

Sometimes it seems that Aunt Lillian wants to be the only person to share the limelight with her two sons.

There used to be a big poster at the depot Jimmy Carter headquarters with pictures of the two books written by her children—*Why Not the Best,* by Jimmy Carter, and *The Gift of Inner Healing,* by Ruth Carter Stapleton—and a sign proclaiming, "Miss Lillian Is Here 10 A.M. to 2 P.M.—Autograph Party. Miss Lillian Carter Will Be Here In Person To Autograph."

And she did sit for four hours to push the books of Jimmy and Ruth, which made great souvenir purchases from Plains.

After one of Aunt Lillian's old friends, Rudy Hayes, managing editor of the Americus *Times-Recorder,* collaborated with another journalist, Beth Tartan, to write a very complimentary book about Aunt Lillian, *Miss Lillian and Friends,* Miss Lillian was not pleased.

In fact, Rudy told me that Aunt Lillian had not spoken to him for months. I felt that this was very unfair because Rudy had been a good friend and had helped Jimmy in every way for years.

Miz Lillian absolutely refuses to do what is expected of her. When she was traveling in Ireland with her "Friendship Force" group, a cameraman was trying to get a good picture of her as she sat on the throne of King William of Orange, in Dublin Castle.

"Say cheese," he told her.

"Peanuts," she shot back tartly.

When she arrived at University College in Dublin, she was greeted by a leprechaun and a thousand stomping students who filled the auditorium with their chanting of "Good old Lilly!"

She commented to the students that she was disappointed because she heard they "always throw things at the university's guest speakers."

They responded by sailing paper airplanes in her direction as she spoke.

18 · BUCKSHOT BILLY

No commentary on Billy would be complete without his definition of a redneck. He says, "A good ole boy is a guy that rides around in a pickup truck and drinks beer and puts 'em in a litter bag. A redneck's a guy that rides around in a truck, drinks beer, and throws 'em out the window."

In Plains, Jimmy grew up hearing another definition of a redneck, however, contained in this story: A tourist came to town and a redneck told him, "I had to shoot my dog."

The northern tourist said, "Oh, that's too bad. Was he mad?"

The redneck replied, "Well, he weren't none too pleased."

There are many family stories about Billy's drinking. One that Billy himself enjoys telling concerns the time he had been drinking heavily at a friend's house prior to a fishing trip. As the evening ended and he prepared to leave, he picked up two cups from the table, one containing his bourbon and one containing the minnows he was taking with him on his fishing trip. In the night he got thirsty.

In the morning, when he woke up, the cup with his bourbon was still there but the cup with the minnows had been drained dry.

I wonder what history will have to say about Billy Carter— William Alton Carter III. The short-range view of him is that of a loose-talking, beer-drinking, hard-smoking, irreverent yokel. He likes to project this image, as it has made him almost as popular with the general public as his brother, the President.

But there's another Billy, too. I want to talk about Billy as a businessman—one of the most capable and smartest businessmen that I know, the man who skillfully built his family's peanut business into a multimillion-dollar operation.

Of course, he does not run the business now but this, too, is part of family history. I would say he could estimate a truckload of peanuts within three hundred pounds of what they actually weigh. You can't learn this from schoolbooks.

He also had the kind of personality that farmers could relate to, and I must say, he was much better at handling farmers than Jimmy was. Not that they didn't respect Jimmy, and even come to him for advice, but Billy had that sunny personality and cracked the kind of jokes they loved. Billy was more a part of the farmers he dealt with. Jimmy always seemed a little removed and on a loftier plane.

Billy had to spend an enormous amount of money to comply with the Environmental Protection Agency in regard to pollution resulting from his peanut-shelling operation.

I understand it cost about $1.2 million for warehouse improvements during the past few years largely involving a new peanut-shelling plant with facilities for additional storage.

I have been told that Jimmy designed the plant and Billy supervised the construction. I understand the shelling equipment cost about $800,000, 22 percent of which resulted from rulings by government agencies OSHA and EPA.

Federal inspectors kept dogging Billy's footsteps and he was constantly complaining about "too much government regulation and red tape."

For example, Billy said he had to spend $400 for guard rails for the top of a grain elevator that one man might have to inspect perhaps once a year. He felt that was $400 totally wasted.

Billy was also not happy at the prospect of higher minimum wages. He hired seventy-five men and women at peak season and claimed that if the minimum wage went up he would have to lay off people. Now the problem is no longer his. Until the business is sold, it's the problem of the trusteeship headed by Charles Kirbo.

Toward the end of his regime, Billy was complaining that it took his office workers nearly 15 percent of their time just to fill out required government forms.

Billy really understands his brother more than his brother knows and he has a sixth sense about things. Even while Cousin Jimmy was enjoying the "honeymoon" period in the White House, when 65 percent of the public was shouting its approval of his first hundred days, Billy was predicting within the family that Jimmy would not be an extremely popular President.

Billy said that Jimmy would be too concerned with getting things done to be popular. He would make enemies by not compromising. And Billy was so right.

Toward the end of his first year in office, a Harris poll showed that 57 percent of those polled were no longer sure Jimmy had the "basic competence for the job" of President and only 32 percent felt he was competent and handling things right.

Billy may pretend not to know what's going on in the political world, but he reads the papers pretty carefully. He just knows it is better not to get involved in his brother's business of running the country. So when reporters were pressing him on what he thought about the Panama Canal last fall, Billy said, "It's a good way to get from one ocean to another."

He simply refused to let anyone know whether he agreed with his brother's goal of turning the canal over to the Panamanians.

As I see it, the brothers seem to have a little agreement that they will not comment in public on the job the other is doing. This began back when Jimmy was constantly traveling to drum up support for his presidency, way before the primaries. At that stage, he was grateful to have a competent businessman like Billy handling the family warehouse.

In fact, Billy had increased the business so efficiently that it became a $5 million enterprise. Jimmy would go in to visit with Billy and talk, over a cup of coffee, but it was more a matter of Billy filling him in than Jimmy telling Billy what to do. Billy had outgrown his teacher and didn't need to be told. In fact, Billy was getting a little hot under the collar that his share of the family business was only about 15 percent—the rest being owned by Jimmy and Miz Lillian.

That is the inside story of why Billy split from the peanut business and went to work full-time being a businessman on his own and making personal appearances lined up by his Nashville, Tennessee, agent, a sharp young man named Tandy Rice.

And I believe this also explains why Jimmy has said nothing about Billy's branching out. To be able to criticize his younger brother, Jimmy would be on firmer ground if he and Aunt Lillian had made Billy an equal partner with them. Since this was not done, Billy's feeling was that he was free to make his own way.

When it looked like Billy's sale of beer on Billy Beer Day would top five thousand dollars, Billy heard a man saying, "Greed has taken over this town."

Billy called him on it, asking, "Who did you say has taken over?"

Billy was about to get mad when he realized he was the beneficiary. The man was looking him right in the eye and repeating the word, "Greed, that's who has taken over this town."

"Oh, greed," said Billy with a broad smile. "I know that guy. He's a good ole boy."

I am not the one who counts Billy's money but the word around Plains is that Billy made about a half million dollars in 1977 from his Nashville and presidential connections, which made him a great attraction at paid public appearances.

Billy says freely that he has no fear of Jimmy disapproving of anything he does. "It don't bother me if Jimmy's staff bitches a little," he says. " They don't tell me what to do and he don't tell me what to do."

And that's the way it's going to be.

Even his Amoco gas station, which is an eyesore, junked up and needing paint, has become a landmark for tourists who have waited in line for gas for up to thirty minutes just to be able to say that they bought gas at Billy's station.

Billy used to make fun of the fact his brother was governor, just the way he now makes fun of the fact that his brother is President. When reporters asked him what it was like to stay overnight at the Governor's Mansion, Billy said he didn't know. "I got lost," he said, "so I spent half the night talking to the security guard."

Billy always had a little contempt for Jimmy for not being a beer drinker like he was. And Billy said, "Since he's running for President, he drinks scotch and I've never trusted a scotch drinker."

The truth of the matter was that Jimmy was not much of a scotch drinker either. He just occasionally had one if everyone else was and he could nurse a drink for hours.

When Jimmy announced the appointment of Atlanta lawyer Griffin Bell as Attorney General at a press conference, he again tried to poke fun at Billy by saying that "since JFK had appointed his brother Attorney General, maybe I should give the nod to Billy."

Then he added that until Billy got his law degree, he would ask Bell "to serve until Billy can become qualified."

In his retort to Jimmy, Billy's reply was:

"Either Secretary of State or Secretary of Agriculture would do."

It was really a minor miracle that the press started to appreciate and become friends with Billy. Around Plains, Jimmy was apt to hold the press at arm's length and not be as relaxed and intimate with them as Billy was.

And, of course, the press couldn't go on a beer or bourbon toot with Jimmy the way they could with Billy.

Actually, some members of the Carter clan had been a little apprehensive about Billy—would he put the family in a bad light? Would he give the impression that the Carters were a bunch of rednecks? Billy's language was so quaintly ungrammatical and his clothes were so casual—he prided himself on wearing farmer's clothes—that they had reason to be concerned.

But a funny thing happened. The press was bored. There was nothing to do around Plains except wait for Jimmy and sit around talking or having a beer. Not only did Billy enjoy trying out his latest quips, and sarcasms, on the reporters, but he sold about the only beer in town, at his gas station.

The only other place that sold beer was a beer joint off Main Street. The press found themselves getting addicted to Billy's brand of humor as they sat around drinking his beer. Besides, they had the excuse, for their editors, that they were working on getting some inside dope on the candidate.

I must admit that they also cultivated me to pump as much information out of me as they could.

However, with my duties as state senator and those of running a store, I could not give them the amount of attention Billy could. Besides, being a state senator, I was not as lighthearted and felt the weight of state problems on my shoulders. It's good the press had both of us for balance.

I'll never forget the wild day in Plains when Billy launched his "Billy Beer," which is brewed by the Falls City Brewing Company of Louisville, Kentucky.

I was at the town council the night Billy got permission to hold the gala opening at Plains and no one put up any objection. Someone asked jovially, "You're going to give free samples, aren't you?"

Billy chuckled and allowed that he was. Even Jimmy's triumphant return as Democratic nominee was no competition to Billy Beer Day October 31, 1977. A huge yellow-and-brown striped balloon around a hundred feet tall hovered in the air.

A rock band from Macon, Georgia, Larry Hudson and the Stylists, sang a song entitled "Billy Beer," and there were games going on constantly in a "Peanut Olympics."

There were such competitions as peanut tossing, peanut relay races, shelling and eating contests, peanut guessing contests, and a lot more. I had thought that perhaps Miz Lillian would sit this out because of her expressed feeling against commercialization in Plains, but she not only showed up but wore a Billy Beer yellow T-shirt. She drew the line at drinking any. Always frank, she said she tried one of his beers and got diarrhea.

I think the thing that amused me the most, however, was that there was not an empty beer can on the ground afterward—souvenir hunters had scooped up every one.

It was ironic that though the celebration was in our town, Billy was no longer a citizen of Plains, because he had moved his family away near Buena Vista. Mayor Blanton fixed that by making Billy an honorary citizen of Plains. Billy hawks his beer everywhere.

Billy even appeared on a program paying tribute to Elizabeth Taylor, who was raising money for a hospital wing to be built by the Variety Clubs Children's Charities.

It was one time he was not charging for his appearance but he managed to do a little good public relations work for his beer company. Bob Hope told Elizabeth Taylor he had a surprise guest for her and in walked Billy Carter, to the delight of the audience.

Hope said to Billy, "What's the good word?"

Billy said, "Six-pack."

Bob Hope said, "Six-pack? But that's *two* words."

"Not if you drink them fast enough," retorted Billy, to the amusement of Elizabeth and all the guests.

Later, when Elizabeth was thanking all the guests for coming, she helped Billy's redneck image by saying, to the surprise of many, that she was pleased that she had seen Billy Carter and to find that he had two shoes on.

In Plains we cringe a little when we hear Billy being the butt of still another joke, and another, as when Redd Foxx said on his TV program, "There is a new Billy Carter doll out, you pop its top and it burps."

If it will help sell beer, Billy doesn't mind using even the Bert Lance affair for comedy.

In fact, Billy is getting to be a pretty good stand-up comic. In one exchange with Bob Hope, Billy said, "I just wrote a check for $400,000 to get into the beer business."

Hope said, "Do you have that kind of money in your checking account?"

"Oh no," said Billy. "I just have nineteen dollars."

"Well," said Hope, "you can't write out a check for four hundred thousand dollars with only nineteen dollars in your bank account."

Billy said with a little smile, "You can in Georgia."

Billy's emphasis on beer has made beer a general subject of humor in Plains. In fact, there is even a Bert Lance beer joke: Bert Lance is putting out a beer. It's called overdraft.

About the silliest costume I ever saw on Billy was a dunce's hat made of Billy Beer pop tops that had a streamer that came down and tied under the chin. And with it there was a pop top little vest.

I couldn't believe that Billy would do it simply for the love of beer, though as soon as the beer was out, stores competed with each other to be the first to carry it. For a time, only one store in Washington, D.C., was able to get Billy Beer and they happily sent a case of it to the White House, so the President could see what his brother "hath wrought."

Plains citizens, who were used to the sight of plain ole Billy with a can of beer in his hand, got a laugh when the state of Virginia banned the sale of Billy's Beer because it carried the name of a *living celebrity.*

According to that state's Alcoholic Beverage Control Commission, the ABC "may withhold approval of any label... that infers endorsement... by any prominent living person."

Going a step further the commission chairman Archer Yeatts, Jr., added, "We feel it highly improper for Mr. Carter to endorse a label selling beer in Virginia. I don't care what it is, I think it is downgrading to the office of the President of the United States."

Though I somewhat share the commission chairman's feelings about the dignity of the presidential office, it would seem out of his jurisdiction to ban the sale of a beer that merely has a *first name* on it, as the beer's official name, even though it does carry Billy's testimonial which says: "I had this beer brewed up just for me. I think it's the best I ever tasted. And I've tasted a lot. I think you'll like it, too."

At this writing, the war of the Billy Beer is still being waged in Virginia. Twelve Virginia distributors filed an appeal before the ABC Board asking for an exception in the case of Billy Carter because Billy Carter was not "a living celebrity."

Paul Brown, who represented the distributors, claimed that Billy Carter was only a "self-confessed redneck and country bumpkin who couldn't even win an election for mayor of Plains, Georgia."

I have always been very supportive of Billy, helping him get any project through the Businessmen's Association that I could. I genuinely like Billy and think he has come a long way from the rebellious little kid who had to leave school for disciplinary reasons.

I admire Billy because he didn't just become a dropout. He came back and graduated with his class, even though his marks were deplorable. But the thing is he had guts to do the right thing and not jeopardize his future.

Today Billy is a big businessman. He has come a long and rocky road—and he proves that you can make good even though some people have called you a clown.

Actually Billy has always loved his image as a clown and Georgia "good ole boy."

He cherishes his image as a fellow who just won't conform to the town. But the image isn't 100 percent true. Underneath all that bluff and humorous sarcasm is a fellow who knows how to handle farmers and city slickers when he has to, and a fellow who built his brother's peanut business to a value several million dollars greater than when he started running it, after Jimmy became heavily involved in politics.

People think that Billy has always had the gas station that he has made famous. That also isn't true. He bought the Amoco station from the Jenningses who ran it until just a few years ago.

When the Jenningses wanted to sell, Billy had the good sense to know it was a good moneymaking proposition, and Billy improved on gasoline sales vastly by promoting himself as the picturesque fellow with a beer can always in hand.

That's the evolution of Buckshot Billy into Mr. Bigtime.

But before the evolution, I think there was a little bitterness in Billy that made him want to be completely different from the rest of his family. Everyone was working so hard at being an overachiever that it made Billy want to show he was the opposite.

With fame comes danger. When Billy's phone rings, his office doesn't know what to expect because a few times there have been threats of one sort or another, such as a bomb threat. If he can avoid it, Billy doesn't even bother to talk on the phone.

His wife, Sybil, or one of his kids or an employee takes messages for him. That's how we differ. My name is still listed in the telephone book. This means I get messages meant for every other variety of Carter who is unlisted.

I hope I can continue to do this. I feel that Plains has been so good to the Carter family that there should always be a Carter or two in the phone book.

If you ask me, Billy Carter does have a yen to be in politics—not like his brother in state or national politics, but just local politics. In fact, he proved it by running twice for mayor of Plains. The current mayor is also the barber of the town as well as working in the control tower of a nearby airport.

Billy, who had much more time to campaign, should have won

but he lost both times. Two things worked against him—his flaunting of beer drinking in a highly religious town and his uninhibited language.

The second time Billy ran, he should have coasted in on his brother's coattails because the Plains election was in December 1976, when Jimmy was the President-elect and the most popular man in America.

But Billy used too much humor and ran a campaign based on trivia. His big point was that if he won, he was going to tear down the Christmas tree in the center of town. He objected to it because it was made of plastic and he called it a twenty-five-foot-monstrosity.

The town was proud of its huge man-made tree and did not appreciate Billy's negativism. When he lost, Billy mysteriously said he always kept his campaign promises. And just as mysteriously, the Christmas tree disappeared. There was a lot of bitterness and Georgia police did come around to question Billy about the missing tree.

However, witnesses were able to show that Billy had been out of town on the night in question and it remains an unsolved case.

A "P.S." to that Christmas story of 1976 is that a few days before Christmas, Billy Carter and some of his cronies appeared with a twenty-foot cedar Christmas tree and proceeded to set it up in the middle of town. They even gave it a typically Billy touch by topping the tree with a beer can.

Billy knows the power of politics because it helped him get his beer license. Some years back, he ran for alderman and won, and after he was installed, the council voted to give him his beer license. He did not get reelected and he claimed it was because all the churches were angry at him for selling beer.

But his beer license was still intact and he thumbed his nose at the churches.

When Billy aimed a little higher and ran for mayor but lost, he said, "The only way I'll get me elected is if I can get all the beer drinkers to come out and vote and get all the Baptists to stay home."

Continuing his appearances at political functions, Billy was asked by his brother, the President, to attend the Alabama Conference of Black Mayors, which he did.

However, not without getting in his usual digs that "my being there will hurt my image as a redneck."

Another time, during Jimmy's presidential campaign, Billy was asked to meet Senator Talmadge during one of his visits to Plains.

Billy rode in the front seat of one of the Georgia state patrol cars.

When asked by a member of the press if that was the first time he ever rode in a patrol car in an official capacity, Billy replied, "Let's put it this way. This is the first time I wasn't required to ride in the back seat."

Billy has a fine title now, though he is not mayor, as he wanted to be. In 1977 he was elected president of the newly formed Merchants Association in Plains. I am the one who nominated him.

There were twenty-nine merchants and businesses represented, all determined to seek a united spirit of cooperation and better business practices.

I made the motion that Billy be named president and he was elected without opposition. As one merchant put it, "We are striving to put our best foot forward for all visitors coming to our town."

The first thing that we did, under our new president, was to plan for the comfort of five to ten thousand visitors estimated to stream through Plains every day.

On December 6, 1977, the Welcome Center was officially opened at Plains and First Lady Rosalynn came for the ceremony, attending with Mary Beth Busbee, the wife of the governor of Georgia.

It was a very windy day and I have a delightful picture of Rosalynn laughing as she tries to save her hairdo with a big scarf while Mary Beth watches skeptically to see whether wind or ingenuity wins.

I remember when Billy was born and Jimmy had to give up being the only son. It was hard for him to adjust, but Jimmy had been baptized into the church and he was taking his religion seriously. He tried to keep envy out of his heart.

Everyone was spoiling and petting Billy in a way Jimmy had never been spoiled. Jimmy had always been forced to do his best to please his daddy but Billy pleased his daddy by just smiling or walking beside him.

And Billy and Uncle Earl became inseparable. I remember I would be working in my daddy's general merchandise store when father and son would come in for shoes. It was very funny to me that I would have trouble finding a shoe that Billy liked. He didn't seem to like anything. But just as soon as his daddy liked a particular pair of shoes, that was the only one he would have.

I think Billy's new image is unfortunate. Yet I don't know what Jimmy can do or what he should do. There has always been a situation between the two brothers in which Billy wants to show that "nobody tells me what to do."

And now he has added, "Not even the President of the United States tells me what to do."

Billy put a five-thousand-dollar price tag on himself for each appearance at such things as a belly-flop competition, a peanut olympics—where he participated in a sack race with Yogi Bear—and a swamp buggy competition. Each antic that was announced in Plains in the summer of 1977 seemed more ridiculous than the last.

Not all the events were smashing successes either, and in one place, King's Island, Ohio, almost half his audience walked out on him.

As his brother struggles with the serious problems of government and world peace, Billy is photographed drinking beer which bears his own name, or is surrounded by buxom TV beauties of the *Hee-Haw* show. The fact that he earned about a half million dollars the first year in his role as First Brother and First Clown of the nation does not make up for the loss of dignity.

Billy did not need to earn his money in this outlandish fashion. Behind the mocking grin there is a good business brain. Billy was making a small fortune running his family's peanut business before he decided to try for the bigger fortune.

Of course, I laugh as loudly as the next person when he spouts off his witticisms, and I like him immensely.

Or when he shows up in one of his sweat shirt and sneakers outfits and proclaims, "I refuse to reveal the name of my tailor."

Billy has always been a great jokester and he has sometimes delighted the family with his pungent sense of humor. Until the presidential campaign, he counted on us to be his good audience. I really believe that Billy could have made a fine stand-up comedian in the tradition of Bob Hope or Red Skelton.

Perhaps, after Jimmy is out of the White House, he can still go into comedy as a *serious* career. But I do believe that the timing now is a little wrong.

As I've mentioned, I think that one reason Billy has gone into the personal appearance business is that he was only a 15 percent owner of the family peanut business—the rest of the company belonging to Jimmy and Miz Lillian. When Charles Kirbo became the trustee for all of Jimmy's business while Cousin Jimmy is president, Billy was made the supervisor of the whole enterprise.

But he was not happy. He went to Kirbo and tried to buy the other partners out, but Kirbo turned him down. At that point, Billy used a few choice words and got out of the business altogether, leaving Kirbo to find another supervisor.

Billy had three women raising him—his mother and two much older sisters—but he seems to have a chip on his shoulder about women. He seems to relate to male visitors around Plains much more than to female ones.

He also shows an unusual independence with his wife, Sybil, talking as if he feels he owes her no explanations.

Plains has given her high marks in forebearance because she never tries to change him—even when he brags that he starts every Sunday morning by drinking a beer with his breakfast. Sybil has done a fine job in raising their children and handling the business any time he is gone. In the old peanut days she acted as bookkeeper for Billy, just as Rosalynn did when Jimmy headed the company.

As a baby, Billy developed a stutter which he has never completely overcome. Aunt Lillian used to coach him to try to get him over it, having him read with a lighted candle in front of his mouth. I don't believe he stuck with the candle routine very long.

Billy doesn't like being questioned by female reporters over the issue of women's rights. When discussing his opposition to ERA, he admitted he stood alone: "I've got a brother that's behind it, a sister-in-law pushing it, and four daughters that I sure don't want to see drafted." Once he commented he'd read that hogs were smarter than most women.

There was only one time that I saw Billy react with tears instead of ribald humor. That was when a spark from a vending machine ignited fumes from a gasoline truck that was parked at his gas station, causing an explosion and damage to his station.

Billy had been playing softball with the White House reporters and staff when it happened and he rushed to the station. He was so overwrought that he started throwing punches at a cameraman who was taking pictures and Billy had to be dragged away.

The thing that is most touching, and what gave Billy's true feelings away, was what he said as he stood crying, "It's the only damn thing I have in the world."

To me this said that though Billy was earning money running the family peanut business and though he owned a percentage of it, he did not feel a part of it.

And then later, Billy snapped back to his old self, hiding behind humor and explaining the accident this way: "It all started when

Jimmy was losing the ball game. You all set the station on fire so we wouldn't win the game."

Billy might be fun-loving and irreligious, but he does have a kind heart. I remember one cold winter day when Billy passed an accident on the highway near Plains. Instead of just driving on as others were doing, he rushed to the aid of the people in the two cars involved.

One car had careened into a tree after the collision and there was blood everywhere. Billy saw that there was a little infant bleeding and in danger of shock and freezing before help could come. He took off his own coat and wrapped the child in it.

Then to soothe and reassure the little one, he carried it with him, talking to it as he tried to help others until the ambulance got there. He may have saved the child's life.

Though Billy never completed his education past his first year of college, his mother instilled in him and all the Carter children the love of books. Billy will spend as much as forty or fifty dollars at a time on reading matter.

Billy sometimes reads a whole book if he wakes up in the middle of the night and can't sleep. He frequently wakes up in the middle of the night—evidently, even Billy worries. He's had responsibilities for a long time, ever since he was a bridegroom at eighteen.

Billy had a checkered educational background. For drinking beer in school, the principal threw him out and he went to a military school for a year. He returned to graduate from Plains High School—almost at the bottom of his class.

Billy just wouldn't study and he had a girl friend, Sybil, younger than himself.

Right after graduation, he ran away to the Marines, coming back only long enough to make Sybil a bride, at fifteen—almost sixteen—and take her with him.

As a marine, he wanted to be the toughest, and he was always getting into scrapes. Once, when on leave, he tried to lick five or six sailors. As he puts it, "I found out I wasn't as mean and tough as I thought." But from all I've heard, he is a very good barroom scrapper.

Billy's temper is well known around Plains. Some of us figure he just never learned to control it like other kids did. When he was born he was so much younger than everyone else that he was treated like an only child, pampered and adored by both his parents.

I don't believe he ever got spanked by anyone other than a maid around the house. He likes to talk tough saying that he is on his way to go and punch somebody in the nose and get thrown into jail. Everyone always tries to calm him down—Sybil or some of his buddies—and usually nothing happens.

Ever since Billy's father died, when Billy was only thirteen, any stunt he pulled was excused on the grounds that he had lost his father. He had been the apple of his father's eye. From what I can figure out, Billy really thought he could be the head of the family and run the peanut business, even though he was barely in his teens.

He had been very upset when brother Jimmy, the bigshot in his fancy uniform, came home and said he was taking over the business.

But Billy found it was hard to compete in the outside world. Billy left the Marines in 1959 and went into construction work and then sold paint in Macon, Georgia. He tried going to college at Emory University in Atlanta for a while, but decided it was not for him after he flunked English.

It was then Jimmy gave him the opportunity to get into the family's business and grow with it. The year was 1962, when Jimmy was running for the Senate. It turned out to be a good arrangement. Jimmy did the politicking and Billy did the "peanut pickin'."

But getting back to Billy and Sybil, even though she was only fifteen when she married him, she was a very mature and caring person. She herself admits that one reason she married Billy when they were both so young was that after Billy's father died, Billy needed someone to take care of him and she just felt it was up to her.

In a way, she still acts a little maternal toward Billy, sometimes beaming approval and sometimes mildly scolding him like a disapproving mother.

Sybil opens Billy's fan mail and with a crowd around, she will tease him about the fan letters he is getting from eighty-year-old women. She, naturally, is not thrilled that Billy's picture is always being taken with some young beauty queen—a Miss Peanut or a Miss Doughnut—or the beauties on the *Hee Haw* program. But she is aware that things will change one day and all that Billy can grab now will help put those kids through school and make a good life for the family.

People ask me how many beers Billy drinks in a day. Since I don't count them, I have to take his word for it that it's about a dozen, in other words, two six-packs.

As a father, Billy is very permissive and he enjoys his children, just as if he is one of them, and they enjoy him. They ride around in the pickup truck with him and are very angry if they are in a crowd and a tourist who doesn't recognize them makes some snide remark about Billy's drinking habits.

Billy once got a pet spider monkey for his kids and it was a house pet, along with their pet rabbit. Billy was just as amused as his children when the spider monkey would treat the rabbit like its personal horse and ride around on its back.

But one day Billy quit being amused because the monkey bit him. Sybil insisted it was time for the monkey to go. But they didn't destroy it. They simply gave it away and Billy was happy to report that he had seen the good ol' monkey riding around on the back of a dog that belonged to its new owner.

Strangely enough, for a rambunctious, rough-talking, free-wheeling man like Billy, his six children show every sign of becoming well mannered, gentle, and polite individuals.

The eldest, Kim, twenty-two at this writing, is both talented and exceptionally pretty. She has a lovely singing voice and is also able to get up and speak impromptu at town meetings.

Jana, nineteen, is full of life and has a lot of friends. Buddy, seventeen, the oldest boy, whom Billy gave my daddy's nickname to, because he was so fond of his Uncle Alton, is turning into a good businessman like his daddy and the rest of the Carter clan. In his spare time, he works at the family gas station.

Marle and Mandy, fourteen and ten, are nice kids, and Earle at age one, is the pet of the whole family and of the town, as one daughter or another carries him around with her while she runs errands. It's a very nice and well-balanced family and I give Sybil's dedication and firmness a lot of credit for it as well as Billy's warm, loving attitude toward them.

He tries to keep it more or less secret but Billy actually did join the Plains Baptist Church when he was twelve years old. But if anybody points this out to him, he quickly defends his record by saying he's only been back six times.

Any time Billy can take a poke at Baptists, he does, even though his children go to the Baptist Church. He always says that when he dies, he is going to be buried by a Methodist preacher who will tell nice lies about him and he throws in that at his funeral, he wants to have Tom T. Hall, the country singer and composer, sing his song about "Faster horses, younger women, older whiskey."

I will never cease being grateful to Billy because of what he did when Daddy Alton had his heart attack and Dr. Frank Wilson in Americus said he would have to have a pacemaker—and very quick.

Billy, who was named for my daddy, was right there at the hospital to do anything he could to help. He even beat my wife, Ruth, there.

I remember how I and Daddy's wife, Betty, left for the hospital in Atlanta and Billy rushed to get Daddy's clothing and was right behind us.

He even stayed at Emory Hospital in Atlanta with Uncle Buddy, as he called him, until he knew he was going to be all right, with that new pacemaker.

Billy has a special feeling for my wife, Ruth, dating back to the time she was a schoolteacher for one year. She taught him math in the ninth grade.

Ruth said she was amazed at how quickly Billy could grasp algebra and that he was able to understand something in one day that others took two and three days to learn. If he got bad grades in school, she said, it was just that he wasn't motivated.

There is a question raised now and then about whether Billy is prejudiced against blacks. He has said quite frankly that he considers himself still to be a little prejudiced. However, Billy has had good relationships with black employees and the black citizens of Plains.

He used to fly with a black pilot, Bill Turner, out of Peterson Field, the Plains airport, during the presidential campaign, and grew very fond of Bill.

During the campaign, Billy said there were just two famous people he wanted to meet—former astronaut John Glenn and the seven-foot-tall black Atlanta Hawks center, Walt Bellamy.

Both wishes were granted.

One day someone was kidding Billy about getting chummy with blacks and Billy said, smiling, "I know, I'm going to ruin my redneck image."

19· SISTER GLORIA, SISTER RUTH

Jimmy's father loved all his children but he certainly did not treat his four children equally. Two he smothered with affection. They were Billy and his younger daughter, Ruth, whom he named for the biblical character.

Uncle Earl's favorite passages from the Bible were from the story of Ruth in the Old Testament. Thus, the name Ruth. He really doted on Ruth and could not get over her beauty. Ruth is a glowingly beautiful woman—even today—and she was a beautiful child.

It was almost as if she were like some little fairy princess come from another world into that family. Uncle Earl kept telling Ruth that she was the most beautiful child in the world and I'm afraid that was a sometimes a little hard on Sister Gloria, who was cute and vivacious, and excelled in her own way.

As it turned out, it was also hard on Ruth later on when she grew up, to adjust to the fact that there were other equally beautiful girls in the world, too. And that not everything would come to her on a silver platter.

The fact that she became the kind of person who could give spiritual help to vast numbers of people and write a book like *The Gift of Inner Healing* attests to the fact that a greater beauty lay inside her than even her physical beauty.

It is also a tribute to both sisters that they became, as adults, loving friends and not competitors. In fact, just as Ruth helped Jimmy, so was she there in Gloria's hour of need.

Yes, looking back, it wasn't easy to be a Carter daughter, whether you were the favorite or not.

Gloria Carter, Jimmy's lesser known sister, grew up, married and divorced, and now is married to Walter Spann, a local farmer. In fact, they live on the same road as I do, State Highway 45, south of Plains. We live less than a quarter mile apart.

225

Gloria is entirely different from Ruth, who is three years younger than she. For example, Gloria does not like to be around crowds of people the way Ruth—and Jimmy—like to be.

She likes being hidden away on the farm. In a way, it was a fine thing that Gloria had the opportunity to widen her horizons by working on the editing of her mother's book, *Letters from India*. That gave her a chance to travel, oftentimes with Miz Lillian to publicize the book and it opened up a whole new world.

But now, at this writing, Gloria complains that she does not want to be part of that kind of world anymore and is content to be back on the farm.

The family has always worried a little about Gloria—me among them—because of the tragedy in her family. It is that she has a son who was tried and sentenced to serve time in a California prison.

William Spann—called Tody—who is now about thirty-one, was convicted of armed robbery committed while under the influence of drugs.

For years, Gloria had lived a life of emotional upheaval never knowing what would happen next.

She had tried to hold up under the strain of a son who was not like other children. For a time, she enrolled him in a special school which featured therapy as well as classes under a controlled environment.

It was not cheap and she worked as a secretary to afford it.

Before the school, her life had been a nightmare of wondering where Tody was. Even at fourteen and fifteen he would stay out until all hours or not come home for days at a time. She grew haggard as she spent her time hunting for him. He had been expelled in the eighth grade, so Gloria had been very happy to find a special school for boys with problems.

There's no doubt about it. Gloria has had the hardest life of anyone in the Carter family.

She eloped with a fellow named "Soapy" Hardy, whose only previous work before entering the Air Force had been soda jerking.

She married in 1945 and returned home alone in 1949 with a little child—Tody—and a broken marriage. A divorce followed, and before the year was over, Gloria had met and married Walter Spann, a prosperous farmer.

Walter cared enough to adopt Gloria's little son. But Tody seemed bent on self-destruction from an early age. He resented his step-father, would not obey his mother, and made a fool of everyone who tried to help him. Psychiatrists could not help.

I remember when Cousin Jimmy tried to straighten him out and gave him a job. Tody repaid him by disappearing in a company truck. Once it was Billy Carter's car that he took and abandoned in another state.

All of this, of course, hurt Gloria very deeply because she loved her son and didn't want her family to turn against him.

It was after he was out of the special school that Tody started bumming around the country and getting into more and more serious trouble. When the phone rang, it was frequently Tody to say he was in jail again.

Gloria was exhausted physically and emotionally and depressed. Once when she thought she could stand it no longer, she had gone to see Ruth at Fayetteville.

Ruth tried to give Gloria the same kind of help that she is famous for having given Jimmy when he lost his first bid for governorship. But Gloria would have none of it.

As Gloria herself admits, she shooed Ruth away saying she didn't want to hear about Jesus or anything connected with religion or prayer and what she really wanted to do was just get one good night's sleep.

To get this good night's sleep she went to Ruth's lakeside cabin. Since she was all alone, she looked for something to read and everything in print was of a religious nature. In sheer boredom she opened a little book of Gertrude Keehn's radio talks.

Almost immediately, her eye hit a line that changed her life. It was the same thing that Ruth had been getting at but Gertrude Keehn was saying it in a way that she could understand.

The line was: "Give your problem to God for sixty seconds, and rest your mind."

Suddenly she found herself talking directly to God and admitting she couldn't cope with her son and asking the Almighty to "take my son for ten seconds and let me have some peace."

Those were ten seconds that gave her an entirely new feeling of peace. And suddenly the world looked beautiful again. She had been so busy worrying about her great problem that she had lost sight of the beauty of the world.

Today Gloria is still enjoying the world although her son is still in prison. She enjoys life from the back of a motorcycle. Her religious experience prompted her to suggest that she and her husband both get motorcycles as an exciting hobby that has the added thrill of enabling a person to pass close to the beauties of nature and viewing them much more intimately than from a car.

Gloria now feels that God has her son in His hands, such as he has her in His hands and somehow everything will be all right.

Gloria has also become very interested in the State Legislature and when the State Senate is in session has written to me in Atlanta to give me her views on matters in which she is interested. I've always found her reasoning interesting and logical and I always welcome her letters for their frankness of expression.

During Jimmy's presidential campaign, Gloria had a shocking experience when someone phoned her and, disguising his voice, threatened to tell the press about Tody unless she paid hush money.

She had already satisfied her own mind that the voters were going to vote for Jimmy and not her son, Tody, and as for herself, she had the new strength the Lord had given her to face whatever embarrassing revelations came out because of the press's interest in the whole Carter family.

Without a moment's hesitation, Gloria told the mystery caller, "Say whatever you like—I won't pay you any money."

The story did come out but Gloria was right—the voters were voting for Jimmy, not Tody.

Even as this book goes to press, there was again troubling news for Gloria from the California prison in Soledad. Bill Carter Spann was complaining that his guests at the prison were being searched before being permitted to visit him, and a prison spokesman, Phil Guthrie, explained that it was for good reason.

The reason for the search, Guthrie said, was that there was a strong suspicion that Bill was involved in drug trafficking or possession.

Gloria is an intensely talented woman who could have been many things. She could have been an artist. She took a correspondence course in art and was so good she taught in her home until Walter put a stop to it.

For a time, she also taught art one day a week at Plains High School and at Buena Vista.

Now Gloria just satisfies her artistic yearnings by painting flowers and butterflies on her blue jeans.

Another career that Gloria could have had was accounting or tax work. For a time, after going to business school, she was a bookkeeper in Americus and also helped Jimmy on his warehouse books.

Many farmers had her make out their farm taxes. She worked for me sometimes at my antique store auctions.

I felt sorry for Gloria during the presidential campaign because I knew how much she wanted to help Jimmy. But Walter made no secret of the fact that he didn't want his wife involved with the fun-loving Peanut Brigadeers.

However, Gloria did manage to get Walter's permission to go on one Peanut Brigade trip to Florida. She also did some letter writing on Jimmy's behalf.

It's a rather touchy subject in the Carter clan that Walter did not seem interested in any part of Jimmy's campaign except for a quick moneymaking scheme—the selling of square-inch plots of genuine Plains Carter land.

Soon after Jimmy was elected and Plains began to flourish with tourists, Gloria and her husband became involved in a souvenir land-selling deal in which tourists were offered a square inch of land for five dollars.

The tourist was given a nice little certificate, and the deed was duly recorded in Sumter County. Of course, at this price per square inch, an acre of land will bring several million dollars—which sounds like a slick scheme to get money, but actually it is a cute idea and gives the tourist a small piece of property which becomes a valued souvenir of Plains.

As soon as Jimmy heard about this operation, he reacted immediately and negatively, indicating that the operation bilked people out of their money in selling a square inch of land for five dollars. The press carried his remarks nationwide as to his displeasure.

A day or so following this news coverage, it was reported that Jimmy's brother-in-law Walter Spann had sold the land to the company that was selling the squares.

J. D. Clements, Jr., a friend of Jimmy's and mine, came out to my home and explained the operation to me. He said that he had stock in the company and that he felt the company would be a great success.

I was sorry to see Gloria singled out to stop making money in souvenirs because, after all, Brother Billy was also cashing in on the tourist influx in a less imaginative way with his gas station souvenir shop. Frankly, I didn't see anything wrong with the land-selling enterprise and would have liked to have expressed my opinion before he blasted it.

However, out of loyalty to Jimmy and his expressed opinion, I did not want to issue any statements publicly about it that would add fuel to the fire. Many reporters and TV people contacted me urging me to comment on the "Big Inch" operation, but I refused.

Later, I understand, Jimmy did call Gloria and told her he was sorry that he had acted hastily and flown off the handle, stopping her little enterprise.

I understand other companies have done the same type of promotion in other communities with great success and without criticism. In fact, another company in Plains has been selling land for eleven dollars per square inch. I understand they did fairly well and have many "satisfied" customers, but they have now stopped this business.

I know they had a big signboard on Highway 280 just a few miles east of Plains for a while advertising the square inch souvenir land.

State Senator Norwood Pearce of Columbus was the attorney for the company that Gloria and Walter were connected with. Senator Pearce is a good friend of mine in the Georgia Senate.

Many people still come in my antique shop inquiring about the five-dollar-per-square-inch souvenir land and wanting to buy several square inches as souvenirs of Plains. I tell them that it is my understanding the company is no longer in operation.

To my knowledge, this is the only souvenir business taking advantage of his fame that Jimmy objected to.

When my father died, Gloria spent much time at my father's home answering the phone, accepting visitors who were offering words of condolence, and making herself helpful. I'll never forget her generosity to Betty, my stepmother, and me during this time of great sorrow.

The story of Ruth is the opposite of Gloria's. Instead of searching for love, she was, from the beginning, almost smothered with love.

Ruth realized eventually that her father's excessive love for her and praise was not beneficial.

Ruth herself admits that hers was a lopsided childhood and that she felt "too much love" from her father and "insufficient love" from her mother, which caused her to be "emotionally crippled" as an adult.

When she got married, she used to go running home from Americus every time her feelings were hurt, and they were always being hurt because no man could measure up to her father and his treatment of her.

Having been so spoiled by her father, Ruth was not ready for the responsibility of taking care of a husband and children. When she lived at home, she had not even had to wash her own stockings and underwear—Uncle Earl had servants for that.

Ruth had only to be pretty and cheerful and her father doted on her every word or whim.

The girls, Gloria and Ruth, had a mother who was independent and strong-willed. When they were teen-agers, she was apt to be off doing things for strangers.

It was especially hard for Ruth because, to the annoyance of her mother, she could always go to her daddy to get what she wanted. For his favorite child, there was nothing Uncle Earl wouldn't do. Years later, after Ruth had become a faith healer, in order to heal her own conscience, she went to her mother and sought her forgiveness for their differences in the past.

This did much to relieve the tensions in the Carter family between the womenfolk.

Ruth spends more time with her mother now than in the old days that were filled with resentments and that inspired Ruth's husband, Bob Stapleton, to keep the strong-willed women apart from each other as much as possible.

Before she could find her inner strength, however, Ruth suffered great anguish and almost wrecked her marriage to Bob Stapleton, a fine man, who is a veterinarian in Fayetteville, North Carolina.

In fact, the reason they live there, and not in Americus, so the family story goes, is that Bob took her away so that she could not go running back to her daddy every time they had a spat.

The move to Fayetteville saved the marriage but Ruth was far from happy and eventually was seeing psychiatrists. One thing she learned was that she was filled with resentment against Bob because he had fallen asleep and not been there when she was giving birth to one of her children.

Rosalynn Carter could have been bitter, too, over a similar incident but that wasn't her way. What happened was that she had a very difficult first childbirth and Cousin Jimmy was at a movie waiting it out.

When Jack was born in 1947, Rosalynn and Jimmy were in Portsmouth, Virginia, and the baby was born in the Navy Hospital in Norfolk. Rosalynn was only nineteen years old and Jimmy was told that the baby wouldn't be coming until the next day. He left the hospital and went to a movie and that's when the baby was born.

In Ruth's case, it was not until she was "born again" that she was able to erase the bitterness from her heart about being "deserted" in childbirth. She did it by reliving the incident and pretending that Bob *had* been there.

Before her "rebirth," she went to doctors and psychiatrists who were unable to help her. Then she laid her whole burden and emotional wounds before Jesus and suddenly she felt her depression lift and her wounds become healed.

What she did for herself she is now helping others do for themselves—inner healing therapy.

As a housewife, she had tried to escape responsibilities, but after her own inner healing and religious experience, she went back to college.

Religion was terribly important to her and she began Monday night prayer meetings which grew in popularity as other people were helped by her counseling.

First Ruth gently helps a person to look inside and find where the guilt lies. It can be very painful, like the exposing of a raw nerve. But once the person is reexperiencing the incident that led to the feeling of guilt, that person is ready for Ruth's "ministery of inner healing," and they pray together and ask the Lord to take the burden.

Ruth was deeply involved in nondenominational healing before Jimmy ran for the presidency so she cannot be accused of riding on his coattails. In fact, she would be very careful not to talk about her brother when she was lecturing on faith healing, or talk about faith healing when she was campaigning for her brother.

It was pretty hard to do because people followed her wherever she went. At faith healings they would be wanting to know what her brother was really like, and when she was campaigning, reporters and others would try to get her to talk about her religious beliefs.

Even though she grew up as a Baptist, Ruth feels that she must work outside of any established denomination because Jesus looks at all people of all religions and has love in his heart for everyone.

For many years this made her unpopular with churches and many called her a "false prophet." But she kept doing what she felt compelled to do—help those with emotional troubles—no matter what anyone said about her.

She has not changed.

Many people expressed shock and displeasure when, after Jimmy was in the White House, Ruth became friendly with and converted Larry Flynt, the publisher of *Hustler*, a pornographic magazine, to her way of thinking, even celebrating Thanksgiving with him and his family.

They felt she should talk only to nice and noncontroversial people, but as Ruth Stapleton explained, she deals with anyone who needs her.

She ministers to those who are sick in spirit and cares not what their former lives were. When they are healed they lead a new life. Larry Flynt, the publisher, had tears in his eyes as he declared to the world that he had changed completely as a result of the ministry of Ruth.

Even when she was a child, Ruth didn't care what others thought. She played with black children, as Jimmy did, but boys were given more freedom in those days and little white girls were not supposed to play with anyone but other little white girls. It took courage.

Though she still is not the kind of woman who is interested in the details of housekeeping, the way her sister-in-law Rosalynn or my wife is, she has matured into a good wife of a different sort.

Her weakness has become the strength of her children, who look after their mother and run the household when she is there and when she is away.

So much attention is given to Ruth that her husband gets overlooked but he is a wonderful fellow, easygoing and able to look after their four children while she is out ministering.

Bob Stapleton's business partner is Willard Slappey, a first cousin of Jimmy and me, who already had an animal hospital going in Fayetteville before Bob joined him. Not only do they take care of small animals at the hospital but they care for large animals on surrounding farms.

It is interesting to me that, in her way, Ruth is following in the footsteps of her mother, being just as completely absorbed in ministering to man's mind as Miz Lillian was in ministering to the physically ill, no matter how poor they were or rejected by society.

Ruth's latest project is to establish a place where people can come to be spiritually healed. She calls it the Inner Healing Center, Holovista Ranch. But so that people will not write me to ask how they can go there, let me give the address of her center: Inner Healing Center, Behold, Inc., Box 53757, Fayetteville, North Carolina 28305.

I have not seen the place but Holovista, which means "whole life," is a thirty-acre ranch near Dallas, Texas.

20 • "ONCE IN LOVE WITH AMY"

When Jimmy was running for governor, sometimes my wife, Ruth, would have his young daughter, Amy, at our house so that Rosalynn could keep up with her speaking schedule. Amy was just three and yet she had a great curiosity about everything and wanted Ruth to read her many books.

Rosalynn, busy as she was when she came to pick up Amy, still treated her daughter with great respect. If Ruth was in the middle of a story, Rosalynn would wait patiently until Ruth had read to the very end.

A more selfish mother would not have cared how Amy felt and would have just said, "Come on, let's go."

Amy was always free to bring her little friends to go swimming in our pool but she would always call Aunt Ruth to ask if it was all right. Ruth would always serve cookies and something to drink.

Once, after Jimmy was elected, Amy called with the same question but saying that this time she would bring the refreshments. Ruth told her it would not be necessary for her to do that and as usual served the cookies that she had herself baked—Amy's favorites being peanut-shaped ones with peanut butter filling.

Ruth's favorite story about Amy involves Amy's reading matter on one afternoon that she was spending at our house. Amy had gone through all the little Golden Books that Ruth had saved through the years and her own reading matter that she had brought along.

Ruth couldn't believe her eyes when Amy picked up the book *Heloise—All Around the House,* and started reading it. She was not being bored by all the household tips but really interested. When it was time for Ruth to drive her home, she kept on reading *Heloise* all the way home in the car.

When they arrived at Amy's house, she asked to keep the book so she could read some more.

Ruth told her to finish it and return it the next Sunday at church.

But when Sunday came, Amy had to report that she had put it up for safekeeping and couldn't find it anywhere. Weeks later she found it in the back of her mother's car when they opened it to put in some groceries.

According to all reports, that is Amy's current problem—misplacing a lot of her personal belongings such as shoes, coats, and books.

The first year in the White House, Rosalynn tried to give Amy a very normal Halloween, just as if she'd been in Plains. In fact, Rosalynn even sewed Amy's costume herself—a cat costume.

Closer to home—over in Calhoun—Jimmy's son Jack and his wife, Judy, tried to give their two-year-old toddler, Jason, a normal Halloween, too. They did it with the help of two Secret Service men.

On trick-or-treat night, little Jason would go up and knock on certain selected doors and ask people, "Do you want to see my gorillas?" Then the two Secret Service men wearing gorilla head masks would step forward and make like gorillas.

We have always enjoyed every holiday in the Carter family, Thanksgiving, Christmas, New Year's, birthdays, and anniversaries. Halloween has always been a special favorite because the children were so excited about their costumes. Every year there is an annual Plains Halloween Carnival, sponsored by the Junior Women's Club and the Plains Lions Club.

Prizes are given for the best boy costumes and best girl costumes. Things are quite different now. As a boy, on Halloween, we would go on hayrides in a wagon pulled by two mules. At the carnival party we would bob for apples, dunking our heads in a tub of water to grab an apple with our teeth.

After I was grown and had children of my own, Ruth, my wife, would take Connie, Laurie, and Hugh, Jr., trick-or-treating every Halloween. In my day we didn't knock over outhouses if someone refused to treat, but we would turn over chairs on the front porch if no sweet was forthcoming or if no one was home.

Ruth would take the kids many places including Cousin Jimmy's house, and Rosalynn would take her little ones various places including ours. Jimmy and I would be content to stay home and dish out the treats to those who rang our bells.

How different Halloween was in 1976, right after Jimmy won the election. Amy attended the carnival as usual but now she was accompanied by her bodyguard, whose nickname was "Little Joe"—the only name I ever heard him called.

Amy took part in all the little competitions and other events with her cousin Mandy Carter, Billy's daughter. There was the usual apple bobbing, ring tossing, dart throwing to burst a balloon, a fishing pond for prizes, fortune-telling, a scary haunted house with many noises, and even a game of bingo.

I was the auctioneer. My job every year is to auction off the cakes that the ladies have baked for sweet charity. Sometimes, if the mood of the crowd is right and my spiel amused them, I might get as high as fifteen dollars for some cakes. But the average price would be about two dollars.

With Amy this night were two of her favorite female relatives—her Grandma Allie and her sister-in-law Caron, Chip's wife.

After the carnival Little Joe herded Amy, Mandy, and the rest of their little ghost and goblin crowd on their trick-or-treat rounds. This time the houses he took them to had been carefully selected in advance. Amy's favorite treat was chewing gum.

The Halloween theme was also used at Amy's last birthday party in Plains before moving to the White House. Her birthday is October 19, so the theme is appropriate.

Amy's first Halloween in the White House was a doubleheader. She was also celebrating her tenth birthday. A bunch of her playmates from Stevens, her school, came for a Halloween party and after a pumpkin carving contest, they sipped the usual punch and ate the usual party fare.

And then they saw the original Frankenstein movie in the White House private theater.

One of the pumpkins was mighty funny. It had a "Carter grin," with many teeth, and Daddy Jimmy, who claimed he had carved it, posed with it for an amusing picture.

Sometime after the children's party, Amy received a gift from her parents that would really amaze the children of Plains—a genuine sled for the coming snowy season. Jimmy had promised that Amy would be able to use the sled a lot at Camp David, the presidential retreat in the Catoctin Mountains in Maryland.

It's really to Jimmy and Rosalynn's credit that Amy is not more spoiled than she is. Wherever she goes people want to give her things. Back during the campaign, there was a donkey used at a ceremony at Warm Springs that involved Jimmy Carter. Amy fell in love with the donkey so later in the day it was brought to Plains for her. But, wisely, she was not allowed to keep it.

When many gifts were sent to the Carters they were stored in a trailer until Jimmy and Rosalynn could decide what to do with them.

Amy was not too impressed or overwhelmed. She went there to look for some of her missing things—some magazines and books she had ordered. Sure enough, they had been delivered to the trailer by mistake. She didn't try to grab any gifts.

She took the reading matter meant for her, got into her car, locked the doors, and read happily out of sight of the tourists.

The nation was aghast when Amy took a mystery-story book to the table to read at a formal state dinner. But those of us who know her in Plains were not surprised. Once Amy went to the ladies' room after Sunday School and stayed in there for a great length of time. People were starting to worry about her. It turned out she had been finishing up a story in a magazine that she had just gotten.

Many people wondered why Jimmy and Rosalynn would let Amy take a book with her to read at their first formal dinner—the one for the Mexican President and his wife. The truth of the matter is they were using a little psychology, getting Amy to see that life in Washington was really a lot like life in Atlanta or Plains.

It was just the normal thing for her to do—read if she got bored with speeches and grown-up talk.

Jimmy and Rosalynn did a lot of other things to help Amy adjust in those first months at the White House. For one thing, Jimmy and Rosalynn took her along when they went to inspect the new $59-million Children's Hospital National Medical Center, which had been in the process of building for many years.

To help Amy get over any remaining shyness, the new President playfully showed Amy the facilities in the therapy room for recuperating children and then picked her up and tossed her on a water bed, where she giggled and bounced around.

That was three months after Jimmy took office. Eleven months after, Jimmy was still being the average, normal father. He took several hours off to attend a violin recital at St. Patrick's Episcopal Church, where Amy, for the first time, showed what she could do on the violin.

Afterward, Jimmy and Rosalynn joined the other proud parents for cookies and punch and conversation about their offspring.

Jimmy even attended a pre-Thanksgiving dinner served by Amy's fourth-grade class at Stevens Elementary School in Washington, and I don't believe he got any indigestion. Then there was the day he found himself attending a special assembly at her school.

Dressed in yellow ballerina costume, so I am told, but wearing stocking feet instead of ballet slippers, Amy danced the role of a shopkeeper in the child's ballet named *Doll on a Music Box*.

The Carter family was tickled at Amy's pride at being a ballet performer. So pleased was she that she kept waving at her daddy from the stage now and then to make sure he was watching, even once when she was actually dancing.

Amy has a mind of her own and it is a liberal mind. What is more, she knows how to handle her Grandmother Lillian. This is one story that made the rounds of the family, when Miz Lillian was taking care of Amy while Rosalynn and Jimmy were involved in the presidential campaign.

Amy asked, "Grandmamma, can I have Elizabeth come over on Saturday to play with me?"

Miz Lillian asked, "Is she black?"

Amy immediately responded in a scolding tone, "Grandmamma, you're not supposed to ask that."

Amy was a chip off the Carter block and I could see, in my mind's eye, Jimmy playing freely with his little black friends, when he was her age.

Lillian was probably just being curious. She had encouraged Jimmy to play with black children, but Amy was taking no chances.

Even though Amy is the daughter of a President, she still is a little girl, with likes and dislikes, and interests similar to any other ten-year-old whose family may not be constantly in the limelight. She enjoys eating at McDonald's or Hardee's whenever the occasion arises, and like most other kids who take their lunch to school, she likes to swap something she has for something tasty someone else might have.

Amy's taste in TV fare is not too sophisticated. Her favorite show, when last I heard, was *The Flintstones*.

The White House may not appreciate my telling it because it may bring on a deluge, but in the interests of First Family history, I want to tell what Amy collects. She collects comic books and she collects dolls of every description.

Amy does not need expensive games to keep her occupied. She and her friends used to make up their own games and if she has a tree house to climb into, she is perfectly happy all alone with a book.

Amy likes to read mysteries, biographies, and science books. This makes her daddy wonder if Amy may grow up to be a scientist as he was when he was involved in atomic science.

One of Amy's helpful hobbies is washing the car. She gets into the act with anyone else who is around, but sees to it that she is in charge of the water hose.

Since Rosalynn is a fine seamstress and makes some of Amy's clothes, even at the White House, she had hoped that Amy would take to this womanly art. So far Amy has tried some needlepoint work but prefers the more mechanical type things. She loves to operate film projectors and record and tape players.

Though she is a tomboy, Amy is not totally without romance in her soul. In fact, it was hard to know, in Plains, who her real boyfriend was. She had a clever technique, like a Scarlet O'Hara southern belle, of telling several different boys that she liked them so they all would huddle near thinking they were the one.

I have it on good authority, though very hush-hush, that her favorite boyfriend at Westside Elementary School was Scott Roberson. I believe that his mother drove one of the school buses for the Sumter County School System, for a time. At Westside, Amy's schoolteacher was Mrs. Jan Williams, whom she adored.

Scott is very smart in school and quite an athlete for his age, excelling in softball and football.

Before Amy moved to Washington, he used to take her skating or to a movie sometimes on the weekend. Of course, his parents took them.

Like Amy, Scott also was blond-headed.

Amy seems not to have found a new boyfriend as yet, now that she is at a different school—the 109-year-old Thaddeus Stevens Elementary School in Washington—but she does have a close girl pal, Claudia Sanchez, who is the daughter of a Chilean Embassy cook.

Amy is a bit of a diplomat herself, I hear from the White House. Around the other kids, she doesn't talk about her father being President. Only because at home their parents question them about Amy do the other children know that somehow Amy is special and because of the presence of the Secret Service.

Everyone knows that when her Daddy was running for the presidency, Amy earned pin money with a lemonade stand. Few people, however, know the whole inside story of her business enterprise.

In the first place, it wasn't just Amy who was in the lemonade business. She had two equal partners, her next-door neighbors, the brothers Gnann—John, nine, and Sidney, seven. They had a good idea and they started out nicely.

They charged a modest five cents a glass for their pink lemonade, serving cups of it from a cardboard box. Then Amy supervised the building of a better stand of wood, propped on some old bricks. The kids painted their names in a row along the bottom, "John Amy Sidney," in the order of age, and above it, painted their new price, "LEMONADE 10¢."

The stand was positioned right between Amy's house and her partners', because that was where the action was with tourists driving and walking by and reporters keeping a constant watch whenever Carter was there. The kids' business boomed.

They did very well but kept getting more and more greedy and raising the price, and the price of lemonade went up to fifteen cents and then a quarter. It was Sam Donaldson, the famous ABC White House correspondent, who gave Amy the idea of diversifying and adding sandwiches because he was hungry.

Amy and her sidekicks rushed into the candidate's house and emerged with mostly peanut butter sandwiches, and a few of pimiento cheese. To their surprise the peanut butter sat there while the pimiento cheese quickly sold at fifty cents apiece.

When there was a little grumbling eventually at the lack of variety, Amy came up with tuna fish sandwiches and charged a dollar apiece. Then the kids got greedier and upped the price of the peanut butter and cheese sandwiches to a dollar and tuna to a dollar fifty.

I think about this time Jimmy and Rosalynn got a little concerned. They wanted Amy to have fun and learn a little about business but they didn't want her to gouge the public.

Meanwhile, Amy had discovered a new source of wealth. The reporters wanted to borrow her Frisbee to kill time and exercise while waiting for Jimmy to emerge from the house, on the occasions he was home, between campaign trips.

Amy, getting the hang of business, said, "You can use it if you pay for every quarter of an hour."

They established a price for fifteen minutes and Amy, not trusting anybody's time sense or watch, got the timer from her mother's kitchen to make sure nobody cheated.

Sometime before the end of July 1976, everybody in charge of Amy, including the Secret Service, thought it was time for Amy to close shop. I don't know what her total earnings were but I do know that many days she made as much as twenty-five dollars.

The situation had gotten just a little out of hand. Her parents feared the outlandish high prices Amy was getting from eager reporters was spoiling her and keeping her from learning the true value of a dollar.

Though she no longer has contact with the press, in the White House, she does see her old lemonade stand partners. In fact, her favorite Christmas present was a gift from them—a huge pet hermit crab.

During the presidential campaign, Jimmy would get the sympathy of every mother in the crowd by telling how much he wanted a little girl and had to argue with Rosalynn for many years before he got his wish. As he would put it, "Rosalynn and I had an argument for fourteen years and I won."

The inside story is a little more complicated. First of all, it was Miz Lillian who started campaigning for a little girl. But Jimmy, too, had oftentimes told me he wanted a girl.

However for years, Rosalynn did not conceive. There was a good-sized tumor on Rosalynn's ovary. It was removed and that's when Amy came along—twenty-one years after their marriage.

A most cherished possession that Cousin Jimmy and Rosalynn brought with them to the White House is Jimmy's favorite painting—a portrait of Rosalynn and Amy. It was done by Thornton Utz, a painter who came to Atlanta to do a portrait of Governor Carter.

Utz lives in Sarasota, Florida, where he has a studio. While visiting at the Governor's Mansion in Atlanta, he watched Amy play and he watched Amy's mother, Rosalynn, affectionately hug Amy. He was so inspired that he returned to his Sarasota studio and, from memory, started painting Rosalynn holding Amy on her lap.

That early portrait became so special and unique to Cousin Jimmy and Rosalynn that they brought it along to the White House, where I saw it when I visited in the family quarters.

Amy was a fourth-grader when her daddy ran for President. I'm sure that at school in the spring of 1976, before Jimmy got the nomination, a lot of the kids didn't really think that Amy had a chance of being in the White House. They saw her more as the lucky kid of a former governor.

But from what I hear, they did envy her the chance to travel the way she did during some of the primary campaigns—even though Amy told us *she* did not like it. Some of her classmates had never been outside of Plains, or at least no further than Americus or Albany.

To them, Amy was just a little girl who had to wear glasses and who had a rock collection and a doll collection. She also had two cats,

Misty, the one who went on to make animal history at the White House, and Sausage, who seems to have disappeared from her life.

Eventually, Amy got a little jaded from being on the go so much. According to her teacher at Westside Elementary School in Plains, Mrs. Jan Williams, Amy went on one field trip with some of her friends to Magnolia Springs and took two rolls of pictures but didn't even bother to have them developed.

When it was time for Amy to leave Plains for Washington and her new life, Amy's classmates at Westside gave her a going-away party. The President-elect and Rosalynn and the two grandmothers attended, and all eighty-three of Amy's classmates got to shake the hand of the man who would be President within a very few days.

The children had a present for Amy. It was a charm for her charm bracelet.

It was Jan Williams who helped Amy change her mind about the Secret Service men. It was one of the things Amy most dreaded about having to come to Washington. She didn't want to have any men following her around. But Mrs. Williams took the time to discuss it with her several times and point out how lucky she was to always have someone to drive her and a car at her disposal.

She decided that she was lucky because not many other nine-year-olds always had someone to talk to and drive them around.

Of course, she soon learned that she wasn't going anywhere unless her mother or daddy had given permission, even if there was someone to drive and a car to take her.

Once when her dad had given her permission to go to the movies she happily ran out and got in the car. No one had notified the agents, however, so Amy sat in the car for quite a while until an agent on duty asked why she was sitting in the car. When that matter was finally resolved, she realized that in the future the agents would have to have at least a five-minute notice for Amy's future activities.

Amy is an independent child who really had to adjust to the fact that she would be accompanied everywhere by two security agents, who had to be notified of her plans at all times.

Amy has learned to take a gentle ribbing from the agents. One day, they were telling her that they were going to wear tuxedos in colors to match her long dresses, which she wears for evening events at the White House.

It was a big change for a little girl who had enjoyed getting dirty climbing trees and digging in the ground. And had enjoyed going without shoes. Now she knew that in Washington she would have to be all prettied up whenever she was in public. She would even have to quit blowing big bubbles with her chewing gum outside the family quarters.

But when the family returned to Plains on those first weekends, Amy made the most of it. She dressed up as a "hobo" and sat in Mrs. Williams' front yard waving at tourists who didn't dream hers was one of the faces they were coming to Plains to see. To add to her own amusement, she had painted her face with lipstick and eye shadow to fool the tourists, and just to be a ham.

Amy has always shared her toys and games with her friends and anytime she received anything that she could share with her classmates, she never hesitated to do so.

Once when Barbara Walters visited Plains to interview the Carters, she brought along a large chocolate bunny for Amy which Amy promptly shared with her classmates by cutting it up into small enough sections to be distributed to all the students.

Another time the Carter family received a case of apples from some friends and the following day Amy took a bag of them to school and gave all the teachers at the Westside School an apple.

Just about everyone in the Carter family has had a crack at authoring a book or helping bring about a book one way or another. I guess it was bound to happen that it was finally the turn of Amy Carter, aged ten, to be the star of a book.

Not too big a book. In fact, only a thirteen-page book, but the original printing was 200,000 copies. Helping to assure that this masterpiece, entitled *The White House,* would be a success was the fact that Daddy Jimmy wrote the introduction for the pictorial story of Amy Carter's "tour" of the White House.

Once, First Lady Jacqueline Kennedy was recorded making a historic walk through the White House, but she only wore one outfit for the whole walk-through. Amy appears in different outfits, even an evening dress as she comes down the grand staircase of the White House to show where state visitors descend for the reception on a gala evening.

Besides Daddy, Amy had two more helpers—Nan Powell, the wife of her father's press secretary, and Nancy Moore, the wife of a presidential assistant, who did the text writing.

And the photographers taking pictures of such scenes as Amy sitting on the President's lap in the Oval Office are none other than

Amy's brother Jeff and her sister-in-law Annette. I was amused when someone in Plains said the book should be called *All in the Family.*

Mrs. Jan Williams is a good friend of ours and now and then we talk about what an interesting and alert little girl Amy is. Jan recalls how Amy would go to visit her and always rearrange the little figurines in her aquarium.

She would always complain that it was not right, and in fact, "it's weird," to have birds and a cat in a fish tank.

Amy liked to work at cleaning the aquarium so much that she got her own aquarium and reported to Mrs. Williams that she had decided to have a cat figurine in her own aquarium after all.

Sometimes Jan would bring Amy over to our place so that they could swim together, if Ruth didn't have time to watch Amy at the pool.

Once in Jan's class, the children were told to write an important letter to someone and Amy announced that she was going to write to Uncle Hugh because he was a state senator and ask him about the drug problem, which she did.

I believe I sent her enough material to keep her class busy for a long time.

The thing that sticks in my mind most about Amy is a conversation she had with her teacher about what it would be like to be handicapped. They had been reading about it and afterward they had discussed whether, if a person had a choice, it would be better to be blind or deaf.

After some thought, Amy said she would rather just not be able to talk. Jan Williams commented that for Amy silence would be a real hardship because when she is with someone she knows and really likes, there is not a moment of silence.

During the inaugural, Jan Williams went to Washington with Amy and stayed with her throughout the ceremonies.

In fact, the day after the inaugural, Jan took Amy to the Smithsonian. Amy was having a wonderful time just being an inquisitive little girl when a family hurried over and a lady commented that she certainly looked like Amy Carter.

Jan replied, "I've been told that many times."

Amy had been cringing but now she brightened a little, realizing that she could avoid recognition. The woman stood awhile longer just looking at Amy and said, "Is she your little girl?"

Jan said yes she was, neglecting to add, "from my classroom."

Here I am in front of my antique store in Plains. It has become the most photographed antique store in the world because Jimmy always stopped here first in his visits home.

To fishermen I am known as the "Worm King of America." Because I ship so many worms, the Plains Post Office advanced to a second class post office.

Your Ticket for Four Years of
Good Government by all Georgians

JIMMY CARTER FOR GOVERNOR

FUND RAISING BARBECUE SUPPER
AND RALLY

Eve Park Baseball Field, Tifton, Ga.
8:00 P.M., Thursday, August 27, 1970

Please come and have this souvenier ticket validated
SPONSORED BY SOUTH GEORGIANS FOR CARTER

Isn't it time some-
body spoke up for
YOU?

Donation
$5.00

N° 1341

Jimmy was using the peanut image even in his successful race for the
governorship of Georgia in 1970 for which I was campaign manager.

That's me with the glasses, second from the left, just after Jimmy was
sworn in as Governor of Georgia. Shaking Jimmy's hand is Senator Julian
Webb, who is now on the Court of Appeals of Georgia.

Jimmy was a hard-working governor who attended few purely social events. Here we both attend a party at the home of Representative Ward Edwards.

My daughter Connie has always been a little ham. Here she is pretending her monkey doll is biting her finger, and she's in pain. It was taken about 1955 when she was three.

Carolyn Carter

My wife and I on a night out at the Hyatt-Regency in Atlanta in 1976.

Amy is a complicated child, wise beyond her years, yet trying to enjoy childhood. Here she is with her cat, Misty Malarky Ying-Yang. It surprises me when I realize how much she resembles Laurie when she was the same age.

Daughter Laurie was the quiet one in our family, but you wouldn't know it by the picture of a two-gun cowgirl taken in 1954.

Billy Carter is about the only Plains businessman who did not paint up and fix up his place of business when Jimmy was running for President, but tourists love the beat-up, unpainted look of his filling station and flock there by the thousands to buy gas and beer.

This is how Plains looked during the campaign—wild!

Amy caught on quick and anytime it looked like someone else was about to ask her if she was Amy Carter, she would turn to Jan and ask her a question, calling her "Mother."

Jimmy and Rosalynn are happiest when Amy gets no mention in the newspapers. One incident which distressed the First Family and the White House was an ad in a magazine showing Amy looking a little bit sad. The headline said, "You Can Help Save Amy—Or You Can Turn the Page."

It had been meant to be a funny spoof of the "Save the Children" ads and under the picture was a coupon for sending money to "Over-privileged Kids, Inc." so that Amy could spend two weeks living among "real people" in Laurel, Maryland.

The address given was that of the Democratic National Committee.

The magazine explained it had only been joking but the White House and the Save the Children Federation were not amused and Save the Children called the ad "a disservice to the desperately poor whom the legitimate charities like Save the Children are trying to help."

They were concerned that the ad was making light of charities and that people would not take as seriously their legitimate and very touching ads which show the face of an underprivileged child of some faroff land with the plea that "You can help save [this child] for $16.00 a month or you can turn this page."

I asked what had happened as a result of the spoof and whether money had come in for Amy and learned that money did indeed come to the Democratic National Committee and was turned over to the Save the Children Federation. That happened in July of 1977 and the Carters have protected Amy from exploitation carefully since then.

Amy's claim to fame right now, according to her own words, is that she can hang upside down from a tree. Everybody thinks that little Amy is just a bookworm, who takes a book to the table with her, even when there's company at the table. But that's only one part of Amy.

The other part is the tomboy Amy. She's happiest on a bike or trampoline, or playing kickball or football or bowling, and she feels about animals the way her Daddy did when we were kids. She wears her cat Ying-Yang—for short—draped over her shoulder the way her Daddy used to wear his squirrels on his head.

What is the White House going to do to Amy? I don't know. It is making her just a bit bratty in that she passes judgment and doesn't hesitate to say that this and that are "dumb" or show her contempt for various people.

But maybe she'll be saved from it by the calming influence of Rosalynn.

I'm not trying to say that Amy is mean. Quite the contrary. She is very kindhearted and when she loves someone, she almost overwhelms that person. I'm thinking of the black woman who was her baby-sitter back at the Governor's Mansion—the woman who was serving a sentence for murder.

I know Mary Fitzpatrick. I remember her well because she also, on occasion, looked after my grandchildren. Amy felt the goodness of this woman in spite of the one bad deed she had committed, and bestowed her love on Mary like a blessing.

The Carter family rehabilitated Mary but I give Amy most of the credit. It was very touching that when Amy came to the White House, one thing she had to leave behind was Mary, who had been a trustee at the prison, permitted to work in the Governor's Mansion.

A girl with less depth would have forgotten Mary since everyone wanted to be her new friend. But no, Amy prayed for Mary and wrote letters to her. Jimmy and Rosalynn were so touched that they used their influence to get Mary under their care and supervision.

And now Mary is at the White House and Amy looks after her as much as Mary looks after Amy. When Amy studied a book to prepare her for becoming a member of the First Baptist Church in Washington, she shepherded Mary through the same experience.

And when Mary Fitzpatrick was baptized in the same church, Amy was the first person to hug her and congratulate her.

Incidentally, Amy was baptized at the age of nine, the same age as her father was.

One action Jimmy and Rosalynn took to try to keep little Amy from being spoiled any more than normal was to pass the word that the press could no longer interview her. She was off limits.

That is why there suddenly was a dearth of stories about Amy and her life at the White House. I guess it was quite a letdown for the press, after they had made her famous and put her lemonade stand on their press beat.

I remember when Amy was the only member of the family who did not want to come to the White House to live. Her daddy had a long talk with her and she had a whole list of reasons—Mary

Fitzpatrick wouldn't be there, and neither would her friends, and where would she ride her bike?

Jimmy had answers for all that—Mary could come visit. Amy would have a whole classroom of new friends and she could ride her bicycle on the big White House grounds and at Camp David.

But still Amy wasn't happy. How could she go and leave her tree house? And would there be room for her huge dollhouse?

Daddy Jimmy promised to personally design another tree house exactly like the one she already had. And as for the dollhouse, he personally carried it on moving-in day. He was a pretty good daddy.

The dollhouse now sits in a large hallway near her bedroom which is the same one that Tricia Nixon used to have. Amy does have a special friend to share her dollhouse and her imaginative games. It's not a celebrity's child, but, as mentioned earlier, the daughter of the cook of the Chilean Embassy, a little girl named Claudia Sanchez, who goes to the same school Amy attends.

Cousin Jimmy never ceases to marvel at the delight of having a little daughter after raising only sons. He claims that it's Amy who keeps him feeling young and Amy shares all her thoughts and her knowledge with her daddy. One night she had a dream about God and was able to report just how God looked—"He's an old man and he has a brown beard."

Amy insisted that she had seen the beard correctly and it was, indeed, brown.

Amy was very concerned, when she was coming to Washington, that her cat have all its certificates and papers from the vet so that she could take it out of the country if they ever went traveling, or if some dogcatcher came around looking for stray animals.

Even so, as she sat in the plane on her way to Washington, she remembered that she had left all her cat's credentials in her teacher's car. The cat didn't worry about it and slept nearly all the way to Washington.

Part Five

CAMELOT SOUTHERN STYLE

21 · THE MEN AROUND CARTER

Georgia is certainly well represented at the White House. There are just five persons who can see the President at any time and only one of them is not a Georgian. The exception is Zbigniew Brzezinski—nicknamed Biggie.

Jimmy had met Biggie when Jimmy was governor and Brzezinski was head of a "think tank" group that was part of a Rockefeller foundation. Biggie helped Jimmy formulate his foreign policy when he was a presidential candidate and became so indispensable that he ended up at the White House as successor to Henry Kissinger as National Security Affairs adviser, the title Kissinger had held in his early days with Nixon.

The other four who have immediate access to Jimmy at the White House are Jody Powell, who is press secretary, Hamilton Jordan, his top administrator, Frank Moore, congressional liaison man, and Stuart Eizenstat, domestic policy adviser.

I learned that Jody is the President's favorite comic at the White House, always good for a chuckle. When Jody was invited to appear on a TV comedy show, *Saturday Night Live,* Jimmy was amused at Jody's comment, "I'll let you know if I decide to make an ass of myself on national television for an extended period of time rather than briefly, as it has been up to this point."

Feeling as he does about casualness, Jody applauds Jimmy's de-glamorizing and deglorifying of the office of the presidency and his efforts to bring it down to earth. But Jody was the one who was able to put a humorous twist to it to tickle Jimmy's funny bone: "We've often said that if we could reduce by 10% the extent to which people in Washington take themselves too seriously, it might be more important than a zero-based budgeting."

Jimmy had to take a little teasing about all the economies my son, Hugh, Jr., was instituting at the White House. And someone asked how it affected his own expenses.

Jimmy replied, "The only item Hugh has challenged so far is my six hundred dollars for toothpaste."

Though Hugh, Jr., is not one of the Big Five who can see the President at any time, he does have a position of importance at the White House.

One day when President Jimmy was visiting Plains, he stopped in my store to tell me what a fine job Hugh, Jr., was doing at the White House. In the first week at the White House, Hugh, Jr., had more than earned his yearly salary just by cutting a few of the unnecessary frills.

"He's quite a guy," said the President. "He's saving the federal government a lot of money and he's just getting started."

I felt pretty proud as I recalled that little Sonny had gotten his first taste in business as a "worm farmer," helping me raise worms. Today, he is an efficiency expert at the White House, charged with studying every phase of White House expenditures to see where economies can be instituted.

This has given him a new nickname in Washington and one that does not anger him at all—Cousin Cheap. He has a second job that is not as controversial or well known and that is to be a liaison with former presidents and presidential families—Gerry Ford, Richard Nixon, Lady Bird Johnson, Mrs. Truman.

The contact with past presidents is turning out to be very pleasant. He and ex-President Ford hit it off so well when Hugh, Jr., went to Vail on White House business that they ended up playing tennis together.

Sonny is an excellent tennis player and it is amusing to me that he flew about two thousand miles to play tennis with an ex-President, but at this writing has not yet played tennis with the Man right at the White House—Cousin Jimmy.

When Hugh, Jr., went to work at the White House, he asked that the President treat him as if he were not a Carter and that's the way it has been. When I came to visit, he was not a drop-in guest at the living quarters of the White House. While I was there, the President and Rosalynn naturally invited my son to have dinner with all of us.

This is what Jimmy would have done had he been dining with the parents of any other White House aide. Hugh earned his presidential appointment the hard way. He graduated as an industrial engineer from Georgia Tech and went on to receive his master's in business at Wharton in Philadelphia.

Though he works at the White House at a salary above $50,000, this is a reduction in earnings from his previous position in private industry, vice-president of John H. Harland Company, a check-printing company.

Hugh, Jr., has always been an expert at using the things around him to best advantage. For example, when he received his master's degree in business administration, he did his thesis on worm-farm production in the United States—the business he had grown up in—and they thought so much of it that it was added to the library at Wharton.

Hugh, Jr., has well earned his nickname of Cousin Cheap. He is the one who deserves the credit—or blame, depending on your viewpoint—for deglamorizing the life of a White House aide and getting rid of all the expensive frills that once went with the office.

It used to be that almost all the White House aides had one or two TV sets in their offices, ordered any magazines or newspapers they wanted, and had chauffeur-driven limousines.

The first thing Cousin Cheap did was remove three hundred TV sets from the Executive Offices. It was such a drastic cut that only at the end of the haul-away exercise did he suddenly remember to save one set for his own office, so that he could have it when needed in line with his job.

About forty thousand dollars of the taxpayers' money was saved by cutting out the extra publications such as newspapers and magazines which were delivered daily.

Much money is also being saved by making aides drive themselves to work in their own cars, and Hugh, Jr., has ordered twenty limos removed from the White House motor pool.

Also money was saved by selling the Presidential yacht, *Sequoia*, which Nixon and LBJ, in particular, used to keep ready at all times on the Potomac, as a sort of floating nightclub. Since Jimmy Carter does not drink, except for an occasional glass of wine as a toast at a chief-of-state dinner, the yacht was not his style. Instead he enjoys going to Camp David with his family.

Many people are curious to know just what sort of things my son handles in regard to the president. I know that one trip Hugh, Jr., made to Vail, Colorado, was to arrange for former President Gerald Ford to come to Washington to participate in the ceremony at which Jimmy Carter signed the Panama Canal Treaty.

It was important because Ford's presence at the treaty-signing would give bipartisan sponsorship and strengthen the chances of the treaty being ratified in Congress.

As a second kind of involvement, Hugh, Jr., handles special requests that come from former presidents or their families. For example, Gerry Ford's executive assistant, Robert Barrett, requested that the cost of the Ford telephone switchboard be part of the White House communications budget.

Hugh, Jr., studied the matter but true to his nickname, Cousin Cheap, felt it was in the interest of the country to say no. The reason was that it would cost five thousand dollars a week. But the ex-President was not miffed at Hugh, Jr., and they continue to have a warm relationship.

There are many things Hugh, Jr., does to save money that the general public doesn't realize. For example, saving on the cost of shipping the presidential limousine. Hugh, Jr., discovered that the Secret Service was planning to fly the limousine to Roanoke at the cost of several thousand dollars.

He arranged that it be driven to its destination at a cost of two hundred dollars. The President's car, it seems, is frequently transported ahead of his arrival by plane or helicopter.

In the interest of economy, no longer can groups of staffers use Camp David, the presidential retreat in Maryland, as a recreational place. Hugh, Jr., is studying ways in which to cut the cost of operating the presidential retreat and already the number of aides and stewards have been diminished.

No detail of White House costs is too small for Hugh Carter, Jr., to study. Among the minor economies he has instituted is to get rid of expensive rag paper note pads on which White House staffers used to take their notes.

Now they use ordinary paper.

Though Hugh, Jr., has a smiling exterior, he is grimly serious in his recommendations, and he has a keen perception to see what is absolutely necessary for efficient operation of the White House and what can be eliminated.

When I teased old Cousin Cheap about lowering the standards, he laughed and said most of the Georgia gang now working in the White House are not used to frills anyway. He said most of them have it better now than they ever had it before and he included himself.

Of his office, he said, "I've never had as nice an office as this—light blue walls, dark blue carpet, a sofa, several comfortable chairs, an impressive desk, and a wall of built-in bookcases containing only six books."

He chuckled as he commented that his set of government regulations looks pretty lonely but he had boxes of books at his apartment and no time to even unpack them and bring them to the office.

Hugh, Jr., also commented, "I don't think Ham Jordan has ever had an office as nice as his is now, either."

In previous administrations, top-level aides ordered the redecoration of their offices as a mark of status. Those days are gone. "We will do any redecorating on a need basis," Cousin Cheap has announced.

When several reporters asked Hugh, Jr., if it was true that he was cutting frills just for show, he answered, "Come back a year from now and see if we aren't doing the same thing."

Cutting frills is, of course, the most spectacular and newsworthy thing that Hugh, Jr., does, but as assistant for administration he supervises well over two hundred employees at the White House. He acts as presidential liaison with the Secret Service, Federal Protective Service, Honor Guard, and other military personnel connected with the mansion.

Hugh, Jr., oversees the mail that comes to the White House. The mailroom has around 170 employees who receive, analyze, classify, and, often, answer the President's mail.

Automatic pens are sometimes used to sign Jimmy's name to routine letters up to twelve hundred times per week. There are twenty-five or thirty form letters on tape. These letters are reproduced in large quantities so that congratulations, thank-you notes, etc., can be received by people from the President. Some of these same letters have been used in the White House for twenty years.

The White House receives about fourteen thousand letters per day, ten thousand of which are addressed to the President. Forty-five percent of these are referred to government agencies and twenty-five percent to members of the White House staff. Many letters are answered by simple printed cards—these are suitable for framing.

During the presidential campaign Hugh, Jr., worked up to twenty hours a day. He helped organize the Peanut Brigade, which was so instrumental in Jimmy's election.

After the election was over, Ham Jordan asked my son to stay on with the administration. At first, there was the problem of nepotism—would his assignment to the White House constitute a violation of the antinepotism law?

White House counsel Robert Lipshutz, who was just joining the White House staff, sought the opinion of his outgoing predecessor,

Philip Buchen. Together they checked and determined that under the law enacted by Congress in 1967, federal officials are barred from giving their relatives jobs, but exempts everyone more distant than a first cousin.

Fortunately, Cousin Cheap, as my son, is a second cousin which puts him on the legal side of the law.

Hugh, Jr.'s, starting salary of about $50,000 when he entered the White House at age thirty-four sounded big back in Plains. But, of course, in Washington, D.C., with its high living costs, it was a different story; rents are extremely high.

Some say that Hugh Carter, Jr., and President Jimmy Carter are quite alike and that they both have the same orderly technician's type of mind. Some say that when you look at the President, you see the kind of person Hugh, Jr., will be in another twenty years.

That may be so, but Hugh, Jr., will not be found in politics. He has said many times he has no interest in a political career and looks forward to returning to the business world after Jimmy leaves the White House, or after Jimmy no longer needs him.

Part of the time the President calls him Sonny, as he used to in Plains. But now and then, when he catches himself, he calls him Hugh, in keeping with the dignity of the position. It is rather amusing to hear a $50,000-plus specialist being addressed as "Sonny."

Like other members of the Carter family, Sonny has always strived for perfection, without letting it show. He is an earnest, low-keyed, and efficient businessman.

Hugh, Jr., has little time for dating or socializing since he went to work in the White House. However, for several years before even going to the White House, Hugh has dated Glenna Garrett, a Delta Airline stewardess.

I would say that Charles Kirbo was and still is Jimmy's closest adviser and closest friend. This was the lawyer who befriended Jimmy in 1962 and won him his state Senate seat when he proved that ballot boxes had been tampered with during the voting.

That was the start of a friendship and trust. And it would still be the same after Bert Lance had departed Washington in the autumn of 1977. Kirbo served as Jimmy's volunteer chief-of-staff when Jimmy was governor but he did not come to Washington to take an administration job, as he could have.

Instead, he preferred to be just an unofficial adviser and friend, as he practiced law in Atlanta. Kirbo is a senior partner in the King, Spalding law firm.

I am a friend of Kirbo's as well but what he probably doesn't know is that I have a strange tie-in with his household helper, his cook. "Son Coon," as he is called—his real name is Mack Wilkerson—comes home to Plains nearly every weekend. He also likes to reminisce about "Mister Jimmy" now that his boss's best friend has become President. Son Coon likes to tell how relaxed Jimmy is around the house when he stays at the Kirbo's.

Son Coon was not used to such informality and he told how startled he had been the first time he prepared breakfast for the governor, who had stayed overnight, and Jimmy had walked in to the breakfast table in his bare feet.

Once I asked Son Coon what Mr. Kirbo had said to him the morning after Jimmy won the presidency. Son Coon said, "Mr. Kirbo patted me on the back and said, 'Our boy got it.'"

Many people thought Bert Lance was the strongest single influence on Jimmy Carter's presidency. I can remember the first time I ever heard of Bert Lance.

During the 1970 campaign, when I was busy telephoning for Jimmy all over the state, the Atlanta campaign headquarters called me and said that Bert Lance, who was then a banker in Calhoun, Georgia, wanted to offer Jimmy some advice in regard to banking laws which he might encounter when he became governor. The Atlanta headquarters asked me to call Mr. Lance, which I did.

I took notes on his conversation and passed them on to Jimmy. I later met Lance in the headquarters in Atlanta and we grew to be great friends. I found him to be one of the most knowledgeable men that I have ever known.

Most people outside the state of Georgia don't know that Jimmy pushed for Lance to be commissioner of transportation when he was governor and Bert was elected for the job by the State Board of Transportation.

Bert served as commissioner until he resigned to run for governor, with the blessing of Jimmy, who could not succeed himself—though the law has been changed since then.

Lance was defeated in his try by George Busbee, who is the governor at this writing.

As a commissioner of transportation, Lance was very much liked by the Georgia legislators and was effective in getting them to pass legislation which improved the highway system in Georgia. He was smart and affable and honest.

I was not at all surprised when Jimmy chose Lance to be his director of the Office of Management and Budget. They had a long personal and business relationship. As I later read in the paper, Jimmy Carter's business had been borrowing money from Lance's National Bank of Georgia.

This is standard procedure in the peanut business. The warehouse owner has to borrow money to pay farmers for their peanut crops. The money is made when the peanuts are processed and sold to users and manufacturers of such things as peanut butter.

Of course, since they had business dealings and worked together at the State House, when Jimmy was governor, it was natural for Jimmy to continue to lean on Lance for advice during the presidential campaign.

Several times Jimmy traveled on the private plane owned by Lance's bank. Knowing how much of a stickler he is to obey the letter of the law, I'm sure that he did not realize the bank had not been reimbursed for these campaign trips. But as soon as the information came out in public, Jimmy immediately reimbursed the bank, out of his own pocket.

The news came out in such a way that it appeared that Jimmy was trying to get something for nothing, but that is not his way. I remember many times during the campaign he would tell someone to make sure that something was paid for, for the campaign, even though it might be a small amount.

There were many things that helped Bert and Jimmy become such good friends. Jimmy identified with Lance because Lance was a self-made man, having worked his way up in the banking business from the start of teller at the age of twenty, at the First National Bank of Calhoun.

Lance married the daughter of the president of the bank, but he could have been a small-town banker the rest of his life. Instead, he became president of the National Bank of Georgia, headquartered in Atlanta.

Lance was also a member of the Georgia Business and Industry Association and the Atlanta Chamber of Commerce. His influence on

President Carter was as a trusted and proven friend, a shared background, and proven confidence. Bert Lance shared also with Carter an awareness of the dangers of inflation and they spent much time discussing it and how to combat it.

Being a warmhearted person, Jimmy did not turn his back on Lance when he was in trouble with Congress over his banking practices. Even after Lance felt it would be for the good of the country for him to resign, since the inner workings of the government had ground to a halt over the investigation and hearings, Jimmy stood by him.

In fact, Jimmy continued to play tennis with Lance and to entertain him at the White House. This, too, is Jimmy's way.

Something good comes out of almost everything and even the embarrassment of the Bert Lance hearings had a positive effect. The banking practices of America were examined and found to be much too lax. What Lance had done other bankers also did—making loans casually and extending credit to members of one's own family.

As a result, banking procedures will be tightened, making banks sounder and stronger.

The man Jimmy picked to replace Bert Lance as Director of OMB, James T. McIntyre, is someone I have known and worked with for many years. Perhaps our friendship started on a bit of a sour note because our first meeting was when he came to me and wanted me to introduce a bill in the Georgia Legislature I had no interest in. But soon I grew to respect his ability.

As governor, Jimmy asked McIntyre to head his newly created Office of Planning and Budget. McIntyre did such a good job that Jimmy's successor, Governor George Busbee, reappointed him as budget chief. The only thing I can hold against McIntyre is that originally, he was a Maddox appointee—deputy state revenue commissioner 1970.

It is fascinating for students of politics to learn that as soon as Jimmy became President, he made Robert Strauss special trade representative—they had had a love-hate relationship for years. Strauss gave Jimmy no help toward the presidency when he really needed it.

In the early days, Strauss seemed to regard Jimmy as a man with only peanut qualities.

But one of the times it was a love relationship was in 1972 when they joined forces to try to stop the nomination of George McGovern, knowing that would be a disaster.

That was when Carter was still governor of Georgia. Even so, Jimmy let the word get around that he wouldn't mind being Vice-President whether McGovern or Hubert Humphrey won—a suggestion that got a big laugh.

Strauss and Jimmy didn't succeed in stopping McGovern, but Jimmy helped Bob Strauss become chairman of the Democratic National Committee—a step up from Strauss's previous position as committee treasurer.

The way Jimmy did it was by organizing a group of Democratic governors, after the 1972 election, to get rid of McGovern's choice, Jean Westwood, and install Bob Strauss instead.

It was a narrow victory. But there was no reward. Jimmy felt he deserved the credit but Strauss thought that Senator Scoop Jackson had been the deciding force.

At any rate, instead of throwing his weight toward Jimmy in 1975 and early 1976, Strauss worked toward getting the presidential nomination for Scoop. Only after Jimmy had worked his tail off and had the nomination in the bag did Strauss jump aboard his bandwagon.

Not only that, but in the early days of Jimmy's presidential ambition, Strauss had gotten hold of Hamilton Jordan's blueprints for Jimmy's projected presidential campaign, so the inside story goes, and had laughed himself silly at the notion that Jimmy thought he could make President. I was aware that Strauss was not one of Jimmy's favorite people.

But politics being what they are, and Jimmy being a man who wants the best man for the job, no matter what he used to think of him, Strauss was invited to join the new administration.

I would say that Hamilton Jordan [pronounced Jerden] is Carter's No. 1 man in the White House—Carter's "man with ideas." At age thirty-four, Hamilton Jordan is skilled in politics and in running campaigns, and idolizes Jimmy—always has.

The first time I met Hamilton Jordan was in 1966. But when, in 1970, he and I worked together in my worm farm office in Plains setting up Jimmy's gubernatorial organization campaign, we had a close relationship, with Hamilton calling me up excitedly when he had a favorable report about some prospective county chairman he had found. Since I would preside at the Sunday afternoon strategy meetings, I appreciated the way he would keep me informed of all the particulars.

Hamilton is boyish-looking and seems even younger than his age. Someone has said that when Jordan whistles "Dixie" he sounds like Gomer Pyle. He looks a little like him, too. Hamilton likes to crack jokes and he still makes people feel good by asking their opinion about various matters. I think he learned this from Jimmy.

Cousin Jimmy is a good listener—someone said he listens with a "blowtorch intensity"—and he likes to make the people he is conversing with do most of the talking. Jimmy well knows this flatters a person and motivates him.

Hamilton Jordan doesn't give you the vaguest clue of what's on his mind. My guess is that in the back of his mind, he's already planning his strategy for Jimmy Carter's reelection campaign in 1980.

Hamilton's office is a couple of doors down from the President's in the West Wing of the White House—the one H. R. Haldeman used to occupy in Nixon days. Ham has a large wooden desk and bookcase facing the wall in his office that was previously installed there by Haldeman.

He has a large oval table with leather chairs in a comfortable arrangement near a fireplace. Hamilton's office is a Rube Goldberg dream—it's loaded with gadgets. He has a fan to pull up the smoke in the chimney of his fireplace.

He has a console on his desk that lists the exact location of the President and his family at any given moment. And this is only part of his setup. There are all sorts of buttons. He is one of the few persons permitted to have a television in his office; it is hooked into the White House cable system.

Hamilton Jordan can sit in his office and monitor Jody Powell's press briefings in the White House press room. He can also rerun last night's TV news.

Every morning Hamilton holds a conference of his political staff which is very informal and where all kinds of ideas are thrown in for consideration.

Hamilton Jordan was the son of a well-to-do insurance agent in Albany, Georgia. He grew up in the midst of politics. His grandfather was Hamilton McWhorter, who had been president of the Georgia Senate and a close buddy of Senator Richard Russell. In fact, Hamilton had gotten early experience in politics by coming to Washington to work in Senator Russell's office.

When Ham could not get into the Army because of flatfeet, he joined the International Voluntary Services and went to Vietnam anyway. After six months in Vietnam, a traumatic change occurred when Ham developed a large lump on the back of his head. It was diagnosed as black water fever and he was sent home.

When he got well he went to work at a bank in Albany, Georgia, but he hated banking. To get away from banks he volunteered to help Jimmy in 1966. He did all the filing, and typing. But gradually he started giving his ideas to Jimmy and eventually they had long talks together more and more frequently.

Jimmy lost but Hamilton did not lose faith in him. In fact, he had grown to idolize him as "the man who goes to church on Sunday and believes it." When Jimmy ran again in 1970, Hamilton Jordan was as enthusiastic as ever and was a tireless worker.

At first he was lost as executive secretary to the governor—the job Jimmy had given him—but he soon caught on and did a commendable job.

I saw him at the White House and it was a strange feeling to realize that he was now the top aide to the President, giving away jobs—important, sensitive, high-level jobs—deciding who should be the head of an agency, member of a board, or director of this and that.

In the middle of a discussion about the progress in the hiring of women and minorities, Hamilton jumped up and snitched some candy from his secretary Eleanor Connors' candy jar. Someone commented that Eleanor should keep some licorice candy in the jar for Vice-President Mondale.

The thought went through my mind that life in the White House is not too different from the way it was at the Georgia State House.

In his spare time Hamilton liked to listen to albums of Bob Dylan, an acquired taste he shared with Jimmy. I am told he can sit for hours listening to Dylan—especially his favorite, "Only a Pawn in Their Game," about the murder of Medgar Evers.

Plains, Georgia, and parts around the Peach State have certainly taken over Washington. I got a kick out of reading how the "Georgia Mafia" were wandering around Washington like lost souls, trying to find southern-style restaurants and houses under the $100,000 class. They did better at finding restaurants than they did on houses.

Hamilton Jordan found a house on Capitol Hill in the $100,000 class and Jody Powell found one in Northwest Washington at about the same price. Bert Lance got himself something even more elegant to live in. At that time, it looked like he and Mrs. Lance would be doing the most entertaining in the administration, next to the White House. In Atlanta their stately home had been the center of a wonderful social life.

Hamilton Jordan has not had a completely carefree life. As a child, he had to sleep with special braces on his legs because he had been born with misshapen legs.

Some wonder who is more important, Jody Powell or Hamilton Jordan. They both are "indispensable men" to Jimmy. They are such good friends that the press frequently refer to them as the Bobbsey Twins. If one is there, the other cannot be far behind.

Jody Powell, Jimmy Carter's press agent, is often called one of Carter's whiz kids. But beneath the down-home charm of Jody Powell and Hamilton Jordan, they are tough, smart, and loyal to Jimmy. They both came from towns in Georgia no more than forty miles from Plains.

The most important thing Jody does each day is meet with reporters assigned to the White House. He spends several hours each day preparing for this, including a brief session with the President.

Jody Powell is No. 2 or No. 1½ man around the White House, just a half step behind Hamilton Jordan in importance to the President. Jody is just a year younger than Hamilton—age thirty-three. Jody is either getting more civilized or conservative because he's now wearing a tie to work, I noticed when I visited the White House not too long ago. He used to roll up to the White House in his eleven-year-old Volkswagen, looking like a Georgia cracker. But when the newspapers started making fun of his appearance and the way he put his feet up on the office furniture, he began to shape up.

From Jody Powell's window, he can watch reporters come and go on their way to the press office. The press can ask every kind of embarrassing and needling question and he must continue to reply with tact and good humor. He will answer the same question asked over and over again by different reporters who hope to break down his reserve and flush an angry retort or presidential secret.

Jody's father, Joseph Lester Powell, was a farmer with five hundred acres of peanuts and cotton. Jody's mother, June, taught civics in the Vienna (Georgia) High School. Powell was a liberal man and hated Lester Maddox's racist politics.

He encouraged Jody in his interest in politics and was proud that his son worked in the governor's office. In 1975 Jody's father learned that he had terminal cancer. Unwilling to let others watch him waste away, Joseph Powell took his gun and shot himself.

I had known Joe Powell and done a lot of antique business with him. He had sold me coffee tables that he had made out of wagon wheels. Once I sold him a two-horse wagon which he bought only for the wheels.

He stripped the wheels off and left the body of the wagon for me to dispose of.

I ended up in the hospital with a ruptured disk because of one of Joe Powell's coffee tables. I was helping a lady load one of the wagon-wheel coffee tables that she had bought into her car. I remember lifting my side well over my head and taking most of the weight on me. The sprain became more severe each day, and Thanksgiving Day was very painful. By Christmas I could not stand up and went to St. Joseph's Hospital in Atlanta, where I was put into traction.

That didn't work and a myelogram turned up the fact that the ruptured cartilage was pushing against the nerve going down my right leg. Dr. Bill Moore, one of the South's leading neurosurgeons, performed an operation which was a complete success.

I was up and walking in two days and back at the State Capitol at my Senate duties within ten days.

Young Jody Powell had many triumphs and letdowns in his life, too. He was a Civil War buff and liked to draw Civil War battles and read constantly about the Civil War. He had a spectacular high school record and entered the Air Force Academy in Colorado.

But on Christmas Day of 1964 when he had only one semester to go before graduation, he returned home to Vienna. He had been caught cheating on a history exam. Jody never talked about it then, but his mother said it turned out for the best, in that he rose above it and has a better career than he might have with the military. The closest Jody comes to talking about the military that could never be is to comment wistfully that he thinks he would have been a good pilot.

Instead of the Air Force, Jody ended up getting a degree in political science at Georgia State University in Atlanta. Like Hamilton Jordan, Jody, too, went into work he disliked, in this case, the insurance business.

Politics drew him like a magnet, and by stroke of luck and southern hospitality, Jimmy Carter and Jody got together in 1969. It happened when Jody was writing a paper on southern populism, just at the time Cousin Jimmy was getting ready to begin a populist-style campaign for governor of Georgia.

Jody liked the man who seemed to appeal to farmers and who wasn't a racist. Jody wrote Carter discussing his campaign and Carter invited him to Plains. Carter liked Jody's thinking and hired him as his driver and general flunky to help him do a little of everything during the 1970 governor's campaign.

They spent endless hours together and often would even sleep in the car after a hard day of campaigning, when there wasn't time to find a place to sleep.

Sometimes Jody was so exhausted he would stay awake smoking while Cousin Jimmy slept in the seat beside him. Two times his cigarettes caught Jimmy's pants on fire. To do penance, Jody promised that if Jimmy won the election, he would quit smoking.

And he did—for about ten days.

In a way, Jody is the "Billy Carter" around Jimmy—the kid brother substitute. He dresses sloppily, like Billy—going around with vest unbuttoned, no jacket, and in shirt sleeves with tie at half mast. He has the same kind of brashness in speaking his mind and earthy vocabulary, using four-letter words and picturesque language.

Some say Jody dares to say what the President is too pious to say, just as Billy does. Jimmy reacts the same way to Jody's language as he does to Billy's, chuckling a little and saying he is not offended.

But whereas Jimmy might only think harsh things, Jody would and does dare to say them.

There was a letter from an antibussing leader who called Governor Carter a "gutless peanut brain." Jody replied:

"Among the many burdens that fall upon a governor, one of the most exasperating is having to read barely legible letters from morons. I respectively suggest you take two running jumps and go straight to hell."

If Jody has any fault, it is that he is too good-hearted and promises things he can't deliver. All during the presidential campaign, the reporters begged for interviews with Jimmy. Jody would promise and set up the time and then he couldn't deliver.

The reporters would be on his neck. But so relaxed and tolerant would Jody be, taking their abuse, that they would forgive him and start pleading with him to set it up again.

When the election returns came in and it was clear that Jimmy Carter was the winner, it was only Jody Powell who got the special treatment of a long sincere and eloquent look and then a hug. There were no words. Carter's eyes were saying it all—how much he felt he owed to Jody.

One of the most important people to go along to Washington with Cousin Jimmy was Frank Moore. He had filled in for Jody and worked for the governor as executive secretary when Hamilton Jordan had come to Washington to represent Jimmy. That was when the chairman of the Democratic party had made Jimmy head of the Elections Committee on a national scale to help elect Democrats to Congress.

Since Jimmy was stuck in Atlanta in his gubernatorial duties, he sent Hamilton to work full-time at the committee.

It was a wonderful national assignment which gave Jimmy and Hamilton the inside story on political situations all over the country. Much that they needed to know in order to win a presidential election was learned through that important assignment.

Meanwhile, Frank Moore did such a good job as executive secretary to Jimmy that he brought him to Washington to be the liaison with Capitol Hill.

Stu Eizenstat is Jimmy's top domestic adviser. Technically, he heads the Domestic Council but probably this office will be absorbed under the reorganization program and other functions will come under Stu's control.

I have only met Stu a couple of times, but I know that Jimmy has great respect for him and his abilities. Though only thirty-four, Eizenstat supervises a staff of twenty professionals and twelve secretaries—probably the largest support group in the White House.

Stu's memos are among the best the President receives because this aide spends hours perfecting them and thinking through the concepts put forth in them. And as Eizenstat puts it, "I never tell the President anything without also telling him what it will cost."

Eizenstat is one of the "Georgia Mafia" who did not come from the area around Plains. He grew up in Atlanta, was an All-American basketball player at Grady High School, and later attended Harvard Law School. He has always been highly active in the Jewish community.

One of Stu's rules for himself is that he always tries to come up with a decision or report within the time limit of forty-eight hours, so he is a man the President can really count on.

Stuart Eizenstat and his staff must answer letters referring to issues of the day.

The President himself gives his signature about fifty times a day, on important official letters, letters to friends, and autograph requests. Besides that, he signs legislative bills into law and documents such as missions.

Greg Schneiders was one of Jimmy's top advisers, who didn't happen to be part of the "Georgia Mafia." Greg was a nice-looking twenty-nine-year-old restaurateur when his brother gave him a ticket to one of our fund-raising luncheons in Boston, in July of 1975.

Greg was so impressed with Jimmy that he volunteered to help set up a Carter for President Headquarters in Washington, D.C.

This put him in close contact with Peter Bourne, who was in charge of setting up the Washington office. Bourne was so impressed with Greg Schneiders' brightness and eagerness to work that he put him together with Jody Powell, who needed help with the press.

So he was in on the ground floor and he was the only man around, from what I hear, who didn't get excited, lose his temper, or get flustered. Carter noticed these qualities and soon he was taking Schneiders along with him to be a jack-of-all-trades.

Greg kept the wrong people away from Carter, without antagonizing anyone and he was a comfortable fellow to have sitting in the next seat on a plane.

The press used to laugh that Greg was "Mr. Step 'n' Fetch It," but the menial jobs paid off. From simply holding Jimmy's coat, he ended up making comments and suggestions that Carter listened to and took seriously.

When Jimmy was elected and going to the White House, he was planning on having Greg as his appointments secretary, until the FBI did its routine investigation. It found that Greg had been sued a few times for debts incurred in his restaurant business.

Also, the press at about the same time was making public the fact that Greg had a "female roommate" who wasn't his wife. The new President had made a big point of saying that he respected family life and that he hoped that everyone living together who wasn't married would get married.

The story has a happy ending. Greg was given a clean bill of health as to his personal financial honesty and integrity. He was ap-pointed director of special projects for the White House. As for his roommate, he married her, and Jimmy danced at his wedding.

22 · A TASTE OF DANGER

Since I've become somewhat acquainted with the Secret Service officers who protect Cousin Jimmy, I've been fascinated with how thorough they are and how they operate.

When Jimmy attended church after he received the nomination, there would always be one or two Secret Service people at every door. Also, inside the church one would sit right behind him and there was usually one on his left side across the aisle.

The Secret Service would always check the church building for bombs before Cousin Jimmy would enter and they even looked under all the shrubbery around the church. They used a walkie-talkie extensively.

Once in church I saw a man approach Cousin Jimmy with a brown envelope after a church service. Someone immediately radioed the Secret Service officer nearest the man to check him out and the envelope as well.

The Secret Service officer did. I stood there and watched. There was no danger, but it pays to be careful and the Secret Service was taking no chances with the President's life.

The Secret Service officers are very studious individuals. They talk very little. They want all the information they can obtain but they never report back to you concerning the outcome.

I find from gradually getting to know some of them that they are human like anyone else. The men like good-looking women and are not immune to meeting them whenever you care to introduce one to them.

I got on a first-name basis with one Secret Service man and I learned to admire him very much. His name was Louis Sanchez and he spoke fluent Spanish. Louis was about twenty-six years old and single.

I kidded him a good bit about meeting a nice girl here in Plains and getting married. He would always blush. He was very devoted to his work and he liked Jimmy. Knowing how Jimmy likes to speak Spanish and even reads a Spanish Bible, I told Louis a good way to get Jimmy's attention was to talk with him sometimes in Spanish.

I think Louis was a little bashful about doing this. He admired Jimmy very much and would have given his life to protect him, if necessary. Louis was transferred to some other part of the Secret Service, away from Plains.

He came back by to see me a few months later. He said he had just been away doing his summer training in the Reserves.

Once in the summer of 1977, security really heated up when what looked like a remote-control bomb was discovered in a flower bed near the Plains Baptist Church. Several ladies, who were interested in flowers, fortunately found the device and alerted the Secret Service stationed in Plains.

It seems the device had been planted in the flower bed several days before the ladies found it. There was a battery, a radio, and a container of mysterious white powder all taped together.

Someone had gone to a lot of work to construct this apparently life-endangering bomb. Though the experts took the powder for examination, we never learned what they had found out about it.

Almost as soon as Jimmy had been sworn in as President, the threats against his life began. A man who had lost his government job and who lived near Washington was arrested for making threatening comments and saying that "if I had a gun, I'd shoot the President."

The last I heard he was undergoing psychiatric treatment.

Then there was the story that got into the papers about another young man who somehow slipped by all the guards and Secret Service men and wandered around the White House, actually sticking his head into the President's Oval Office.

He asked if that was the way to Mark Siegel's office and President Jimmy casually answered him, directing him to the right office. From what I hear, the whole security system of the White House was reviewed and overhauled at this point.

Since I still have a listed phone, it means that I get some of the crank calls with sinister messages for Jimmy. Sometimes, my wife, Ruth, gets the calls. Both of us have been instructed on how to handle them.

My wife got one just before Jimmy went to Chicago to attend Mayor Daley's funeral. A young-sounding man called our home saying he was calling from New York City. He gave her his name and the telephone number of his parents.

He said he was in a phone booth, and that number would be of no consequence. Anyway, he said, "Please don't let Jimmy Carter go to Chicago. He'll be killed." He said he just had that gut feeling that something was going to happen, that he was working with the Robert Kennedy campaign when he was shot, and he just had a feeling that something would happen to Jimmy.

He even went on to say that Daley died when there was nobody in the room with him. At that time, Ruth had not yet read the newspaper of the day, and she hurriedly read it while waiting for the Secret Service to call back.

Sure enough, everything he told Ruth of events surrounding Daley's death were true; the fact that he had just gone for a checkup and died in the doctor's office.

Ruth had called the Secret Service in Plains immediately and told an agent the story, expressing the hope that she wasn't worrying him with petty little nothings.

The Secret Service people had said they always wanted to know every little thing of suspicion. When the agent called back, Ruth had to recount every detail of the story again.

Of course, being very new in all the recent happenings and unaware of all the procedures, Ruth then became very concerned about Cousin Jimmy and was very anxious to call him. But the Secret Service man calmed her and told her that hundreds of such instances occur and he didn't think the President was in any real danger.

It was as early as October 1975 that two Secret Service officers arrived in Plains, trying to look inconspicuous. In a town of 683 people, two well-dressed strangers in knitted suits and with Yankee accents, wearing dark sunglasses, did not exactly go unnoticed.

Since everyone knew that Jimmy had taken a notion to run for President the next year, people were quickly pointing them out as the Secret Service.

In a little while after I'd noticed those two well-dressed strangers, two men entered my antique store trying to look casual and looking even more conspicuous. I did a second take and almost burst out laughing. They were the same two men. Only this time, they were wearing bib overalls like you see on the *Hee Haw* television show—brand-new and stiff.

They still stuck out like sore thumbs. I said, "Oh, you fellows must be some of the Secret Service assigned to guard my cousin, Jimmy."

They looked at each other and shook their heads. They had gone to great lengths to blend into the town, visiting Ernest Turner's general store for inconspicuous clothes and they still weren't making it.

An event took place on November 8, 1975, that alarmed the Georgia state troopers. That was the date Cousin Jimmy publicly announced in Plains that he was seeking the presidency. As Jimmy was making his announcement, twenty-two-year-old Larry Williams was observed in the act of what seemed to be pointing a rifle at Jimmy.

Larry acknowledged that the rifle had indeed been pointed toward Jimmy but said that he was merely trying to get a better look at him through the telescopic sight of his .308-caliber hunting rifle.

Larry was handcuffed to a light pole and later taken to the Plains police office where he was detained for several hours.

Jimmy refused to press charges. Afterward, Cousin Jimmy was much concerned about the welfare of Larry and his wife, who was pregnant.

All of Jimmy's relatives have the problem of strangers trying to get us to slip messages to Jimmy at the White House. Ruth Stapleton, his sister, says that strangers are constantly appearing at her doorstep in Fayetteville, North Carolina, with letters and messages insisting that she get them to the President.

I have the same experience every day. Hundreds of people try to reach Jimmy through me. I just have to do the best I can. If I think it is important enough, I try to get the message to Jimmy. If not, I politely excuse myself.

One woman called Jimmy Carter, collect, at my home three times one night. The operator had a very hard time convincing the woman that Jimmy Carter was in Washington at the White House being President, and not at my home in Plains.

Soon after Jimmy had won the Democratic nomination, a woman came into my antique shop one evening on auction night. The antique auction had not yet started and I had gone home to freshen up and get a bite to eat, as I always did.

She told one of my clerks that she had come to Plains to kill "Jimmy, first and if not him Billy, second, and if not him, Hugh, third." My faithful clerk, Cecil Rathel, got her out of the store immediately and down the street to a café where there happened to be a state patrolman.

The patrolman took her to Americus to jail. The woman didn't have a gun. But she had left a sack of clothes and incidental items in my antique shop. They questioned her thoroughly, and since she seemed harmless, they put her on a bus for her home in California.

That is the last I've ever heard of her. The story I was able to piece together is that the woman had hung around Plains for about two weeks prior to the Saturday night on which she made her move. In fact, she had attended our church twice.

During the governor's campaign of 1970, one thing kept us all worried about Jimmy—his disregard for his own safety in airplanes. Some of the family would always go down to see Jimmy safely off on his campaign tours, taking off from the dirt field airstrip, and we would hold our breath and say a silent prayer.

Not only was Jimmy fearless, he also showed loyalty. He had one pilot who insisted on taking him everywhere.

He wanted Jimmy to fly with him in his plane, *all the time.* And Jimmy did fly with him most of the time.

Frankly, I think by then Jimmy could have flown the plane himself, as he usually sat up front with the pilot and he knew a lot about flying anyway and also knew radio procedure.

One of the safest pilots to fly Jimmy around during the presidential campaign was Tom Peterson, who operates the Peterson Airport outside of Plains, and is a very capable young man. Recently my daughter Laurie's husband, Ed Tharpe, soloed from Peterson's field. Ed took flying lessons from Pete.

There were all kinds of amusing things happening in Cousin Jimmy's early days in the White House. Once it seemed that someone had made off with Jimmy's suit jacket, right out of the Oval Office.

Secret Service men couldn't crack the case for hours. It turned out that Jody Powell, who is kidded for being the sloppiest dresser around the White House, had simply flung both his and the President's coats over his arm as he left in his usual rolled-up shirt sleeves.

I am very sorry that bloodshed had to take place at Plains soon after Jimmy became President. I am referring to the incident of the Ku Klux Klan holding a rally in Plains. I want to explain about that.

First of all, the people of Plains had nothing to do with the rally. The whole incident would not have happened had the City Council checked up on the person applying for the permit. I understand that the application had been made out for a permit for a bluegrass festival with a music show and patriotic display plus activities.

It turned out to be a Klan Rally and ended in tragedy with some thirty-nine people injured. Klansmen were on the grandstand when a small sports car sped through the field and smashed up underneath the grandstand.

The speakers fell like rag dolls as the platform dropped. The car tore into the crowd around the grandstand as well. There were about 250 people in all at the rally.

Many of the people in front of the stand were hit by the car, some injured badly. There were many broken bones, whiplash, cuts, and serious bruises.

Bill Wilkinson, imperial wizard of the Invisible Empire of the Klan, was quoted in the *Ledger Enquirer* newspaper of Columbus, Georgia, as saying the Klan chose Plains for the rally because "we want to help these people keep blacks out of their church."

The Plains Baptist Church became the center of controversy in the fall of 1977 with racial tones involved along with a lot of other things. The big question going around this community now is whether someone in the Plains Baptist Church invited the Klan here then and also if that same person invited them again this time. Also, who was the person or persons who extended the invitation, if one was extended?

I stayed away from the affair completely and ignored it. When I heard the rally was going to be held, I felt that the City Council could still cancel the permit based on the fact that they did not know all the facts when they granted the permit.

But the mayor and City Council refused to take action; the rally was held, along with a cross burning.

The President deplored this tragedy when he heard of it. I'm sure that he was very disappointed that such an event would take place in his hometown.

We urged prayer for all those hurt at the rally in our new church that Sunday night—Maranatha Baptist Church of Plains.

23 · A CAMPAIGN IS A FAMILY AFFAIR

One day in October of 1974 I saw a car coming up the long drive to my house. It was Governor Jimmy Carter and he was alone. He usually had a state patrol bodyguard with him but not that day.

He got out of his car and knocked on my back door. He had on blue jeans and sneakers. I couldn't imagine what he wanted.

When I went to the door he asked me if he could come in, saying he had something to tell Ruth and me.

I invited him in the den and he and Ruth and I sat down for a chat. He said that we were the first family members that he had told beside his mother. He said he wanted all the family to know first. By this time I was getting excited and anxious for him to get to the point as I couldn't imagine what he was going to say. Finally, he blurted it out, "I am going to run for President of the United States."

I said, "What!" I couldn't believe my ears. I knew that he was measuring himself against other candidates and feeling just as qualified, but thinking is one thing and action is another.

There was no peanut smile on his face as Cousin Hot explained why he was determined to run two years hence. He said he was sure the timing was right.

I said, "Why do you think you can win?"

Jimmy said he had talked to many of the presidential hopefuls and many of them had spent the night at the Governor's Mansion in Atlanta. He had studied them and their words and their political philosophies. He said he felt on safe ground and was just as qualified as they were for the office.

We discussed the problem of being a southerner. He would be breaking a precedent dating from the time of the Civil War, although you could have your choice in calling Lyndon Johnson a southerner or a western man.

Jimmy said his problem would be to get the American people to realize that a southerner from Georgia could perform as President just as well as a person from any other part of the United States—and that, if he could get that idea across, he could win.

I looked at my old buddy. He seemed so eager and so serious and full of confidence that I could not bring myself to tell him about the doubt I felt about the fulfillment of his great dream. A President from the Deep South?

Hardly! And yet, who was I to say? Jimmy had done other unbelievable things—like commanding a submarine and becoming governor.

I had helped him win his race for the governorship and no matter what I thought, I would help him now.

I said, "Jimmy, I'm willing to help you in any way that I can."

He smiled. He said, "I want you to look after the home front for me."

"Fine," I said. At that time, I didn't know what he meant but after he won the Florida primary I learned what he meant. I was to be the person who explained Jimmy Carter.

Newspaper reporters, photographers, and book writers from all over the world began to converge on Plains to find out about this man named Jimmy Carter who was well on the way to becoming the Democratic front-runner.

About 95 percent of the media people were directed to me for interviews and information. I sent some of them to other members of our family for additional information. I know that I spent six to eight hours a day in interviews for several weeks, after he announced his candidacy.

So this explains one of the things Jimmy meant when he said he wanted me to look after the home front. That early press reaction meant a lot to his success as a presidential candidate.

There was one other question Jimmy asked before he left my house that historic day in October 1974. He wanted my opinion as to when he should announce his candidacy for the presidency. I suggested he announce it while he was still governor before the end of his term.

He decided to announce in December 1974 at the Civic Center in Atlanta.

The more I thought of Jimmy's chances of getting the nomination of the Democratic party, the more possible it seemed. Jimmy was a quick study and, after all, he must have learned an awful lot about the inner workings of the party in his position as chairman of the National Democratic Party Campaign Committee for 1974.

In this job he had learned all the special problems of every state and of the congressional districts of every state. He knew what each state wanted.

Jimmy's strategy was simple but would require a tremendous amount of work: *Make a total effort all over the nation.* Knowing how thorough my cousin could be, I shuddered as I thought of the work involved. Sure enough, after Jimmy finished his term as governor in January of 1975, he visited over half the states and met thousands of people, many of them very influential.

By that I mean these were people, each of whom could exert influence on thousands of voters.

It was too much to do visiting a state only once. But he went back to certain states again and again. He continued traveling all over the country until he had developed certain intuitive feelings about what people were looking for in their next President.

He was keeping lists of things that rankled people and those that he agreed with became part of his credo. Some of the things seemed only of minor importance until one thought about it and then realized it was not a small thing at all.

Such as, "No public official should accept anything of value."

And, "We should have minimum secrecy in government and maximum personal privacy for citizens."

And, "Public financing of campaigns should be extended to members of Congress."

And, "The mechanism of our government should be understandable, efficient, and economical."

Then, borrowing from his approach to state government reform, which had cut administration costs in half, "We need to abolish and consolidate hundreds of obsolete and unnecessary federal programs and agencies."

Jimmy had thoughts on the problems of every segment of American life—the need for a comprehensive education program, the need for a comprehensive national health program, the finishing of the basic U.S. Interstate Highway System.

The correction of gross tax inequities. The need to open our political doors so that people will know what their politicians are doing. The need for eliminating waste and inefficiency in national security and the ultimate goal, of nuclear curbing weapon capability among all nations.

These were some of the things Jimmy listed after learning what the people worried about, and these were some of his goals for the future, should he be in a position to help make needed changes.

Getting Jimmy elected to the White House was a family affair for us and each of us helped in any way possible, if only to baby-sit Amy for a while or pass out literature. As I had done in the gubernatorial campaign, I worked with the press, feeding them the things they needed to know about Jimmy and about the family and about Plains.

My daughter Connie was part of the Peanut Brigade. I believe it was in March or April of 1976 that she went with the Brigade to Baltimore—each of them, of course, paying their own expenses as part of their contribution to Cousin Jimmy.

I enjoyed hearing all about that trip when she got back, and must say youngsters are more nervy than we used to be in our days of timid politics.

Connie was in a car with Dick Fleming, a fellow from Atlanta, who I believe is with the administration now in Washington. An NBC crew was following them. They would really ham it up for the benefit of the cameras.

They would pull up beside people at red lights and yell into other cars and pass out pamphlets. At shopping centers they'd do the same and make such a commotion they'd get on the national news. Connie had a microphone strapped around her waist and clipped to her collar so that when she walked up to a person to talk to them, they could not see it and wouldn't know they were being recorded.

The funny thing about the mike was that it could transmit from her car to the NBC van. Dick and she didn't know that until they had been riding around for a long time. Suddenly Connie got nervous about their lack of privacy.

They were riding down the street when Dick said of California Governor Jerry Brown, Jimmy's main rival in Maryland, "You know, I really think that Jerry Brown is a twirp!" And that was one of their milder statements.

Connie got nervous and said, "Dick, do you think that they can hear us back there in the van?"

"I don't know," he said. Then Connie said into her mike, "If anyone else is partaking of this conversation, let it be known by waving your arms and legs out of the windows of a van!"

All of a sudden they looked behind them and arms, legs, cameras, and just about everything else you can think of were waving furiously out of the windows of the NBC van.

The van driver also started blowing the horn. Needless to say, after that Dick and Connie stopped running down the other candidates, and settled for telling how great they thought Jimmy was. But even so, the NBC gang had their fun threatening to make a Nixon-type tape exposé out of it!

Don Oliver, the NBC commentator who was following in the van, became a good friend of Connie's. That little incident had broken the ice. Later in Plains, she invited him to my house for lemonade and a swim. Everyone sat around talking about the campaign and swimming was forgotten.

Another thing that she and Dick Fleming did in Baltimore was to barge in on a bull roast political rally for all the local candidates. They had heard that Jerry Brown was going to attend and give a political plug for himself so the brigade had assigned Dick and Connie to counteract Brown's appeal.

It had been raining that day so they put on rain slickers that practically dragged on the floor and they looked like clowns, Connie said, as they ran around taping Jimmy Carter posters all over the bull roast area. She recalled that they had managed to tape a Jimmy Carter poster over each keg of beer.

The people in charge were so confused by what they were doing that they were afraid to stop them.

Getting bolder and bolder, Connie and her buddy taped posters on the doors and walls, then started putting brochures on the tables and talking to people, above the sound of the rock band that was playing.

Some people, she said, were very friendly and others furiously tore up the brochures saying Jerry Brown was the only good candidate.

Connie said she learned that in campaigning it doesn't pay to argue with anyone and so she would just smile and turn to someone else.

The plot began to thicken when Dick sauntered up to the band-leader and asked him if the presidential candidate's young cousin, Connie Carter Collins, could make a little speech to the crowd.

"I almost died when I found out what Dick had done." There was no way she could back out. The bandleader introduced her as a celebrity who had come all the way from Georgia.

"Well, I certainly wasn't a celebrity," Connie said, "but I went up there with my very southern accent and my funny rain slicker with its Jimmy Carter posters all over it and I just started talking.

"I told those people that I had come all the way from Georgia on my own expense to tell them how much I believed in Jimmy Carter.

"I told them that he was a compassionate, hardworking man who would make them a great President. It couldn't have lasted more than forty-five seconds, but it was the biggest speech I've ever made. I was shaking like a dead leaf on a tree.

"And Daddy," she added, "I was so startled. Many of the people started asking for my autograph. Can you imagine anyone wanting my autograph because my name is Carter?"

Connie admitted that eventually campaigning "gets in your blood—once you start you just can't stop."

The hardest part, she found, was what Rosalynn Carter had done a lot of—house-to-house campaigning and leaving brochures. If no one came to the door, Connie would write, "Sorry we missed you. Hope you will vote for my cousin," and sign her name.

Everyone who worked for Jimmy now takes a little credit for his presidential victory but Connie staunchly maintains that it was the notes that all the Peanut Brigadeers wrote that did the trick.

As it turned out, Jerry Brown won in Maryland in spite of the Peanut Brigade and I teased Connie about that. She said, "Yes, I know, Jerry Brown beat us miserably in the Maryland primary, but I'll always consider it a victory because I know we did turn some people around!"

Connie was also glad that she had been in Baltimore one of the times when Jimmy needed her and all the support he could get. Jimmy was speaking and getting a lot of heckling from the crowd for his stand on the amnesty issue.

Connie was waiting by the ropes so that she could catch him when he came out. During his speech, her group had positioned them-selves so that each was beside a heckler. They would just stare the hecklers up and down to the point where they got embarrassed to shout out. They shut a lot of hecklers up that way.

When Cousin Jimmy came out from that ordeal and caught sight of Connie, he grabbed her and hugged her and shook hands with a few of the Brigadeers who were with her. Connie said, "I realized he must have been awfully lonely out on that highway." She meant the campaign trail, of course.

As Jimmy's spokesman to the press on family matters, I kept getting all the flak about how hard it was to get an interview with Jimmy through Jody Powell. Jody would be a good fellow and say, sure, sure, he could arrange it but then the interview would never happen.

Reporters would fly hundreds of miles to be at the right place at the appointed time for just a fifteen-minute interview but it wouldn't take place.

It is hard to believe how furious some of the reporters could get when they felt they had done everything to cooperate and still were out in the cold but I think a reporter of *Rolling Stone* was probably the angriest—at least he found the most effective way to express it.

What happened is that he had arranged an interview, not through Jody Powell, but through Ham Jordan, to see Carter during the Florida primary. He had flown from Colorado to Orlando, where the interview was supposed to take place.

But there was no interview. Jimmy was not available and Hamilton wasn't there to work it out. The reporter went to Ham's hotel room and banged on the door but Ham would not open it.

The reporter, in his fury, set the door on fire using lighter fluid from his cigarette lighter.

I was always getting reports of the anger of the press, wherever they went with Jimmy. And if this is what it was like for the winner, I wonder what it must have been like for the losers.

Take the time Jimmy went to Hollywood.

Cousin Jimmy got the royal welcome when he went to California as a candidate. Warren Beatty entertained for him in his own apartment at the Beverly Wilshire Hotel. But the press got very angry—and were still talking about it when I saw them later in Plains—because Beatty had decreed that even Carter's arrival for the party could not be filmed. Few reporters got in.

I found out later what the party had been like anyway. Louise Lasser, who was the star of the series *Mary Hartman, Mary Hartman*, was lying on the floor to be comfortable and other guests were almost as relaxed—Peter Falk, Dennis Weaver, Carroll O'Connor, and George Peppard.

It turned out it was George Peppard who had been so against the press that his friend Beatty had gone to a lot of trouble to keep them out.

The press was not happy either about the treatment they'd gotten at another fancy party thrown for Cousin Jimmy by Lew Wasserman, the producer of *Jaws,* the spectacularly successful movie. Later I sat at the same table with Lew, the head of MCA (Music Corporation of America), when we both were guests at the White House.

The media was furious that Wasserman kept them roped off and isolated from the guests in a room far away from the party. Chairman Robert Strauss of the Democratic party had arranged the party and the press people were angry at him, too, for their shabby treatment.

A few reporters were supposed to be a pool and give the others a fill-in on everything they saw, but they, too, were kept away, except for a brief look at the dinner table. Lew told them that even the names on the guest list were strictly private.

I guess even Cousin Jimmy was a little nervous when he came upon this scene of opulence because, as I got the story later, when Jimmy arrived at the door he looked around a little nonplussed and said, "Ah, this reminds me of Plains."

His hosts wanted to know what he meant by that and he explained, "All these trees."

Before the busy night was over, the press covering Carter managed to get their feelings across to him and he was gentleman enough to apologize to them. And maybe sensing their contempt for the limousines he was riding around in, while talking about being the common man's choice, he quit using a limousine the next day.

At the start of the campaign, Jimmy wanted four young men who would be available so that one could travel with him at any given time. Hugh, Jr., went on Jimmy's first campaign trip and Jimmy came back saying he wanted Hugh, Jr., to go with him all the time.

Hugh, Jr., feels so close to Jimmy that he could almost read his mind on what he wanted and have it for him before he said a word. To my knowledge, I don't believe the other three men went on the trips after all, as Jimmy's aides.

Little by little, Jimmy was getting his act together and the *underdog* was feeling stronger all the time.

One of Jimmy's best campaigners never said a word. He didn't have to. It was that monster peanut with its big toothy grin. All he did was stand there and Jimmy always tried to position himself so that this character Mr. Peanut—"The World's Largest Man-made Peanut"—

would show up in the picture with him.

The monster peanut is fourteen feet high and weighs 450 pounds. It is built out of hoops, chicken wire, foil, and foam. It was unveiled at Evansville, Indiana, at a political rally for Jimmy in 1976 during the campaign.

Carter saw it and fell in love with it. He said he wanted it. Loretta Townsend, who was one of its designers, was getting the peanut in shape for gift-giving when two men kidnapped the peanut and smuggled it to Plains without Mrs. Townsend knowing about it.

When Billy Carter saw it, he said, "This is the ugliest peanut I ever saw in my life." The Secret Service drilled a hole in it to make sure it contained no bombs, as it was always near Jimmy when he spoke or held press conferences on the depot platform in Plains.

It became the world's most photographed peanut because of its famous location. Tourists hacked out pieces of it for souvenirs. Mrs. Townsend came to Plains recently and repaired it, coated it with fiber glass to protect it and installed a commemorative plaque.

It has now been removed from the famous old Depot platform and has been placed in front of Mrs. Reese's new store, where it can be properly cared for.

The campaign put a spotlight on Plains as the new year, 1976, rolled around. The townspeople realized that it was time to shape up and they looked around. The row of stores on Main Street were badly in need of paint. Even worse was the Plains High School, where Jimmy had gone to school and graduated.

Patches of paint were falling off the walls and there was even widespread termite damage. Back in 1972 Jimmy Carter was the number one person on a list of forty-four who had actually sued the school board for neglecting the public schools in favor of private schools.

Cousin Jimmy had been governor when he led the legal action protesting that the Board of Education had slashed the county's school tax rate by two-thirds in Sumter County, making it impossible to keep up the schools properly.

As the suit put it: "The defendants [the board members] have placed their loyalties to the private schools of Sumter County above their public duties as members of the Sumter County Board of Education and have engaged in a . . . conspiracy under color of state law and their official positions to injure and destroy public education in the Sumter County public schools."

After two years of struggle to upgrade the public schools, we were shocked that the suit was dismissed.

During the summer of 1976 as tourists started straggling in a few at a time, and then in constantly greater numbers, the Town Council took action and put a clean coat of paint on everything right along Main Street.

There was a town campaign to encourage homeowners to make Jimmy proud of his hometown. The hardware store did a brisk business in paint and nails. Pillars that had been crooked for years were suddenly standing straight, and signs that you could hardly read were suddenly legible again.

One who failed to shape up, paint and fix up his place of business, was Billy Carter.

The Billy Carter filling station continued to be an eyesore with a tumbledown look and a shabby bench for the town jokesters to take their ease as they worked at getting rid of a six-pack of beer.

At this writing, I can look across Main Street at Billy's filling station, which is almost directly opposite. It is unpainted and tumbledown-looking but the tourist cars pour through it in a never-ending stream so that they can say they bought their gasoline from the President's brother.

They also get out of the car and go inside looking for Billy. But he is seldom there. They settle for buying a can of beer and they save the can for a souvenir.

People wonder whether I contributed any money to Jimmy Carter's presidential campaign, or whether I was solely a campaign worker. Some have asked and some have hinted broadly.

I don't mind telling that I contributed the maximum to his campaign, one thousand dollars.

I actually contributed several hundred dollars more but according to rules and regulations, all of my donations over a thousand were refunded to me.

To show how things worked in the primaries and give the reader a taste of primary politics, let me just tell the sneaky but brilliant way Jimmy won in Florida, one of the pivotal victories.

Jimmy had innocently urged the major candidates to stay out of the Florida primary, saying he alone could eliminate their chief competition, George Wallace. Even Congressman Andrew Young came to Florida and campaigned among the blacks for Carter. Many of the major candidates were pleased to skip Florida, because they thought it was just a "stop Wallace" movement.

But Jimmy knew better. He had it all figured out. He knew if he did stop Wallace in Florida, he would be well on the way to the presidency. Florida was a cross section of all people from all over the nation. Wallace had carried it big in the last presidential election. Jimmy knew he had to have the Wallace vote, and taking Florida not only proved he could do that but that a cross section of the nation was willing to vote for him.

Scoop Jackson recognized Jimmy's strategy too late. He rushed to Florida and tried to make a big splash in the race but he was far too late.

Jackson had more money than Jimmy and he had more support from labor but the people wanted something different this time. Jackson had that old-fashioned look of short hair and every hair in place. Jackson was businesslike and brusque.

The people wanted compassion, looks, charm, and an honest smile and they found it in Jimmy Carter.

Jackson was often late in arriving. Jimmy respected people too much to be late. He always arrived ahead of time, no matter what the situation. This is one of the most important assets a politician can have—punctuality in making the scene.

And there were other reasons Carter swept the Sunshine State. More time was spent there by Jimmy and his family than by any other candidate. More organizational work was done in Florida. Phil Wise, of Plains, did a tremendous job of running Jimmy's campaign in Florida. He had good voter contact through his fine handling and relations with the news media.

And I must not forget the Peanut Brigade, which was especially effective in north Florida.

After the Florida primary, "We're No. 1" rang throughout the nation among Carter supporters, and many people began to get on the bandwagon who had never thought he had a chance before.

As for Wallace, he stayed on the campaign trail until after Michigan, hurling a lot of insults at Jimmy Carter. But after Jimmy won Ohio, Wallace was the first big politician to phone and endorse him. That's politics.

Incidentally, my son, Hugh, Jr., and I both worked on that Florida primary. Hugh, Jr., and Mrs. Dot Padgett were cochairmen of the Peanut Brigade drive in northern Florida. They invited me to fly down and meet the group at a large hotel in Jacksonville and to act as master of ceremonies for a grand final rally for Jimmy.

We held the meeting similarly to the ones we had held when we were having the Sunday afternoon meetings near the close of Jimmy's gubernatorial campaign in Atlanta in 1970. It was a great meeting and I left there that night feeling certain that Jimmy would win Florida.

After Jimmy won the Florida primary, thousands of tourists and newsmen began to pour into Plains to find out where this miracle boy came from and to learn something about him.

Cousin Jimmy's strategy was to run in all the primaries. He wanted to build an overwhelming lead in his number of convention delegates and take them to the July convention. His strategy worked.

I called hundreds of delegates myself on Jimmy's behalf, especially uncommitted delegates. Based on their reaction, I felt Jimmy had everything going his way.

I continued to call until one day Jimmy came into my antique shop and sat down in an upholstered chair. With a big grin he said, "Well, Beedie, you can stop your calling. Governor Milton Shapp [of Pennsylvania] has just endorsed me and I have more than enough delegates to win the nomination."

It was one of the most soul-satisfying moments for me of the whole campaign.

Still, I knew there would be much work ahead. I almost developed a boxer's cauliflower ear holding the phone to my ear so much as I raised money for Jimmy's campaign. Somehow we always squeaked through.

By far the most memorable fund raiser of the whole campaign was a family affair—the Million Dollar Supper held at the Pond House, owned by Aunt Lillian, on October 2, 1976. Actually, the total amount of money raised in this Plains "spectacular" was $1,110,000.

In all, 222 guests gave $5,000 each. Counting all the volunteers and helpers, and even freeloaders, there were about 400 partaking of a most unusual array of food.

The way the "catering" had been handled was this: Mrs. Maxine Reese, one of our most loyal Carter supporters, had asked over one hundred volunteers to each prepare enough supper for five persons.

Some prepared fifty servings instead of five, so the reader can imagine how much food we had.

A V-shaped table was set up in the backyard of the Pond House to hold the food and there were tubs more waiting for space on the table. There were two tin washtubs of iced tea. The barbecue pit was decorated with clusters of grapes, ears of dried corn, apples, and pumpkins.

A huge trough was filled with ice and bottles of champagne and Chablis. On a special stand was a tremendous cake with a miniature White House on top.

The airports of outlying towns and Plains were doing a landslide business with private planes coming in from all over the United States. But even hardened party-goers looked a little stunned as they saw the mountains of food:

Barbecued beef, southern style; fried chicken; roast turkey; glazed ham; southern-style stew; and chicken pot pie. That took care of the meats.

For vegetables there were butter beans, string beans, black-eyed peas, corn pudding, baked beans, English peas, turnip greens, sweet potatoes, corn on the cob. Then there were various salads—green salad, potato salad, gelatin salad, deviled eggs, cucumber salad, pickles and relishes—plus corn bread, rolls, biscuits, pies—expecially pecan, southern style, and peach pie—and every variety of cake.

Of course, it would not have been complete without the tureens of peanuts that stood everywhere.

I got to talking with a charming woman, and was much impressed as she mentioned something about their seven houses around the world—two in Spain—and how they had flown in by chartered jet from their farm in Lexington, Kentucky.

As she introduced me to her husband, I realized who this charming woman was—Mary Lou Whitney, wife of philanthropist Cornelius Vanderbilt Whitney.

The Whitneys, as much as anyone, enjoyed the music of the Gritz—a blue-grass rock band from Furman University of Greenville, South Carolina, who played and sang on a stage bound by bales of straw.

And the Whitneys laughed uproariously as Lynn Moon, a beautiful girl from Buena Vista, Georgia, sang, "Peanut Pickin' Politickin' Man."

Then Jimmy gave a short talk about how much nobody knew who Jimmy was. The crowd roared with laughter when he said he wished those "searching for Jimmy Carter" could be here now.

My elder daughter, Laurie, was pregnant and not able to do as much for the campaign as she wanted to. Even so, she stayed at the depot many days helping at the campaign headquarters and she took home hundreds of envelopes to address.

At the inaugural, Laurie was so obviously pregnant that when she got into the big bus which was taking us from the Capitol Hill swearing-in ceremony to the parade stands near the White House, Chuck Robb immediately got up and gave her his seat. As son-in-law of former President Lyndon Johnson—and husband of Lynda Bird, who was also along—he was given the courtesy of Jimmy's Courtesy Shuttle Service.

In fact, the President-elect had arranged for all of us family members and friends such as the Robbs to have lovely picnic lunches to eat en route to our choice seats for the parade.

Victory had come hard. There had been a time a group had a slogan they called ABC—"Anybody But Carter." Sometimes Jimmy or Rosalynn would be heckled. They just learned to cope. It was a little harder on Rosalynn. She was so sincere that she wanted to stop and explain and try to change the heckler's mind.

She was a small determined figure handing out little packages of peanuts and literature. When I saw her later at the White House, dressed for a formal dinner for the Shah and Empress of Iran, I thought how different the backgrounds of these two women were.

And then I suddenly felt very proud as I realized that Rosalynn had earned her position at the White House every bit as much as Jimmy had.

Incidentally, Rosalynn once said that before she started campaigning, the only President she had ever seen had been President Truman—and that at a distance, when he was christening a ship somewhere that Jimmy was stationed.

Jimmy could poke a little fun at the fact that Rosalynn was doing so much campaigning to influence women's votes. As he told the story, a political pollster was going around following up Rosalynn to see which candidate was going to get the vote. At one house a young woman answered the door and the pollster asked, "Madame, what party does your husband belong to?"

The young woman drew herself up and reported, "Young man, *I'm the party* my husband belongs to."

24 · THE WINNING OF THE WHITE HOUSE

Why did Jimmy win?

The first month of the campaign, a staffer had rented a room in Philadelphia in a downtown hotel and set up a news conference. This was in the winter of 1975. No one showed up but the staffer and Jimmy.

Jimmy was not distressed. His confidence was not even dented. And sure enough, soon no room was large enough to hold the crowds.

Why did Jimmy win? People ask me this wherever I go. How could a man who was virtually unknown beat an incumbent President? How did it happen that the least known of the list of potential Democratic candidates got the chance to administer that knockout punch?

There are many answers—Watergate disillusionment and all the others you've heard ten times over. But I choose one word: confidence.

I recall Jimmy told someone on one of his earliest campaign trips, "You probably think I'm crazy but I'm going to be the next President of the United States." He was the most confident man I've ever seen in a campaign.

His confidence was infectious. His power to motivate people cannot be exaggerated. Other staffers working for other Democratic candidates worked fairly hard, but the Carter volunteers worked with zealous determination for even twenty hours per day when necessary—which was often.

I'm sure none of the other candidates approached the campaign with such scholarly attitude as Jimmy. Just as he was determined to enter every primary so that he would leave no stone unturned in seeking the nomination, so was he determined to know how every President before him had conducted his campaign.

And not only the campaigns of the winners. Jimmy studied every presidential race checking what techniques the winners and the losers had used and what their attributes had been, their speaking styles, and their platforms.

So when he patterned himself to a certain extent after Jack Kennedy, he was picking a winner closest to his own attributes and philosophies, and with a style that would be comfortable.

One of Jimmy's biggest enemies right from the start was Lester Maddox, who had been a cross Jimmy had to bear all through his governorship. As his lieutenant governor, Maddox had put in a bad word for him whenever he could, and he was doing it again.

The instant Jimmy Carter received his party's nomination, in July 1976, Maddox vowed he would support President Ford or Ronald Reagan, or whoever got the Republican nomination in the next month.

"He's the most totally dishonest person I've ever met," said Maddox, proceeding to dispute Jimmy's claim that his reorganization of the state had saved the taxpayers any money. Claiming that Carter lived in a "dream world," Maddox predicted that Jimmy would be a wild liberal "far to the left of Kennedy, Johnson and McGovern," and that he would impose national health care and cut defense to a dangerous level.

By contrast Julian Bond, the black state legislator, complained about Jimmy's "self-righteous air" and claimed he was "Nixonesque" in that he "wraps himself in the flag."

A man who had written speeches for him for just a few weeks—Robert Shrum—wrote an article claiming that Carter and his campaign advisers were cold and calculating.

To this latter charge, I said, "That's what campaigns are. One must not be a stargazer, but be coldly practical to win a campaign."

Actually, I found Jimmy was anything but cold around people. Because of his warmth and magnetism, crowds would almost fight each other to get close to him.

Jimmy Carter made his share of boo-boos but I don't think the *Playboy* interview was one of them and I'll tell you why. A lot of the entourage, press, and followers of his day-to-day campaign were saying in early October that Jimmy was bombing and the crowds were no longer coming to see him. He was talking to a bored handful of people.

He was giving the same speech over and over and they were tired of his goody-goody sound, like a preacher. A lot of tourists, too, were telling that Ford was pulling ahead because he had the prestige of the White House behind him and had just sat tight making no mistakes, like the ones Carter had.

"I'm going to vote for Ford because, at least, he's a human being. He's not trying to be too perfect like Jimmy is."

Well, all of a sudden Jimmy wasn't perfect anymore! I think Jimmy realized that there was no excitement or glamour about him, when he was just a good, God-fearing man satisfied with his life and completely in love with his wife.

Then the story came out in *Playboy*'s October 14, 1976, issue quoting Jimmy as saying, "I've looked on a lot of women with lust. I've committed adultery in my heart many times. This is something that God recognizes I will do—and I have done it—and God forgives me for it.

"But that doesn't mean that I condemn someone who not only looks on a woman with lust but who leaves his wife and shacks up with someone out of wedlock."

Wow! Suddenly Plains and the nation were buzzing about Carter. Every reporter wanted to know what he meant. I am sorry if the quote hurt Rosalynn's feelings—and I have it on good authority that it did—but I'm almost sure she owes the fact that she is in the White House to Jimmy's shocking statement putting himself in the category of millions of other men who can't have every woman they desire, but look anyway.

Suddenly, Cousin Jimmy was saying to the nation that he was not above other men and he did not consider himself above the crowd, even though he had not been sexually disloyal to his wife.

As Jimmy told the *Playboy* reporter, "Christ says, don't consider yourself better than someone else because one guy screws a whole bunch of women while the other guy is loyal to his wife."

Suddenly, Jimmy Carter was like a Hollywood celebrity—everybody wanted to take a look at him—the one who told it like it is. The women saw him as a more glamorous figure and a few told me they would like to see him look with lust at them.

Some women said Jimmy was getting more like Jack Kennedy every day and they hadn't realized how really sexy he looked.

What a lot of the press didn't understand was that Jimmy really was telling the truth when he said he feels he is not better than other people simply because his lust for his own wife keeps him from doing anything about his lust for other women. Also what Jimmy was saying was that he was harder on himself than on the people around him and he does not expect everyone to live by his standards.

He feels that God does forgive men their transgressions and God is man's judge, not Jimmy Carter.

Rosalynn stuck with her perfect answer, no matter how the press badgered her, "I trust Jimmy completely." But she had an amusing moment when some woman asked her if men and *women* had equal rights to lust.

Rosalynn agreed that women did indeed have an equal right to lust and I can just imagine Jimmy's face when he read that line.

Sometime later Rosalynn explained what she thought Jimmy was trying to do. "I think Jimmy was simply telling people that God does not expect anyone to be perfect but he loves us anyway and he forgives the person who has a personal relationship with God—the one who asks for forgiveness."

I liked what Rev. Bruce Edwards said about Jimmy's statement in *Playboy,* "I think the truthfulness of these statements in the interview is an indication of how deep his religious faith really is instead of how shallow it is, as some people would challenge.

"I think if you looked beyond the colloquialism that he used, he had some very deep theological thought about the way he views other people and that most people would do well to practice."

Lust might be a word in Jimmy's vocabulary but he never even told a dirty joke. About the only joke that could qualify along that line is this one:

I once knew a young divinity student who was very proud of his pure reputation. He always went to church, studied hard, never had dates, and he wanted to be sure that everybody thought that he was very, very holy and very pure.

One night he went into a restaurant. The restaurant was crowded. He sat down at one of the booths and after a while a nice-looking young girl came in and she looked all around and she couldn't find another place to sit so she sat down with him.

He was very embarrassed and he leaned over and he said, "I'm glad to have you here. I'm a divinity student and I don't have dates but I think we can sit together because the restaurant is so crowded."

And she screamed at the top of her voice, "To your hotel room!"

He said, "I didn't say anything about a hotel room, I just said that I'm glad that we're sitting here together here in the restaurant."

And she shouted, "To spend the whole night?"

And he said, "You've embarrassed me terribly. What are you talking about?"

And she said, "Well, to tell you the truth, I'm a psychology student, and my professor said I had to say something startling to someone I met to see what his reaction was. I didn't mean any harm by it."

And he shouted at the top of his voice, "Fifty dollars?"

My own favorite Jimmy Carter campaign story deals with the lack of loyalty in the world—and a parallel could be drawn to voters, as a parable:

There was a certain maid who came over to New York to get a job and couldn't speak good English, and she couldn't get a job. Finally, this doctor and his wife—very fine people without any children—thought they would do her a favor by letting her take a position in their own household.

She was a good servant, very well behaved, but after she had been there about two years, they had really gotten to rely on her. She was not married, she came in and told the lady of the house in her fumbling English, "I am very sorry to tell you this, but I am going to have a child."

The lady of the house said, "Well, that's just not possible. You are not even married."

The maid said, "Nevertheless, miss, it is true. I guess you want me to leave."

The lady of the house talked to her husband, and they finally decided that the maid was such a fine servant, and they needed her so badly, and they loved her, and she didn't have anyplace to go.

So they said, "You go ahead and have your baby and we will adopt it as our own."

So in a few months the baby came, and sure enough, the doctor and his wife adopted the baby as their own.

About a year later, the maid came back again and she said, "You don't know how I hate to come back, but I've just discovered that I'm going to have another baby."

And the lady of the house said, "Well, enough is enough; you'll have to leave."

Then the lady talked it over with her husband and told him that the maid was going to have to leave, and the husband said, "Look, just a minute. We already have this baby, and the maid takes care of the family, she nurses us, she knows us, I think we ought to give her one more chance. We don't want her to be abandoned here with this other baby."

So the maid had her second baby, and the doctor and his wife took it under their care, too. In a few months, the maid came back to see the lady of the house again. She said, "I hate to come to talk to you," and the lady of the house said, "Now look, I'm sure you're not going to have another baby."

And the maid said, "No, ma'am, I'm leaving."

And the lady of the house said, "How could you possibly be leaving when we've done all for you we possibly can to make your stay here more pleasant? We've helped you when you've needed it, and so forth."

And the maid said, "I just made up my mind. I ain't working for nobody that's got two children."

Sometimes Jimmy didn't need to fight against the criticism of others—he could be his own worst enemy. There was the very serious blunder he made during the campaign concerning "ethnic purity" from which he refused to back down.

What happened is that in the Pennsylvania primary Jimmy threw out a line about maintaining the ethnic purity of neighborhoods and not upsetting the ethnic purity by imposing change.

Civil rights people and just average voters became alarmed and said he sounded like Hitler with his talk of "ethnic purity."

This could have destroyed his Pennsylvania primary chances—maybe his whole campaign as well—had it gone on indefinitely.

When Jimmy gets stubborn, there is just one person who can handle him and that is Rosalynn. She sat him down and argued with him until he understood how he had sounded. And once he understood, he quickly tried to remedy the situation, making his open-mindedness clear and being careful to clarify what he had meant, but reiterating his belief that everyone had a right to live where he wanted to.

Nobody knew, better than I, how unconcerned Jimmy had been about color or ethnic origin. He had stood almost alone at his church, pleading for blacks to be permitted membership.

Looking back, I recall that the first pronouncement Jimmy made as governor of Georgia at his inaugural address in 1971 had been against racial discrimination. It had stirred the nation and been widely circulated in the newspapers.

I was there within a few feet of him when he made the statement. I looked around just after he made the statement. There were smiles and nods of approval on many faces and there were frowns of disapproval on some:

"I believe I know our people as well as anyone. Based on this knowledge of Georgians, north and south, rural and urban, liberal and conservative, I say to you quite frankly that the time for racial discrimination is over."

Billy Carter was the member of the family who campaigned least for his brother. Jimmy's three sons—Jack, Chip, and Jeff, all in their twenties—flew all over the country campaigning.

My three children campaigned also. I campaigned from my antique shop and went out to speak any chance I got, as well as acting as Jimmy's liaison with the press. Miz Lillian campaigned comfortably from a rocking chair in front of the Carter headquarters at the depot.

Only Billy Carter stood around in blue jeans and casual shirt chuckling at the commotion around him. "When he was governor," Billy said, "Jimmy and I came to an agreement—I would run the business and he would run the state. As far as I'm concerned, that still stands. He can run the country and I'll run the warehouse. He's not going to tell me how to run the warehouse and I'm not going to tell him how to run the government."

Now and then Jimmy would make sure that Billy was not left out completely and he would invite him to watch the returns come in.

It was in the Wisconsin primary that Billy Carter most annoyed the Carter forces by deserting them in Milwaukee to help the Udall campaign. He helped hang Udall posters drinking bourbon all the way—and then made himself at home at the Udall headquarters which was celebrating victory prematurely.

Billy kissed the candidate's wife and helped celebrate, too, as she danced around.

As it turned out, it was all a terrible mistake. Not only did Billy not belong but Winged Victory didn't belong there either. She went flying back to Carter headquarters and Billy ended up celebrating his brother's victory at still another party with strangers standing at the bar of the Marc Plaza Hotel, in Milwaukee.

But at least Billy did announce that he was going to vote for his brother—not because he was a Democrat or a blood relative, but because he was "the smartest man I know." I remember when Billy liked to infuriate his family and friends by proclaiming that he was voting the Republican ticket.

When Billy got dressed up during the campaign, he made sure he didn't have the conservative look of his brother. A favorite suit of his during the campaign was a green one that he wore with a lime-green tie. Other times he didn't wear a suit at all, but just shirt and jeans.

During the campaign, Billy claimed he wasn't going to do anything but stay home and tend to his peanuts, but he did, in effect, campaign to keep Plains as it was, a town with a pleasant small-town atmosphere. In fact, he headed a group that went to Johnson City, Texas, home of the late President Lyndon Johnson, to see what does happen to a little town that produces a President.

He looked over the LBJ tourist attractions with their neon lights, costumed dummies in their outdoor displays, and he was distressed. Lady Bird Johnson gave a barbecue for Billy and his friends and I guess she told him the facts of political life. He came back to Plains still alarmed and voiced his conclusion, "This damn town's going to be a junkyard or, worse yet, another Miami Beach unless somebody can stop it."

I am happy to say that the Town Council has done a good job in stopping it. Visitors see, not a bright and flashy town like Johnson City has become, but just a small town, looking like it always has, except for clean paint and a few tour buses going by.

Even before the primaries were well under way, the seer Jeane Dixon was predicting that Jimmy Carter would be the next President. We all protested that we didn't believe in such things, but we found it heartening.

As it turned out, the famed Jeane Dixon was right about Jimmy, but she made a slight error concerning whom he would defeat as the Republican candidate—Ronald Reagan!

It was surprising to see the divergent types who were won over to Jimmy Carter's camp. When Phil Walden, the "Music King," millionaire head of Capricorn Records, declared he was going to work for the election of Jimmy Carter for President, as early as 1975, his friends in the music industry said he was "fiddling the wrong tune."

Carter, they said, didn't have a chance. Walden just smiled and said that Jimmy would win and he would be "the best damned President of the United States since Thomas Jefferson."

It's hard to estimate how much influence rock stars had in winning votes for Jimmy but the Allman Brothers alone raised $50,000 in one benefit in Providence, Rhode Island, while Walden's groups raised over $100,000.

The concert donations were eligible for federal matching funds. Other rock groups who worked hard for Jimmy were the Outlaws, the Marshall Tucker Band, and Charlie Daniels.

Jimmy Carter scored many firsts in his remarkable rise to national fame and the presidency.

He won eighteen primary elections, for example; and he was the first graduate of the U. S. Naval Academy to become Chief Executive.

Though Jimmy and Rosalynn place their faith in the Lord, even they are a little superstitious. Rosalynn wore a green coat that she felt was lucky and Jimmy wore his red lucky tie. People kept wondering why Jimmy didn't have a greater variety of ties but it was just that he felt more confident in that red one.

The official color of the campaign was green, the color that Rosalynn used a lot in her house and in her wardrobe.

It's strange, what little things suddenly become important and precious when a man becomes President or even runs for the presidency. Suddenly all the little notes Jimmy had sent me were very precious to me and I regretted having thrown any of them away: the notes from the governor to me as his floor leader, and the notes from one member of the family to another.

I was not the only one suddenly saving everything. Fellow senators would tell me they had a letter from the governor dated 1971 and they were going to frame it.

Highway commissioner Tom Moreland, who had received a note from Jimmy thanking him for the good job done on the sidewalks of Plains, told me he had kept the letter from Governor Carter and was glad he did.

It was discovered that Jimmy had written his name in some freshly poured cement on a sidewalk at Georgia Southwestern College in 1942 and this became a sort of shrine to the students.

They say, "Names are votes." The candidate who can recognize the greatest number of people and call them by name is bound to be the winner. Potential voters who wander around at a rally, unrecognized, don't go away enthused about the candidate. Someone has to pay attention.

I remember the night in December 1974 at the Civic Center in

Atlanta when Jimmy was greeting people as a candidate for President of the United States, announcing his intention, even that early in the game.

I was standing at the door, with other close friends of Jimmy, welcoming people as they came in and trying especially not to let anyone important get by without recognizing them.

Someone tapped me on the shoulder and pointed out one person that we had let get by. It was Martin Luther King, Sr. He was wandering about unrecognized in the huge crowd. I immediately went over to him and introduced myself and told him how happy we were to see him there in support of Jimmy's candidacy for President.

He seemed most appreciative that I extended him that attention and I, frankly, believe that particular meeting had a big influence on his giving Jimmy the enthusiastic support that he gave him throughout the long and hard-fought presidential campaign.

I think Jimmy Carter was the closest we could get to the Abe Lincoln tradition in a modern President. It wasn't that he didn't have a better home to live in than Lincoln, but there was the same striving to learn and the same rock-hard work.

Lincoln split rails. Jimmy Carter never had an allowance, never had a penny given to him by his daddy. Every cent he had, he earned because this was the tradition of both my father and his. As Jimmy put it, when he talked to groups, he felt a special privilege in just having the chance to succeed.

"I'm the first child in my Daddy's family who ever had a chance. I used to get up at four A.M. to pick peanuts. Then I would walk three miles along the railroad track to deliver and sell them. My home had no running water or electricity."

No one who has not been around can understand how hard he was willing to work. When Ruth Stapleton told him she was getting fatigued from all the campaigning, Jimmy told his sister, "Honey, I can will myself to sleep until ten-thirty A.M. and get my tail beat, or I can will myself to get up at four A.M. and become President."

It is part of our family legend now that when Jimmy was nine, he bought five bales of cotton at five cents per pound. The little businessman stored it, as he heard grown-ups do, waited until the price tripled, and then sold.

We once figured out how much work Jimmy Carter did to finally win the election for governor. In the four years that he campaigned, after Ruth bolstered his morale, Jimmy made 1,800 speeches. And he and Rosalynn shook 600,000 hands.

When Jimmy was in the presidential race, many people would grab him and thank him for something he had done for them, long before he knew he would ever be a candidate for the highest office. Once it was a man who was so choked up he could hardly speak, but he just wanted to say thanks.

Jimmy understood and patted him. Afterward, he explained the man had come to him for help a long time ago when his daughter, who had been a battered wife, had shot her husband after a brutal beating.

Sometimes it would be a farmer to whom Jimmy had extended credit when no one else would. Jimmy had great faith in people and they would seldom disappoint him.

Billy, Jimmy's brother, who took over the business while Jimmy ran for office over a two-year span, was a "good ole boy" who made the farmers laugh and slap their knee, but it was Jimmy they would come to when they were in trouble.

His compassion was evident in the State House, too, when he chose a female inmate of the state prison to take care of Amy, who was three years old when he became governor. People were shocked to think that the governor would trust a prisoner, an acknowledged criminal, who admitted she had murdered a man, to take care of his most precious possession, his only daughter.

But Jimmy had perfect faith. So impressed was I with his faith that I had no qualms about letting this rehabilitated "felon" take care of my own grandchildren.

Jimmy had many heroes and loved to quote them.

From Adlai Stevenson, Jimmy gleamed this nugget: "A hungry man is not a free man."

From President Woodrow Wilson: "Democracy is not so much a form of government as a set of principles."

From Lyndon Johnson: If our Constitution "doesn't apply to every race, to every religion, it applies to no one."

Jimmy's presidential campaign was doubly interesting for me because it was fun to see how many things he had said to me or others suddenly took on new meaning as he said the same thing during the campaign.

For example, how natural it was for him to be religious: "Christianity is like breathing." And what he said about himself: "I have never desired to be better or wiser than any other person. I think my greatest strength is that I am an ordinary man who has worked and learned and lived his life with his family and made mistakes and tried to correct them without always succeeding."

All through the years I have known him, I have observed that Jimmy Carter can adjust and improve. I have never seen him refuse to listen to someone else's side of the question. If you proved he was wrong he would adjust.

There was a nice openness about Jimmy that people would like. Word would get back to me of things he had said that showed he wasn't putting on airs, and always knew who he was.

In California when someone asked him whether he had ever been to California before, Cousin Jimmy responded, "Well, it's the first time I've been to California when anyone noticed I was here."

Jimmy and his staff have figured out that all told, he made 2,100 speeches during his presidential campaign. This was about double the number he made to get the governorship.

Most of his speeches of course, were stump speeches—informal remarks at hundreds of political receptions and rallies.

The press corps used to complain about the sameness of his speeches. I have heard Jimmy tell them, "I am not speaking for the entertainment of the press corps." His most famous words said over and over, "There are a lot of things I would not do to be elected. I wouldn't tell a lie. I wouldn't make a misleading statement.

"I wouldn't betray a trust. I wouldn't avoid a controversial issue."

In the early days of the campaign, many reporters coming to Plains told me that Jimmy Carter had more intelligence than anyone we had had in the White House recently, and frankly, they said they were going to vote for him. But somehow they could not experience the closeness that they had found in following some other presidential candidates.

Jack Kennedy and LBJ, especially, had singled out certain reporters and had been very close with them—leaking good stories to them. I don't believe Jimmy did this.

On Election Day, Billy managed to tone down his pride in his brother by masking it with a bit of humor. "Jimmy's still upset because I decided not to take Secretary of State. I want to be his director of Alcohol and Firearms."

Prior to Jimmy's acceptance speech, Billy was asked if he would be in attendance and he replied, "I'm not sure. I have heard him talk before."

25·IT'S PRESIDENT JIMMY NOW

If you have to be a part of a presidential inauguration, the best way to see it is from the winning side. Our hotel rooms at the Washington Hilton were simply alive with fresh flowers and baskets of fruits and candies. The hotel was the center for the presidential family and Vice-President Mondale's family, and everything the management could do had been done. Later I learned that Chip Carter, the President's son, had been instrumental in arranging for our comfort.

The first of the inaugural festivities was the Mondale reception and as soon as I arrived and had greeted the new Vice-President and Mrs. Mondale, Rona Barrett started to interview me on camera for ABC. Laurie and Ed, and Connie and Leon really enjoyed this. One of the problems throughout was that the press was so busy trying to pump the Carter family for information, that we family members had trouble seeing and participating in what was going on.

We were there to enjoy ourselves and to celebrate but the press were there to work—and especially work us.

But somehow we managed to enjoy it all anyway and have a few words with many of the stars we had seen in New York at the convention. There was Connie swooning over Paul Newman again, and there was the handsome Freddie Prinze looking and acting very cheerful. Who would have dreamed on this happy occasion that his death was very near.

Cher and Gregg Allman were there. Gregg had been very kind and helpful to Jimmy when Jimmy needed it most. Linda Ronstadt and Aretha Franklin were also there and we saw and spoke to Roger Mudd of CBS news, a family favorite.

When we got back to the hotel at 1:00 A.M., we found out how important it was to have fruit and snacks available. We had gone to a reception and a gala without having had time to eat. And we hadn't eaten since the snack on the flight to Washington that morning.

The day of the inaugural, Thursday, January 20, was bitterly cold and we were glad that a bus was waiting outside the Hilton to take the Carter and Mondale relatives to the swearing-in ceremony. All the way to the Capitol people waved and pointed at us.

The traffic was truly like nothing we had ever seen before. When we got near the Capitol it was just easier to walk through the crowds to our seats. My daughters and their husbands sat to the right of the podium on the ground, in front of the inaugural stand. They said they had a perfect view.

Ruth and I sat with the President's immediate family, on the podium.

The three-hour parade that passed before the presidential reviewing stand was the most beautiful parade I have ever seen. The Army, Air Force, Navy, and Marine bands were the greatest and so were the various school bands who showed their pride in their new President by marching in perfect formation.

The greatest hit of the parade of floats and bands was the simple act of Jimmy and his family walking down the avenue—Rosalynn and the President holding hands much of the time. And that moment when the President—still a father above all else—stooped down to tie little Amy's shoelace. I think Jimmy's walk was meant to show the world how humble he feels.

In his hour of excitement, he would have hated sitting like a "king" in a limousine making little royal hand gestures at the crowd.

Jimmy has the kind of energy that makes him hate to sit still at such exciting times.

He was that new breath of fresh air.

And we all got a belly full of fresh air that day with him. It was really cold—about 10° F.—on the President's reviewing stand right in front of the White House.

The inaugural ball was like a family reunion of Georgia relatives and friends. We attended the ball at the National Guard Armory—which was the offical one for Georgians— and the one at our own hotel, the Hilton.

The floor was so crowded dancing was almost impossible and people screamed to be heard above the music. By now, my women-folks were starting to fall apart. Connie had developed a bad cold and all of us were wheezing a little. Even so, we ignored our scratchy throats and kept right on screaming and backslapping.

How many more times would a member of the family become President of the United States?

One of the happiest persons at the inaugural from Plains was Rosalynn's hairdresser, Bernard Womack. Bernard still fixes my wife's hair every Saturday. In fact, he and my daughter Laurie were in the tenth grade together and he would come to our house with her after school so that she could help him with his math.

Already, he showed signs of being a fine hair stylist and when he was through doing homework, he often did my wife's hair right at home.

When Rosalynn became First Lady of Georgia, Bernard went to Atlanta to do her hair for the Governor's inaugural ball. During the presidential campaign, Bernard would come from Americus, where he had his beauty shop, and take care of several members of the family.

He would cut Jimmy's hair, fix Rosalynn up, and take care of my wife's hair as well.

During the inaugural festivities at Washington, D.C., Bernard showed us an article and laughed as he pointed out how another fellow was trying to steal his thunder by saying he was doing Rosalynn's hair. But actually Bernard fixed the First Lady's hair three or four times during inaugural week.

He was quite a regular at the White House in the early moving-in days. On one occasion, Gregg Allman and Cher were there and Bernard had a nice chat with Cher as Gregg played the piano.

As soon as Jimmy got in the White House, Republican Congressman Barry Goldwater, Jr. started taking potshots at the peanut farmer saying, "I wasn't worried when I saw all the Carter relatives moving in with him at the White House. After all, who else is going to help him plow the White House lawns to put in this year's peanut, 'tater, and corn pone crop?"

Jimmy just grins and bears that kind of humor. He knows that the peanut has been very good to him in giving him an image that every adult and child recognizes instantly.

The early news from the White House was sometimes amusing. Word trickled back to Plains that Jimmy was going to upgrade the operation of the White House even in the matter of grammar.

He circulated a memo among his staff complaining about the misuse of the pronouns "I" and "me." The memo began, "There is a persistent error which continues to cause a problem for Susan and me (not Susan and I) in correspondence & memos coming to the Oval Office."

The Susan referred to was Susan Clough, the President's secretary.

Even after this memo an error managed to slip by. In another memo addressed to the President, and concerning some legal matter, there was a reference to the "Attorney genetal."

Jimmy sent the memo back with a note in the margin that he wished his staff would not describe Attorney General Griffin Bell this way.

When Jimmy became President, a lot of people wondered if his show of affection wasn't a little phony. President Kennedy, though considered a man of warmth, had never shown affection to his wife in public, had never even kissed her good-bye in front of strangers.

Yet here was Jimmy kissing friends and kissing Rosalynn and other relatives freely in public. Jimmy and I came from a place where affection was openly displayed. My wife, Ruth, reminded me the other day that one first-grade teacher, Miss Annie Ruth Ray, would let any or all of her little children kiss her good-bye after 3:00, when the first-graders had lined up to go home.

Displays of affection are part of the customs of the South.

Now that he was "President Jimmy," he was fair game and everyone was taking potshots.

They had a whole list of particulars on why Jimmy was a "fashion disaster." His jacket was too big. The jacket was too long. The pants were too short. You could see where the trousers had hung on the hanger.

His shoes looked like a farmer's, they said. As far as I could see, this would only assure Jimmy that he was properly dressed since he wants to look like the common people and not a dude or dandy. I'm sure Jimmy Carter was not envious that Vice-President Walter Mondale did make the best-dressed list of the Custom Tailors of America. He'd figure one administration man on the list was enough.

From what I hear, Jimmy hasn't changed a bit. He still concentrates with classical music. I understand that even at 9:00 or 8:00 in the morning or even earlier, when his first visitor of the day—Zbigniew Brzezinski—comes into that little work-study next to the Oval Office, Mozart records are already playing.

Another composer whose music Jimmy likes to work to is Beethoven.

Whatever Jimmy Carter does as President, he is going to be criticized for it. When Jimmy took his first move to open relations with Cuba for the first time since the Kennedy administration, detractors said, "Ah-ha, the President is trying to help the Coca-Cola Company!"

Coca-Cola is the largest user of sugar (one of Cuba's exports) and its headquarters is in Atlanta. Carter enemies immediately pounced on the fact that when he was governor, Jimmy had taken trips promoting the state in which Coca-Cola planes had been used and that the chairman of Coca-Cola—J. Paul Austin—had given a luncheon at the "21" Club in New York City to raise funds for Jimmy's presidential campaign.

The enemies pointed out that Coca-Cola has a special interest in resuming relations with Cuba because Cuba holds over $27 million worth of its properties, which were confiscated during the Castro take-over.

In June of 1977 Austin flew to Cuba to meet with Fidel Castro and upon his return, briefed the President on what he had found. One would think that this was pretty clever of Jimmy, to learn all he can about a nation with whom the United States would like to resume full business and diplomatic relations.

But no, even some members of Congress got angry about that briefing, maintaining that the President was trying to circumvent Congress, especially the Senate Foreign Relations Committee and the House International Affairs Committee, which are supposed to guide the President on naming of ambassadors and overseeing foreign trade.

What I'm trying to say is that I try not to get too excited and I caution the family not to be too upset when our relative in the White House is blasted every other day in the newspapers.

Of course, we don't have to worry about Billy getting upset. Even as his brother's stock sinks, his goes higher and higher.

Since Billy has become "First Brother of the U.S.A.," his sales have zoomed—both of beer and of gas. Some tourists even offer to pay a dollar for a beer can if Billy Carter has drunk from it.

But for Jimmy almost everyone was complaining about something. Women's groups were complaining that of seventy high posts such as ambassadors, only a handful were women.

Others complained that Jimmy was more concerned about human rights in other countries than he was right in the United States. Even the President's style of speaking came in for severe criticism and a headline in a Washington newspaper read, "Carter's Faults as

Speechmaker Hinder Effort to Lead U.S."

It will be interesting to see how Jimmy handles the Congress. Other Presidents, like LBJ and Kennedy, would visit on Capitol Hill and sit around being a good ole boy. Jimmy is not a backslapper or a horse trader.

If that has to be done, it will have to be Jimmy's staff who do the backslapping for him.

Jimmy is sometimes better at campaigning for himself than for other candidates. He wanted very much to help a Virginia friend, Henry E. Howell, become governor of the state. He made speeches for Howell and even Jack Carter, his eldest son, came up from Georgia to campaign for him. Howell not only lost, but so decisively that he said he was through with politics.

On the other hand, his endorsement did not hurt the New Jersey incumbent, Governor Brendan Byrne, who retained his seat.

Many people were surprised when Jimmy brought his children and their wives to live at the White House. So much of a fuss was made about the cost of feeding them that he had to issue a statement saying that the food for Jeff and Chip and their wives would be paid for out of his own pocket.

The family understood why Jimmy and Rosalynn wanted their sons near. It was supposed to be a reward for their having given up time from their own lives to campaign for Daddy.

Jimmy and Rosalynn desperately wanted to make up for the years when politics had kept them from enjoying their children. They were determined to make the White House one happy family—the sons living on the third floor, one floor above the family rooms occupied by Rosalynn and Jimmy.

And what is perhaps most important, Rosalynn and Cousin Jimmy felt that the kids really needed them. They were not as mature as they would have been had they not lived in the Governor's Mansion where everything is done for them—they had not fully learned how to cope with the everyday problems of life.

Since the law does not permit a father in the government to hire his own son, Chip was lucky to get a job at the Democratic National Headquarters, helping line up speakers for fund-raising events. The salary was not fabulous but adequate—eight thousand dollars. However, had he not been living at the White House, it would have been poverty row for him, as he himself said.

Perhaps someone else would make a big thing of that job and

build it into a larger salary, but Chip was happy to leave it and try something else—the peanut business in Plains.

Jack was the only Carter who did not come to Washington. He has the greatest independence of any of the sons and is determined to make it on his own.

His wife, Judy, is also very energetic and independent. I was not surprised when I heard that she had joined *Redbook* magazine as a contributing editor. But Judy is not just trading on her name. She has been writing for magazines starting in college—Agnes Stott and the University of Georgia.

She also has written for a magazine called *Learning*.

We all were delighted to hear every scrap of information about what it was like for the young folks living in the White House. We were amused to get the news that it was so cold on the third floor of the White House that Jeff and Chip and their wives had all taken to wearing thermal underwear.

And each couple had decorated their apartment quite differently. Chip and Caron had chosen a modern decor while Annette and Jeff won my vote by carefully picking authentic antiques such as a straight-backed chair that Lincoln had used and an inkwell that Thomas Jefferson had used.

The first party of the young folks was given by Jeff and Annette for friends from Plains and everyone wore blue jeans, the dress-up fad in their quarters.

The young wives were especially thrilled by their White House assignment—to fill in for Rosalynn Carter when the First Lady has more than one event to attend. Since Cousin Jimmy has decreed that he will not attend the traditional dinner given at the embassy of a foreign dignitary, the night after the foreign dignitary has been entertained at the White House, the young couples frequently go in the President's place, as his emissaries.

Even presidential children are not immune to the marital difficulties that beset other couples.

Around the Governor's Mansion Chip was known as a ladies' man. His daddy thought marriage would settle him down and was pleased when Chip chose Caron, a stay-at-home, quiet girl whose father was a farmer in nearby Hawkinsville.

When Chip, at age twenty-six, came to the White House to live with his wife, he still hadn't really settled down and the gossip columnists had a field day reporting that he was seen in this or that nightclub, naturally in the company of girls. Caron was pregnant so she wouldn't have gone to nightclubs even if she liked them—which she didn't.

The most surprising report that we got in Plains was that Chip was competing with the governor of California, Jerry Brown, for the attention of Linda Ronstadt, the popular rock star. That was mighty high flying.

I know that Jimmy and Rosalynn were both very upset over Chip's behavior, just when he was becoming a young father.

There was one traumatic weekend when Caron went with her in-laws to Camp David and Chip arrived later and seemed very happy to be back with Caron. After that, a wonderful opportunity arose for Chip to take his place as a responsible family man. Billy Carter, Chip's uncle, was making so much money in his personal appearances, that he no longer wanted to be bothered by the peanut business.

It was Chip's chance to show what he could do. With the blessing of his parents, he took Caron back to Plains and became part of the warehouse business.

I kept an eye on the couple and prayed that they would be able to compromise in their life-styles and save their marriage by becoming more alike—Caron going out more and Chip going out less.

I certainly could not adopt a holier-than-thou attitude, however, since my own son, Hugh, Jr., was the first member of the younger Carter clan to get a divorce.

Though Chip may have troubles in his personal life, he's known in the family for being very warmhearted and concerned about the pain of others. When he accompanied his grandmother, Miz Lillian, to India, he was very distressed about the conditions he found and kept asking, "What do the people do to survive?"

It's hard to remember that Chip is really James Earl Carter II, named for his father. But whether he eventually follows his father into politics, as some believe he will, it is far too soon to know.

Jeff, twenty-four when he entered the White House, the youngest of the Cousin Jimmy sons, was completing his schooling at George Washington University. The reason he was a little older than most college seniors was that he had interrupted his education two times.

First when he quit school to work on a barge for a year, and second when he joined the family on the campaign trail.

Jeff, like all the rest of the Carters, is pursuing his own special interests—geography, conservation, and photography.

At first, friends around the White House were amused at the poor quality of the pictures Jeff was forever snapping of his father in an effort to become another David Kennerly, the noted photographer of the Ford administration.

But soon he was taking such good pictures that there was talk that he would be publishing a photo album of the presidential family, and that a publisher had all but signed him up.

But at this writing, word has trickled down to Plains that Jimmy put his foot down at one more member of the immediate family cashing in on the family name.

Jeff's full name, incidentally, is Donnel Jeffrey Carter—the first name being the same as my brother's. Jeff's wife, Annette, is also a photo buff. But her degree at the University of Georgia was in home economics and interior design—her mother-in-law's special interest.

In his early days at the White House, Cousin Jimmy did not have too much time to come to Plains, but when he did he would head first to my antique shop to pay his respects to Daddy and me.

May 31, 1977, is a visit that stands out in my memory. It was a Tuesday morning and this was the first time he had been back to Plains in about two months—so we were very glad to see him.

He greeted both of us with a big hug, Dad first and then me. When he hugs a person and looks deep in their eyes, it is almost a religious feeling. It's as if Jimmy can look into a person's heart and see what is there and you feel his compassion.

It is a tremendous feeling to have a President of the United States walk down the streets of your town, population 683, and have him enter your store with the multitudes following him.

It's not the easiest thing to talk naturally when news reporters have their pencils out scratching down everything you say and tourists are listening in and TV cameramen are taking pictures and the Secret Service is looking at you as if you're under suspicion.

No, it's not the easiest thing to be your natural self, but I try.

I told the President that I had heard on national television that morning that he was coming to Plains to see how junky the town had become. He flatly denied it and said that, to the contrary, he thought the people of Plains should be commended for keeping the town as clean and friendly as it was.

He said he knew it was a tremendous undertaking for us to meet and welcome the thousands of visitors that we have coming here continuously. That made me feel pretty good.

I then took a different tack but pursued how he could improve the town. I suggested that he try to arrange some way for people to park near his home for a few minutes so that they could see at least part of the house through the trees and take pictures of what they could see.

Many people, I said, told me they drive thousands of miles to see the home of the President and they are very disappointed when they cannot see his house. He agreed with me on this suggestion and promised that he would try to work something out.

As we talked further, I asked Jimmy how my son, "Cousin Cheap" or "Frill Cutter," was doing. Jimmy laughed and complimented the great job that Sonny was doing as administrator at the White House.

I asked the President if he still planned to build a helicopter pad here in Plains and he told me that because of the great expense involved he was about to drop the idea and to continue to use the Peterson Airfield.

I then asked if Hugh, Jr., was responsible for any of this suggestion, and Jimmy said laughingly that he probably was.

We talked about a few personal matters as best we could under the circumstances.

Jimmy had one bit of news before he left. He said the Secret Service wanted to build a tall fence around his house, but he had said no.

I was glad he had.

Everyone wanted to touch Jimmy,
I noticed during the campaign.
They really related to him.

Miz Lillian holds up a poster of an angry peanut about to bite off the tail of an
elephant. The caption says, "Do it, Jimmy!"

After this picture was taken of Hugh, Jr., and me at the Democratic Convention in New York in 1976, my son worked night and day, helping organize the Peanut Brigade among other things.

This was one of my convention passes at the exciting Democratic Convention in New York, 1976:

THE DEMOCRATIC PARTY OF THE UNITED STATES IN CONVENTION

Robert S. Strauss/Chairman
New York City
Madison Square Garden
July 12-15,1976

HONORED GUEST

MONDAY JULY 12

6295

Among my souvenirs.

This is my favorite picture of Jimmy Carter and his family.

Tears and cheers on victory morning, sun-up at the Depot platform in Plains. We had waited all night for Jimmy to return from Atlanta. I'll never forget how choked up Rosalynn and Jimmy were. Ruth Carter Stapleton, to the right of Jimmy, shed happy tears too.

This is the most informal picture I've seen of Rosalynn. She was at Plains for the opening of the new Welcome Center and a high wind was ruining her hairdo. The First Lady struggled to pin down her hair with a scarf.

President Jimmy and Rosalynn visit in the back of the antique store with Daddy Alton and me. The sign on the wall is helping to get our Marantha Baptist Church built.

As fate would have it, I was present at the White House when the Shah of Iran and Empress Farah Diba were greeted by angry demonstrators outside the White House, and I, too, felt the sting of tear gas released by the police. Left to right: the President, the Shah, the Empress, the First Lady, my wife, and me; taken in the Green Room at the White House, November 15, 1977.

When I visited the White House as a sleep-over guest, the President interrupted his working session with Vice President Mondale to greet us and visit a while. Left to right: Hugh Carter, Jr., Assistant to the President for Administration; Vice President Walter Mondale; Hamilton Jordan, Assistant to the President; State Senator Hugh Carter (me); Mrs. Hugh Carter (my wife, Ruth); President Jimmy; and Glenna Garrett (friend of Hugh, Jr.).

A happy trio on the south lawn of the White House, out of sight of tourists—
Rosalynn, Cousin Jimmy, and Amy.

26 · THE TRUTH ABOUT THE PLAINS BAPTIST CHURCH SPLIT-UP

The world by now knows that the Plains Baptist Church is tragically split. Though I was one of the leaders of the splinter group, which marched off and formed a new church, I still grieve for the togetherness that all the Baptist people of Plains once shared.

I'm sorry the split had to coincide with Cousin Jimmy becoming President but that's the way it was. And the fact that he was President added to the tension which made the split inevitable. He himself says so.

The Plains Baptist Church, a beautiful old building, became famous because that is where Jimmy Carter worshiped and taught Sunday School. It was his Sunday home.

He was proud of it. It had been founded in 1848 with just twenty charter members and he knew its history as well as I did—how its first split had occurred in 1871 because freed slaves had left to form their own church.

The second split which took place a little more than a hundred years later also involved blacks.

I began leading the singing in our church back in 1956 when Rev. J. R. Harris was pastor. Rev. Harris was not well physically and I consented to lead the singing to help him conserve his strength for his sermons.

In many small-town churches such as ours, the music effort is all volunteer. Before our split I had led the singing for eighteen years.

All through the years, when I have been leading the singing and sitting in the choir, at some point in the service, Jimmy and I have always had a little reassuring smile that we gave each other.

This smile was a regular contact that meant a lot to each of us and we have sometimes talked about it. We have always lived very busy

309

lives and sometimes we would go all week without seeing or talking to each other. That little smile at church, which was our little ritual, renewed our confidence and security in the affection of the other.

Jimmy always appreciated the work of the various members of the church in making each Sunday a success. One woman especially worked hard to get the music just right and arrange for all the specials. It was Mrs. Carol Anderson, who played the organ and piano as well as selecting the hymns.

Now and then, when he was especially moved by the music, Jimmy would stop on the way out to pat Mrs. Anderson on the back or kiss her on the cheek and congratulate her for a wonderful music performance.

"The Old Rugged Cross" is my favorite hymn, followed closely by "Amazing Grace." Rosalynn's grandfather, Uncle Cap Murray, used to tell me that "Amazing Grace" was his favorite song.

I think about him every time we sing it. We served together on the Deacons' Board for many years. He has been dead some years now but the song also has become the favorite of Jimmy Carter— making it a frequently used song even with dance bands.

Jimmy and his wife and family all join in in singing the hymns.

One sermon at Plains Baptist Church especially impressed Jimmy and he never tired of mentioning it. The question had been posed from the pulpit, "If you were arrested for being a Christian, would there be enough evidence to convict you?"

Jimmy had decided that there would not be enough evidence to convict him and it made him stop to think of ways he could change for the better.

Then that incident, I believe, was followed by the conversion experience in the autumn of 1966, when he and his younger sister, Ruth, went for that walk in the pine woods. She had asked him if he was willing to give up everything for Christ, even his politics, and he had thought about it for what seemed a long time before he said yes.

Having freed himself from pride and political ambition, he found that he had new peace of mind.

In the late spring of 1967, Jimmy did lay missionary work in Massachusetts and Pennsylvania. He went with Milo Pennington, a peanut farmer from Texas. With this trip, Cousin Jimmy experienced a sense of release, assurance, and peace with himself.

He also spent several days working among Spanish-speaking families in an area of a New England city, representing the Plains Baptist

Church, speaking in Spanish to the Cuban-Puerto Rican people. Jimmy had learned Spanish in the Navy and he speaks it well.

He had now definitely put his religious faith first in his life. He was learning to be less self-centered. And I think that only when he had learned to see the other person's problems, too, not just his own, was he ready to go on and become governor of Georgia and then President of the United States.

Then as soon as Jimmy became nationally famous and it was known that he was running for the presidency, everything changed. And not for the better.

I hated to see so many extraneous matters influencing the congregation's attitude toward the church. Things like TV cameras, a desire for publicity, the feelings of certain members about race, and the personal life of our minister Reverend Bruce Edwards.

Reverend Edwards had done a very charitable thing by adopting a partly Polynesian child, not too long before the presidential election.

Then there was the storming of the door by the black activist, Reverend Clennon King—no relation to Martin Luther King, Jr., that I know of.

Reverend Clennon King headed a congregation called the Divine Light Mission at Albany and he claimed to want to become a member of the Plains Baptist Church, but when Reverend Bruce Edwards tried several times to get King to come to his study and talk about joining the church, King refused.

Everything that King did delighted the Republicans, especially when King suddenly insisted that his application for membership be acted on the Sunday before the presidential election.

Somehow out of difficulty comes some good. King did perform a service in that he forced the Plains Baptist Church to take a new look at the confusing anti-black-agitator policy of 1965.

I will never forget that crucial Sunday of November 14, 1976. The church seemed under siege with Reverend Clennon King waiting on the steps, three Ku Klux Klansmen parading up and down outside while inside President-elect Jimmy Carter and his family huddled with the membership, leading the forces of right.

The question before the house was whether to fire Reverend Bruce Edwards.

Jimmy and Rosalynn looked relaxed and happy from their vacation at Saint Simons Island, where they had gone after the exhaustion of the campaign. Cousin Jimmy was calm and even cheerful as he spoke time after time, calling on the members to open their hearts and their church doors.

He said, "Anyone who worships Christ should be allowed to come to our church." He even threw in a little humor, saying, "You know my brother Billy never comes to church but if we passed a resolution that said no one who sells beer can enter this church, he'll come."

Most important, Jimmy said the real issue was whether to keep blacks out of the church. He maintained that on scriptural grounds they should not be kept out.

Jimmy's words had a soothing effect and in a great outpouring of love toward our new President, the congregation voted 120 to 66 to open its doors to anyone of "good faith." We set up a "Watch-Care" Committee to screen new members.

And at the same time, our church voted to keep Reverend Bruce Edwards as minister.

There was great rejoicing and Rosalynn cried a little. Sandra Edwards, the minister's wife, was also overcome. I thought that now the wounds of the church had been healed. And so did Jimmy and Rosalynn. But we were all wrong.

The story really starts long before this—back in 1965. I want to tell the whole story and get it off my chest and also because so many church people around the country have written or visited me to talk about our church situation.

To understand how misunderstandings and complications arose, it is necessary first to go back to August 15, 1965. Y. T. Sheffield, my old coach and math teacher, now deceased, served as moderator of a conference in the Church in the absence of the pastor, Reverend J. R. Harris—also now deceased—who was on vacation.

Motion was made, seconded, and carried by the unanimous vote of the twelve deacons and pastor present that it be recommended to the church that the ushers refuse to admit any "Negroes or any other civil rights agitators" to all worship services in Plains Baptist Church.

The motion was seconded.

However, in discussion Jimmy Carter spoke in opposition to the motion. J. D. Clements, Jr., spoke in favor of not voting on the motion. A motion was made to table it and it was defeated.

The motion was carried—for, 54; against, 6.

Members of Jimmy Carter's immediate family and one other church member voted against the motion.

This motion was interpreted by many people to mean that *no*

Negroes would be admitted to any services in the church at all, regardless of who they were.

I interpreted this motion, however, to mean that any *civil rights agitators, black or white,* would be refused admittance to any worship services. I was among the fifty-four who voted for the motion.

There is quite a bit of difference between these two interpretations. At the time the motion was passed, there were many attempts to integrate churches in this area of Georgia by groups of civil rights agitators who were not interested in the feelings of the people; they were only interested in seeing if the integration could be accomplished.

I can remember several attempts at a church in Americus, Georgia, in which there was a lot of publicity and turmoil.

We, at the Plains church, did not want to have this upsetting condition at our church and I feel that this was the basis of the above motion—to avert unfortunate incidents which were unnecessarily called for.

Most blacks in this area want to worship in their own churches. They do not try nor do they wish to attend the white churches.

Actually, as far as I know, no Negroes or whites who were civil rights agitators had tried to enter our church before 1976.

We have had many Negroes who were *not* civil rights agitators attend services at Plains Baptist Church between August 1965, when the controversial motion was passed, and 1976, when all the recent controversy started. As far as I know, no black had ever been denied admittance to our church.

Through the years, Jimmy Carter has run for governor and President, and this 1965 conference in the Plains Baptist Church and his vote on that day has been an important topic among people all over the world.

On October 31, 1976, a black from Albany, Georgia, Reverend Clennon King, came to the Plains Baptist Church and was not admitted. Regular worship services had been canceled. Reverend Edwards held a news conference that day contrary to the advice of at least one deacon, myself.

In asking him not to hold the press conference, I tried to impress on him the possibility of more hard feelings and more controversy. Reverend Edwards did not heed my advice and I, along with the rest of the world, listened to his press conference. I was very disappointed at his action and with his remarks.

Reverend Edwards told reporters that the word "nigger" had been used several times at a deacons' meeting held on October 24, 1976, in discussing the *August 15, 1965,* much publicized decision made by the church in regard to refusing to admit civil rights agitators, black or white, to all worship services in the Plains Baptist Church.

On the afternoon of October 31, 1976, a deacons' meeting was called and twelve deacons voted to recommend to the church that Reverend Bruce Edwards resign. Deacon Tim Lawson, however, had second thoughts about making the decision unanimous.

I would like to say here that, as a deacon, I voted to ask the pastor to resign because I had asked him to please not hold the press conference that he had held a few hours before.

That night I realized that I had made a mistake at the deacons' meeting in voting to recommend that my pastor be dismissed. I resolved that night to reverse my decision and to stand up before the church at the next conference and explain my reasons and to publicly ask my pastor to forgive me.

I felt that we both had made a mistake, he in his unprecedented press conference, and me in my vote made in anger. It was now time for forgiveness and frank admittance that a mistake had been made.

I hope that the reader realizes that the eyes of the world were on Plains Baptist Church at this time. Not just the United States but people all across the world were watching our actions; it was just before the presidential election.

I would like to say that throughout this time I kept in constant touch with Jimmy by telephone through my son Hugh, Jr., who was traveling with Jimmy in his campaign. I knew Jimmy was very interested in his own church where he, too, had been a deacon and a member most of his life.

On November 14, 1976, a conference was held in Plains Baptist Church with about two hundred members present. President-elect Jimmy Carter was also present. Aunt Lillian, and others of his family, also attended.

Ernest Turner, chairman of the Board of Deacons, acted as moderator. The moderator read the letter from the Board of Deacons asking the pastor, Reverend Bruce Edwards, for his resignation.

I asked the moderator to be recognized. I was recognized and moved that we *not* vote on the recommendation of the Board of Deacons which asked the pastor to resign.

My motion was seconded by Jimmy Carter. Discussion followed and here are my remarks:

Mr. Moderator, ladies and gentlemen ... If we vote to back the Board of Deacons and ask Reverend Bruce Edwards to resign and continue to keep the doors locked we are going to split our church into pieces and attract hundreds of people who will come just to see if they can attend, the agitators and also the curiosity seekers.

In my opinion, we are not acting like Christians when we lock the doors to people who want to worship. Now, membership in *our church is a different question and I have a later motion which was approved unanimously by the Board of Deacons which will establish a Watch-Care Committee to investigate and approve persons who apply for membership in our church.*

I think we have all acted too hastily—both the pastor and the deacons. I am ashamed of my vote at the last meeting of the Board of Deacons where we voted to ask Reverend Edwards to resign.

Reverend Edwards, I ask you to forgive me here, publicly before this conference. After much thought and prayer, I think this was a tragic move we made in writing a letter asking you, our pastor, to resign. In my opinion we do not have sufficient reason to ask you to resign.

I think Reverend Bruce Edwards is a fine preacher and I think most all of us loved him dearly before all this trouble began. He's made some mistakes, but so have we. He's talked too much to the press. He's used some words in his press conference that I don't think any of us approve of.

But I still don't think we have sufficient reason to ask him to resign.

If he resigns, and he might do this—I couldn't blame him after the way we have treated him—I certainly don't know where we would ever find another pastor that would suit us as well as he does. Good pastors are few and far between.

This statement is from my heart—the way we act in our church, at times I wonder if we are really Christian in our actions.

We are about to let one black tear this church to pieces.

I just can't stand to see this be done to our church, and God's church, and it's our job to protect it.

I know many of you probably want to speak, but I want to explain quickly, my motion. If you vote "Yes" on my mo-

tion—there will be no vote on the deacons' letter of request to Reverend Bruce Edwards to resign. He will still be our pastor.

What his action will be, will be up to him. He might resign. But I hope he will not.

Thank you, Mr. Moderator."

The motion failed 96 to 100. But I will always feel that the consideration of the motion was fruitful as the next motion, to dismiss the pastor, failed.

Following the narrow defeat of my motion, a motion was made, seconded, and *defeated* that the pastor Reverend Bruce Edwards be dismissed. The motion failed, 84 to 107.

I then made a motion upon recommendation of the Board of Deacons that a Watch-Care Committee be established to consider all applications for membership in our church.

The motion was seconded and carried unanimously. It was agreed that all persons wishing to join our church would be referred to the Watch-Care Committee who would examine them and make recommendations back to the church whether to accept or reject.

The next motion was a historical one. Jerome Ethredge, who is now a missionary to Africa, moved that we open the doors of Plains Baptist Church to all people who want to worship Jesus Christ.

It was seconded by Kim Carter—Billy Carter's daughter. The motion passed 120 to 66 and in essence, wiped out the August 15, 1965, controversial closed-door policy motion.

A motion was then made, seconded, and carried that, as the church clerk (custodian of the records), Hugh Carter meet with the press in front of the church and announce the results of the conference. Hundreds of people waited outside the church including a large number of newsmen and television personnel.

Another conference was held on February 20, 1977. Reverend Bruce Edwards was moderator and 149 members were present. The conference was a *called* conference. It had always been the custom in our church to announce a *called* conference at least a week ahead of time and announce the matter or matters that would be taken up at that conference.

It was customary at a called conference to take up *only* the subject or subjects that had been announced. Whereas, at a *regular* conference, held quarterly in the Plains Baptist Church, matters that are brought up are not restricted to those announced.

The February 20 meeting was ostensibly called for the purpose of deciding $376.50 be taken out of the miscellaneous fund of the budget to pay for the balance due on some corn that had been sent to the Children's Home, an institution supported by Baptist churches.

After the matter of the corn was settled, one of our members, Dale Gray, arose and moved that Reverend Bruce Edwards be dismissed as pastor of the Plains Baptist Church.

I want to impress upon the reader that I told the conference that this motion seemed to be completely out of order because this was a *called* conference and was for the purpose of deciding on paying for some corn and *not* for so important an issue as voting to dismiss our pastor.

There was much discussion and many motions. There were two motions to table and two motions to adjourn by those seeking to put off the vote until all the church members could be notified that such an important matter would be taken up.

I urged the conference to put off action on such an important motion for at least one week so that all church members could be notified that this matter would be voted on. I explained that this hasty action today would be regretted.

It was evident that the group favoring the dismissal of Reverend Bruce Edwards had done their homework and had people present whose names were on the church roll, eligible to vote, but many were members who I had not seen in the church in years.

Every motion was defeated that would have delayed the dismissal motion. Since Reverend Bruce Edwards saw that he was going to be dismissed, he got up and resigned with the following motion:

"Because of the future of this church and because of the discussion and action here today, I hereby resign, effective April 30, 1977, and request that I be given an indefinite leave of absence beginning immediately."

The resignation was accepted and the damage had been done.

I frankly felt that our church had been left in a shambles, and that Reverend Bruce Edwards had been "crucified." I still feel this way.

Many of our members left the church in frustration. I tried to continue attending the church and the deacons' meetings and tried to carry on the jobs that I was elected to, praying and hoping that the cold atmosphere and hate would disappear and the problems would work themselves out.

I had been a deacon for thirty-one years, been the church clerk for twenty-eight years, and had led the singing for eighteen years. I also had several other important committee assignments.

I was baptized in the Plains Baptist Church in July 1930, when I was nine years old, and my wife was baptized there in 1931. My son was baptized there in April of 1951, Laurie in January of 1956, and Connie on July 23, 1961.

The church was an integral part of our lives. We had been taken to the church as children by our parents, and we had brought our own children up there. Over half of the social gatherings and activities in a small town centers around one's church.

Jimmy Carter was baptized at the Plains Baptist Church in 1935. Rosalynn, formerly a Methodist, was baptized there in August of 1954. Jimmy's mother, Lillian, and his father, Earl, were also baptized there. So were Jimmy's sisters, Ruth and Gloria, and his brother, Billy.

Jimmy and Rosalynn's three sons were also baptized in the Plains Baptist Church.

It is difficult to express an opinion or give advice or say what you would do if a situation was such and such. It is even more difficult to know what to do if you're in the middle of a situation, as I was Sunday after Sunday. It was during this time that the feelings and emotions of confusion and even hate prevailed in the Plains Baptist Church. It is very sad to see the church that you have attended all of your life in such a state.

I attended my last deacons' meeting on May 1, 1977. I left the deacons' meeting that Sunday afternoon thinking and hoping that we could heal the wounds and bring our church back together again.

I was called on to lead the closing prayer, and after the prayer, two of the deacons told me personally that they appreciated the things I had said. I left the church feeling much better about the whole situation.

I understand that that same afternoon some of the deacons and former deacons met to distribute to the press and others a paper entitled, "The Silent Majority of Plains Baptist Church Is Heard." I'm not sure who wrote the paper, but it is my opinion that the harsh wounds might have been healed to some extent if this paper had *never* been published and distributed.

This paper was a personal attack on Reverend Bruce Edwards and myself. As recorded in the Atlanta *Journal* in a story by Jeff Prugh of the Los Angeles *Times*, Bruce Edwards says, "They got my job. What else do they want? It's like rubbing salt in my wounds—and they did it in a cowardly way, without anybody signing it.

"The church did not issue the statement—it should have been voted on by the members. The sad thing is, they believe they're right. They don't feel any emotion for somebody who's already lost his job. I want the world to know that this statement is filled with half-truths and lies!"

As for the most controversial points that applied to me, the report said, "Reverend Edwards, Senator Carter and several others have been the cause of most of our disagreements by making irresponsible, disruptive and misleading statements to the press contrary to the best interest of Plains Baptist Church."

I flatly deny this allegation and I leave it up to the American public to be the judge, as to who completed the schism.

I further quote from the report: "We further disagree with Senator Carter's statement that we have crucified Reverend Edwards." As I most definitely believe *he was "crucified,"* I do not apologize for this statement to anyone.

Bruce Edwards was without a job because of the action. I see no better way to describe how he was treated than to say he suffered deeply and was "crucified." The reasons they gave for wanting him to resign are half-truths and lies, in my opinion.

As I see it this whole controversy in the Plains Baptist Church was based on an "antiblack" feeling, an "anti-Carter" feeling, and an "anti-Bruce Edwards" feeling, plus a longtime feeling of jealousy that has built up between certain families in this community.

It is a sad state of existence when sane people will allow such "anti" feelings to split the Lord's House.

I submitted my letter of resignation to the chairman of the Board of Deacons, Mr. Ernest Turner, on June 10, 1977. It read as follows:

Dear Friends:
I hereby submit my resignation effective today, June 10, 1977, as: Deacon, Church Clerk, Song Leader.
I also resign from all committees on which I serve.
Through prayer and attendance at church and Sunday School and at the Deacons' Meeting on May 1st, I had hoped that I could continue to attend the Plains Baptist Church which I loved so dearly and where I have been a member since 9 years of age.
Then the report entitled "The Silent Majority of Plains Baptist

*Church Is Heard" was handed to me. This completely convinced
me as to what my decision should be.*

*I will be glad to turn over the Church records to whomever
you elect to replace me and if you like, I will explain to him or her
the operation of the job as there is much more work to it than it
appears.*

*I will constantly be praying for each member of the Plains
Baptist Church and I wish for you, the best.*

> *Sincerely*
> *(Signed)*
> *Hugh Carter*

The time had come for action. A meeting was called.

About fifty people started the Bottsford Baptist Mission in a vacant church building belonging to the Lutheran Church in Plains.
The building is about five miles south of Plains, just off Highway 45.

The first service was held on May 22, 1977. Tim Lawson, who had
been a deacon in the Plains Baptist Church, served as moderator. He
opened the meeting that morning with these words: "Good morning,
this is the Lord's Day and we are here to worship."

Suddenly something clicked, something magical happened. We
were indeed joined together. It was a thrilling moment as we realized
that we had almost lost sight of our objective, worship of the Lord.
And now all controversy was behind us, we were able to worship
freely.

There were seven young people in the choir. We sang songs like
"Nothing but the Blood," "What a Friend We Have in Jesus," "Trust
and Obey." Reverend Bruce Edwards and his wife were in attendance. He suggested that we call our congregation "The Bottsford
Baptist Mission."

We decided this was a good name until a new name could be
constituted. Reverend Jimmy Hayes preached the morning and evening services. The scripture for his morning message was Mark 6:5
and 6. His subject was "Where There Is No Vision."

We also sang as the offertory song, "Give of Your Best to the
Master." The closing song was "I Gave My Life for Thee."

On that inspired first day, the piano was played by Mrs. Ida Lee
Timmerman, a lady who had been a member of the Plains Baptist
Church for more than fifty years. She was about eighty-seven years
old.

Tim Lawson led the singing. Service was held again at 6:00 P.M. on May 22, 1977. There were forty-seven people present.

Services were held again on May 29. Sunday School was at 10:00 A.M. and worship services were held at 11:00. The Reverend Earl Duke gave the morning message.

Reverend Fred Collins, a former pastor of Plains Baptist Church, delivered the message for the services held on Sunday evening, May 29. After the message, a brief meeting was held out in the churchyard with those desiring to attend and we tentatively offered Reverend Fred Collins three hundred dollars per week, subject to the approval of the majority of the mission, to move to Plains and become our permanent pastor.

Reverend Collins informed us that he would let us know after much prayer, consideration, and meditation. He accepted our offer and began his ministry at the Bottsford Baptist Mission on Sunday, June 26, 1977.

Although names for the new church were discussed, nothing definite was decided. Reverend Collins thought that this subject merited much prayer and thought. He also stated that our church needed to be legally incorporated.

All favored constituting a church immediately.

Regular services were held at Bottsford Baptist Mission on June 19, 1977, Reverend Bruce Edwards as the preacher for the morning and evening services. These were the last sermons he would preach in Plains before assuming a pastorate in Hawaii.

We all regretted seeing Reverend Bruce Edwards and his family depart our community. He was truly a Man of God.

Reverend Bruce Edwards gave one final message, a statement that I will never forget. He said that Reverend Fred Collins had phoned him and during the conversation said, "I have come to the conclusion that the Christian's lot in this life is to suffer."

Easter of 1977 sounded a sad note in the Carter family. The President would not come to Plains for Easter services and I am sure it was because of the trouble at the church. The church hatred and dissension had made him a stranger in his own town.

Helping found a new church has not made me beloved on all sides, either. In fact, as an aftermath of the church trouble, violent things started to happen around our home. First, two plate-glass windows of our home were broken.

Then someone maliciously damaged our swimming pool. On another occasion our home was shot at from some distance away. And for nine straight Sunday nights, garbage was thrown in our front yard. Whoever threw it there knew every move of our family.

One Sunday night my son-in-law, Leon Collins, and I hid in the bushes near the road and waited until after 10:00, but no garbage appeared. Yet Monday morning it was there. So it had to have been deposited there after we'd all gone to bed.

The next Sunday we were at church in the early evening and returned home about 9:00 and the garbage was already there.

Even my wife has had church problems. She was harassed by telephone calls which the telephone company traced.

Newsmen would call me or come into the store every day to ask which church Jimmy would attend when he came back to Plains for a visit—the Plains Baptist Church or the new Maranatha Baptist Church of Plains, as we had finally named it. I would reply truthfully that I didn't know, that it was a difficult question for me to answer because he had friends at both places.

The climax came in August 1977 when the President was expected home for several days' visit. Newsmen and television stations were gathering at both churches and it was a madhouse around Plains. No one seemed to remember that the main reason Jimmy was coming was to attend the Murray family reunion, which is held every year.

He always accompanies Rosalynn to her family reunions, just as she always accompanies him to his. My wife, Ruth, and I are always invited to this reunion dinner of Rosalynn's side of the family.

Over and over I explained to the media that I didn't know what the President would do. Jimmy had three choices. He could go to Maranatha or Plains Baptist Church, or he could avoid the whole issue by only attending the Plains Methodist Church where the Murray reunion dinner is always held.

Sunday, August 7, 1977, was the day of high drama in Plains. The question that had the town buzzing was "Where will Jimmy attend church?" I had sent him a personal invitation by mail to attend worship services at Maranatha.

Since all the people in our new church are his people and love him and believe as he does, I just felt he would be more at home there. When he came by my antique shop to speak to me and Dad on Saturday, he acknowledged that he had received the letter but he still didn't say definitely that he would attend.

However, he didn't have to say because advance men for communications for the White House and Secret Service men had come to see me to get the location of our church and other details. However, it is a trick of the Secret Service sometimes to make it seem that the President is going to be one place and then show up at another for security reasons.

The tourists were keeping watch on both churches to be sure they wouldn't miss the arrival of the President.

At Maranatha, we had about a hundred people inside the church and another hundred outside—newsmen, TV people, and tourists. My wife and I had brought my daddy and stepmother and our daughter Connie Collins with her husband, Leon.

What a thrill when Cousin Jimmy arrived, and we all settled down to hear Reverend Fred Collins preach a great sermon. By wonderful coincidence, it was the second birthday of Jimmy's grandson, Jason Carter, son of Jack and Judy. It is our custom at church to sing Happy Birthday to whomever has a birthday during that week while the person having the birthday stands at the front of the church and puts a coin or bill into the Building-Fund Treasury box for each year of his life.

Since Jason was a visitor, and only two years old, we did not make him put in his little pennies into the birthday box. But he did it anyway, as the congregation sang. Some children, who are regulars, wait for their birthdays so they can proudly put in a coin for each year.

A fifty-year-old man usually puts fifty dollars into the church box and is happy to help celebrate his birthday by adding building blocks to the new church.

Reverend Fred Collins, our pastor, preached a truly inspired sermon on how different lives turn out differently and how some people are tempted to blame God for not having the wonderful things happen to them that happens to others.

I looked at Cousin Jimmy and realized that he represented both sides—he was a man who had had wonderful things happen to him and he had also known bitter defeat.

Later, though he had already been to two churches, he did not act impatient as he waited quite a while for the food to be served at still a third church, the Plains United Methodist Fellowship Hall, where the family reunion is held each year. Lunch consisted of fried chicken, ham that my wife, Ruth, had made, deviled eggs, and iced tea, with canteloupe for dessert.

At the reunion, Jimmy acted as if he hadn't a care in the world and as if he weren't upset over the sad state of our church affairs. He kissed the ladies, clapped the men on the back, and even paid attention to all the small fry, who were anxious to take a new look, now that he was a genuine President of the United States.

I thought it was diplomatic and fine that Cousin Jimmy combined the old with the new, attending Sunday School class at Plains Baptist Church, as he always had done, and then coming to pray and worship with us at Maranatha.

I felt touched that our new church was being blessed by the President when he said:

"Bless this small and new church. We are separated, we all pray, not out of a sense of alienation and hatred, but out of love and re-dedication to Thee. Help all the tensions to be alleviated."

It was a happy day when Carol Anderson moved over to the Maranatha Baptist Church of Plains. Her daughter, Jill, was baptized into the new church and the baptism took place in my swimming pool, which, at this writing, is still officially used by the church for the ceremony which involves complete immersion.

Jill was eleven when she was baptized on October 2, 1977.

With Carol back at the piano, as she had been at the Plains Baptist Church, Mrs. Ida Lee Timmerman retired from that post. But Ida Lee is now honored as the oldest member of the new church, having been born April 27, 1890.

For the last two weeks of his life, however, my daddy was the oldest member—eighty-nine against her eighty-seven.

It was sad that the first funeral to be held at the Maranatha Church was for my own daddy, Saturday, January 21, 1978. Jimmy came from Washington for it, right after delivering his first year's State of the Union Address, and Rosalynn was with him.

Carol Anderson played two favorite hymns—"The Old Rugged Cross" and "The Saviour Is Waiting"—but this time there was no singing of the songs Jimmy and I had sung so many times before.

The comforting thing was to know that when he died, Daddy Alton *was* a member of the new church. He had come to the conclusion himself and had requested membership of Reverend Fred Collins. And it was acted on that very night at the regular weekly prayer meeting.

Two weeks later, to the day, he passed away.

I knew that Jimmy could not hide behind a diplomatic attitude forever. He is too much of a straight shooter. Before he returned to Plains for Christmas 1977, reporters asked him if he felt a "greater affinity with members of the Maranatha Church" than of his old Plains Baptist Church. Cousin Jimmy finally confessed in public, "Yes, I do. Most of the members who voted with me on the controversial issue of allowing blacks to attend services did move out of the old church and I feel more compatible with that group."

But Jimmy continued to be diplomatic in spending some time at both churches so that he would touch base with all his friends and relatives.

At this writing, we now have sixty-eight members and our building fund has jumped to $35,000. On impulse I had sent a little note to Billy Graham, telling him about our new church and building plans and back came this letter:

BILLY GRAHAM

December 19, 1977

Dear Senator Carter,

Thank you for yours of December 6. Please excuse the delay in replying but we have been in the Philippines and in India for the past several weeks, and I am dictating this as I pass through the airport here in the United States en route to other commitments overseas. Thus the brevity of this reply.

We are, of course, standing behind the President with our prayers as he carries a heavy load of responsibility, and also for you our Senators and Congressmen, that you may have great wisdom from God Himself and strength to meet the burdens upon you.

We are overextended financially at the moment but will contribute $10,000.

Cordially,

Billy Graham

The Honorable Hugh A. Carter
The Georgia State Senate
P. O. Box 97
Plains, Ga. 31780

We are planning to start building soon, knowing that somehow the Lord will sustain us in our effort to complete his house of worship. My heart is warmed as I report that plans are already being made to landscape the property on which the church will rise.

The new church will face many financial problems. A home for the pastor must be built and a new church building must be erected, costing about $250,000 total. But I believe the Lord will provide and the church will grow and prosper as it is founded on *love for* and *faith in* God.

Our church welcomes all contributions, large or small and the names of all contributors are added to our honor roll. The address is Maranatha Baptist Church, Plains, Georgia, 31780.

Already, as I write this book, one of the members, Lilloise Sheffield, the widow of Jimmy's and my well-remembered and beloved coach and math teacher, has given the church eleven acres of land to build the new church. The land was appraised at $20,000.

Members continue to labor mightily for the church building and the sum is slowly rising. I have contributed substantially and am continuing to contribute substantially each week and will do so until the steeple has risen to its final height.

Though Chip and Caron Carter are not yet members of the new church, as soon as they returned to Plains after living in the White House, they gave $250 toward the building fund.

I know that all things are possible and this church will come to pass. We have named our church Maranatha for a good reason. It is an Aramaic word found in First Corinthians 16:22, which means:

"Our Lord cometh."

27 · I SLEPT IN THE LINCOLN BED

Most people wonder what it's really like to visit the White House family quarters—that sacrosanct second floor which is off limits to the tourists.

I was among them—but now I know.

I'd been to the White House during the inauguration, of course, but that was before Cousin Jimmy had really settled in. Then he was as much a stranger there as I.

But finally, after Jimmy had gotten used to the place and it was really home, I was invited to come share a beautiful moment—a formal dinner for the Shah of Iran and his Empress.

How could I know that it would be an awkward time, to say the least, when the White House seemed almost "under siege."

How could I know, when I received an invitation to come stay at the White House awhile and attend a formal White House dinner, that I would hit the jackpot and be at the White House when screaming and chanting of protesting students never ceased and tear gas made an arrival ceremony for the Shah of Iran an ordeal.

I will never forget the look of the marching students with paper bags or masks over their faces, like something out of a nightmare, and the screams of their leaders giving a chant which was repeated by the marchers, over and over and over, endlessly. All through the night, as Ruth and I lay in the Lincoln bed and tried to sleep, the chanting went on.

Overhead, helicopters with armed troops circled the White House without pause, ready in case the trouble should deepen and greater violence break out. Before that night would be over—November 15, 1977, several dozen people would be in hospitals—both the supporters of the Shah and the enemies of the Shah, who hid their identity by covering their heads completely.

How different it had seemed when we were just getting ready to come to the White House. Hugh, Jr., had worked out the date of the visit with the President and had called to tell me that the engraved invitation was on the way. He said that the President wanted us to stay in the Lincoln Room at the White House and attend the state dinner given by him and Rosalynn for the Shah and Shahbanou of Iran—as he called the Shah and Empress—on the night of November 15.

Ruth and I were thrilled to receive the invitation and we began to make plans to attend. I even almost broke down and bought a dinner jacket for the occasion. But, all through the years that I have been state senator, and even when Jimmy was governor and I attended parties at the Governor's Mansion, I prided myself on being an average man who rented a tuxedo.

So, though my wife, Ruth, gently pushed me toward a store, I sidestepped and arranged for my usual rental.

Getting from Plains to Washington, D.C., is not an easy thing. We drove thirty-five miles to Albany, Georgia, parked the car, and took a plane for Atlanta. We had been up since 5:00 and we left Albany at 7:23 A.M., arriving in Atlanta at 8:00 A.M., and departed Atlanta for Washington at 9:40. We arrived at the National Airport in Washington at 11:23, about thirteen minutes late.

Hugh, Jr., was at the airport to meet us with his girl friend, Glenna Garrett, a stewardess with Delta Airlines. Sonny had arranged for us to see the President at 11:55 so we had to hurry to the White House to be there on time.

I was rather thrilled to realize that my son did not have to stop and clear us with anyone but simply ushered us right into the West Wing of the White House and to the President's Oval Office.

Before we walked in, Hugh, Jr., introduced us to the President's personal secretary.

The President's secretary, Susan Clough, was a lovely blonde who has a fifteen-year-old son though she is only thirty-two herself. She also has a fourteen-year-old daughter. She has a great sense of humor and in a teasing way was calling Tim Kraft the President's *"former* appointments secretary" because he had been late by ten minutes and forced the President to wait that length of time.

The President's hatred of lateness, it seems, has not diminished since his gubernatorial campaigns.

Jimmy was not in the Oval Office as we entered, but in the smaller office adjoining it, where he likes to sit and do most of his work.

Sonny pointed to the presidential desk and commented that it was one that had been used by President John Kennedy.

As we were approaching the little office, out stepped the President, all smiles. He exclaimed, "Beedie, my buddy!" and grabbed me and I grabbed him. We gave each other a bear hug—we were both so glad to see each other. He took me then into his small private office and showed me the beautiful paintings on the walls. All the time he was asking me about Daddy and how things were in Plains.

I told him Dad was fine and working every day. His pacemaker had been changed but he was doing great and was only in the hospital one night. I told the President that all the newspaper stories about his—the President's—aging so drastically were certainly not true and he looked wonderful. His hair was perhaps a little thinner and had a little more gray, but otherwise he looked like the Jimmy of the campaign days.

I also reminded him that the papers said that Rosalynn looked younger and more beautiful. He agreed that this was true. Jimmy truly loves his wife and is quite proud of her. He never hesitates to brag about her and I admire his great love for Rosalynn.

The President then escorted Ruth and me into the Oval Office for pictures, several of which were taken in front of the famous fireplace.

Vice-President Mondale walked in. We had attended parties and met on several occasions, but Jimmy introduced us again as he told Vice-President Mondale that I helped him get elected governor of Georgia and served as his Senate floor leader while he was governor.

We stayed for a few more minutes and I had to pinch myself to realize that there I was, a country boy from Plains, making myself at home in the White House, talking to the President and Vice-President of the United States at the same time.

I was fascinated by the background of Fritz Mondale. He seemed to be almost a Carter, so closely did his background fit in with Jimmy's and mine. He had a quaint nickname—nobody calls him Walter—and he had grown up in small towns, including Elmore, Minnesota, population 837.

He knew all about farm chores and odd jobs and he had once even spent a summer vacation as a pea-lice inspector. Sunday School had been as important to him and his wife Joan as it has been to Rosalynn and Jimmy and Ruth and me.

I learned that there was even a born-again experience in his family, though a little different from Jimmy's experience which involved his sister, Ruth. In Fritz's case, it had been his father, who had been out alone plowing a field when he had his moment of spiritual rebirth.

My good friend, Hamilton Jordan, also dropped in to say hello. Later, someone showed me an item in a Washington newspaper saying that the President had interrupted his busy schedule to go out immediately and speak to his cousin, Senator Hugh Carter, when he found out that he had arrived.

I had noticed two trays of food outside the door of the Oval Office. They were there for Jimmy and Fritz Mondale to have a working luncheon together after we left.

As for our own lunch, Hugh, Jr., and Glenna took us to the White House Staff Mess which is run by Navy personnel. I saw some of my old friends there—Jim McIntyre, who was serving in Bert Lance's place, Jack Watson, Herky Harris, Robert Strauss, and others.

At 1:30 P.M. we were guests of Max Cleland, head of the Veterans Administration. I served several years in the Georgia Senate with Max and we were delighted to see each other again. He is a triple amputee but this certainly does not dampen his spirits. He is doing a splendid job as head of the Veterans Administration.

Hugh, Jr., told us that Joan Mondale had invited us over to the vice-presidential home. We were scheduled to be there at 3:30 P.M. This was a real treat and an opportunity that few are afforded. I was pretty beat by then but wouldn't have missed it for the world.

We drove immediately to the Vice-President's home in Sonny's Elite Ford. It crossed my mind that if my son hadn't been such a stickler in finding ways to economize, we would probably be arriving in a chauffeured limousine.

The guard at the gate was expecting us and welcomed us, directing Hugh, Jr., to park right at the door. I was a little disappointed because Joan Mondale, who had become a friend through the campaign days, was not there. She had been called away but she had left a note for Sonny. It was handwritten on beautiful stationery which carried a little lithograph of "the Vice-President's House" at the top:

Dear Hugh:

I am so disappointed I cannot be here to give you and your parents a personal welcome. You are in good hands with Gayle— she knows the house and the art work.

Make yourselves at home and enjoy it all!

Sincerely yours,
(signed) Joan Mondale

Gayle was Gayle Bauer and she did indeed give us a fine tour of the home. A big collie met us at the door when we arrived.

The dog was blind from old age but very friendly and lovable, named Bonnie. There were two cats, one sleeping on the sofa, a calico cat named Squirt, and her son, which was a much larger cat, brown and white, sleeping under the coffee table, named Kitty.

The Vice-President's house is a Victorian residence and was built in 1891 as the home of the superintendent of the Naval Observatory. President Hayes and his advisers chose the site because it was away from the traffic. It sits on the top of a pointed hill and has a huge sloping yard all around it.

I was especially impressed by the beautiful dining room table added by Vice-President Nelson Rockefeller. Mrs. Mondale has had the opportunity to choose the arts and craft for the home which she feels was an opportunity to showcase the range and quality of recent American art.

After seeing the vice-presidential home, we had grown weary as we had been up since 5:00 A.M., so Hugh, Jr., took us to his condominium town house in Arlington, Virginia. We spent the first night there with him.

His place is beautiful and convenient to Washington. The house is furnished throughout mostly with antiques he has obtained from our antique store in Plains as well as other antique stores.

Hugh, Jr., had arranged for us to attend the National Symphony at the Kennedy Center and to sit in the President's box. Aaron Copland was conducting and this concert was in tribute to his seventy-seventh birthday.

The next morning, we were to move into the White House and we took all our bags with us. There was a nightmarish quality from that moment on as we approached the White House. The marchers were everywhere, hooded figures, and for a while I wondered if we would have trouble getting onto the White House grounds.

In front of the White House a row of mounted police faced Lafayette Park keeping the students away from the White House side of the street. They were jeering at the police and waving sticks.

The mounted police sat on their horses and made no move to make contact with the students. Nor did they seem to pay any attention to the shouting and chanting or to the placards and banners that said, "Down with the Shah," and "Kill the Shah," and "The President is entertaining a killer."

The noise reached a crescendo as the guests were arriving. It seemed to be coming from just beyond the White House fence. On top of that was the roar of the low-flying helicopters.

As I looked up at the helicopters I noticed the men on the White House roof. There appeared to me to be teams of snipers up there standing by with rifles in case of trouble.

I could see in the distance that many of the demonstrators had big long white sticks and they were hitting each other.

Many wore hideous masks and the signs for and against the Shah were waving wildly. There was the constant chanting by the demonstrators over loudspeaker apparatus. The most persistent was the yell of "Down with the Shah."

Later I learned that in the bitter and bloody violence, ninety-six demonstrators and twenty-eight police officers were injured—some seriously.

I was told that one estimate of the demonstrators was four thousand anti-Shah and fifteen hundred pro-Shah. When this was taking place, close viewers said that children and old persons were especially frightened.

The crowds were eventually dispersed by the police. However, during the remainder of the day and into the night, the protesters milled around the Ellipse and Lafayette Park shouting slogans and arguing with the police and each other.

The arrival ceremony for the Shah and Empress was scheduled for 10:30 A.M., but it was slightly delayed and I was told that the visitors were being brought in a different gate in order to avoid the marchers. Security was very high. Hundreds of additional White House police and Secret Service men were everywhere.

There was a tremendous crowd of friends and official Washington as well assembled on the South Lawn for this arrival ceremony. Ruth and I waited outside the White House with Hugh, Jr., Glenna, and some members of the staff. Then the President and Rosalynn suddenly came out the South Portico because they had been informed the car containing the Shah and Empress was arriving.

Cousin Jimmy showed Rosalynn where we were standing and they both waved to us from a little distance. It was the only relaxed moment in a very formal event. For a moment Rosalynn showed how delighted she was to see us and then she became very formal and dignified as the car was rolling up.

The background noise accompanied everything as the demonstration of protesters was raging some four hundred yards away.

All of a sudden, we saw what appeared to be smoke coming from the crowd of demonstrators. It turned out to be tear gas fired by the U. S. Park Police, to disperse the crowd. I noticed the smoke started blowing right toward the speaker's stand and us. We were only a few yards from the speaker's stand, which had been set up on the lawn, red carpet and all.

Rosalynn seemed to be the most distressed by the tear gas. The President showed no signs of discomfort; he did not hesitate, but kept right on with his speech. The Shah was the first I saw to take his handkerchief out of his pocket and begin to wipe his eyes.

By the time Jimmy finished his remarks and turned the podium over to the Shah, the Shah was composed and ready to make his speech, which he did without hesitation. Jimmy had taken his handkerchief out of his pocket and given it to Rosalynn. However, Jimmy never did use the handkerchief.

He simply wiped the tears from his eyes with his hand. Using his ingenuity to overcome a bad moment, his first words were that he was sorry and had to apologize about Washington's pollution.

Jimmy told me later that tears were streaming from his eyes but he knew with tear gas it was best not to wipe the eyes. Rosalynn said that she was a little concerned at first as she did not know what the tear gas was and she felt maybe they should leave and go inside at once but that Vice-President Mondale whispered to her and said it is only tear gas and it won't hurt anything once it passes over.

Fritz Mondale was busy wiping his eyes also. The gas covered all the spectators and we all began to stream tears. I could feel my face burning all over where I had shaved only a couple of hours before.

About two dozen mounted police on horses forced hundreds of the bottle- and stick-throwing students back as the tear gas floated onto the White House lawn, toward the group welcoming the Shah on the White House grounds.

In spite of it all, the President and Shah, acting as if nothing was out of the ordinary, trooped the line inspecting the military guard. Then after the ceremony was over—the whole ceremony had lasted about fifteen minutes—the President and First Lady took their guests to the White House balcony for pictures and a customary wave to the crowd below.

From the balcony, Rosalynn signaled for us to meet them inside at once. It took several minutes for Hugh, Jr., to work us through the crowd and back to the Green Room, where they were waiting for us. Jimmy introduced Ruth and me to the Shah and Empress and we then went into the hallway, where the cameramen and press and many others were waiting to watch the presentation of a gift—a fabulous needlepoint tapestry of George Washington.

The Shah made an impressive presentation speech and Jimmy made a short speech accepting the gift on behalf of the United States. The Shah explained that the handwork portrait of the father of our country had been meant to become a bicentennial gift to coincide with the nation's bicentennial celebration in 1976.

But it had taken two full years to complete the needlework and that explained the delay. There were 250 stitches in each square centimeter.

Senator Herman Talmadge had invited us to lunch in the Senate Restaurant, so after the arrival ceremony for the Shah we struck out for Capitol Hill. It was a relief to get away from the turmoil around the White House.

It was a lovely luncheon in the private senatorial dining room and I couldn't help but notice that the cost of the delicious trout dinner was only $2.75. The Senate Restaurant is run on a nonprofit basis. We all started off the meal with the famous Senate bean soup, which I noticed was only 45¢.

The next stop on our agenda was to visit the Capitol on a tour which Vice-President Mondale had set up, especially for us, through the sergeant at arms of the Senate, Nordy Hoffman. His assistant, Peggy Mandjuris, escorted us on the tour of the Capitol building.

Out of all the beautiful rooms in the Capitol, my favorite is the small President's Room, where all the bills used to be signed. I understand that this room is still occasionally used for that purpose. The furnishings are beautiful—chandeliers and paintings and an impressive Lincoln table.

Peggy told us that the decorative walls and ceiling took the artist five years to paint. When I told Jimmy, later in the day, how fond I was of this room, I learned that he likes it, too, and was as impressed with it as I had been.

Weather permitting, many of the bills are now signed in the White House Rose Garden, where there is more room. It is also more convenient to the President's Oval Office.

We talked awhile longer to Nordy Hoffman and learned much about the Capitol building itself. I asked him if he was a friend of

Fishbait's, now retired. He said yes, but that he did not intend to write a book like Fishbait did.

After we got back to the White House, Rosalynn was more relaxed and gave us a little tour of the second floor, where she and Jimmy and Amy live, and then the third floor, where her son Jeff and his wife, Annette, have an apartment. I also saw the apartment that Chip and Caron used when they lived at the White House.

We headed back for the Lincoln Room. Rosalynn pointed out that the Queen's Room was just across from the Lincoln Room. She said that Jimmy's mother preferred to stay in the Queen's Room when she visits but that Allie Smith, her own mother, always stays in the Lincoln Room as we were doing.

There we were at last, Ruth and I, alone in the Lincoln Bedroom. I never dreamed I would ever be spending a night there.

But it was happening. I was exhausted and wanted to lie down for a few minutes and nap, but as an antique dealer, I was driven to absorb the look and feeling of the room. I could still hear the muffled sounds of the demonstrators across the street screaming and chanting their slogans of hate.

On the table on Ruth's side of the bed was chocolate candy and fresh fruit—oranges, bananas, apples, and grapes. There were two windows in the room. Just outside the window nearest my side of the bed, magnolia tree limbs were visible.

Even with the distant shouting, I heard birds singing on the magnolia tree. Neither Ruth nor I smoke, but there was a cut-glass case on the table on my side of the bed with a single cigarette in it.

The room was decorated primarily with American Victorian furnishings from the 1850–70 era. President Truman had made the decision to install bedroom furniture in the room from the Lincoln era. The rosewood bed was most beautiful, over eight feet long and almost six feet wide. I was told Mrs. Lincoln purchased the bed in 1861, along with other furniture.

There is a little shadow over whether Abraham Lincoln actually used that bed but better authenticated is the fact that several other presidents did—Woodrow Wilson and Theodore Roosevelt.

Mrs. Teddy Roosevelt liked the marble-top rosewood table in the middle of the room which appears to be designed to match the bed.

Both pieces of furniture have ornate carvings, including fanciful birds, grapevines, and flowers. This is typical of the Victorian style and era. I was told by one of the aides that from 1830 to 1902 the

Lincoln Bedroom served presidents as either an office or as a Cabinet room. Lincoln himself used it as both.

During the Teddy Roosevelt renovation, all presidential aides' offices were moved to the newly constructed West Wing and the second floor became part of the private family quarters for the President.

I had always heard about the rocking chair near the window which duplicates Lincoln's chair in the box at Ford's Theater the night of his assassination, so I did spend some time rocking in it, as did Ruth.

Everything in the room fascinated me but especially the holograph copy of Lincoln's Gettysburg Address, displayed on the desk. This copy is made on three sheets of paper and was the second version prepared by Lincoln at the request of historian George Bancroft.

That address was delivered by President Lincoln on November 19, 1863, well over a hundred years ago.

Feeling the respect I do for the priceless antique relics in the room, I hated to see a modern television set in there. But, being part of my generation, I turned it on anyway to watch the news. Almost as fascinating as the Lincoln Bedroom was the Lincoln Sitting Room next to it.

This is the small room in which President Nixon liked to sit with a fire going in the fireplace. And I was told that was the room where he had made Secretary of State Kissinger kneel with him in prayer in a very dramatic scene, before he left office.

At one time—during the Tyler administration—the small room was used as the presidential office. Also it doubled as a bedroom during the Polk administration and office for the President's nephew and private secretary, J. Knox Walker.

One thing that impressed me in the room was a small desk in front of a window. It had been used by James Hoban, the original architect of the White House.

Ruth and I began dressing about 6:30 for the 7:30 dinner. Rosalynn had told us where to come for the brief intimate reception for the Shah and Empress at 7:20 in the family quarters before descending to the East Room for the reception preceding the state dinner.

It was a pleasant little meeting of the honor group with the President and Vice-President and their wives. The Empress looked sophisticated and stunning and I was proud to see that Rosalynn was equally as beautiful, and held her own against the exotic visitor from the Middle East.

The Empress was wearing a dazzling blue-and-gold brocade gown and shimmering diamond and sapphire pendant earrings. I noticed that the Shah's eyes were still red from the tear gas but no one mentioned the incident.

Very soon, the chief military escort aide informed Ruth and me that we were to be the first to be escorted down to the East Room, where hundreds of guests waited. We went down on the elevator, and the escort turned us over to another aide, who then escorted us into the reception room. As we entered, we were announced by the aide calling out "Senator and Mrs. Hugh Carter."

Many of our friends who knew us rushed over to greet us—including former U. S. Senator David Gambrell and his lovely wife, Luck. Right after us, the other couples from upstairs were announced, the President and First Lady being the last to enter.

As they were entering the reception, someone asked the President if it was the first time he had experienced tear gas. Jimmy said, "Yes, and I hope it's my last."

Someone else asked him whether the Shah of Iran was upset about the situation and he said, "No, I don't believe so. I think he has handled it very well."

Then the President and Shah took their places in the receiving line and we all went by to shake their hands and greet them. As I shook Jimmy's hand I whispered to him, "Boy, this is really uptown."

He laughed and agreed with me. For a moment, we were back in Plains.

After the reception in the East Room, we entered the State Dining Room and were escorted to Table 12. To my surprise and shock, number 12 turned out to be the head table. I had no idea Jimmy and Rosalynn had chosen to seat us with them in spite of all the high-ranking dignitaries there.

I did notice that every table had at least one notable or famous person—the Vice-President, a Cabinet member, a member of Congress, a justice of the Supreme Court, or a high-ranking White House staffer.

There were place cards in front of each of us at our table. At my right was Edie Wasserman, the wife of the chairman of the board of Music Corporation of America. Next to her was her husband Lew, whose Universal Studio had made such successful movies as *Jaws,* *The Sting, Airport,* and *Earthquake.*

Next to Lew was the Empress, then President Carter, the Shah of Iran, then Rosalynn, then my wife, Ruth, and back to me.

The centerpieces at the tables fascinated everyone. They had used big chunks of minerals—emeralds, quartz, etc., borrowed from the Smithsonian.

Our centerpiece, combining huge semiprecious stones and flowers, excited a lot of comment and it deserved to. Mixed in with the gems and rising gracefully from them, were miniature yellow and salmon-colored orchids.

I'm glad that I had been warned that there would be finger bowls because I certainly would not have known what those lovely little bowls with floating greenery were. I have heard that some people have assumed they were soup and tried to drink them, and I don't blame them.

Several hours before, when Rosalynn was showing us around the White House, she had taken us to the roof of the White House with a let's-share-a-secret look.

Ruth and I had been amazed to find a little greenhouse up there. Rosalynn had shown it to us proudly, explaining that she and Jeff liked to putter around up there. Then she said, "Look at these geraniums. See these tiny leaves. They are the descendants of the geraniums that the first President to live at the White House used for his finger bowls.

"So when you see your finger bowls tonight, you'll have geranium leaves in them which have been propagated through the years since John Adams." Then she smiled and added, "At least, that's the way the story goes."

The White House roof has another important use. That's where Jeff practices his hobby of stargazing. He and Annette use his fine telescope to observe other planets such as Jupiter with its moons and Saturn with its rings as they appear over the horizon on a clear evening.

Ruth was having an animated conversation with Edie Wasserman and suddenly I heard Ruth say, "I want to come see you in California before it falls off into the ocean."

The Wassermans laughed uproariously. And they have proven their enjoyment of Ruth's company by sending all manner of gifts since that evening, most of which show their own sense of humor—such as a director's chair which is a paperweight and various T-shirts from their movies, *Jaws* and *Big Foot*. At this writing, a costume has just arrived from them which is based on the *Bionic Woman* TV series—which, I confess, is my favorite series. They even sent us a thousand dollars for our Maranatha Baptist Church building fund.

Ruth is getting ready to send some samples of Georgia products, such as pecans.

But to return to the White House banquet, most of the time Ruth and Rosalynn talked as if they were back in Plains and Ruth was filling Rosalynn in on the church situation. Rosalynn asked many questions and seemed genuinely interested in how the Maranatha Church was coming along with its building plans.

But suddenly the Shah and Ruth started talking, and Ruth, who has a fabulous memory, was telling about a friend who goes to the Virgin Islands every year and told her he does business with a relative of the Shah's. The Shah was delighted and said that he, too, knew this mutual friend very well.

A subject not touched on my side of the table was the demonstrations outside the White House. We talked of everything else: the difference of customs in Iran and the United States, the Empress' interest in modern art, and the beauty of the centerpieces.

It was an exhilarating experience to be so surrounded by beauty on all sides—the surroundings in the family quarters in the White House, the elegant hairdos and clothing of the ladies. My wife was dressed in a lovely bright color she called persimmon.

Rosalynn was in black, white, and red. The long skirt of her gown was white. The top was black and the red accents were a red sash and hem edging.

Now and then I could hear a word of earnest conversation between the President and Shah; they were talking about oil and oil prices.

When he turned to me, the President explained why Hamilton Jordan was not at the dinner—he was representing the President at the funeral of Pinkie Masters, a good friend of his and mine, in Savannah, Georgia. I remember I spoke with the President about how saddened I was about Pinkie Masters' death.

Pinkie was one of Jimmy's early supporters when he ran for Governor the first time, and he supported him ever since. He owned a famous bar near the Hilton Hotel in Savannah and was known for his great dedication to Jimmy—he would do anything to help Jimmy.

Way back, I believe in 1974, long before anyone was taking Jimmy's candidacy seriously, Pinky was doing a public relations job as he sold the merchandise in his liquor store.

He would put the bottles in paper bags on which he himself had stenciled the slogan "CARTER FOR PRESIDENT."

Later I learned that while the picketers were screaming and we were partaking of the fancy food, reporters at the White House killed time watching the movie *The Godfather* on television.

Nothing can describe the feeling of grandeur one gets sitting in the State Dining Room which is large enough to seat 140 guests. The ceiling is high and above the fireplace mantel hangs a huge portrait of Abraham Lincoln seated in a pose of thoughtful contemplation.

Dinner music was provided by the Strolling Strings. There were two violinists on each side of our table for quite a long time.

I looked across the table at Jimmy and he smiled at me and I smiled at him. I knew he was thinking the same thing as I—"This is a long way from Plains, Georgia."

I looked around the room and felt warm to see other familiar faces from Georgia—Jimmy's son Jeff and his wife, David Gambrell and his wife from Atlanta, Jimmy Bishop and his wife and the Carlton Hickses from Brunswick, Joe T. Andrews from Milledgeville.

I would not have known the names for the courses without the help of the menu, which was contained in a lovely booklet with the presidential seal in gold on the cover, as well as my name printed by hand:

DINNER

IN HONOR OF

THEIR IMPERIAL MAJESTIES

THE SHAHANSHAH AND THE SHAHBANOU OF IRAN

Sebastiani	*Mousse of Sole*
Pinot Chardonnay	*with Salmon Hearts*
1976	
Charles Krug	*Suprême of Pheasant*
Cabernet Sauvignon	*Wild Rice*
1973	*California Broccoli*
	Watercress and Mushroom Salad
	Trappist Cheese
Hanns Kornell Brut	
	Frozen Praline Crown
	with Chocolate Pears
	Demitasse

My eyes kept straying to the fairy-book Empress and especially the stunning pendant diamond and emerald earrings which moved as she swayed so gracefully. I found myself counting the number of diamonds in one of her earrings and was well past two dozen before I realized what I was doing and stopped.

I was sure that some of the diamonds in it were at least three carats. I mentioned the earrings to Edie Wasserman, who also exclaimed over their beauty and commented, "And to think that this must be just one pair in her collection."

Jimmy, I thought, was very diplomatic in the way he referred just once, with light good humor, to the violent demonstrators outside the White House gates, and let it go at that. He started his toast by saying, "One thing that I can say about the Shah—he certainly knows how to draw a crowd."

And that was the only mention made of it. However, I understand that there was a little egg throwing that had followed the Shah's limousine when it had entered the White House gates, at the southwest entrance. This is the back door of the White House, so to speak, and not the Pennsylvania Avenue northwest entrance usually used.

Jody Powell, the press secretary, later confessed that the White House had been slightly misinformed about the demonstrations. They had been led to believe that the demonstrators would be a mixture of well-mannered kids and middle-aged people.

They had not expected such belligerence on the part of both those who supported the Shah and those who opposed him.

This was the Shah's twelfth visit to the White House. On his first visit, in 1949, he had come with 140 suitcases and trunks for a month's stay. That time he had been the guest of President Truman for a while and the Shah had given the President a Persian rug.

In 1962, when he visited President Kennedy, Jacqueline Kennedy had been very clever in the way she had handled the knowledge that Empress Farah was going to wear a dress that contained rubies, and a tiara and necklace of diamonds and emeralds.

Jackie went the other direction completely and wore a starkly simple evening dress.

In 1973, when the Shah visited President Nixon, there were masked demonstrators in smaller numbers and they had chanted, "Down with the Shah."

In 1975, the last time he had visited, before this current visit, the student situation had heated up and about two hundred students were masked and shouting, "The Shah is a puppet."

After the music, strong lights came on and the news media with their TV cameras beamed their lenses at our table. The President rose and gave a formal toast to the Shah and his country, Iran. The Shah responded with a slightly shorter toast to the President and the United States.

It was very impressive—the toast and then the lifting of the glass. We moved, then, back into the East Room for the entertainment of the evening—about thirty minutes of Sarah Vaughan, Dizzy Gillespie, and Willis Conover.

The final touch was to be invited to go to the second-floor family living quarters again with the President, First Lady, and other close friends, after the guests of honor had left for Blair House across the street from the White House.

For a while David Gambrell, the President, and I were off in a corner and Gambrell mentioned that my worm farm was written up in the current issue of *Reader's Digest*. Cousin Jimmy chuckled and said, "Yes, Hugh, and you and I are the only Carters who have been written up in *Playboy.*"

This remark by the President drew a hearty laugh from the group, who now moved in on us. It had been several years since *Playboy* did a short story on my worm business so I was surprised that Jimmy still remembered.

Cousin Jimmy suddenly chuckled and tried to explain why he hadn't talked to the Empress more at the table. "I was sitting between the Shah and Empress Farah. The Empress is one of the most beautiful women in the world. My preference was—well, I won't tell you. I'll let you guess.

"I was going to talk with her about oil prices," he chuckled again, "but Lew Wasserman was talking to her about movies and I don't have to tell you what the Empress' preference was."

We were all pretty tired and stretched out in various comfortable chairs. Ruth was in the most comfortable chair of all. Jimmy stood around looking at her and then sank down into the sofa closest to her. She suddenly noticed all the telephone buttons beside her and realized she must be sitting in the President's chair, where he could grab the phone for important calls.

"Oh, Mr. President, I'm in your chair. Let's swap." Jimmy gave her a mock dirty look for suddenly getting formal with him and said, "Oh, no no. You be Mr. President."

They laughed and we suddenly recalled Inauguration Day when

it had been the son of Jimmy's sister, Ruth Stapleton, who had sat in the presidential chair. It had happened in the Oval Office where members of the family had been escorted to see where Jimmy would be holding forth from then on.

The new President had gone off with some of his aides, so only other members of the family were in there with a White House staffer who was serving as a guide. Filled with exuberance, eighteen-year-old Michael Stapleton had plunked himself into the President's chair, clowning around by throwing his arms up in the Nixon V for victory sign and yelling that we won.

Suddenly Michael realized that someone had joined the group and was not looking pleased. It was the President of the United States.

It was obvious that the President had arrived with his aides to start working and it was an uncomfortable moment with neither side knowing quite what to do. Jimmy muttered darkly—something about thinking he had left the family in the White House living quarters and Michael got out of there as quickly as he could.

But when he got home he sent the President a note of apology for having invaded his privacy and got a very nice note in return. In fact, the P.S. is now part of family lore. The President wrote: "By the way, Michael, do you know that you're the only one in our Administration who sat in my chair before I did?"

Rosalynn was being asked about the violin lessons she was taking and why she was taking them. She explained that the lessons had originally been intended for Amy but the violin teacher strongly recommended that Rosalynn take them along with Amy as a shared project.

Rosalynn demonstrated to me how you had to hold the violin with your chin pressing the violin against the shoulder—not with your hand. Your left hand remains free to finger the strings.

Rosalynn said that when she first started taking lessons, she got very sore in her neck muscles until she became accustomed to the pressure.

We realized that it was 12:30 A.M. Jimmy himself made the announcement, saying that he had to get up at 6:00. Rosalynn suggested that Ruth and I meet her and Amy for breakfast in the family dining room at 8:00.

I would not be able to see Jimmy for breakfast because he would be gone by then. We hadn't really had a chance for a good talk. Jimmy, tired as he was, kept urging that we stay until Friday and Rosalynn joined and was almost as insistent.

I explained that I had to be in Plains for a scheduled meeting on Thursday. Ruth and I both expressed our extreme pleasure and appreciation for the unique experience and their lovely invitation. I said that Hugh, Jr., had lined up one more busy day of sight-seeing for us the next day and I already had memories enough to last a long time.

I wanted to tell Cousin Jimmy that I had been asked to write a book about our relationship and the family history, but somehow this wasn't the time. He had much more important things to think about and those demonstrators were still screaming away outside the White House. It could wait. Besides, this book had to be completely mine and totally objective.

Also the thought had crossed my mind that if I told Jimmy about the book, he might feel obliged to offer to help me by remembering things for me and I certainly did not want to impose. Not even my son knew about this book.

In the Lincoln Room the dark four-poster bed and the rich old furniture gave a heavy and ponderous feeling and the shadows in the room reminded me that Lincoln's ghost was supposed to walk here.

If the ghost walked that night, we were too exhausted to see him. We fell asleep talking about this fantastic day of violence outside and grandeur inside the White House.

During the entertainment some of the guests had been talking about the fact that trash fires could be seen burning on Pennsylvania Avenue in front of the White House. Some Iranian students had thrown a match into newspapers and placards.

My last memory as I drifted off to sleep was of the droning of the helicopters and the far-off voices of the chanters, grown quieter now.

In the morning we packed hurriedly and rushed to breakfast with Rosalynn and Amy. Amy was doing some last-minute studying and we were all trying to find the answer to a history question for her—"Who were the Tories?"

She was supposed to have the answer written out for her history class before she got to school. We talked about it during breakfast and still could not decide on an adequate answer.

Amy made up her own mind and, I suppose, wrote the answer on her way to school. She ate quickly and hurried off. I asked Rosalynn how Amy got to school and she said that the Secret Service always took her.

The rest of us relaxed and had a more leisurely breakfast of grapefruit, coffee, scrambled or poached eggs on toast, bacon and sausage.

I was happy to learn that none of Amy's fears that she would be lonely in the White House had come to pass. According to Rosalynn, she has many friends, some of them from back home—the children of Press Secretary Jody Powell and legislative aide Frank Moore. That way, she still hears the Georgia accent she is used to.

And she has the children of her class from Stevens School. Rosalynn told how sometimes after their violin lesson, they go shopping at Sears. This way Amy is maintaining a wholesome approach toward money and careful shopping.

Sometimes they also go to a McDonald's hamburger place for a snack. A big deal for Amy is a stop at a pizza parlor and that usually is her Sunday treat.

After breakfast Rosalynn wanted to know what we'd like to see of the White House and we ended up with a tour that I'm sure few people ever get. We saw the laundry rooms, for example. And the kitchens. And the flower room where the bouquets had come from for the decorations of the night before.

I had read about a bowling alley. Rosalynn took us there. A single lane, but nice. Rosalynn said they often bowled and that Amy was a good bowler.

There are three chefs who work in the stainless-steel kitchens in the basement. Rosalynn says she checks the menus for the week making some changes. She says that she finds much more important things to do than worry about menus.

However, she makes sure that the menus contain a lot of vegetables because Jimmy likes them, along with simple meat dishes.

Ice cream is still a favorite dessert rather than pastries.

Hugh, Jr., told me his favorite room in the White House is the Map Room, which was used by President Franklin D. Roosevelt as a situation room to follow the course of World War II.

It was redecorated in 1970 as a reception room in Chippendale style. Among the things that impressed me in the room is a silver pitcher once owned by President Martin Van Buren and a portrait of Benjamin Franklin completed in 1759 in London.

The room contains a number of nineteenth-century landscape paintings. A small mahogany lap desk for traveling, bearing the initials of its owner, Thomas Jefferson, stands on a Philadelphia Chippendale chest and is most impressive.

Probably the most notable among the Chippendale pieces in the Map Room is an elaborately carved highboy on the wall opposite the windows. This piece alone must be worth thousands of dollars.

Every time I look at an antique I think about its value. This is natural since I am an antique dealer and operate an antique store.

The barbershop is no longer exclusively used by presidents and their top male aides. They now laughingly call it the "Unisex White House Salon." One day a week, a man and wife team, who have a unisex hairdressing shop on Capitol Hill, come to the White House barbershop in the basement and snip and set the heads of both men and women working at the White House.

It isn't cheap to get your hair done at the White House. A shampoo, styling, and blow drying is twelve dollars for men and eighteen for women.

Cousin Jimmy does not use this beauty parlor team. He uses the regular White House barber, Rodrigues Morales.

While I was there, I was amused to hear how everyone conspires against Jimmy to keep his hair long the way the voters liked it during the campaign. It seems that Jimmy keeps wanting to have it cut short and so he will tell Susan Clough to call the barber and tell him he's coming down and wants his hair cut short.

She does as she is told and then Tim Kraft, his special assistant for appointments, goes to another phone and calls the barber to warn him not to cut more than a trifle of the President's hair.

Poor Jimmy—if he really wants it short—he is going to have to cut it himself.

Hugh, Jr., had shown me the movie room the day before. Rosalynn said that they saw about three movies a week there. She said Jimmy usually went back to his office to work after supper, unless they saw a movie. She said that she encouraged the movie attendance as much as possible for him to rest and relax.

I told Rosalynn that Hugh, Jr., had told me that he had attended one movie there when Chip invited him. Rosalynn told me to tell Sonny that he had an open invitation to attend the movies there anytime he wanted to.

I was returning to Plains with messages for some of our townspeople. In the flower room the florists inquired about Mrs. Clarence Dodson, who had come from Plains to supervise the decoration of the White House for Jimmy and Rosalynn's inauguration festivities.

Rosalynn spoke of Wayne Dean, an interior decorator from Americus who had come to the White House to help her redecorate a couple of rooms. We know him well since he is the designer who helped Ruth and me decorate our house.

I had a few moments to speak with Jeff and Annette, and their devotion to each other was very evident. Jeff told me he was doing well in school making all A's. He has always been a very intelligent boy, and in the same grade in high school as my daughter Connie.

At 9:30 Sonny arrived to take us on a little tour of Washington sights.

It was interesting that the Shah was also leaving Washington the same day I was. Traditionally, the head of a foreign state gives a return party at his own nation's embassy the night after he has been entertained by the President.

But because Jimmy Carter changed the rule and announced that he would not attend these return dinners but would send another member of the family, as his representative, the Shah left early rather than take a chance on the President not showing up.

Some of the masked demonstrators were still outside and looked pretty grim. I was told of many other demonstrators who come and exercise their First Amendment rights with a more humorous flair. There was one who came and performed rain dances in bare feet every day until he tired of it.

Another man came with printed signs insisting that the Secret Service was sterilizing the public with cosmic rays and that FBI Director Hoover had been murdered with cosmic rays.

I was also told that I had missed one of the most picturesque White House demonstrators, a woman-hater who comes with his bicycle demonstrating against women. Both he and his cycle are completely covered with signs telling how he has been abused at the hands of women.

The FBI Building was first and by luck our guide, named Art, was from Brunswick, Georgia. He said he hoped to become a special agent.

From the FBI Building we drove to Arlington Cemetery, where we visited John and Robert Kennedy's graves, as well as taking a short tour of the cemetery. We visited the Tomb of the Unknown Soldier and witnessed the changing of the guard.

After that, it was time to go to the airport. I was glad that our visit had ended on the solemn note of the Arlington Cemetery. We had seen the present—having been eyewitnesses at the Iranian incident which will be talked about for years to come—and we had seen the past at the graves which attested to traumatic moments of history.

28 · A PRESIDENT'S HOLIDAYS ARE LIKE NONE OTHER

I think it shows Jimmy's love for Plains and all he left behind there, that he left the glamour of the White House with its stunning twenty-foot Christmas tree, to return to Plains, where he bought and paid for his own little Christmas tree—fourteen dollars.

That tree—the one he and Rosalynn enjoyed in their own home on Christmas Eve—was only ten feet high. It was a Virginia pine, which, however, had been raised in Georgia.

The most interesting thing to me was that after the selection and before the tree was cut down to bring to his house, one of the workers slept all night beside that tree to keep someone else from buying it.

But there was no Christmas tree in the center of town to greet him as there had been the year before, when he had been President-elect. The town was just afraid of having it disappear again as it had the year before when pranksters had done their bit to liven the Plains Christmas season.

Instead, every telephone pole blossomed out with red Christmasy lights and green decorations.

As someone said, "Let's see them pull up the telephone poles!"

The security around Jimmy was especially intense at Christmastime in Plains. I noticed it when I went to the airport to greet him and again to see him off when he went back to Washington, after the holiday, prior to taking off for his goodwill European trip.

The security was even more tight around the church. Secret Service men stayed all night at the Maranatha Church, where Jimmy and Rosalynn were coming to worship on Christmas Sunday. I have never seen tighter security around Jimmy and I felt bad that, because there had been some threats, he was unable to have a free and easy holiday, but that's what it means to be President.

In spite of the security, however, Jimmy still made a point to come and visit my daddy, who was just home from the hospital, after a small setback. When Jimmy came out of his Uncle Alton's house, about three hundred people had gathered to wait for him to appear.

Jimmy's first Christmas in the White House did not escape without a note of criticism from the press. He had sent out Christmas cards with the message of "Merry Christmas."

Since many persons to whom a President sends cards are not Christians, it is not considered diplomatic to be mentioning Christ on the card.

It was typical of Jimmy Carter to create a great outpouring of love from the White House at the holiday season by sending out over sixty thousand Christmas cards. I was told that this is the largest number that have ever been sent from there, though Nixon was not too far behind. The John F. Kennedys only sent a little over two thousand.

When I was visiting the White House in November 1977, great preparations were already afoot for the President's first Christmas at the White House. Even though he would be leaving it behind, for a second Christmas tree in Plains, a huge Christmas tree would be installed in the Blue Room with ornaments made by retarded children and adults all over the United States.

Each person making an ornament for the White House, through the mental health foundation or center of his town or city, would receive a certificate telling of his or her contribution to White House Christmas, 1977.

Rosalynn put a lot of work into making Christmas a very special thing full of pride for several thousand retarded boys and girls and adults.

I received a photograph of how the tree had turned out with its unique decorations. It was truly beautiful—a twenty-foot fir, touching the ceiling, covered with 2,500 ornaments.

Some of the unique ornaments have probably never been seen on a Christmas tree before. Someone had made a Swiss cheese out of Styrofoam. Someone had knitted an "Eye of God" out of yarn. And there was also a Star of David made of yarn.

Then there were the things that were not too surprising on a Christmas tree—chains of peanuts from Georgia, little wreaths of Hale Koa nut pods from Hawaii, corn-husk dolls from Indiana, and little plaques decorated with designs of corn kernels and other seeds from Iowa.

The project was coordinated by the National Association for Retarded Citizens. Though only 1,500 persons received certificates, they represented the 6 million persons who are a part of the association.

Why had Rosalynn departed from the tradition of commercial ornaments? As she explained it, "Jimmy and I wanted to show that retarded citizens are talented, too, and we recognize their right to develop their talents."

It had been Rosalynn's own idea, and I think she deserves a lot of credit for it, to get the NARC to undertake the Christmas tree ornament project. It had been one of the first things she did after becoming First Lady.

How much food is involved in White House Christmas entertainment? When I saw the White House kitchens, in November, plans were already being made for Christmas. To have a plentiful supply for congressional and press and all other parties; the amounts being planned were two hundred cakes, eight thousand cookies, twelve turkeys, twelve Virginia hams, and three hundred gallons of punch.

In the midst of their own multitude of Christmas parties, Jimmy and Rosalynn had to pause to fly to Fayetteville,, North Carolina, to attend the wedding of their nephew, Sydney Scott Stapleton, the son of Jimmy's evangelist sister, Ruth, on Saturday, December 17, 1977, to Carol Lee Gainey.

Then they had to fly back to be in time for one of their own parties—for the White House staff.

It's a pity that Cousin Jimmy could not even attend a wedding without there being a noisy demonstration outside the church. This was a group shouting and carrying banners saying, "Free the Wilmington 10" and "Human Rights Begin at Home." There was also a farmer's rally and a four-hundred-vehicle tractorcade disrupting Fayetteville.

The tractors carried big signs saying, "CRIME DOES NOT PAY AND NEITHER DOES FARMING," and "THE FARMER FEEDS YOU THREE TIMES A DAY."

In order to quiet the demonstration and hear the farmers' case, North Carolina Representative Charles Rose, who was attending a prewedding breakfast with President Carter, left the breakfast and joined the farmers.

Congressman Rose expressed the President's "deep feelings and sympathy" for farmers and assured them he was studying the situation.

Before that several thousand farmers chose Thanksgiving holiday and drove their tractors to Plains to picket the President's home and demand higher prices for farm products. Jimmy was not at Plains that weekend but having his Thanksgiving dinner at Camp David.

I greeted them and tried to let them know that I would deliver their message to the President.

Jimmy and Rosalynn enjoyed the wedding, as best they could, and gave Sydney and his dental hygienist bride a gift of a silver serving spoon carrying Jimmy's signature on one side and "The President's House" on the other.

Then Jimmy and his party slipped out the side door of the church so that they would not pass the demonstrators on their way back to the airport. Afterward, Jimmy said he could not intervene in the Wilmington 10 case because it was still in litigation in North Carolina courts.

Jimmy left behind a strange souvenir for a family who had staged a postwedding rehearsal dinner at their home. He autographed the fireplace mantel of their home with a felt-tip pen.

John Beard, the owner of the home, a pawnshop owner, who keeps his own helicopter parked on his lawn, felt well repaid for all his trouble.

Beard had gone to great pains to make this a memorable occasion. Trying to give the wedding a white-Christmas effect, he had brought in snow-making machines, which also decorated the lawn. It never got cold enough to make snow.

The presidential party partook of a huge buffet dinner at Beard's home but he was so busy making sure everything was all right, he never did get to break bread with the President.

But the autographed mantel made up for everything.

In the old days at Plains, Jimmy and Rosalynn were exhausted if they had to attend more than three or four Christmas parties—and maybe participate in some caroling. But at the White House, their first year, they had to give fifteen parties before taking off for Plains and quieter festivities.

There was a party for the Secret Service and White House guards, a party for the White House press corps, a party for Congress, and a party for the Carter volunteers, to name a few of the outstanding ones.

One of the most important parties, as far as Rosalynn and Jimmy were concerned, was the Christmas party at which Amy met the children of the whole diplomatic corps in Washington. That was the 1977 White House party for diplomatic children of the five to eleven age group in all the embassies. Amy, at age ten, was among the oldest children attending.

The entertainment involved clowns, and Amy had a special treat when one of the clowns made her up as "The Littlest Clown." He painted round pink spots on her cheeks and dressed her in a ruffled clown costume. On her head was a pointed clown's hat.

Amy, I hear, was pretty shy about that and not at all thrilled about the attention and being perched up on the stage in the East Room where 430 children from ninety-six countries could see her looking "funny."

But Amy's daddy and mother, who came into the room, didn't think she looked funny or ridiculous but simply marvelous. And Helen Hayes, the actress, who had come from New York, said, "You're a real trouper, Amy," which made Amy feel much better.

The "First Lady of the American theater" was the narrator for the children's entertainment, provided by the Pixie Judy theatrical group of New York.

One of the six-year-old guests confided a desire to Rosalynn to give Amy a kiss and Rosalynn, much amused, brought the two children together.

One of the things Amy was able to show her guests was her huge gingerbread house liberally covered with powdered sugar snow and flanked by gingerbread Christmas trees. It sat on a huge sideboard in front of a mirror in the State Dining Room, where the cookies and fruit punch were spread out.

It took two military aides, standing on each side of the tempting gingerbread house, to keep the little ones from taking a few nibbles as Hansel and Gretel did in the fairy tale.

At the time of my visit, the law stated that government officials could keep only gifts worth fifty dollars or less. Any gift over that value had to passed along to the chief of protocol at the State Department to become public property.

However, the plan was to have the fifty-dollar maximum changed to one hundred because of inflation.

It was interesting to me that one of the first things Jimmy had done on taking office was to spread the word to foreign chiefs of state, through our State Department, that he would appreciate gifts being kept below the fifty dollars. Every time a new foreign visitor was expected, the Protocol Office again explained about the American law.

Jimmy and Rosalynn have received some lovely gifts from chiefs of state that they have been able to keep, such as books, musical records and tapes, and for Rosalynn, one lovely glass rose.

Little Amy got lucky, too. She was permitted to keep some little Russian wooden dolls.

Much is reported in the press about gifts that a First Family receives from a visiting head of government. But little is known about what the President and First Lady give to foreign chiefs of state.

When Rosalynn made her Latin American trip, she gave beautiful glass sprays of dogwood blossoms which were made by a Georgia glassblower, Hans Frabel. She also gave leather-bound copies of Jimmy's Organization of American States human rights speech.

Knowing how musically inclined the Mexican First Lady is, Rosalynn gave her another southern hand-crafted product—a dulcimer.

Cousin Jimmy usually gives a foreign visitor two gifts—a framed photograph suitably autographed and a landsat book of NASA photographs of earth taken from one of our satellites. I believe the name stands for land and satellite—thus, "landsat."

One of the things that amazed me on my visit to the White House was to learn that there is a gift room for the storing of gifts that come from the public, until some disposition is made of them. One of the problems my own son faced as head of the Office of Administration was what to do about the five hundred to a thousand gifts the Carters receive every month from the general public.

At first, unless they came from personal friends, the gifts were returned to the sender. But it was soon obvious that many people were deeply hurt to have some gift they had labored upon with loving care bounced back to them. So a new policy was instituted of giving the gifts to charity or to the U. S. Archives, whichever seems to be more appropriate.

Things that are useful like homemade quilts, potholders, and children's clothing and games now go to charitable organizations, such as orphanages.

Money, however, is still returned to the sender. If there is no return address, the money goes to the general fund of the Treasury.

One of Hugh, Jr.'s, innovations is to keep a computerized list of all the donors and their addresses and the gifts they have sent. Each person gets a nice little note telling what has happened to his gift.

When I was at the White House I learned how every single thing was being recorded in the computer from a child's puzzle valued at a dollar to a piece of Waterford crystal from the Irish government valued at several hundred dollars.

While Jimmy and Rosalynn were off seeing the world, Amy learned a little about skiing. One thing she learned was that you have to aim away from a tree. But she came up smiling and everyone agreed she was a good sport to hold back after a big bump.

While she was away a gift of a six-foot-tall dollhouse arrived at the White House for her. It was a special gift from a little girl in Milwaukee, the grandchild of a Hungarian refugee, John Varga.

Varga had made a fully furnished dollhouse for his granddaughter, Lisa, and Lisa had been so thrilled with it that she had wanted Amy Carter, whom she heard so much about, to have one just like it, with parquet floors and window boxes with flowers.

It took months to build and furnish, and when John Varga arrived in Washington, no one was there to receive the dollhouse so carefully transported in the back of his truck.

Hurriedly, several presidential assistants rounded up two legislators from Varga's state—Senator William Proxmire and Representative Henry Reuss—and staged a nice presentation complete with photographers to take pictures to show to the presidential family.

The sad part of the story is that Amy will only be able to play with the dollhouse for a little while because it is too valuable a gift for the White House to accept. But the happy ending is that the dollhouse will be sent for permanent display to the Georgia Museum after being shown for a while at the National Archives in Washington.

Unusual gifts pour in from the public. One of the most unusual was a pair of reindeer from Finland. These were accepted by Amy and then turned over to the Washington Zoo. But what Amy was permitted to keep was a little Finnish stocking cap with pretty design that had been sent along for her, too.

Members of first families remain famous through history for the things that are named for them. There is still an Alice Blue for the daughter of President Teddy Roosevelt and there is the Jacqueline Kennedy Garden at the White House, which keeps her memory bright for all the tourists who walk through the White House. Now I hear there is a Rosalynn green.

And already little Amy Carter will be remembered in history for having a poinsettia flower named for her. This honor was announced during the Carter family's first Christmas in the White House.

The horticulturist, Paul Ecke, Sr., who made the announcement said it was done in recognition of President Jimmy's conservation efforts. Ecke said "Amy and her generation will require all the encouragement they can get to face the challenge of conservation in the future."

I was sorry to see Jimmy's first Christmas homecoming clouded by still more "tractorcades" of farmers trying to drive their tractors as close as they could get to the President's home.

When he came to see me as his first stop on his walk around town, the first morning home, we talked very seriously about the farm situation.

I couldn't believe my eyes when my son sent me a White House press release which showed that just my conversation with Jimmy, when he stopped in the antique shop, was being treated as news.

Not the part of the conversation which had dealt with his curiosity about the Jimmy souvenirs and which ones were most popular with tourists, but the conversation we had about the angry farmers and their tractorcades.

Just because I would be curious to see such a press release, too, I'm going to share it with the readers. But before I turn to that, I want to mention what happened to the things that Jimmy picked up and looked at.

Even before he had left my shop, people had snatched up everything he had touched and bought them, some asking me for a slip of paper to confirm that the President of the United States had handled the item.

The transcript of our conversation, which was dated December 22, 1977, and slugged, "For immediate release," follows verbatim:

THE WHITE HOUSE
INFORMAL CONVERSATION BETWEEN
THE PRESIDENT AND HUGH CARTER

HUGH CARTER'S ANTIQUE SHOP

MR. CARTER: *On this farm thing, you know, they came in over here; couldn't get anybody to give them a welcome. I went over there.*

THE PRESIDENT: *I am glad you did. I mentioned you in my press conference.*

MR. CARTER: *I know you did. I heard it. That is great. But, you know, I knew you were for them, but it was hard for me to—they were a little angry. They wanted you down here. They started shouting, you know, "We want Jimmy. We want Jimmy. Where is Jimmy?"*

THE PRESIDENT: *We have got a letter to a farmer. I know they have got the headlines in the Columbus paper. I just wonder if they got it in the Atlanta paper. Have you looked at it?*

MR. CARTER: *I haven't gone through this yet. I just got it. You want to look at it?*

THE PRESIDENT: *No, I don't—there it is. I just wanted to be sure it was covered.*

I got a letter from a woman in Baxley, a widow, and her young son, on the farm. So I just sent her a seven-page telegram explaining the way I felt about the farm program.

The new bill that we passed didn't go into effect until October, and it will take care of a lot of our problems. Of course, we have still got a serious problem when we don't make a crop. And land prices, as you know, have leveled off. They were going up 10 to 15 percent a year, which kept prices going up. They have kind of leveled off. And also farmers have a tremendous capital investment, much more than the average businessman.

MR. CARTER: *That is true. Another thing, you know, Jimmy, some of them need to keep their cool. You know , a lot of them are getting mad, and I think this is wrong.*

THE PRESIDENT: *I think they had some violence in Texas.*

MR. CARTER: *I know. I saw it on TV.*

THE PRESIDENT: *As long as farmers let the consumers know they have got a problem, that is good. But if they ever turn the consumers against them, they will be worse off than they were before. What is best for consumers is to have the farmers strong and have a sound financial base. Prices are fluctuating so wildly.*

END

Eventually, as I knew he would, Jimmy did have a face-to-face confrontation with the farmers—but only a delegation from the several thousand who had assembled. He invited them to his home and they had a frank talk.

Though the farmers had asked for "100 percent parity," Jimmy told them that he was opposed to that large amount because it would drive up American farm products to the point where they would not be competitive on the international market.

Jimmy further assured the farmers that farm prices were bound to go up because of increasing world population and the limited amount of farm land.

However, the farmers were not happy and left muttering that they might have to follow the lead of the Arabs in getting increases by withholding crops just as the Arabs did with oil.

In January 1978, a group of us were sitting around reviewing Jimmy's first year in office. Some wondered if Jimmy wasn't discouraged with all the trouble that he had had in trying to accomplish anything in office—his energy bill torn to pieces in the Senate, his tax reform plans in trouble, the Panama Canal Treaty ratification in doubt.

And worst of all, the polls showed that his popularity had dipped below 50 percent.

I said no, Jimmy was not discouraged. I said I have seen him in similar situations in Georgia when he was governor, when it appeared that everything was going against him. But his determination and confidence brought him out on top, again and again.

I think things look a lot better abroad thanks to his nine-nation tour and I am sure the goodwill he generates wherever he goes will bring other countries more toward our way of thinking and a greater understanding among all peoples of the world.

Jimmy is a good man and a good fighter. He fights doubly hard because he feels that he is right. But a lot of heartache lies ahead of him for the very reason that he thinks that being right should be enough.

I hope and pray the country and the Congress can learn to understand Cousin Jimmy the way I do. He is not a "go along to get along" kind of person, the way House Speaker Rayburn used to train young politicians to be.

He is not a compromiser. Compromise is barely in his vocabulary. He is a man who drives doggedly toward what he believes is right without bowing and scraping or begging for favors.

If the nation can understand this style of politicking or statesmanship—take your pick—we may have a great new world.

INDEX

Carter, Laurie Gay, 72, 80, 86, 87, 88, 130, 235, 271, 286, 299, 301, 318
Carter, Lillian (Miz Lillian), 4, 27, 30, 31, 41-42, 46, 51, 63, 65-66, 67, 68, 76, 86, 91, 97, 128, 147, 154, 159, 178-179, 182, 183, 184-186, 187, 195-208 *passim*, 211, 213, 219, 220, 226, 233, 238, 241, 293, 306, 314, 318
Carter, Littleberry Walker, 167-168
Carter, Lulu Pratt,168-169
Carter, Magdalen Moore, 165
Carter, Mandy, 223, 236
Carter, Marle, 223
Carter, Mary Ann (Diligence), 168
Carter, Moore, 165
Carter, Nina Pratt, 22, 26, 28, 33-34, 46, 168-169
Carter, Rosalynn Smith, 4, 8, 11, 12, 23, 30, 41, 56, 60, 63, 64, 65, 66, 67, 68, 69, 73, 74, 75-76, 77, 78, 79, 86, 88, 92, 93, 94, 97, 105, 109, 112, 118, 120, 121, 122, 130, 131, 132, 148, 149, 153, 158, 159, 177, 178, 179, 180-194 *passim*, 198, 199, 200, 218, 220, 231, 234, 235, 236, 237, 238, 239, 240, 241, 245, 246, 278, 286, 289-290, 292, 295, 300, 301, 302, 305, 306, 311, 312, 318, 322, 324, 329, 332-333, 335, 336, 337, 338, 339, 343, 344, 346, 348, 351, 352, 354
Carter, Ruth, *see* Stapleton, Ruth Carter
Carter, Ruth Godwin (Baby Ruth), 5, 8, 24, 56, 62, 69-70, 73, 76, 81, 83-84, 85, 93, 94, 102, 106-107, 119, 130, 131, 132, 133, 143, 147, 156, 191, 198, 199, 200, 201, 204, 224, 234, 235, 268, 269, 273, 300, 302, 318, 322, 323, 327, 329, 332, 334, 336, 337, 338, 339, 342, 343, 344, 346
Carter, Sybil, 86, 216, 220, 221, 222, 223
Carter, Thomas, Jr., 165
Carter, Thomas, Sr., 163, 164-165
Carter, Wiley, 164, 166-167
Carter, William Alton III, *see* Carter, Billy
Carter, William Archibald (Billy), 167, 168, 170-172

Carter, Worm Farm, 18, 101-110
Carter's (Hugh) Antique Store, 2, 17, 18, 102-103
Cash, Johnny, 17
Cash, June, 17
Cato, Marguerite Wise, 63, 64
Cato, Robert, 63
Cheese ring recipe, 94
Chester, Mr., 55
Church, Frank, 151
Clark, Jack, 30, 46
Clark, Rachel, 30-31, 46
Cleland, Max, 330
Clements, J.D., Jr., 229, 312
Clough, Susan, 301, 328, 346
Coca-Cola Company, 302-303
Coleman, Julia, 54-58, 61, 62
Coller, Alma Hall, 49
Collins, Connie, *see* Carter, Connie
Collins, Fred, 321, 323, 324
Collins, Leon, 88, 156, 157, 299, 322, 323
Columbus *Ledger* (newspaper), 57
Connors, Eleanor, 261
Conover, Willis, 342
Cook House, 12, 26, 204
Copland, Aaron, 183, 330
Corn bread dressing recipe, 99
Cosell, Howard, 201
Cousin Beedie, *see* Carter, Hugh, Sr.
Cousin Cheap, *see* Carter, Hugh, Jr.
Cousin Hot, *see* Carter, Jimmy
Crickets, 103-105
Crickubators, 110
Crowe, Carl, 113, 114
Currer-Briggs, Noel, 163

Daley, Richard, 268-269
Davis, Alvin "A.D." (Knock), 31
Dean, Ross, 20, 52
Dean, Wayne, 346
Deriso, Jimmy, 146-147
Divine Light Mission (Albany, Ga.), 311
Dixon, Jeane, 294
Dodd, Lamar, 88
Dodson, Mrs. Clarence, 346
Dolvin, Sissy, 51-52
Dominick, Guy, 110
Donaldson, Sam, 240
Downer, Mr. and Mrs. T.R., 26
Duke, Earl, 320
Dylan, Bob, 261

362